The
KENNEDY
WIVES

Triumph and Tragedy
IN AMERICA'S
MOST PUBLIC FAMILY

AMBER HUNT and DAVID BATCHER

LYONS PRESS
Guilford, Connecticut
Helena, Montana

An imprint of Rowman & Littlefield

For Hunt, whose smile lights my way
—AH

For Mom, Betsy, and Emily, with love
—DB

Lyons Press is an imprint of Rowman & Littlefield

Distributed by NATIONAL BOOK NETWORK

British Library Cataloguing in Publication Information available

Library of Congress Cataloging-in-Publication Data

Hunt, Amber.
  The Kennedy wives : triumph and tragedy in America's most public family / Amber Hunt and David Batcher.
    pages cm
  Includes bibliographical references and index.
  ISBN 978-0-7627-9634-2 (alk. paper)
  1. Kennedy, Rose Fitzgerald, 1890-1995. 2. Kennedy, Ethel, 1928- 3. Onassis, Jacqueline Kennedy, 1929-1994. 4. Kennedy, Joan Bennett. 5. Kennedy, Victoria Reggai, 1954- 6. Kennedy family. I. Batcher, David. II. Title.
  E843.H86 2014
  973.922092'2—dc23

                    2014034236

CONTENTS

CONTENTS

PART I
Rose

1

FROM THE CRADLE

Josie Fitzgerald was afraid her baby might not last the week.

The summer of 1890 was brutally hot, and in the week following Rose Elizabeth Fitzgerald's birth, 284 Bostonians would die—almost half under the age of one. But Rose was as hearty a girl as a mother could hope for. She not only survived that first week—she would live until 1995.

She would marry a man named Joe Kennedy, who would become one of the richest men in the nation. She would have nine children between 1915 and 1932, and she'd raise them in homes in Boston, in New York, in Florida, and on Cape Cod. Traveling to Paris for shopping would become routine, just one of the many coping mechanisms she'd use as she learned to look the other way; her husband cheated on her with hundreds of women. She'd see politically ambitious Joe named ambassador to the United Kingdom in 1938 and live in England on the brink of World War II. She'd pray the rosary and attend mass with great devotion. She'd return to the United States, the family name in tatters, after her husband's outspoken support of appeasement cost him the ambassadorship and seemingly any hope of a political future.

She'd write thank-you notes with scrupulous fidelity. She'd tragically lose two children to aviation disasters in the 1940s and see a third child institutionalized for life after a botched lobotomy. She'd hobnob with popes and drink tea with royalty. She'd see her remaining children marry, one by one, and watch as her three sons became a mid-twentieth-century political powerhouse. She'd see her Jack elected president of the United States, her Bobby named the country's attorney general, her boy Teddy elected to the Senate. She'd advise world leaders and play hostess at the

White House. She'd attend funerals for two sons, killed less than five years apart by assassins' bullets, and a funeral for her husband, who died more than seven years after being immobilized by a stroke. She'd walk three miles a day and take bracing ocean swims. She'd stand by Teddy after a car accident off a bridge in Chappaquiddick left a young woman dead and his name splashed across the front of every tabloid in the world.

She'd write letters to her adult children about points of grammar. She'd watch one daughter marry a movie star and struggle with alcoholism. She'd watch another, inspired by the experience of having a special needs sister, found the Special Olympics. She'd watch her dozens of grandchildren struggle and achieve in politics, business, media, and philanthropy. She'd watch Teddy reach for the presidential nomination (and be relieved when he didn't get it). She would bow her head and accept God's will. She would become a writer, a media personality, a symbol throughout the world of grace and fortitude in the face of tragedy, an example of service to country and humanity. She would see her name become an indelible part of American history.

In that stifling bedroom in North Boston, shy, pretty, sweet-natured Josie could not know it, but her daughter would see wonders.

2

BETWEEN JOE AND HONEY FITZ

As teenagers in the first decade of the twentieth century, Rose Fitzgerald and Joe Kennedy fell deeply in love. Rose's father responded by sending her to a convent in Holland.

The protective father in question was career politician John Francis "Honey Fitz" Fitzgerald. Born in 1863 in Boston to Irish immigrants, Honey Fitz would come to cover the waterfront of Massachusetts politics; he served on the Boston Common Council, in the state senate, then for two terms in the US House of Representatives, then for two (noncontinuous) terms as the mayor of Boston. A short, powerfully built man with intense blue eyes, he was a born politician who loved to work a crowd. He crooned "Sweet Adeline" at nearly every campaign stop, "was loud, brash, unrestrained on the stump, an indefatigable backslapper and handshaker." He married the lovely but much more retiring Josie Hannon in 1889 and Rose, the eldest of their six children, was born on July 22 of the following year. Josie was a deeply devout Catholic, and she inculcated strict adherence to the religion in the children, as would Rose a generation later with her nine children.

If daily mass and praying the rosary were habits Rose inherited from her mother, her father transmitted his love of campaigning. Shy Josie mostly abdicated her role as political wife in favor of raising her children. "Mother had a limited capacity for the official social swirl," Rose would later write, and from an early age, the energetic, outgoing, articulate Rose served as her proxy. "I've been in the limelight since I was practically five years old," she was fond of saying. As a teenager, she was covered by the local newspapers as she joined her father on many public appearances.

When not appearing at campaign stops with her flamboyant father, she was attending a series of Catholic schools, where the nuns further instilled in her the importance of personal, daily devotion to the faith.

Rose's upbringing was Victorian, an era and ethos that from our vantage seem archaic, restrictive, and conservative. Women actualized themselves, according to Victorian mores, in motherhood. The one progressive impulse in the Victorian era was the new insistence that girls should be well educated—that they be so in order to better raise educated *sons* was taken for granted. It seems that Rose never seriously questioned any of this. "As motherhood is the greatest and most natural God-given gift for women for posterity," she would write in the 1960s, "it would seem that the birth and rearing of children in the way which to us seems most ideal, would be the most satisfying and the most rewarding career for a woman." In motherhood, she believed, was real power: the power to mold a child. "Her words will influence him, not for a day or a month or a year, but for time and eternity and perhaps for future generations."

As a girl Rose's intellectual verve was undeniable. Graduating from Dorchester High, south of Boston, at only age fifteen, she set her sights on Wellesley College, an elite, all-women's liberal arts college outside of Boston. Her father vetoed the idea: Even after two years of additional convent schooling, he claimed she was too young. Wellesley was also a secular school, and it would not do for an Irish Catholic political figure to send his daughter to a non-Catholic institution. Instead, she took classes at the Sacred Heart Convent in Boston and improved her piano skills at the New England Conservatory of Music.

It was around this time that Rose began dating the son of Patrick J. Kennedy, a banker, liquor importer, and a force in Boston's ward politics. P. J., as he was known, was often at odds with, and occasionally a wary ally of, Honey Fitz. Fitzgerald didn't like him, and he didn't like the Kennedy boy either.

The boy, Joseph Patrick Kennedy, was a couple of years older than Rose, a tall, athletic, handsome student at Boston Latin, a prestigious boys' high school that was a feeder school to Harvard University. While not a star in the classroom, he excelled in athletics: a year-round athlete, he played football, basketball, and baseball and captained the tennis team. He was gregarious, charming, and well-liked, already popular with young ladies by the time he started dating Rose. Excluded from many Protestant economic and social institutions, Irish Catholic Boston was, at the time, a tight and interconnected population. The Kennedys and the Fitzgeralds had been vacationing in the same spot—Old Orchard Beach, Maine, a popular resort for Boston's Irish Catholics—since Rose was eight. In 1906, Joe invited her to a high school dance. "He was a very good baseball player," Rose later remembered. "He didn't drink and he didn't smoke . . . and then he was a very good polite Catholic." Rose was sold. Her father, emphatically not. He refused to let her go.

And so Rose invited Joe to a dance at Dorchester High. What followed was a furtive courtship, enabled by many friends and even Honey Fitz's chauffeur. "It took teamwork and conspiracy, because we needed reliable allies," she would remember. "During that last year at Dorchester High, and the following year, when I was commuting to Sacred Heart, Joe and I managed to see each other rather often. Less often than we would have liked, but more often than my father was aware of." Though she risked incurring her father's wrath, her early relationship with Joe was remarkably innocent, in keeping with the time for a respectable, Catholic girl. They attended lectures together, met each other at friends' gatherings, and took walks, which were almost always chaperoned.

But in 1908, Honey Fitz, wounded by losing reelection to the mayor's office, separated the couple by sending Rose to the aforementioned Dutch convent. He took Josie, Rose, and her younger sister Agnes to Europe "for what Rose presumed was a brief vacation." The family toured Europe for more than two months, seeing England, France, Switzerland, and Germany in rapid succession. It's unclear exactly when Honey Fitz told the girls that they'd be left at Blumenthal, a Sacred Heart convent school near Belgium. In her memoirs, Rose would only write, suggestively in the passive voice, that "toward the end of that summer, it was decided Agnes and I would stay on for a year of school."

Despite the abruptness with which they found themselves enrolled, Rose and Agnes adjusted to life at the international school. The atmosphere was Spartan and severe, but the education topflight. Rose sharpened her German and French by conversing with the many native speakers of each among her classmates. She stifled her intense feelings of homesickness and hit the books, all the while keeping Joe's photo on her writing table. Rose was allowed to return to the States in 1909, when her father decided to run again for mayor of Boston.

After more than a year away, her passion for Joe was as intense as ever, as was Honey Fitz's disapproval. Not yet realizing the hopelessness of his efforts to snuff out the romance, he again sent her to a convent school, this time in New York City, and then on to Manhattanville College. At Manhattanville she studied without ever receiving a degree, as the school wouldn't have the state certification to award degrees until years later. It was very different from the Wellesley that she had so ardently hoped to attend.

"Rose's gender clearly fettered her education," wrote Rose Kennedy biographer Barbara Perry. "She possessed an inquiring intellect, a facility for languages, and a prodigious academic work ethic, but her father confined her to stultifying convents and Catholic finishing schools." Although Manhattanville was not Wellesley, Rose nevertheless developed an abiding affection for it, and she found it perfectly suitable years later for her own daughters, Jean and Eunice.

Rose also showed her intellectual energy, not to mention her frenetic, find-a-way enthusiasm, in her establishment of the Lenox Avenue Club (later the Ace of Clubs) in 1910. Barred as a Catholic from WASP social clubs like the Junior League, Rose simply started her own, and she insisted on giving it intellectual heft. The meetings usually featured a guest speaker on some political or social issue, and a premium was placed on knowledge of current events, as it would later be at the Kennedy dinner table. Rose was decidedly not a feminist: She would hold, throughout her life, the belief that a woman's most natural fulfillment was found in the raising of children. But she believed fully in the ability of women to engage their minds with—and form educated opinions on—issues facing the larger world.

The same year, 1910, as Joe Kennedy was toiling at Harvard, Honey Fitz narrowly recaptured the mayor's office and Rose prepared for her society debut. Since she was the daughter of the mayor, her debut reception, attended by more than five hundred people, was covered by the Boston newspapers. Joe and his parents were in attendance, though Honey Fitz still had not accepted Rose's choice of a beau. When Joe invited Rose to Harvard's junior prom in 1911, Honey Fitz forbade her to accept, despite the fact that she was almost twenty-one years old. And he employed his usual strategy for keeping the two apart: He got his daughter out of town. He sent her to Palm Beach, Florida. Then he sent her to Europe for six weeks. He prevailed upon her to accompany him on visits to Chicago, Indiana, New Jersey, and all over Massachusetts. He took her to Central and South America. He did everything in his power to keep Rose separated from Joe Kennedy.

Joe graduated from Harvard in June 1912 and, after a stint as a bank examiner for the state, became, at age twenty-five, the youngest bank president in the United States. He ably took the helm of Columbia Trust, the small East Boston bank his father had founded. In the meantime he continued to see other women. According to Joe Kennedy biographer David Nasaw: "At Harvard and after graduation, Joe remained faithful to Rose in the way that men of his generation and class remained faithful to their best girls. He did not court other marriageable women, but neither did he remain chaste awaiting his wedding day." He dated chorus girls and was remembered by contemporaries as "a ladies' man."

If Rose knew about Joe's proclivities, she most likely wasn't overly bothered. Despite the piety of her upbringing, she was raised in a home where a husband's infidelity was more or less normalized. As a teenager, Rose knew perfectly well what it meant that her father was away so often, and why it angered her mother. In 1914, as Fitzgerald commenced yet another reelection campaign, his rival, James Michael Curley, threatened to release details of mayoral corruption and of Honey Fitz's affair with a cigarette girl named "Tootles" Ryan, who at twenty-three was the same age as his daughter. Fitz had no choice but to drop out of the race.

It was around this time that Rose decided that she would marry Joe, Honey Fitz be damned. "I had read all these books about [how] your heart should rule your head," she later wrote. "I was very romantic and no two ways about it." On October 7, 1914, the two married in the private chapel of Cardinal William Henry O'Connell. The reception, a relatively small affair with only seventy-five guests, took place at the Fitzgerald home in Dorchester.

Their three-week honeymoon, bookended by brief stays in New York, included seeing the 1914 World Series in Philadelphia followed by ten days of horseback riding, golf, and tennis at the Greenbrier Hotel in White Sulphur Springs, West Virginia, and a short trip to Atlantic City. At the end of October, they returned to Boston and moved into their new home at 83 Beals Street, in the suburb of Brookline.

3

NINE LITTLE HELPLESS INFANTS

"THEY DID COME RATHER RAPIDLY," SHE LATER SAID, TYPICALLY DRY. "And there were a good many of them."

Her first five children were born within six years. "When I look back now, I wonder at the size of the job," she'd write much later. "And I think that when we stood as a blushing, radiant, gay young bride and groom, we were not able to look ahead and see nine little helpless infants with our responsibility to turn them into men and women who were mentally, morally and physically perfect." Perfection is a tall order, but it never would have occurred to Rose to try for anything less.

By the time their first child, Joe Jr., was born, on July 25, 1915, Rose and Joe had settled into their Beals Street house. "It was a nice old wooden-frame house with clapboard siding," she'd remember. "Seven rooms, plus two small ones in the converted attic . . . only about 25 minutes from the center of the city by trolley, the usual means of transportation in those days. There was a sense of openness in the neighborhood . . . fine big shade trees lining the sidewalks."

Having grown up with a maid and a cook, it was important to Rose to hire help immediately, and they employed a housekeeper who cooked and cleaned and lived in the attic space. As soon as Joe was born, they hired a nurse to care for him. Rose only occasionally breast-fed; as a society woman out and about, she didn't want to be home every three hours, and the immunological benefits of breast milk were not yet known.

The second child, John Fitzgerald Kennedy, was born on May 29, 1917, and her first girl, Rosemary, on September 13, 1918. Both would challenge Rose's ideas about the perfectibility of her children and her sense of control. Jack was sickly and underweight nearly from the beginning, and at the age of two and a half he nearly died from scarlet fever. (It would be the first of four times in his life that he would receive last rites.) Rosemary, it would gradually dawn on Rose and Joe, was developmentally disabled, or "retarded," as it was called then. Efforts to create a normal life for Rosemary, to help her keep pace with her siblings and to make her feel included, would be one of the central focuses—and ultimately, heartbreaks—of Rose's motherhood.

As the brood grew, Rose's motherhood took on a managerial quality. With nurses and nannies, Rose employed a team approach. Decades later, when the Beals Street house was opened as a historic site in 1967, she remembered:

I conceived the idea of having a card catalog which I bought up the street here, and I put their names and the dates of their birth and their weight and the time they had a Schick inoculation for diphtheria or scarlet fever, whatever it was, when their tonsils were taken out . . . whether there were any complications. Anyone could look up and find out that Jack had his tonsils out in New Haven when he was at school there . . .

The data she kept on her notecards was exacting. "I used to weigh them every week," she later said, "and keep track and then give them more nourishment if they were losing weight, give them an extra glass of milk or cream in their milk." When Joe became ambassador to the United Kingdom in the 1930s, she took the card catalog along with her. "When I got to England I showed it to some reporters, and they thought it was American efficiency," she said. "But I just said it was Kennedy desperation because I couldn't possibly keep track of all of them."

While Rose toiled as coordinator and troubleshooter at the Kennedy home, Joe's career and fortune evolved. He left the presidency of Columbia Trust in 1917 to become assistant general manager at the Fore River

Bethlehem Shipbuilding Corporation's plant; his position there, oversee-ing the production of naval vessels, kept him out of uniform in World War I. "Joseph P. Kennedy was not a shipbuilder," wrote Nasaw. "But he was young, smart, ambitious, disciplined, and well connected; he knew how to negotiate a contract, read a balance sheet, and get things done in Boston."

It was an enormous project, employing thousands of people and bringing in millions of dollars in government contracts. To cite one example of Kennedy's get-rich ingenuity: One of his responsibilities as assistant manager was to award the contract for the plant cafeteria, which would serve the tens of thousands of plant employees. Kennedy quietly formed a privately held company, the Fore River Lunch Company, and awarded the lucrative contract to himself.

The sixty-five-hour workweeks that his ambitions required strained the young marriage. It wasn't so much that Rose needed or expected his help with the children: "I ran the house. I ran the children," she insisted. It seems that she simply missed her husband, resenting his long hours away, both at work and, she almost certainly knew, unwinding with the attentions of other women. In 1920, while pregnant with her fourth child, Kathleen, she even briefly moved back to her parents' Dorchester home. The time away lasted only a few weeks. Honey Fitz, though certainly no fan of Joseph P. Kennedy, was a steadfast believer that a woman's role in marriage was to put up with whatever the husband did; he'd certainly asked his own wife to put up with quite a bit. He convinced Rose to return to Beals Street to resume her responsibilities as wife and mother. She would never acknowledge their break publicly or, for that matter, that there was ever any friction in the marriage at all. Throughout her life, she would show an amazing ability to present her family as she wanted it seen. She did this with great confidence, even when asserting something that would strike the most casual observer as patently suspect. "You never heard a cross word," she said of her marriage. "We always understood one another and trusted one another and that's it."

After the war, Joe went to work as a stockbroker and manager for the Boston office of Hayden, Stone, a Wall Street brokerage firm. It was here that he'd begin playing the stock market in earnest, using his considerable wits—and a great deal of inside knowledge—to grow his fortune. He also dealt in real estate on the side, buying theaters all across New England, and began his ventures into the film industry, enterprises that would gather force as the 1920s continued. It was around this time that he hired Edward Moore as his assistant. Moore would become his right-hand man, secretary, and confidante; in fact, in 1932, Rose and Joe would name their youngest child after him. His wife, Mary, similarly became Rose's closest friend, and the childless couple became as familiar to the Kennedy children as their own parents.

After Kathleen was born on February 20, 1920, the Beals Street house became cramped. The Kennedys moved to a larger home, just a few blocks away, in 1921, and Eunice was born there on July 10. Their household also expanded with the addition of more manpower: "In addition to maids, cooks, and nurses for the new babies, Rose hired governesses to assist with the older children." The Moores were also frequent helpers, allowing Rose to travel. She needed the time away, as Joe was rarely around.

It developed that the two usually vacationed separately. Joe almost always wanted to golf in Palm Beach in the winter, and Rose had other ideas. "I thought that was a terrible waste of money, to be always coming to the same place," Rose later wrote, "but he used to say that he worked hard during the year and he wanted to come and rest someplace. He didn't want to be coming to Europe where he'd have to wait around for customs and changing planes . . . " In 1923, for example, Joe took his two-week Palm Beach vacation in January. In April, Rose and her sister Agnes took a two-month trip to California. When she was on her way out the door for this trip, an almost six-year-old Jack famously cracked, "Gee, *you're* a great mother to go away and leave your children all alone." It's not clear whether young JFK ever castigated his father for his much more frequent absences.

Young Jack was puckish, a lanky instigator. Throughout his youth, he was a source of both frustration and amusement to Rose. "He was a very active, very lively little elf," she would remember,

full of energy when he wasn't ill and full of charm and imagination. And surprises—for he thought his own thoughts, did things his own

*way, and somehow just didn't fit any pattern. Now and then, fairly
often in fact, that distressed me, since I thought I knew what was best.
But at the same time I was taken aback. I was enchanted and amused.
He was a funny little boy, and he said things in such an original way.*

"In looking over my old diary," she wrote to Jack in 1962, "I found
that you were urged on one occasion, when you were five years old, to
wish for a happy death. But you turned down this suggestion and said
that you would like to wish for two dogs instead."

The family continued to grow, but 1923 would also be a year of loss.
That summer, Rose became pregnant with her sixth child. The two eldest
boys—Joe Jr. and Jack—were now in elementary school at Dexter, a private, nonsectarian school within walking distance of their new house.
Rose had originally wanted to send her boys to Catholic schools, but
Joe argued that they needed to expand beyond their Irish Catholic social
circle if they ever hoped to surpass a certain level of political and financial success in the wider WASP world. In September of that year, Rose's
younger sister Eunice died of tuberculosis at the age of twenty-three.
Rose would grieve deeply, if very privately, this loss, while Joe's work kept
him in New York more and more of the time. He was trying to break into
the film industry, and the wheeling and dealing leading up to his 1926
purchase of the Film Booking Offices of America (a deal six years in the
making) meant that he was rarely at home.

That autumn, little Rosemary went to kindergarten with other children her age at the Edward Devotion School, only blocks from the Kennedy house. Though her teacher, Margaret McQuaid, was delighted by
the little girl's grace and manners, Rosemary simply could not keep up
with the other children. "As time went on, I realized she was slow at
school," Rose later wrote. Even before that, Rose had noticed that Rosemary lacked the basic physical coordination of her siblings. She could
not steer a sled, play tennis, row a boat, or roller skate. "I was puzzled by
what this might mean, as I had never heard of a retarded child and I did
not know where to send her to school or how to cope with the situation."
Rosemary would repeat kindergarten the next year, after which it would
be clear that she would never be going on to the first grade.

While this was no doubt upsetting for a mother who believed her responsibility was to raise perfect children, it also brought out the tender side of the strong team culture she fostered within the family. The other Kennedy children "were told that she was a little slow and that they all should help her, which they did do and tried to encourage her." The trouble that they often went to is touching. In 1934 Rose would write to the Choate School, where Jack was attending high school. "Would it be possible for Jack to go to a tea-dance in Providence on Friday, January 19th?" she wondered.

The reason I am making this seemingly absurd request is because the young lady who is inviting him is his sister, and she has an inferiority complex. I know it would help if he went with her. She is fifteen years old, and trying to adjust to herself. I am sure you understand my point of view. It is not tremendously important, but we do all we can to help her.

As we regard Rose's euphemism today—*she has an inferiority complex*—it's easy to read it as Rose being ashamed of having a child with a developmental disability. But that would be a facile reading, only partly true. Rosemary was born into an era when respected voices in the scientific community were claiming that "morons"—as those with IQs between sixty and seventy were newly designated—were a danger to society. It was expected that many of these "morons" would become thieves, drunkards, and prostitutes. Not only did their existence reflect poorly on the genes of their parents, but the females were being forcibly sterilized in many states. There's little doubt that Rose and Joe wouldn't have wanted the stigma that having sired a "moron" would have earned them. But it's also true that they wanted to protect a vulnerable girl from a world that was openly hostile and bigoted toward her.

Sixth child Patricia was born on May 6, 1924, and Bobby the following year on November 11. By this time, Rose's household staff could take over most of the basic feeding and care of the children. Underlining her approach to parenting as the management of an enterprise, she would later write of her firm belief that mothers should spend *at least* one day a week with their children, *to see what methods the nurse is using, what her routine is with them, whether the meals are adequate, or is she giving them the same kind of soup each day so she does not have to think of meal planning, is she putting them to bed too early just [to] be rid of them, etc. If a mother never takes care of her children, she really has no first-hand knowledge of what the nurse is doing.*

A mother inculcated values, beliefs, and habits in a child, but much of the daily care could be outsourced, as it were, given the proper amount of quality assurance.

4

LEAVING BOSTON

As a parent, Rose had the unenviable job of being the taskmaster, the disciplinarian, the one who most often said *no*.

Their mother "was the disciplinarian of all our headstrong impulses, and was sometimes strict," Teddy would later write. "Spankings and whacks with a coat hanger were in her arsenal, as were banishments to the closet."

Their father, on the other hand, got to return to a house that was always ecstatic to see him. "He would sweep them into his arms and hug them, and grin at them, and talk to them, and perhaps carry them around," Rose later wrote. "Also, as each one became old enough to talk . . . he would want that child in bed with him for a little while each morning. And the two of them would be there propped up on pillows, with perhaps the child's head cuddling on his shoulder, and he would talk or read a story or they would have conversations." At least at home, Joe had the easier job: He was a cheerleader to the children, a booster, the parent whose job it was to say *yes*.

It was a contrast Rose only sharpened by withholding physical affection. "Rose touched her children when she spanked them," wrote Laurence Leamer. "She touched them when she adjusted their collars or rubbed a spot of dirt off their cheek before they headed to school. But she did not touch them when she loved them. She did not grasp Joe or Jack, Rosemary or Kathleen or Eunice to her bosom, holding them and telling the child 'I love you.'" In behaving this way toward her children, she was very much in line with Irish American mothers of that time. "These children were Rose's masterwork, and to her mind it was too serious a business to indulge in the excesses of affection." The sole exception was Rosemary, who, because of her disability, got the majority of Rose's physical affection.

Though not outlandish for its time, Rose's parenting style did lead to a strangeness and distance in her relationships with most of her children that lasted throughout their lifetimes. Jack's attitude toward her, generally one of irritation, would never change. Interviewed in 1972, Jack's lifelong best friend, Lem Billings, said that Joe Kennedy's "great warmth and outgoing affection" toward his children "led kids naturally to love as well as honor" their father. "They loved their mother too but in a rather detached way, as she did them." In later life, Jack came to have a "good working relationship" with his mother, characterized by "filial love, but never devotion, and continued feelings of irritation. He really didn't want her around much." From an early age, Jack's personality prickled at formality, reveled in the sloppy *yes-ness* of life, bridled at *no*. Often, his disposition naturally placed him at odds with Rose, who preached the virtue of restraint.

But despite her strictness—or, more accurately, *through* her strictness—she showed the children what they were capable of. "She was a great believer in opening up many opportunities for all of us," Eunice would write. "And though some of those things were difficult, she would compensate by saying you ought to try them."

Rose hoped to make Joe more of a constant presence in their lives by agreeing to move the family to New York. They rented a mansion in the neighborhood of Riverdale in the Bronx, where they lived for two years before buying an estate in Bronxville, in Westchester County, fifteen miles north of midtown Manhattan. Leaving Boston couldn't have been an easy or happy choice for a woman so identified with her hometown, but Rose deemed it worth the trouble to be closer to Joe. Unfortunately, Joe's escalating involvement in the film industry meant that, almost immediately upon his family's arrival in Riverdale in 1927, he started spending most of his time in Hollywood, as he would until 1930.

Joe's business dealings in Hollywood were typically diverse and complicated, but the focus of his work was running FBO, a film studio that he bought in 1926 on behalf of a consortium of investors that he organized. Moving pictures were still in their youth, and there was money to be made. One of the ways Joe did this was to root out inefficiencies in the filmmaking process on both coasts. He centralized the accounting practices of FBO in New York and fired several overpaid studio execs in New York and Los Angeles.

Joe was not indulging previously latent artistic urges; he was muscling in on a new and rapidly expanding market. "He was interested not in making artful or even good pictures at FBO," wrote David Nasaw, "but in making a profit by producing cut-rate 'program pictures,' low-budget westerns, stunt thrillers, and action melodramas and distributing them to independently owned and operated small-town theaters that could not afford to pay premium prices for expensive pictures."

In Los Angeles, Joe avidly pursued his business interests and, just as passionately, pursued actress Gloria Swanson, becoming both her manager and lover. A huge star of the silent era, Swanson was struggling to make the transition to the talkies. Kennedy hoped to manage this transition, and he did so with only limited success. Their coproduction of the epic *Queen Kelly* would be a disaster—one of the most famous uncompleted films of all time—and Swanson's career would subside to regular TV and theater work until 1950, when she would again rocket to fame (and become a camp icon) with her scenery-chewing turn as Norma Desmond in Billy Wilder's *Sunset Boulevard*. Swanson became familiar to the entire Kennedy family during the late 1920s, visiting them in Hyannis Port and at their new home in Bronxville. Joe's ardor for her was ultimately short-lived but flagrant; if Rose knew, her feelings about the affair, like her feelings about so much else, would never be available for public consumption. Rose visited Joe in Hollywood exactly once, in the late spring of 1927. She returned to Riverdale pregnant with Jean.

With Jean's birth on February 20, 1928, Rose now had eight children, ranging from newborn to twelve years old. She instituted a new dining schedule. "Up to age six, [the children] ate an hour earlier than the rest of the family. Rose sat with them and discussed simple topics of interest to toddlers and preschoolers. Then the older children dined together, and she would chat with them about more complicated subjects."

Rose and Joe would always see the family dinner table as a prime location for education and intellectual stimulation. They expected the older children to read the newspaper and have not only knowledge of, but opinions about, current events. Rose "posted articles or documents on a bulletin board, expecting older children to read them and discuss the content at dinner. . . . On Sundays and Holy Days she posed questions about the priest's sermon and Catholic symbolism." According to Rose, the Sunday dinner interrogations ensured that "if they didn't pay attention one Sunday they'd pay attention the next."

When Joe dined with the family, Rose took an auxiliary role. This happened more frequently after 1928, when Joe bought the vacation home in Hyannis Port, Massachusetts, that would, in later years, become the nucleus of the cluster of homes that came to be known as the Kennedy compound. "It was really quite a lot of fun to be at the dinner table with them," remembered nurse Luella Hennessey, who would join the family in 1937 and serve the wider family off and on in some capacity for decades.

Mr. Kennedy was the chairman or moderator of the discussions . . . Mrs. Kennedy sort of led the discussion on feminine and cultural things. Both Mr. and Mrs. Kennedy wanted the children to have a well rounded education, and she often discussed fashion and music and literature, and left it to her husband to handle the diplomatic and government discussions.

Eunice, noting Rose's deference when Joe was at home, put it succinctly: "My mother was more articulate with everything when he wasn't there."

Arriving in 1929, the Kennedys found Bronxville hospitable. Their mansion sat on six acres, walking distance from the Bronxville School the daughters attended; Joe Jr., Jack, and eventually Bobby could ride the bus to the Riverdale Country Day school. The nearby golf course was open to Catholics, and Joe and Rose both enjoyed playing. In the summertime, the family would decamp to Hyannis Port, as they would for much of the rest of the decade.

Joe Jr. and Jack both spent much of the 1930s away at school, and Rose did her best to monitor their health and grades from Bronxville. She was not a mother who hesitated to be in touch with principals and teachers. "The fact has come to my attention that some of the boys at Choate do not seem to know how to write a letter correctly or how to address it," Rose wrote to one of Jack's teachers in 1932. "It seems to me it would be a very practical idea and a very useful one if a short period could be given to demonstrating the different forms."

On another occasion, the same teacher heard from Rose,

I understood from Jack's letter than he is much better and he also said something about eating in the Tuck Shop in order to get "built up." I was a lot worried at that suggestion because the Tuck Shop usually means sweets to me, and Jack has no discretion, in fact he has never eaten enough vegetables to satisfy me. I do not want to bother you, but will someone please investigate this matter a little?

At the age of forty-one, Rose had her last child. Edward Moore Kennedy, nicknamed Teddy, was born on February 22, 1932. Of all the Kennedy men, he would come to most openly express his affection for and admiration of his mother. As the youngest child of the family, he would benefit from more one-on-one time with Rose than any of the older children: His returns home from boarding school would be to Rose the empty nester, rather than to a household bustling with children and household staff. He called Rose "our Pied Piper into the world of ideas," citing her leadership of their dinner conversations: "geography one night, the front-page headlines the next."

By the end of 1931, Joe Kennedy was out of the movie business and no longer trading stocks. He'd been perspicacious enough to recognize, as early as 1923, that the market was overvalued, and in the wake of the 1929 crash, he actually made money via short sales. As a result, the Great Depression was something the Kennedys read about in the newspapers, rather than experienced as much of a daily reality. In 1933, at the depth of the Depression, Joe even bought a third home, this time in Palm Beach. He bought the mansion, a white Spanish-style villa with red tile roof, pool, tennis courts, and large stretch of private beach, for $100,000. Even in 1933 dollars, it was a steal.

Joe's money was safe, but the pessimist in him suspected that the sun might be setting on capitalism. If financial power was about to lose its meaning, he figured, the future lay in political power, and those who wielded it. He became one of Franklin Delano Roosevelt's biggest fund-raisers, hoping that by helping Roosevelt gain the presidency, he might secure for himself a post of some power and prestige. Kennedy had his eye on the Secretary of the Treasury, but he was passed over twice for the position. He fumed privately while waiting for Roosevelt's call.

In 1934, that call finally came when Roosevelt asked Kennedy, despite great public and private opposition, to become the first chairman of the newly created Securities and Exchange Commission (SEC). Politicians and newspaper editors across the country argued that putting one of Wall Street's most notorious manipulators in charge of reforming Wall Street was tantamount to having the fox guard the henhouse, but Roosevelt argued that it took a thief to catch a thief. It turns out that he was correct. By most estimations, Kennedy did an excellent job as the first head of the SEC. And he did it by systematically criminalizing many of the manipulations he had used to build his own fortune. When he resigned in September of the next year, the agency was up and running, having been called by *Time* magazine "the most ably administered New Deal agency in Washington."

Even by Kennedy standards, the 1930s were a frenetic decade for the clan. Joe flew between New York, Hyannis, Palm Beach, and Washington, DC. Rose learned to transfer her entire household—nine kids and a large staff—between three houses while also traveling tirelessly herself. At Hyannis, Rose found a balance between packed, kinetic family life and her need for solitude and reflection. She ordered a prefab cottage, complete with front porch and outfitted with a writing table, and stuck it on the beach. In her little shack, she could read, write, and get some peace away from the bustling household. After one cottage was washed away by a storm, a second was ordered. After the second was wrecked, Rose said, "I started going to Europe, and I didn't need it."

She went to Europe at least seventeen times during the decade, often by herself; this included the trip that Joe gave her in the fall of 1934 for their twentieth anniversary, which tellingly she went on without him. At other times, though, she traveled in the company of the older children, who were learning to travel in the Kennedy fashion: often and lavishly.

It wasn't all shopping and beaches, though. In 1936 Rose and Kathleen (nicknamed "Kick" by the family) went to Russia, or "The Soviet," as Rose referred to it. In Moscow, they visited Lenin's tomb and the czars' palace; they sampled Russian ballet and theater and toured its art museums. Joe Jr. had visited the previous year, and his descriptions had fired her curiosity.

After FDR's 1936 reelection, the president convinced Joe to tackle another administration role, this time as the head of the United States Maritime Commission. After performing the job ably, Joe felt he was in line for something more exalted. The call came late in 1937: Roosevelt appointed Joe as the United States Ambassador to the Court of St. James, the official title for the integral role of US ambassador to the United Kingdom. It was time, after almost twenty-five years of marriage, to move the whole family to London.

5

AMBASSADRESS

In July 1937, thirteen-year-old Patricia was rushed to St. Elizabeth's Hospital in Boston for an emergency appendectomy. She was cared for by a nurse named Luella Hennessey; the Kennedys liked Hennessey so much, they asked her to care for Pat in Hyannis for the rest of the summer. There, Rose thought she fit in nicely: Aside from taking care of Pat, Luella was adaptable enough to pick up a tennis racket, go swimming with the kids, even act as crew in the family sailboat races. She stayed with the Kennedys until September, when she returned to her post in Boston.

In an odd coincidence, Rose had her own attack of appendicitis while visiting her parents in Boston the following February and was rushed to St. Elizabeth's for her own emergency appendectomy. "Her doctor called me and said that she would not be operated on unless I was there!" Hennessey remembered. That evening, when Joe visited Rose in her room at St. Elizabeth's, he asked Hennessey if she would accompany the Kennedys to London, to act as the family nurse and help with the children as they settled in over the first six weeks. She agreed, and would remain with the Kennedys not only for six weeks, nor just through their sojourn in England, but for years afterward.

Sworn in as ambassador at the White House on February 18, 1938, Joe headed to England while Rose took two weeks to recuperate in Palm Beach before organizing the transport of the Kennedy troops. From Florida, she sent Hennessey a note. It read: *Do you understand the art of packing?*

"I wondered why she did that," Hennessey said. "But I certainly learned in London, when we went to the south of France, or went to Switzerland for winter sports; there would be forty-five and fifty trunks and boxes packed for eleven, twelve of us to move." Rose confronted a logistical nightmare anytime she had to move the family en masse; her can-do temperament, along with a sizable household staff, made it possible.

Joe's media profile was at its zenith. By now a multimillionaire with a beautiful wife and nine photogenic children, and fresh from successful stints at both the SEC and US Maritime Commission, he was a press darling. Roosevelt, correctly sensing that Kennedy represented a potential rival should the president try for a third term in 1940, was all too happy to send him across the ocean. Roosevelt also took great delight in putting a plainspoken, even brusque, Irish Catholic into the role of ambassador to England, a spot previously reserved for Anglo Protestants. "Almost invariably they have been chosen for the Englishness of their background and manner," reported the *New York Times*. Joe's appointment was a move designed to create a stir, and it did. Newspapers and film crews covered his New York departure and his arrival in England.

Rose's role, as wife of the United States ambassador, was critical. Representing America at the Court of St. James would require tact, diplomacy, and impeccable manners. It would mean exquisite attention to detail in dress and comportment. It would require minute observance of obscure protocols and an almost archaic level of formality. And all of that under the watchful gaze of the papers and the newsreels. It was, in short, what Rose had been preparing for her entire life.

In March of 1938, Rose crossed the ocean with Kick, Pat, Bobby, Jean, and Teddy; Luella Hennessey, governess Elizabeth Dunn, and all that luggage came, too. Expecting a media circus awaiting the family's arrival, Rose had Eunice and Rosemary wait five weeks to make the trip in order to shield Rosemary from the media glare. Joe Jr. and Jack, both at Harvard, stayed behind for the time being, but they were to join the family that summer.

＊＊＊

The ambassador's residence at 14 Prince's Gate was a six-story, fifty-two-room mansion. Donated to the US government in 1920 by banker and philanthropist J. Pierpont Morgan, it was within walking distance of the embassy and just off of Hyde Park, where Joe went horseback riding almost every morning before work. It had its own elevator, which Bobby and Teddy used as their personal amusement-park ride until Rose put a stop to it. She redesigned the mansion to suit their needs. It would cost Joe a fortune to renovate the residence for a family of eleven; he was able to make peace with that more easily than with his office at the embassy. "I have a beautiful blue silk room and all I need to make it perfect as a Mother Hubbard dress and a wreath to make me Queen of the May," he sneered in a letter to a friend. "If a fairy didn't design this room, I never saw one in my life."

The children were all soon settled into local schools. Eunice, Pat, and Jean were enrolled in the Sacred Heart Convent in Roehampton; Bobby and Teddy went to the Sloane School for Boys, a day school that allowed them to live at the residence with Joe, Rose, and Kick. Kick had decided not to start college in London, opting instead to embrace the London social scene. Rosemary went to the Convent of the Assumption School in Kensington Square, a training center for Montessori teachers. When Joe Jr. arrived in June, freshly graduated from Harvard, the ambassador hired him as his private secretary.

Rose took to life in upper-crust London immediately. Early in their visit, Rose and Joe were invited by the king and queen for a weekend at Windsor Castle. They were lodged high in the castle's tower, in high-ceilinged chambers with sweeping views of the park below. Upon their arrival, Joe looked out the window, around the room, and at his wife. "Rose," he said, "this is a helluva long way from East Boston."

They dined and socialized with the king and queen throughout the weekend, joined by Prime Minister Neville Chamberlain, foreign secretary Lord Halifax, and their wives. Discussions ranged from their children and families to the future of Europe. With war in the air, there's no doubt that Chamberlain and Halifax were eager to get a sense of the opinions and temperament of the man who would serve as the primary intermediary between Britain and the United States. Rose would remember it, decades later, as "one of the most fabulous, fascinating experiences of my life."

Rose's engagements were more or less constant; as the wife of the ambassador, it was her duty to socialize. She threw society debuts for Rosemary, Kick, and Eunice, and, following custom, the young women were presented to the king and queen. Rose spent hours working with Rosemary on perfecting her curtsy, and she was proud to see her eldest daughter show impeccable form when she met the queen. She and Joe went to Ascot, Private View day at the Royal Academy, Founder's Day at Eton, and any number of teas, parties, and balls. She hosted dinners and parties at the embassy, the details of which she agonized over. Rose's sense of correctness—in manners and dress—stood her in good stead on these occasions, and where she didn't know the proper protocol, she wasn't afraid to ask: At one point, she contacted officials at Buckingham Palace to ask when and where it was appropriate for her to wear a tiara. She was informed that a tiara should be worn at any dinner at which a member of the royal family was present.

Not surprisingly, Rose had special admiration for the royals; they confirmed every instinct and opinion she had about what was ideal in public life. "Disciplined, stoical, eternally gracious, they went through life wearing impenetrable masks of civility," wrote Laurence Leamer. "The routine was a matter not of sentiment, deeply felt emotion, but of training, deeply ingrained habits." In the English aristocracy, she found her ideas about child rearing, class, and so much else affirmed.

March of 1939 brought Rose another peak experience when Joe, with the family accompanying him, was sent to the coronation of Pope Pius XII in Vatican City as FDR's personal representative. Pius met privately with the family and presented Rose with a silver rosary. A few days later, seven-year-old Teddy received his first communion from the new pope.

Another bright spot of their term in England concerned Rosemary. Her time at the Montessori school was going exceptionally well; by 1939 the twenty-one-year-old's cognitive impairment remained but the mood swings she had experienced increasingly throughout her adolescence had calmed and she seemed happy, content, and fulfilled. Several factors seemed to be at work. First, Rosemary was told the white lie that if she worked hard enough, she would get a diploma certifying her as a Montessori teacher; this was plain fiction, but it seemed to give her a sense of purpose and satisfaction. Secondly, the nun who worked most closely with Rosemary, Mother Isabel, had a rare connection with the young woman. Finally, perhaps not coincidentally, Rosemary had never had such frequent contact with, or affection from, her father. She brought out in both parents a directness of affection that the other children never saw, and in England she was given healthy doses of it. "You have worked very hard and I am very proud of you and I love you a lot," Joe told Rosemary in a letter. It was a sentence nearly impossible to imagine him writing to any of the other children.

Rose and the children used their residence in London as a base for further European forays. Joe Jr. traveled to Spain, Rosemary to Ireland, and Rose to Egypt, the Holy Land, and Greece. In 1939, Jack took a leave of absence from Harvard and saw firsthand the state of Europe as it eddied into war: He traveled to Romania, Russia, Turkey, Egypt, Palestine, Lebanon, and Greece. After a brief respite with the family in Cannes, he road tripped with Harvard roommate Torb Macdonald through France, Germany, and Italy.

Despite the initial warm reception the Kennedys received, Joe's ultimately mistaken support of appeasement—that if Hitler were allowed to annex large parts of Europe, he would not turn to bloodshed—along with his pessimism about Britain's chances in the event of a war against Germany, soured the British to him. His private clashes with FDR discredited him both to the president and the diplomatic corps, and they made his ambassadorship increasingly untenable. "Try as he might," Nasaw wrote, "he could not quite do what was expected of him. He was simply unfitted by temperament for the position of impartial, impassive listener and reporter, especially at moments of crisis."

By the second half of 1939, Ambassador Kennedy was effectively sidelined and watched in impotent horror as Europe moved inexorably toward war. In the end, Joe's conviction that, no matter what Europe's troubles, they were worth not one drop of American blood, placed him on the wrong side of history. His own political fortunes would never recover.

On September 1, 1939, Hitler invaded Poland; two days later Prime Minister Neville Chamberlain declared war on Germany. Rose, Kick, Bobby, and Eunice boarded the USS *Washington* bound for New York on September 12. Pat, Jean, and Teddy followed on a separate ship. Later that month, Joe Jr. sailed home on the RMS *Mauretania*, and Jack flew home on a Pan Am "flying clipper."

Only Rosemary stayed behind with her father. She was doing so well at the Montessori school that it was decided it would be best if she evacuated with the nuns and her classmates to the Hertfordshire countryside rather than return to the States. Her father spent his weekends at a nearby estate owned by J. P. Morgan and was able to see her often. In spite of Joe's crumbling ambassadorship and the incipient war, they delighted in their time together. She remained in England until June 1940. Joe would stay until the middle of October.

Another member of the Kennedy party had wanted to stay behind in September when the rest evacuated. Luella Hennessey recounted in her 1991 oral history that, while in England, she had fallen in love with a young man and informed Joe that she intended to stay. "We expected to get married," she said.

Joe explained that "it was going to be a long, hard war . . . He gave me quite a bleak picture of the future there, but I still thought that love would take care of everything." After some argument, Joe finally convinced her to sail with the family back to New York, after which, if she wanted to return to London, that was her affair. "You can wait for the boat to turn around and come right back again," he told her, "or you can stay in America."

"I came back with the family," Hennessey continued. "And I was so glad; I knew he was right, because when I arrived in New York, I knew this was my home, and I had no idea of going back again."

"And you had no regrets?" her interlocutor asked fifty years later.

"No," she replied.

"Whatever happened to the young man? Did you ever follow through?"

"He was killed in the war," she explained. "He was a pilot."

6

ROSEMARY

THE LAST OF MANY NAILS IN JOE'S POLITICAL COFFIN WERE THE COM-
ments he made—off the record, he thought—to *Boston Globe* reporter
Louis M. Lyon in November of 1940, shortly after tendering his resignation as ambassador.

"Democracy is finished in England," he said. "It may be here, too."
Given Joe's aspirations to higher office and the patriotic sensitivities of
the body politic as the United States stood at the brink of war, it was a
mind-bogglingly reckless thing for Joe to say to a reporter, on the record
or not.

Over the next several months, Joe tried to back off these remarks
and paint himself as a supporter of the president and neither an appeaser
nor defeatist with regard to England's troubles—through radio addresses,
interviews, and, most importantly, in disastrously muddled congressional
testimony in ambivalent favor of Roosevelt's Lend-Lease proposal. Lend-
Lease sought to arm our allies in their fight against Hitler—to provide
planes, tanks, guns, and freighters—without committing a single American troop. Kennedy agreed to support the proposal in a radio address and
congressional testimony but did so, according to David Nasaw, "in such
a desultory, confused, conflicted manner that it was near impossible to
know whether he opposed or supported it." The press savaged him, and
when they were done, stopped covering what he said and did. His public
life was over.

He and Rose settled into their version of a retirement. Not wanting
to worry about three estates, Joe put the Bronxville mansion on the market in late 1941. Ever after, he and Rose would split their time between

Hyannis Port and Palm Beach. Rose allowed herself a moment of wistfulness, remembering the happy locus of her children's childhoods, before her pragmatic side took over. "I am relieved too to have one less house to worry about," she wrote in a round-robin letter to the kids. "With none of you there, the house was no longer a necessity." The round-robin letters were one of Rose's signatures: she'd write a letter and send it to one of the children; he or she would add a response and send it on to one of the others until it made its way back to Rose.

All of the children were either away at school, working, or in the service. Despite his strong antiwar sentiment, Joe accepted his two eldest sons' desire to join the military. Joe Jr., just finishing his second year of Harvard Law School, enlisted in a special unit of the US Naval Air Corps that recruited straight from Harvard. Knowing that Jack wanted to follow his brother, the perennial golden boy, into the service, Joe pulled strings with a military contact to see that Jack would pass the physical. Given Jack's raft of ailments, from his incipient back trouble to his stomach problems to his yet undiagnosed Addison's disease, passing the physical would have been an impossibility without his father's intervention. Jack was ordered to report to the Office of Naval Intelligence, in Washington, that fall.

Rose, now an empty nester and seemingly uninterested in sitting around in Palm Beach while Joe played golf, planned another trip. In the late spring of 1941, she and Eunice took a five-week trip through South America, including Brazil, Argentina, Chile, Peru, and Ecuador.

With Rose away, Joe continued as the primary parent of Rosemary. Unfortunately, the gains she had made in England seemed to be evaporating, and the war prevented her return to Mother Isabel's convent. She was placed in St. Gertrude's School of Arts and Crafts, in Washington, DC, a school for "retarded" girls that was staffed by Benedictine nuns.

"In the year or so following her return from England," Rose later wrote in her memoirs,

> *disquieting symptoms began to develop. Not only was there noticeable retrogression in the mental skills she had worked so hard to attain, but her customary good nature gave way increasingly to tension and*

irritability. She was upset easily and unpredictable. Some of these upsets became tantrums, or rages, during which she broke things or hit out at people. Since she was quite strong, her blows were hard. Also there were convulsive episodes.

Further, Rosemary was frequently wandering away from St. Gertrude's, which was located in the heart of urban Washington. The nuns had trouble keeping track of her, especially at night, and the Kennedys were terrified that she would make an easy target for predators. Both Joe and Rose were becoming convinced that Rosemary's problems went beyond simple cognitive deficits; they feared that her behavior was being affected by some other neurological degeneration.

Joe consulted with experts in the field about a promising new procedure, developed by Portuguese physician António Egas Moniz and performed in the United States at George Washington University Hospital by Dr. Walter Freeman and Dr. James Watts. The procedure was never promoted as a cure for cognitive disabilities or even mental illness; it was seen as a last resort that would relieve the agitating symptoms of certain psychiatric disorders by severing neural connections between the brain's prefrontal lobes. It was seen as groundbreaking, and would be for years to come: In fact, Moniz received a Nobel Prize for its invention in 1949. For Joe Kennedy, it promised to flatten Rosemary's affect, take away the anger and frustration that tormented her, and offer her some hope of contentment.

Sometime in November, apparently without the approval of Rose, Joe had the procedure—commonly known as a prefrontal lobotomy—performed on Rosemary. She emerged from the operation unable to walk or speak and was moved to Craig House, a private psychiatric hospital in New York, to recuperate. She recovered some of her motor skills at Craig House, but never her ability to speak or her memory. In 1948 Joe moved her to the St. Coletta School in Jefferson, Wisconsin, and never saw her again. Rose and the children wouldn't visit her there either, until after Joe's 1961 stroke left him confined to a wheelchair; even then, they visited without his knowledge.

It's unknown what Joe told Rose or the other children, but it would be twenty years before Rose again used Rosemary's name in a letter to the kids. Reflecting on the time in undated diary notes, Rose wrote of Rosemary's "deteriorating": "It was then we decided that she would be better off for her own sake and for ours if she went to a home where she would be with people of her own mental capacity."

She makes no mention there of the botched lobotomy, but by the time she wrote her memoirs in the 1970s, she was able to speak less euphemistically about what happened to her daughter. She would write:

> *The operation eliminated the violence and seizures, but it also had the effect of leaving Rosemary permanently incapacitated. She lost everything that had been gained during the years by her own gallant efforts and our loving efforts for her. She had no possibility of ever again being able to function in a viable way in the world at large.*

Sometime after Joe's death, Rose addressed the other major issue regarding Rosemary: Joe's unilateral decision to have her lobomotized. "I will never forgive Joe for that awful operation he had performed on Rosemary," Rose confided to historian Doris Kearns Goodwin. "It is the only thing I have ever felt bitter toward him about."

While Rose was the undisputed ruler of her domestic domain, Joe had always made the larger medical decisions for the children, starting with Jack's hospitalization for scarlet fever at age two. His sense of responsibility for Rosemary in particular had only increased since the fall of 1938, when she had been the only child to remain in England with her father. Rose took his single-minded decision as a betrayal, but it was not out of character with their marriage's already established division of labor.

The betrayal, for Rose, was not that Joe acted without letting her weigh in. It was that he had acted, as he had so many times before, on one of their children's behalf, and for the first time the results had been disastrous.

It was only the first tragedy in what would be a very tragic decade.

7

THE MARCHIONESS AND THE
WAR HEROES

As the United States entered the war, Rose became the hub of family correspondence, writing round-robin letters to Kennedy children scattered across the country and the globe. From her perch in Palm Beach or Hyannis Port, she could worry after Jack's stomach, Bobby's grades, Eunice's health, Joe Jr.'s prayer life, and Kathleen's grammar. Since returning from England, Kick had worked her way up from a secretarial position to society columnist at the *Washington Times-Herald*, and Rose sent her qualified congratulations: "I can see improvement in your column," Rose wrote her in 1942, unable to resist noting that the columns contained errors. "Probably typographical," Rose granted.

American soldiers were fighting and dying, both in Europe and in the South Pacific; three of the Kennedy children were called overseas. Jack went from training in Charleston, South Carolina, to commanding a PT boat in the South Pacific in mid-1943; Kathleen sailed to England around the same time as a volunteer for the Red Cross; and Joe Jr., after a post in Puerto Rico, was sent to London in September.

Wisecracking slacker Jack Kennedy showed a valor few would have expected late that summer when he helped save the lives of eleven men in the aftermath of an ill-advised naval battle in the Solomon Islands. His vessel, PT 109, was part of a squadron sent in pitch-blackness to intercept a convoy of Japanese supply ships on August 1. The attack was a disaster, and Kennedy's boat was sliced in half by a Japanese destroyer. Two of Kennedy's crew members were killed, and the other eleven were set adrift.

After clinging to the hull of the ship for nine hours, Kennedy organized the survivors for a swim to a nearby deserted island. (He carried one badly burned man, Pat McMahon, on his back.) The swim took five hours. The men were rescued seven days later, after scavenging for food and surviving mostly on the water they could catch in their mouths during rainstorms. Jack organized an expedition to a neighboring island; there he found a native who took a coconut, into which Kennedy had carved a plea for help, to an Australian naval base. Jack's endurance and heroism are even more impressive in light of his poor health. He wasn't even supposed to be in the military. His perennial back and stomach troubles would have kept him out had Joe not called in favors from his military contacts.

The incident and rescue were picked up by the media worldwide, and Jack, already well-known for being the wealthy son of the former US ambassador to England, became a media darling. Asked later how he became a war hero, he replied with characteristic wryness: "It was easy. They cut my PT boat in half."

Rose found out that Jack had been missing in action only after his rescue; Joe, notified by the navy, had kept the news from her and the other Kennedy children while he awaited more information. Joe often kept worrying news from Rose, not wishing to upset her, and it seems that she did not begrudge him his decision not to worry her with Jack's disappearance. Rose wrote, "We are more proud and thankful than words can tell to have him such a hero and still safe and sound."

Joe Jr., still based in Puerto Rico at the time of the rescue, had a more complicated response. Joe Jr. had been the Kennedys' golden boy his entire life: He'd been healthier, more athletic, a better student, and better looking than his sly, sickly, underachieving brother. Especially since the collapse of Joe Sr.'s political career, Joe Jr. had become the repository of all of the ambassador's political hopes and family ambitions. For the favorite son in a clan that thrived on competition, Jack's sudden shift into the limelight was a shock, and Joe craved more than ever what so many young men of the time craved: to prove himself through wartime heroics. After a brief visit in Hyannis Port for his father's birthday, he piloted his VB-110 across the Atlantic to England, carrying his crew, gear, and a carton of fresh eggs for his sister Kick, whom he'd visit shortly in London.

Stationed in Cornwall, he received a letter from his mother containing a silver religious medal to protect him during his service far away.

While in London, Joe Jr. visited Kick when he could. Despite the hazards of bombing raids and the privations of wartime rationing, Kathleen couldn't be more excited to be back there. She missed it terribly and kept in touch with many of her London friends after her departure with the family in 1939, and now that she was back she spent as much time on the town and at country homes with friends as she did at her tony assignment as program assistant at Hans Crescent, an officers' club in a Victorian hotel in the Knightsbridge section of London. Kathleen wasn't nursing to wounded soldiers as a Red Cross volunteer; she was, she wrote to a friend, exhausted from "jitter-bugging, gin rummy, ping-pong, bridge and just being an American girl among 1500 doughboys a long way from home."

Two weeks after her arrival, she ran into Billy Hartington (aka William Cavendish, Marquess of Hartington) for the first time since her departure four years earlier. They'd met in 1938 at the king and queen's annual Buckingham Palace garden party, just as London's social set was opening its arms for her. He was widely considered the most eligible bachelor in England: polite, self-effacing, funny in a gentle way, he behaved with none of the pompousness of a man set to become the Duke of Devonshire. It was a title held by members of the Cavendish family since 1694 and would make Billy one of the wealthiest men in England upon his father's death. He and Kick had hit it off immediately.

Now, in 1943, it was love at first sight all over again. They spent increasing amounts of time together, and soon enough there was talk of marriage. There was only one problem: Billy was a Protestant, and Kick was Catholic. Billy's parents, the Duke and Duchess of Devonshire, saw how clearly besotted their son was, and they begged Kathleen to convert to Anglicanism. But Kick argued that she couldn't convert. Catholicism, so deeply ingrained by her upbringing, was central to her life. Billy was similarly steadfast in his faith. Though Rose liked Billy very much and was no doubt impressed by his place in the peerage, his Protestantism rendered him, in her eyes, an utterly unacceptable husband for her daughter.

Jack finally returned to the United States in January 1944, barely five months after the PT 109 incident, his health so poor that he flew to the Mayo Clinic in Rochester, Minnesota, even before heading home to see his family. He was told he'd need surgery on his back and was diagnosed with a duodenal ulcer and malaria. When Jack finally arrived in Palm Beach, even normally undemonstrative Rose could not contain herself. "The mere feel of his coat brought her joy," Barbara Perry wrote. "Incredulous at his homecoming, she touched his arms to convince herself that he was really there." Her prayers had been answered: Her "elf" was home safe.

In England meanwhile, Kick became engaged to Billy, and the future Marchioness of Hartington. As far as the difference in their faith went, Joe refused to get up in arms about a difference he didn't see as terribly important. "As far as I'm concerned, I'll gamble with your judgment," he wrote Kick. Rose, however, was mortified at the thought of any of her children marrying outside the faith. And not just embarrassed; literally sickened. After Kick announced that she would indeed marry Billy, Rose wrote in her diary that she was "horrified—heartbroken." She made herself so sick with worry that she ended up spending several days in New England Baptist Hospital.

As stubborn as her mother, Kick cabled Joe. "Religion everything to us both," she wrote to her father. "Will always live according to Catholic teaching. Praying that time will heal all wounds. . . . Please beseech Mother not to worry. Am very happy and quite convinced have taken the right step." On May 6, 1944, Kick married Billy in a civil ceremony attended by the Duke and Duchess of Devonshire and Joe Jr., among others, but not the bride's parents. The eldest Kennedy child sent an icy, six-word cable to his absent parents later that day: "The power of silence is great."

A month later, on June 6, 1944, the Allied Forces invaded Europe. Billy Hartington was called into active duty and two weeks later crossed the English Channel. Joe Jr. delayed his leave to fly support missions for the invading Allies. That summer, while waiting for her son to return on his planned leave, Rose softened. She wrote to Kathleen expressing her wish that she and Billy could accompany Joe Jr. when he visited. She regretted the things she'd said in opposition to the marriage. "However, that is all over now, dear Kathleen, and as long as you love Billy so dearly, you may be sure that we will receive you with open arms."

Joe Jr. wrote home at the end of July to explain his further delay:

No doubt you are surprised that I haven't arrived home. I am going to do something different for the next three weeks. It is secret, and I am not allowed to say what it is, but it isn't dangerous so don't worry. So I probably won't be home until sometime in September.

In truth, Joe Kennedy Jr. had volunteered for a near-suicidal mission—to take out a V-1 launching pad in Belgium. The navy had stripped down a Liberator bomber so that it could be fully packed with explosives. His mission was to get the bomber to the target, turn over control of his plane to two B-17s that were accompanying him, and parachute to safety.

On August 13, 1944, two naval chaplains knocked on the door of the house at Hyannis Port and delivered the news Rose and Joe had dreaded to hear. Joe's plane, they said, had exploded before even reaching its target. "Dad's face was twisted," Teddy would write in his memoirs.

He got the words out that confirmed what we already suspected. Joe Jr. was dead. . . . Suddenly the room was awash in tears. Mother, my sisters, our guest, myself—everybody was crying; some wailed. Dad turned himself around and stumbled back up the stairs; he did not want us to witness his own dissolution into sobs.

Tellingly, Rose's memoirs painted a more stoic picture: "There were no tears from Joe and me, not then. We sat awhile, holding each other close, and wept inwardly, silently." Kick flew home and joined them on August 16. Though devastated, they attempted to stick to their routines and move on stoically. They stayed at Hyannis Port through Labor Day, and the Kennedys continued to have dinner on the front porch, play tennis, and go sailing as if it were a normal summer. In this way, they each grieved privately. After Labor Day, Joe moved into a suite at the Waldorf

Towers in Manhattan, and Rose moved nearby with her daughters into New York's Plaza Hotel, as was becoming her post–Labor Day custom. It was in New York that, on September 16, Kick was informed that Billy Hartington, her husband of only four months, had been shot dead in Belgium by a German sniper. She quickly returned to England, a widow at the age of twenty-four.

Subsequently, Rose wrote to Kathleen about how, after hearing about Billy's personality and ideals,

> *I realized what a wonderful man he was and what happiness would have been yours had God willed that you spend your life with him. A first love—a young love—is so wonderful, my dear Kathleen, but, my dearest daughter, I feel we must dry our tears as best we can and bow our heads to God's wisdom and goodness.*

It seems that Rose dealt with her own grief over the loss of her eldest child, Joe Jr., in a similar way. Joseph P. Kennedy wrote about her to a bereaved friend years later. "With her supreme faith [Rose] has just gone on and prayed for him and has not let it affect her life." Rose mourned, quietly, privately, and with the poise that would come to typify, again and again, the Kennedy approach to grief.

When the war ended Joe Kennedy busied himself with a new venture. In July 1945 he purchased Chicago's Merchandise Mart for thirteen million dollars. At the time, it was the world's largest commercial space, and it would prove to be hugely profitable. Just a few months later, he established the Joseph P. Kennedy Jr. Foundation, named in memory of his son, and gave it a 25 percent ownership in the Mart. The foundation would become the charitable vehicle for the Kennedys' wealth, and over the years it would come to fund research and treatment for persons with intellectual disabilities. On the second anniversary of Joe Jr.'s death, the Kennedy family contributed $600,000—the equivalent of $7.8 million in 2014—to a group of Franciscan nuns to start a convalescent home for "crippled and mentally deficient children."

As Europe rebuilt from the devastation, Rose went to visit Kathleen, who was now well ensconced in London society. Staying with Kick in 1947 at Linsmore Castle, the Cavendish family estate in Ireland, Rose wrote to Joe: "It is beautiful here beyond words, quiet, peaceful, secluded . . . I feel *perfect*."

Back in Massachusetts, Jack had been elected, at only age twenty-nine, to the US House of Representatives in the same district his grandfather Honey Fitz had been elected in the previous century. Though Rose did help with the campaigning in the 1946 election, she participated less than the rest of the family, and certainly not to the extent she would in coming years. The second half of the 1940s seemed to be a reflective period in Rose's life.

That decade, already so tragic, held one final profound heartbreak for her. In 1948 Kathleen returned to the United States for a two-month visit. At the end of it, she announced to Joe and Rose that she intended to marry Peter Fitzwilliam. She'd been seeing Fitzwilliam, a married English aristocrat—and yes, Protestant—ten years her senior, since 1946; now that his divorce was set to become final, the two were ready to wed.

Rose was furious, threatening to disown Kick if she again broke with Catholic doctrine by marrying a divorced man. Joe offered no support either, but was at least open, a month later, to meeting Peter. In France for business, Joe agreed to meet the two in Paris. Kathleen and Fitzwilliam relaxed for two weeks on the Riviera before flying back to Paris in Fitzwilliam's private plane, ignoring warnings that the weather was too treacherous to make the trip.

At his Paris hotel the next morning, May 14, 1948, Joe received a telegram informing him that Kathleen's was one of four bodies recovered from the site of a plane crash on the side of a mountain in the Rhone Valley. She was buried in the Cavendish family plot in Edensor, near the Cavendish ancestral home. Joe was the only Kennedy who attended her burial.

Though Rose spoke little of her feelings after Kathleen's death, she did remember her in a diary entry, dated June 24, 1962. It was fourteen years later, and Rose was on one of her religious retreats at Convent of the Sacred Heart in Noroton, Connecticut. "I heard the grandfather clock chime in the hall," she wrote, "the clock which we had given to Msr. Cushing when we moved to Bronxville . . ." Her handwriting is nearly illegible, and the connection difficult to discern, but the sound called to mind Kathleen, and the "many problems" life threw her way. The entry is in fragments: "Falling in love with Billy. Both young people knew it would be difficult if not impossible to marry—both were young—deeply in love—admirably suited to one another . . ." Fourteen years later, she was turning over the events in her head, wistfully trying to make sense of Kathleen's short life. Rose, though publicly stoic, had room in her life for sorrow, and room for grief. But it was in a mysterious, private part of her, never available for anyone but God to see.

8

ACCOLADES, WEDDINGS, BIRTHS, VICTORIES

AFTER A DECADE OF SO MUCH LOSS FOR ROSE, THE 1950S WERE A RIOT of weddings, births, and political victories. With the exception of Rosemary, all of her surviving children were married during the decade, and all of those matches had produced children by the end of 1960. She saw her eldest surviving son elected, and then reelected, to the United States Senate, and as the 1950s drew to a close, his presidential aspirations gaining steam.

In June 1950, Bobby married Ethel Skakel, a doe-eyed young woman from another large, wealthy, deeply Catholic clan. Ethel's toothy, irreverent exuberance and frenetic, spring-loaded athleticism made her a perfect fit for Bobby and the rest of the Kennedys, and her integration into the family was effortless. Soon after their wedding, Ethel was pregnant, as she would be almost constantly for the next eighteen years.

The Kennedys next joined together for the only truly dark spot in Rose's decade: In October her father, Honey Fitz, died at the age of eighty-seven. Upward of thirty-five hundred people attended his funeral in Boston, including John, Eunice, Pat, Jean, and Teddy. Two mourners were notably missing: Josie, Rose's mother, did not feel well enough to attend the funeral; and Rose herself, shopping in Paris at the time of his death, was not able to make it back in time. Honey Fitz had been ill, and eighty-seven was then, as now, a ripe old age. "In spite of his age," Rose admitted years later, "it was impossible to conceive of life without him."

Though Honey Fitz was gone, Rose was able to engage the political skills she had received from him. Jack ran for the Senate in 1952, and Rose played a more active role in this contest than she had in any of his congressional elections. Jack was running against incumbent Senator Henry Cabot Lodge Jr. It was not the first time the two families had contended against each other for political office: In 1916 it was Henry Cabot Lodge Sr. who had defeated Honey Fitz for the same seat. Further, the Lodges were Brahmins: As a moneyed Protestant family dating from the origins of the republic, they were very much a part of the Boston ruling class that Joe felt had excluded him as an Irish Catholic. The Kennedys participated across the board, campaigning tirelessly across the state. Joe Kennedy, as was his wont, stayed in the background, but his checks spoke loudly enough.

Rose, only the year before named a Papal Countess by Pope Pius XII, drew women by the hundreds, and then the thousands, to hear her speak. She took her impeccable fashion, old world manners, and trim figure (past the age of sixty, she still took obsessive pride in staying slender) all around Massachusetts to great acclaim. Starting with "coffee hours" at private homes, she had to upgrade to larger venues to accommodate the sheer numbers of women who wanted to hear her speak. (The fact that handsome JFK sometimes appeared at these added extra appeal.)

Similar events were anchored by Pat, Eunice, Ethel, and Jean. Rose didn't discuss policy in any depth at these speeches and forums; instead, she told of her travels, prewar London, and the challenges of raising nine children. Only once did her reliable mask of civility slip away. The Korean War was on, and Rose began to speak—very generally—about it at a rally in Worcester, Massachusetts. "Certainly I can appreciate what is happening to the mothers of the boys in Korea," she started. "I lost one son . . ." There was a pause, and then Rose left the stage in tears.

This uncharacteristic loss of composure aside, the "tea parties," as they came to be known, were a huge hit. When Jack won the election by a mere 70,737 votes, Rose believed that the votes she garnered swayed the election. Henry Cabot Lodge Jr. agreed—the reason for defeat, he said, was "those damn tea parties." Both were to some extent correct. Jack's campaign was one of the first to make special efforts to attract both ethnic and female voters; the teas were responsible for attracting as many as seventy thousand voters to the polls alone. "I felt rather like a man who has just been hit by a truck," Lodge said of his defeat.

Though the new Senator Kennedy clearly loved life as a bachelor, he knew that if he hoped to fulfill presidential aspirations, he would need a wife. It was a great relief to Rose, then, for many reasons, when he brought slender, graceful Jacqueline Bouvier to the Cape in the summer of 1952. It was a particularly joy-filled 1953 season for Rose: In May, Eunice married longtime beau Sargent Shriver; in June, Manhattanville conferred on Rose an honorary degree; and Jack and Jackie married in September. (Somehow Rose also found the time that year to travel to Paris and Salzburg.)

The mid-fifties were a blur as more of her children paired off and settled down. After a courtship of only two months, Patricia became engaged to movie star Peter Lawford; they wed in April of 1954 and Pat gave birth to their first child in 1955, just nine and a half months after the wedding. The same year, Rose took the chance to travel around the world—from California to Hawaii to Japan to India and throughout western Europe with her niece, Mary Jo Gargan—before settling for two months on the Riviera with Joe.

Jean married businessman Stephen Smith in 1956. Smith's father, like Joe, oversaw a largely self-made fortune, and the Smiths' Irish Catholic bona fides qualified him, in Rose's eyes, as a suitable mate for her youngest daughter. In 1958, Teddy married Joan Bennett, a blonde bombshell from Bronxville with a good Manhattanville education and musical chops to match. Though Rose was initially unimpressed by the Bennetts' relative lack of wealth, Rose and Joan bonded by talking about music and playing duets on the piano. By the end of 1959, all of her surviving children, except for Rosemary, were married and had at least one child.

———

The fifties were also a time during which the charitable mission of the Kennedy family was coming into focus. Rose's frequent speaking engagements at various Catholic charities and clubs were often to raise money, particularly for youth causes and the research and treatment of what was then openly called "mental retardation." Though it would be the late 1950s before the Joseph P. Kennedy Jr. Foundation would primarily aim its resources at the developmentally disabled, veiled references to Rosemary began appearing in Rose's speeches earlier in the decade. Without context, the audiences had no way of knowing she was speaking about her own child, but it's clear that her eldest daughter was always on her mind. "Sometimes a mother finds in her midst a handicapped child, one child who is abnormal mentally or physically," she said in 1953 when accepting an award for her work with young people from a Catholic charity. "Then, a whole new set of baffling difficulties presents themselves, and then fervently she prays and how diligently she searches every avenue to find an answer to that child's problems."

Throughout the 1950s, the speeches and chats that Rose gave gradually morphed from campaign appearances for Jack to fund-raising appearances for charity and back to campaign appearances for Jack by the later part of the decade. As early as 1957, when she did a short speaking tour of Iowa, Rose started speaking in states that Jack would need to focus on in the 1960 presidential contest. It was typical of Kennedy political savvy that Rose's good works on behalf of the developmentally disabled, while genuine, simultaneously furthered her son's presidential ambitions.

Jack announced his campaign for the presidency in January of 1960. Rose campaigned for him in the lead up to the New Hampshire primary, traditionally the nation's first. After ensuring his resounding victory—he received 85 percent of the vote—they headed to Wisconsin, which promised to be a much more difficult enterprise. Hubert Humphrey, senator of neighboring Minnesota, all but had the state locked up; he was often referred to as Wisconsin's third senator. But the Kennedys, including Rose, fanned out across the state, using their sheer numbers to make the Kennedy name more recognizable in several places at once. Patrick Lucey, then the leader of the state's Democratic Party, remembered that Kennedy's campaign was "just an effective presentation of celebrity. . . . The family was an asset . . . genuinely glamorous as well as glamorized, so the people were anxious to meet them wherever they went." However, Jackie would remember their reception in Wisconsin somewhat differently: "They just *stared* at us, like some sort of *animals*."

Nevertheless, Humphrey felt outnumbered and outgunned by the Kennedy phalanx. The Kennedys are "all over the state," he moaned. "And they look alike and sound alike. . . . I get reports that Jack is appearing in three or four different places at the same time."

On April 5, Kennedy won Wisconsin with 56.5 percent of the vote, thanks in no small part to Rose's help. She sat out the hard-fought West Virginia primary that followed but campaigned for Jack throughout the election, generally campaigning three days on and then four days off, and taking a rest in Hyannis Port in the summer months after Jack received the Democratic nomination. Despite the lighter schedule, it still must have been punishing for a woman who turned seventy during the campaign. By the time Jack was elected, she'd traveled more than thirty-five thousand miles on his behalf, a woman talking to women.

On November 8, 1960, Rose Kennedy's eldest surviving son was narrowly elected president of the United States. The next morning the family gathered in the main house at Hyannis Port for a photo to celebrate the occasion. Seated in the front of the tableau, looking twenty years younger than she was, Rose beamed. Twenty years previous, the Kennedy name was in ruins. That morning she was the mother of the president-elect of the United States. Her eldest living child, whom she'd come so close to losing to illness and to war, was now one of the most powerful men in the world.

9

THE FIRST MOTHER

JACK PRESENTED HIS MOTHER WITH A MAP. THERE WERE FORTY-SIX PINS in it, one for every spot where she'd campaigned, and an inscription: "To Mother—With Thanks." In Palm Beach, as the president-elect prepared for his term and Jackie recovered from the Caesarean delivery of her second child, John Jr., Rose adjusted grudgingly to the constant presence of Secret Service, press, and, anytime she went beyond the perimeter of the estate, gawking tourists and well-wishers.

On January 5, photographer Richard Avedon arrived to capture the next first family. Rose's diary entry captures how disorienting and irritating the interregnum must have been for her, and how, in the midst of it, she coped by attending to details:

> *After my hair had been set and combed out I had to walk back through the living room in my long blue bathrobe. I nodded to one of photographer's assistants and warned her about the loose neckline on Jackie's half-finished velvet dress. I looked out the window to the front lawn and saw someone swinging Caroline, of which I disapproved, as I thought she would be too tired for the photographers. Then I took a quick look at John F. Jr., wrapped in blankets and awaiting his turn to be photographed. And I caught a glimpse of the Secret Service men on the beach outside on the oceanfront.*

The security left Rose baffled about where to enter and exit her own home. Sneaking through the servants' quarters the previous night, she'd surprised a hungry hairdresser apparently helping herself to a salad left on the maids' dining table. "She just threw up her hands and I gave a laugh and she gave a laugh and out I went."

In the days before the inauguration, Washington, DC, disappeared beneath eight inches of snow. Early on the morning of the inauguration, Rose bundled up and walked from the Georgetown home she was renting with Joe, Ann Gargan, Ted, and Joan, to attend mass at Holy Trinity Church. She was delighted to see that Jack, independent of her plans, was attending the service as well. Jack, she thought, "wanted to start his four years in the presidency by offering his mind and heart, with all his hopes and fears, to Almighty God." She didn't approach Jack, staying anonymous and out of sight in the pews. Ever image conscious, she didn't want to risk being photographed in her informal winter bundling.

She and Joe attended the inauguration ceremony, where they were seated in the front row, but at the far end; as a result, "we were left out of everything except the panoramic pictures. . . . Some friends asked me later where I had been during the ceremonies." Still, she was moved by his inaugural address, the weight of the occasion, this culmination of her and Joe's hard work.

That night, for the inaugural balls, she appeared in the same Molyneux gown she'd worn for her presentation at the Court of St. James in 1938. More than twenty years later, she was proud she could easily fit into it, proud her taste was so timeless.

"I was overwhelmed with the joy, the wonder, the glory of it all," she'd say that fall in a speech to the Guild of the Infant Saviour, a Catholic social services organization. "The climax of my life as I approached my 71st birthday."

Rose enjoyed her position as America's Queen Mother, even sleeping in the Queens' Bedroom when visiting the White House. Still, Jack generally found her presence stressful. She joined Jack and Jackie when they visited France at the end of May en route to JFK's disappointing summit with a belligerent, chest-beating Khrushchev in Vienna, but only after she invited herself. "He really didn't want her around much," remembered Lem Billings. "In particular, he didn't want her around on the trip he and

Jackie took to Paris and Vienna, but she asked to go and he let her."

Whether Jack wanted her there or not, she was treated as royalty when they arrived in Paris. She chatted with Mme. de Gaulle about their children, though neither mentioned that both had developmentally disabled daughters. The state dinner welcoming the Kennedys was held at Versailles; the pageantry and protocol must have reminded Rose of the salad days of 1938, when she and Joe were fresh to London and spending weekends with royalty. And Vienna, so rattling an experience for her son, nevertheless also reminded her of her 1911 visit. "I wonder to myself," she wrote in her diary, "if the young man with whom I danced has ever come back and if he too remembered the night in 1911 when, young and gay and carefree, we danced the hours away."*

The president and first lady departed Vienna, and Rose went on to Florence before visiting Pope John Paul XXIII—successor to her friend Pope Pius XII—in Rome. Afterward, she joined Joe for two months at a resort on the Riviera.

The Kennedys gathered for their traditional Hyannis Port Thanksgiving, with dinner for thirty-three. It was a merry scene. "Jack gets a great kick out of seeing Ted dance," Rose wrote, "as Ted has [a] great sense of rhythm, but he is so big and has such a big derriere it is funny to see him throw himself around." Joan played the piano, and Jackie demonstrated the Twist for the assembled mothers, fathers, children, and grandchildren. Rose was happy, despite Joe's insistence on serving squash and sweet potatoes at the meal. (She objected to there being two vegetables of the same color.) Joe carved the turkey, held court, and played with the grandchildren.

The loveliness of the holiday would take on a bittersweet quality in retrospect. Ten days prior to Thanksgiving, Joe had suffered "an attack," as Rose would put it in her diary. He "is not at all himself but quiet, complains about a lack of taste in his mouth and feels blah, he says. For the first time—I have noticed he has grown old." Others at the Thanksgiving dinner noticed he was not quite himself, but Joe, whether out of denial or Kennedy grit, insisted that there was nothing wrong.

---

*The young man to whom she is referring was Hugh Nawn, another Irish Catholic Bostonian. Honey Fitz had hoped that Rose would marry Nawn rather than Joe.

The family gathered again in Palm Beach the next month for Christmas. Presidential business called Jack back to Washington on December 19, though, and Joe took Caroline and saw him off at the airport, where father and son chatted briefly before Jack boarded Air Force One. After dropping Caroline at home, he and niece Ann Gargan went to play nine holes at the Palm Beach Country Club. While on the course, Joe felt faint and disoriented; seeing that his balance was compromised, Ann took him home. He reported feeling better and went upstairs under his own power, where he fell asleep.

Waking just five minutes later, he was unable to speak or move on his right side. He had suffered a massive stroke.

Jackie and Ann rushed with him to the hospital. By the time other Kennedy children started arriving later in the day, he had developed pneumonia, sunk into a coma, and received last rites. Rose could only pace his room and pray. Against the odds, though, Joe survived. He woke the next day and seemed to recognize Rose and the children. By Christmas Eve the doctors declared him out of danger, and by December 29 he was able to sit up. Though he'd never regain movement on his right side or the ability to communicate in words, he was otherwise healthy: His vital signs were good and his heart was strong. After several weeks, he returned to Palm Beach, where niece Gargan, the reenlisted Luella Hennessey, and nurse Rita Dallas would see to his daily care.

Rose resumed her speaking engagements, raising money and helping with Teddy's senatorial bid throughout the state in 1962. The following spring she was with Joe when, entire Kennedy retinue in tow, he was flown north to begin further treatment at the Institute of Physical Medicine and Rehabilitation in New York. She stayed with him at Horizon House, a bungalow on the hospital grounds, specially fitted for wheelchair-bound patients. Every evening, they quietly ate dinner and then watched television together.

Joe's case was overseen by Dr. Henry Betts, who was impressed with the closeness of the Kennedy family, their relentless positivity, and the complete absence of any pity toward their father. He saw a great warmth between Rose and Joe. "My impression was that she adored him," he'd later say. It seemed to him that Joe "was very content" in her presence. Luella

Hennessey saw the devotion, but not the warmth: "She was awfully good to him when he had his stroke," she said. "It wasn't what one would call a normal relationship between a husband and wife. . . . Rose took care of him but there was very little feeling left. It had gone so many years ago."

Months of rehab did little to improve Joe; he could feed himself, and his caregivers became more adept at interpreting his attempts at communication, but he never regained his speech or mobility. Rose's response was complicated. On one hand, she seemed freed by her husband's descent into infantilism—she was able to travel on behalf of Teddy's campaign at her own discretion and was in charge of her own life to a greater extent. On the other, his difficulties upset and depressed her. Letters from that time, though they don't address Joe directly, generally became more irritated, nitpicky, and exasperated.

Frustrated at the tendency of cars to disappear at Hyannis Port, Rose sent a long description of who was allowed to use which car and when. "This is the way [the cars] are to be used," she concluded. "I do not want to be bothered this way at my age, and I do not think it is fair. Please give this to Ethel to read, so every one will understand." In another letter, Rose advised Ethel and Jackie to close the blinds in their homes to avoid the sun fading the furniture. She was both compelled to write such niggling letters, and, simultaneously, exhausted by her compulsion. "I am trying to rest my brain," she wrote wearily.

Later in the summer of 1962, Joe was brought back to Hyannis for what was to be a few weeks of vacation before returning to Horizon House. He never did. Thereafter he was shuttled back and forth between Hyannis and Palm Beach, always in the care of niece Ann Gargan and the staff of nurses. Rose came and went as she saw fit. "Mrs. Kennedy changed a great deal after her husband left Horizon House," remembered nurse Rita Dallas. "Perhaps because a decision had been reached that not only relieved her, but also left her conscience intact." Joe was home, and cared for. Rose was free to live her life.

As an image-maker, she became more involved in Jack, Bobby, and Teddy's political lives than she had been prior to Joe's stroke. Her hectoring letters, throughout 1963, became less about Hyannis household rules and more about how the young men—and their wives—presented themselves to the media and the public at large. "I do not think it is necessary to emphasize the fact that you are both tone deaf or that cultural things do not play such a large part in your life," she wrote to Bobby in April 1963. She also discouraged their publicizing the raucous life of their large family at Hickory Hill, or relying too much on the Kennedys' touch-football games as an anecdotal crutch.

She also stepped into the role of White House hostess on a couple of occasions. The last would be at the state dinner for Ethiopian king Haile Selassie in late August 1963. Earlier in the month, Jackie had given birth to Patrick Bouvier Kennedy five weeks prematurely. The boy had lived only three days, and both parents were devastated. Finally Jack decided that a trip abroad might lift Jackie out of her depression, and he sent her with her sister for a vacation in Greece. Jackie left the day of Selassie's arrival, and Rose happily took over.

Summer became autumn in Hyannis Port. On a beautiful November morning, Rose got up early, attended mass, had breakfast with her husband, and played nine holes of golf. In the early afternoon, she'd been napping when Ann Gargan's blaring TV woke her up. She shuffled to Ann's room to ask her to turn it down.

Ann sat horrified in front of the flickering screen. The news bulletin was reporting that Jack had been shot while riding in a presidential motorcade in Dallas.

Rose's hands trembled and she sank into a chair. "Don't worry," she told Ann. "We'll be all right. You'll see."

The phone rang.

10

"WE ALL SHALL BE HAPPY TOGETHER"

AFTER ROSE RECEIVED THE PHONE CALL FROM BOBBY CONFIRMING HER son's death, she told the household staff that Joe, himself napping, was not to be told of the assassination. She put on a coat and walked along the chilly Hyannis beach alone, praying, asking "Why?"

Teddy and Eunice arrived at the Cape that evening. It was decided that Joe would be told in the morning. When, after dinner, he wanted to watch TV, he was told that his bedroom television was broken, as was the one downstairs.

Rose walked again on the beach, this time with Eunice. "We talked about Jack as if he were still alive," Eunice would remember.

Rose attended mass the next morning, escorted in her black veil past onlookers waiting outside St. Francis Xavier Church. After mass, she returned to the house but couldn't bear to be present when Teddy, with Eunice standing next to him, told Joe that his son was dead. Joe sobbed.

The next morning—Sunday, November 24—Rose, Teddy, Eunice, and nurse Rita Dallas flew to Washington. Joe stayed behind, in the care of his nursing staff and Father John Cavanaugh. The White House was filled with family, friends, and administration officials. Jackie's mother, Janet Auchincloss, noticed that Rose stayed off to the side, the picture of lonely fortitude. Eunice's husband, Sarge Shriver, remarked to Rose that she was holding up admirably.

"What do people expect you to do?" she snapped at him. "You can't just weep in a corner."

On Monday morning, Rose did not feel well enough to walk with the funeral procession from the White House to St. Matthew's Basilica. Instead, she rode behind, in a limousine.

After the burial, she met at the White House with some foreign dignitaries and Kick's in-laws, the Duke and Duchess of Devonshire. She never once, in public, lost her composure.

She flew back to Hyannis Port that night.

In the aftermath of the assassination, Rose had trouble sleeping and would pace in her Hyannis room late at night. Damane and Librium, powerful (and at the time, very popular) antianxiety drugs, helped her sleep, but they were so potent that the night nurses were tasked with making sure she was awake on time for mass. Still, Rose declared, "I am not going to be licked by tragedy, as life is a challenge, and we must carry on and work for the living as well as mourn for the dead."

Though she tried to busy herself in the first six months after her son's death by gathering materials for her autobiography, she generally turned down invitations during that time; it wasn't until March of 1964 that she accepted an invitation to a ceremony marking the renaming of a Paris street in honor of JFK, the Avenue du Président Kennedy. Paris mourned the loss of JFK acutely, and "every place I went the French people were most sympathetic . . ." Rose wrote. "These circumstances made it more difficult for me, as constant reminders often released floods of tears again."

It seems important to point out that Rose—that all the Kennedys— *did* cry. The famous family edict, "Kennedys don't cry," was certainly a command to be tough, no matter what life threw their way. But it was also a dictate meant to protect the Kennedys from the depth of their own feeling, from the combustibility of their own hearts. "I think all of the Kennedys have a great deep feeling for one another," said Father John Cavanaugh. "It's so deep that they do not care much about sharing it with anybody else. They all understand it. They take for granted that the others will understand it. So they're not demonstrative with one another. In fact, they withhold any kind of demonstration because they're afraid, I think, of it getting out of hand." Rose's Victorian formality, coupled with that famous Kennedy admonition, have left the mistaken impression that

Rose was an unfeeling woman. Nothing could be further from the truth. She loved her family and she grieved for them.

It is a sign of Rose's strength that she began to attend more of the hundreds and thousands of dedications taking place across the country for her fallen son, something that could not have been easy. She spoke in several parts of the country after JFK's death, as a way of commemorating him, allowing the public to participate in her grief, and as a way of raising money for the planned John F. Kennedy Presidential Library.

In June, though, her progress out of the valley of grief was nearly halted when a small airplane carrying Teddy crashed in Massachusetts. The pilot and one of Teddy's aides were killed. Teddy narrowly escaped death, and he would spend months in a hospital bed, just as Jack had in 1955. "I guess the only reason we've survived," Bobby said at the hospital, "is that there are too many of us. There are more of us than there is trouble." A rattled Joan marshaled her strength to campaign for her bedridden husband; Rose was all too happy to campaign for Teddy as well, taking her as it did, in the summer of 1964, out of a glum, reflective atmosphere at Hyannis Port. Bobby was running too, that year, for a Senate seat in New York, and Rose spoke frequently on his behalf. In the end, both Ted and Bobby handily won their contests.

Rose also kept a sense of meaning and purpose during this time by speaking more often and with greater candor about Rosemary. Her acknowledgment of her eldest daughter had really begun before the assassination. In 1962, Rose began visiting Rosemary at St. Coletta's. Joe's stroke had immobilized him and had made it easier for Rose to make travel plans without his knowledge. Eunice began visiting, too, and the pair lobbied JFK to make research on mental retardation a major priority of his administration. On October 11, 1961, Jack announced a national initiative on mental retardation, establishing a commission on how to treat and prevent developmental disabilities. Eunice published an article, "Hope for Retarded Children," in the *Saturday Evening Post*, in which she candidly discussed the heartbreak and frustration her mother had faced in trying to find help for Rosemary. The lobotomy was not revealed, but it represented a huge step forward in the family's recovery of their connection to Rosemary.

In a 1963 interview, Rose finally revealed why the Joseph P. Kennedy Jr. Foundation had turned its focus to issues facing the mentally handicapped. "Well, you see the answer to that question is a very simple one," Rose said. "We had a retarded child . . ."

This work continued after JFK's death and throughout the sixties. That included the summer camp that Eunice started in 1961 at her rented Maryland estate. It was a camp exclusively for those with mental retardation; they were children of little means, bussed from institutions in Washington. Resourceful Eunice recruited volunteer counselors from elite Washington prep schools. This summer camp grew throughout the sixties and eventually would expand into the Special Olympics.

Rose became a vocal advocate for persons with intellectual disabilities, raising awareness and money through the media and her speaking engagements. St. Joseph's College gave her an honorary degree in 1965 for bringing funds to research on retardation and serving as an inspiration to the parents of retarded children. The Canadian Association for Retarded Children chose Rose to receive its International Award of Merit for her inspiring example.

In 1966 she and Bobby wielded shovels to break ground on the Rose Fitzgerald Kennedy Center for Research in Mental Retardation and Human Development at the Yeshiva University Albert Einstein College of Medicine in New York. The Joseph P. Kennedy Jr. Foundation contributed $1.45 million toward its construction.

The 1968 campaign season would be the most important for the Kennedy family since Jack's presidential run in 1960. LBJ had decided not to seek reelection, and the conflict in Vietnam was deeply unpopular, leading to regular protests and demonstrations across the country. In March of 1968, urged by the public and driven by his own passionately antiwar stance, Bobby announced that he would seek the Democratic nomination for the presidency.

Rose rolled up her sleeves and hit the campaign trail. Eight days in Indiana followed by three in Nebraska and, after a few days at Lake Tahoe to rest up, on to California and Oregon. The tea party coziness of previous campaigns was less effective in 1968; the issues in this election were war, race, and inequality, vital questions that were creating unrest on campuses and in cities all over the country. But Rose, at seventy-seven, could still win over a crowd telling stories about the boyhood of tousle-haired Bobby. She was, alone among the Kennedy campaigners, immune to the prevailing seriousness.

Bobby carried the primaries in Indiana and Nebraska but shocked himself, his family, and his supporters when he lost the Oregon primary. It was the first time a Kennedy had ever lost an election, and the Kennedys were thunderstruck. Nevertheless, he vowed to fight on in California. By this time, an exhausted Rose was back in Hyannis Port. She waited there for the results of the June 4 California primary.

By the time the results were in—Bobby won California by a wide margin—Rose was fast asleep. It wasn't until early the next morning that the night nurse woke her and told her to turn on the TV.

A televised news bulletin informed Rose Kennedy that Bobby had been shot.

It had happened in a crowded hallway at the Ambassador Hotel, only moments after Bobby left the podium where he'd celebrated his victory in the California primary. The assassin, a confused, unemployed, mentally unstable drifter named Sirhan Sirhan, stepped forward and fired a revolver point blank at the senator's head.

In Hyannis Port, a shocked Rose shouted at the television, "It's Bobby! It's Bobby!" Not knowing what else to do, she went to mass at St. Francis Xavier. At home she struggled to keep her composure and busy herself while she waited for news from California. Bobby was still alive, but brain dead. He was not expected to last much longer.

The next morning she received word that Bobby had died during the night, Ethel and Jackie, along with Teddy, Jean, Pat, and some of his older children at the bedside.

Rose took on the burden of informing Joe that they'd lost a fourth child. Where they'd hidden their feelings in the past, no such effort was made that morning. With no children present to be strong for, Joe moaned and sobbed, and Rose repeated "My son, my son," over and over.

Later that morning, a photographer saw Rose in the driveway of the Hyannis Port house. She was bouncing a ball, like a child, lost in thought.

"It seemed impossible to believe that the same kind of disaster could fall on our family twice in five years," she remembered thinking.

It was impossible for God to leave ten or eleven fatherless children. Why take Bobby when my husband was paralysed, helpless, suffering, satiated with the world's pleasures and responsibilities and ready, almost eager, to go to the Great Unknown. And how could Bobby, so devoted to his children, so absorbed in their fun and frolics and in their sports and studies, be happy in Heaven and away from Ethel who was always with him at home or on his trips . . .

Rose was a Roman Catholic to the bone. She believed in a loving and merciful God, but also a God whose love and mercy were intimately bound up with the mystery of suffering. As she struggled to make sense of the tragedies in her own life, it was through the framework of her Catholicism.

Rose composed herself for RFK's funeral, where she stood stolidly in black, and on the train bearing his body from New York to Washington, where he'd be buried near his brother at Arlington. Thousands of people lined the tracks in observance of Bobby's passing. Rose and Ethel, easily the most devout in the Kennedy crew, gave strength to each other and the family with their conviction that Bobby was now with Jack, Kick, and Joe Jr. Rose would later write, "I take renewed strength and courage in the thought that as Jesus Christ rose from the dead, my husband and I and our sons and daughters will one day rise again and we all shall be happy together, never more to be separated."

A few days later, Rose and Teddy appeared on television from the yard in Hyannis Port. Rose, her voice strong, her posture ramrod straight, and not a hair out of place, thanked "all of you who offered your prayers, affection and condolences at the time of our recent bereavement."

"His death will not discourage or lessen our resolve," she continued. "The thought of his tragedy will not weaken or crush us . . . rather it will strengthen and fortify us."

An AP photo from the occasion is evocative. On the left side of the frame sits Teddy, in a flawless black suit, eyes downcast, the worries of the world heavy on his brow. At the right of the frame is Joe, a shell of a man, his suit hanging loosely, his face an involuntary scowl. At the dead center of the frame is Rose. She looks directly into the lens. In her eyes there is a sadness and a weariness, but more than that, a strength, a steeliness, a defiance. There's no shame in her gaze, no self-pity, and no apology.

11

ON DESTINY

Bobby's death did not weaken Rose's resolve, but it did prompt much reflection and even philosophizing on her part. Approaching her eighties, Rose was trying to make sense of her life, and age provided her the solitude and stillness that allowed her to do so with a new depth.

Preparing for a speech in the fall of 1968, she wrote that God

> has taken three stalwart sons equipped and eager to do his work here on earth, and left me a retarded child who can contribute nothing but must receive benefits rather than bestow. And Joe, who is so helpless— now he cannot feed himself the greater part of the time, requires so much attention. He has done his work nobly and now can contribute nothing—still God leaves him here suffering minor annoyances of ill health daily . . .

"Our family was the perfect family," she continued, "boys brilliant, girls attractive and intelligent, money, prestige . . . But God or 'destiny' just does not allow a family to exist, which has all these star studded adornments."

If acceptance of God's mysterious will was Rose's conclusion, it was not arrived at easily. Her faith, far from being rigid and simplistic, made room for questioning and lamentation, and Rose struggled repeatedly to come to grips with the tragedies of her life. Her conjectures about God— the calculus of suffering, how many "adornments" God can allow—are less theological pronouncements than they are signs of a process, evidence of a vibrant and dynamic faith. Faith was a comfort to Rose; but it also provided a powerful vocabulary for her own struggle to reconcile herself to the capriciousness of fate. The solace that she found in her religion is important, but it was not a solace that faith automatically granted—it was a solace that faith allowed her to *arrive at* via much struggle and questioning. The year of 1969, with its own fresh tragedies, would call upon that faith more than once.

~~~

Late on the night of July 18, 1969, Teddy left a party on the tiny island of Chappaquiddick, just across a small channel from Martha's Vineyard, with Mary Jo Kopechne, one of the aides from Bobby's presidential campaign. The circumstances surrounding the accident remain murky, but it's not disputed that, driving over a narrow bridge with no guardrails, Teddy's Oldsmobile went over the side and into the inlet below. The car landed, submerged, upside down. Teddy sustained a concussion and other injuries, and perhaps it was because of his disorientation that he could not free Mary Jo from the car. Perhaps this—or panic—also factored into his otherwise inexplicable failure to report the accident until the next morning. Mary Jo Kopechne drowned inside the Oldsmobile he left behind.

The media entered a sustained frenzy. That Sunday, the Chappaquiddick incident got more space in the *Boston Globe* than the first moon landing, which was to take place that afternoon. Rose stood by her son, whom she described as "unlike himself . . . disturbed, confused, and deeply distracted" the day after the accident. She wrote condolence letters to Mary Jo's parents and met with them in the Kennedys' New York apartment, where she shared her experience of losing children tragically. She otherwise remained behind the scenes, diplomatic and circumspect in interviews. Ted himself, taking responsibility for the accident and his actions (while never, the Kopechnes insisted, personally apologizing to them), asked the residents of Massachusetts to determine if he should resign. In 1970 he managed to be reelected. While Ted's presidential aspirations had been a question mark since Bobby's death, conventional wisdom now held them moot—the incident had, most felt, permanently ended his chances.

Ted had informed Joe of the accident himself. Sitting down across from Joe in his wheelchair, he took his father's hand. "Dad," he said, "I'm in some trouble. There's been an accident, and you're going to hear all sorts of things about me from now on . . ."

Ted would always hold himself somehow responsible for the fact that, just four months later, Joseph P. Kennedy suffered another series of strokes, fell into a coma, and on November 18, died. Rose, Teddy, Joan, Eunice, Pat, Steve, Jean, Jackie, Ethel, and Ann Gargan were all with him. The funeral was held at St. Francis Xavier in Hyannis, attended by four of Joe and Rose's children and twenty-seven of their grandchildren. Joseph Patrick Kennedy Sr., Rose's husband of fifty-five years, was buried in Brookline, Massachusetts, not far from the Beals Street home he bought in 1915 when he and Rose were young and newly wed.

$\sim$

Condolence letters poured in by the thousands, many containing cash donations for Rose to use at her discretion, whether it be for the Kennedy Library, a memorial for Bobby, or the work of the Kennedy Foundation. "Several people enclosed a dollar bill in an envelope which moved me deeply," she wrote. "One man sent $3.00 and said, 'The poor have so little time. Let us help them.'" For so many the Kennedys stood as examples of service and generosity, rather than only wealth.

Rose escaped the United States for the holidays in 1969: She spent Christmas in Paris with Eunice and Sargent Shriver, who had just been named ambassador to France. Then on to Greece for New Year's with Jackie, Caroline, and John Jr., not to mention Jackie's new husband, Aristotle Onassis. While much of the Kennedy clan (and no small portion of the US public) considered Jackie's 1968 wedding to the Greek shipping tycoon a betrayal, there's little evidence that it bothered Rose terribly much. Or, if it did, she came to peace with it soon enough. Rose's February 1969 diary mentions the happy "lilt" that had come into Jackie's voice since her marriage to Onassis, and her diary in February of 1970 indicated both how much the Christmas in Greece meant to Rose, and how Jackie and Rose's relationship had grown warmer in the years since Jack's death.

"She sent a letter which quite overwhelmed me," Rose wrote,

*with her really heartwarming expressions of the pleasure all of them
shared in my last visit . . . and how utterly unexpected was life's chain
of events—that she and I . . . should now start to share new experiences in an extremely different environment and atmosphere. . . . I
am thrilled, because in this way I shall always be able to contact the
children, to know they all enjoy having me with them.*

Rose also suspected that her presence brought the comfort of famil-
iarity to Caroline and John Jr. "Otherwise," she wrote, "they were more
or less surrounded by Greeks." She would meet Ari and Jackie again in
Paris that spring.

Rose's wanderlust did not wane as she became an octogenarian. In
July 1970 she flew to Switzerland, then to Greece for some time on
Onassis's yacht, the *Christina*, before celebrating her eightieth birthday in
Ethiopia with Jean and Haile Selassie, whose state dinner she'd hosted at
the White House so soon before Jack's death.

Earlier in the year, Rose had cut the ribbon on the newly completed
Rose Fitzgerald Kennedy Center for Research in Mental Retardation and
Human Development at Yeshiva University, an occasion she called "one
of the proudest and happiest of my life." Her work for the intellectually
disabled included her usual speaking engagements and talk-show appearances, but as the 1970s continued, she devoted more of her attention to
the care of her own developmentally disabled daughter, Rosemary. Her
periodic visits to St. Coletta's in Wisconsin continued, and her correspondence with the nuns at the facility reflect how much she cared about the
minutiae of Rosemary's life. The nuns' side of the correspondence paints
a picture of a quiet, simple, and not unhappy life in the rolling hills of the
Midwest.

"It seems the longer [Rosemary] is off medication the more vocal and
expressive she becomes. She at times amazes us with a complete and correct sentence," Sister Mary Charles wrote to Rose in 1971. "We got her a
little yellow canary named Skippy. He sings his heart out the whole day. I
know she likes him as she often says, 'Skippy, Skippy!'"

In June of 1973, Sister Mary wrote, "I try to give her little attentions
during the day; do the little things for her I know she likes—putting a

rose in her hair, talking to her, singing 'My Wild Irish Rose,' which she loves to hear. . . . The three sisters all love Rosemary and each of us do whatever we can to keep her happy. Above all we bear with her moods and emotional upsets with care and concern." The last comment indicates that Rosemary's mood swings were still present, though perhaps less frequent and severe.

One note from Rose to Father Robert Kroll during this period is illuminating. Describing Rosemary, Rose says that "she was progressing quite satisfactorily but circumstances developed by which she was further retarded, and so it is very difficult at times to become reconciled to her present state. However, I try to accept God's will." Though euphemized, it was an acknowledgement of her sense of loss; more than thirty years later, she still had trouble "becoming reconciled."

But she found her peace with Rosemary's condition in her faith. "I do sense and I do believe," Rose wrote, "that Rosemary's gift to me is equal to the gifts of my other children. By her presence I feel that she, too has asked something terribly important of us. With her life itself she too has shown us direction, given us purpose and a way to serve. That has been her gift."

Rose would find the precise limits of her candor when she finally got down to work on her memoirs. In 1972 she received a $1.525 million advance from Doubleday (until then, the biggest advance ever given for a single book) and set to work with ghostwriter Robert Coughlan. To build a narrative of her life, Coughlan interviewed Rose and members of the family at length and went through Rose's archived papers, no small task for a woman who rarely seems to have thrown anything away. Though Coughlan produced the initial manuscript, Rose went through it with a fine-toothed comb, erasing any elements she found untoward, upsetting, or unflattering. The result is her final bit of image making, the crafting of the Kennedy narrative as she wanted it seen. Published in 1974, *Times to Remember* became an instant best-seller. All of the proceeds went to the Joseph P. Kennedy Jr. Foundation.

As Rose got well into her eighties, she could not campaign with the same vigor that she had before. Still, she helped where she could, and she enjoyed the attention. She campaigned in 1970 for Teddy's reelection, his first since Chappaquiddick, and for Sargent Shriver when he was nominated as George McGovern's running mate in the 1972 presidential contest. Exhausted by years of campaigning and worried for Teddy's safety, she was relieved when he decided not to run.

In the second half of the 1970s, Rose's energy diminished markedly. She still took her swims in the Atlantic Ocean off Hyannis, but she had to be helped into and out of the water. Soon she needed nursing help. More and more of her time was spent alone at Hyannis Port and in Palm Beach.

But her life wasn't over. She was at Faneuil Hall in Boston when, on November 7, 1979, Teddy launched his ultimately unsuccessful bid to steal the Democratic presidential nomination from beleaguered incumbent Jimmy Carter. And she visited the Oval Office with Teddy in 1981 for the last time—and the first time since Jack's death—to watch as Ted presented an award for bipartisanship to Ronald Reagan.

On Good Friday, 1984, Rose collapsed at the Palm Beach house and nearly died from a severe stroke. She spent the rest of her days like Joe, confined to a wheelchair. Only speaking with great difficulty, she still said the rosary with Teddy when he stayed with her in Hyannis every weekend.

Rose died from pneumonia on January 22, 1995, at the age of 104, having lived through nineteen presidential administrations, including her own son's; having witnessed the rise of radio, the automobile, the airplane, film, television, and manned spaceflight; having lived at the center of US history during the middle of the twentieth century; having survived two world wars; having traveled to every continent save Antarctica; having associated with kings, queens, popes, and presidents; having outlived her husband and four of her nine children.

She was buried next to Joe in Brookline. Her gravestone, fittingly simple for a woman whose name had come to represent motherhood, philanthropy, and faith, read only "Rose Fitzgerald Kennedy 1890–1995."

PART II
Ethel

1

A LOVE STORY, WITH DETOURS

ETHEL SKAKEL WAS A SKINNY, LOUD-MOUTHED TOMBOY WITH SPARKLING eyes and an ever-present tan when she jubilantly began to conspire with her friend Jean Kennedy. Roommates at Manhattanville College—Rose's alma mater, then located in Harlem—the two girls were good friends with reputations as troublemakers. They came from similar backgrounds, as daughters of wealthy and large Irish Catholic families, into which they each were born second-to-last. They both had rambunctious and revered older brothers who hogged most of their parents' attention. They were both athletic and attractive and, as good Manhattanville girls, were on the lookout for possible husband material. Jean, in fact, was already engaged to a young man named Stephen Smith. As she and Ethel grew closer, she became certain that Ethel would love her older brother Bobby and wanted desperately for Ethel to meet him. Ethel was just as eager.

They plotted, Ethel later recalled, and in 1945, they succeeded: Ethel and her parents joined the Kennedys on a family ski trip to Mont-Tremblant in Canada, where she was formally introduced to Robert Francis Kennedy. Just as Jean had predicted, the two had a competitive sort of chemistry, exchanging an immediate wager over who would ski down the mountain the fastest. Ethel would later say it was love at first sight on her part when she spotted the toothy, five-foot, nine-inch-tall Bobby standing in front of a roaring fireplace.

Less so for Bobby.

Actually, it was Ethel's older sister Pat who first caught Bobby's eye. A disappointed Ethel could only concede defeat. Patricia Sistine Skakel was prettier, quieter, with more book smarts and certainly more feminine appeal. She was even named after a piece of Renaissance art. The sisters were opposites on many levels, right down to the states of their bedrooms: Ethel's was always a mess, like a typical boy's, but Pat's was "soft and refined: French Provincial furnishings, white satin on the headboard, wall-to-wall white fur carpeting in her private bathroom." Pat dated Bobby for two long years. Decades later, Ethel would wince at the recollection: "Ouch . . . That was a black period."

Though there are differing accounts of just how serious Bobby and Pat were—Pat would later refuse to answer when asked if the future attorney general had ever proposed marriage to Pat—by all accounts, it was a heartrending time for Ethel, who was forced to watch from the sidelines as the Kennedy boy with the serious eyes would swing by the house to pay Pat a visit. When he'd spot the little sister, he'd call out a friendly "hi," and she'd respond in kind, "but he never knew how she felt inwardly," journalist Lester David wrote in 1971. "It was a bleak and unhappy time for Ethel and she does not like to talk or even think about it."

In 1947, the cloud would lift and Ethel would get an opening. Bobby left for Israel to write about the War of Independence for the *Boston Post*. While he was away, Pat fell for another boy, Luan Peter Cuffe, and when Bobby returned, it was Ethel's turn to catch his attention. The two were about as opposite in personality as possible: Bobby had trouble finding the right words, so he often just didn't speak. In contrast to his outgoing brother Jack, Bobby rubbed some as uncommunicative. Ethel, on the other hand, was tough to shut up. "She talks and talks: bubbly, informal, slang-larded talk on anything that happens to fascinate her—children, sports, doctors, parties—spoken rapidly in a low, somewhat breathy contralto," wrote David. But soon after the two started to date—which, by proper Skakel-Kennedy standards, largely meant spending time together with other members of their enormous broods—Bobby grew increasingly smitten with the outspoken prankster. Then, in true teenage-girl fashion, Ethel swung the other way, not sure about him. Like her sister, she also had someone else on her mind.

Bobby learned, much to his exasperation, that the woman he wanted to marry was considering becoming a nun.

"How can I fight God?" he asked Jean.

2

THE RISE OF THE SKAKELS

Ethel perhaps seemed an unlikely candidate for a nun. She had been raised in a home without much discipline, alongside brothers who were known to shoot from their windows with air rifles at passersby. But if the seven Skakel children lacked rules while growing up, they certainly didn't lack religion.

The family patriarch was George Skakel, born in Chicago in 1892. His mother, Grace Mary Jordan, was from a slave-owning family in Mississippi. His father, James Curtis Skakel, was a Canadian-born Protestant who didn't care much for Catholics or Jews. Curt, as the father was known, was an alcoholic whose drinking served as catalyst to physical and verbal abuse. "Skakel's temperament was volatile," wrote biographer Jerry Oppenheimer, "and he had a contemptuous air about him and a certain roughness of manner." Gracie, George's mother, had a dark side as well: "Though sweet, refined, petite, and with a lovely drawl and a beautiful command of the English language, Gracie was a racist who railed against the freeing of the slaves and exuberantly supported the Ku Klux Klan," wrote Oppenheimer.

As a young man, George got his first job as a freight-rate clerk on the Sioux City Line of the Chicago, Milwaukee & St. Paul Railway, earning eight dollars a week. His parents were not at all rich, but George was destined to have money line his pockets. After a few years of railroading, he joined a coal-producing firm in Chicago, working as a traffic manager, before serving as an ensign in the US Naval Reserve during World War I. In the early 1900s, George helped establish the Great Lakes Coal and Coke Company in Chicago, which grew to become one of the largest privately held companies in America, making George a multimillionaire. His wealth insulated his family from the crippling market crash of 1929 and the following Depression.

George married Ann Brannack, a chubby woman with a sweet smile and long, lustrous blonde hair. She came from a poor, uneducated family, whose ancestors had left Ireland during the 1840s potato famine. She'd been working in the office at William Howe Co., a coal distributor, where George briefly worked, when the two met. Ann was a tad taller than George and a bit heavier as well, but George liked the cute, boisterous "Liverpool Irish" girl who lived in the blue-collar South Side. He liked less her religion. Ann was a devout Irish Catholic. Her mother, Margaret Brannack, had converted from Episcopalian to Catholicism at her husband's request when Ann was ten years old. As latecomers to faith tend to be, Margaret became die-hard in her religion, and Ann was required to attend early morning mass every day, even if it meant trudging through Chicago in a snowstorm.

"It was a very religious environment that Ann lived in," her lifelong friend, Florence Ferguson Kumpfer, later said. "We used to go to church together every day. The nuns were very strict. Ann was a Catholic's Catholic. Her mother instilled that strong, strong religion in her."

Ann's father, Joseph Brannack, seemed destined to fit an unfortunate stereotype: the hard-drinking Irishman. "He was rarely around," Oppenheimer wrote, "and offered little security for the family, jumping from one menial job to another—hotel worker, night watchman—supporting his family as best he could." Like Curt Skakel, Brannack had issues with drink—a hardship that would lead him and his wife to separate.

Despite George's misgivings about Ann's religion, he courted her, and she believed in him. She was certain he would someday be a success, and so they were married on November 25, 1917, by a Catholic priest. They moved into a house in a Catholic neighborhood in Chicago, and within three months, Ann was pregnant. With each pregnancy, Ann seemed to keep the weight she'd gained, eventually reaching nearly two hundred pounds. In all, she had seven children—four girls and three boys—which she initially raised in a large home on University Avenue in Hyde Park. The first child was Georgeann—a merging of the parents' first names—followed by brothers George Jr., Jim, and Rushton. Next came Patricia, then Ethel—named after her mother's sister and born April 11, 1928, in Chicago's Lying-In Hospital—followed finally by Ann (known as "Little Ann" to her mother's "Big Ann").

The children were young when the family moved east to New York in 1933, hopping from one high-end rental home to the next. For a while they settled in the well-to-do suburb of Larchmont in Westchester County north of Manhattan, renting a mansion on twelve acres of land. The house was impractically huge—so enormous that the family didn't even use many of the rooms. "It was a fabulous place, so big none of us could believe it, and mind-bogglingly beautiful," Rushton Skakel would later recall.

George used the home often to entertain business associates, and Ann was an admirable host. "The parties were always impressive, with a hired staff to serve the finest foods and liquors—especially liquor," wrote journalist J. Randy Taraborrelli. Sometimes the parties lasted all day, beginning when George had breakfast meetings in the morning, and ending after dinner, cocktails, and more drinks at night. George used the house as an extension of his business, and he considered his children—unruly bunch though they were—assets. They weren't ordered to their bedrooms; rather, they were on full display for guests. Potential business partners and clients seemed to embrace the vision as proof that George was a wholesome, happy family man. He became so reliant on the image that it extended outside of the home. "My father practically never went to a business meeting without one of us," Rushton Skakel said. "We'd go into major board meetings at the big companies and we'd be sitting there with all these industrialists and moguls. You'd be the only child in the meeting, and it made a difference with those people. It impressed them and made the meeting a personal, beautiful thing, in their eyes."

As fun-loving a scene as it appeared, "the parties literally every day" had devastating effects, Rushton said:

> *I was 10 years old when we moved to the house on Larchmont. Dad was establishing his company in New York, so my parents had parties,*

parties, parties. That's when Dad started drinking. Dad's alcoholism hit him when we were in Larchmont because of all those parties and all of the drinking that went on. . . . And that's when we started drinking.

Ann loved the Larchmont home for more than the parties. She loved that it was right across the street from the Dominican Day School, a private academy founded by Sister Rose Alma. Ann enrolled then five-year-old Ethel in kindergarten there, and her brothers and sisters in their respective grades. Rose Alma attempted to provide children from families like the Skakels with order and discipline—the exact opposite of what they were getting at home. George and Ann weren't much for imposing rules on their brood; they traveled so much that Georgeann had earned the nickname "the little mother," and she often was burdened with watching over the younger six children alone.

The Skakels stayed in the Larchmont mansion for about two years, settling briefly in another huge house a few miles north in a small town called Rye. The boys enrolled in Canterbury, a monastic Catholic boarding school across the border in Connecticut, and, like a young John F. Kennedy before them, hated it and its impossible rules. Jack, who received "poor" and "fair" assessments in his Latin, science, and religion classes, asked to transfer to another school; the rowdy Skakel boys were asked to leave.

Eventually, the clan headed a few miles north to Greenwich, Connecticut. There, George bought a twenty-five-room mansion that he got for a bargain because of the struggling economy. The three-story brick home had belonged to Zalmon Simmons, one of the richest men in town —impressive status in one of the richest towns in the country. Simmons, who had made his fortune developing the country's first mass-produced mattresses, had built the home on a 164-acre estate known as Rambleside that became famous for its elm trees, azaleas, and countless iris bulbs. The mansion interior "featured hand-painted chinoiserie wallpaper, black marble floors with inlaid copper, and a study paneled with pine that had been stripped from a venerable mansion in London." The library measured almost sixty feet long and had a black marble fireplace, teak floors, recessed bookcases, Corinthian columns, and bay windows that looked out on grounds of stately elms and boxwoods. Inside the main house were six double bedrooms, three staff bedrooms, two single bedrooms, a master suite with its own sitting room and fireplace, a glass-enclosed sleeping porch, a billiard room, six baths, and a playroom for the children. Outside the main house, there was a guesthouse, a teahouse, two servants' houses, a stable for horses, and a garage built for six cars.

After Simmons died in 1934, during the Great Depression, his wife began selling off the estate in chunks. The mansion sat idle for a while, as most people in the midst of the economic downturn simply couldn't afford such a luxurious home. But then, most people weren't George Ska-kel. He paid Simmons's widow less than $160,000 for a ten-acre chunk of the estate that included the main house. For another forty thousand dollars, George got all the Simmonses' furnishings, too. After George moved his family in, he added a seventy-five-foot swimming pool to the property.

There, the wild parties would continue. The children would play football on the lawn and set off firecrackers during dinner. Fully dressed guests would end up drenched in the pool. Ann would adopt an absolute menagerie that would roam the acreage and greet amused visitors: dogs, cats, turtles, lizards, chickens, ducks, pigs, sheep, and goats. Years later, Ethel would re-create these scenes in every sense at Hickory Hill, the house she shared with Bobby and their ever-growing family.

3

THE GIRL WITH THE RED CONVERTIBLE

Though the Kennedys and Skakels both shared nouveau riche status, they handled it in very different ways. The Kennedys *acted* more like typical old money. They were wealthy but tempered in their spending. They didn't just hobnob with the upper crust, they became its top layer. They visited popes and sought ambassadorships and emphasized order and structure and discipline. "Dinner was at 7:15 and it did not mean 7:16," Ethel would later say of her in-laws. The Skakel home was hardly so orderly. "At our house, you didn't know whether you were going to have supper at 5 or 10," Ethel said.

Nor was Rose Kennedy's stern emphasis on scholastics mirrored in Ann Skakel's child rearing. Ethel, in fact, was a mediocre student, doing just enough to skate by, first at Greenwich Academy, and then at the Convent of the Sacred Heart in Maplehurst. By the time she reached Manhattanville, her less-than-studious habits had long been solidified. "Every morning at college—even at college, imagine that—from 8:30 to 9, I read the odds about the racetrack," Ethel recalled. "If only my tests would have been about the race horses instead of history. I would've had an A." She added, with a laugh: "I wasn't a very deep thinker."

In Ethel's senior yearbook—class of 1949—she's described with flourish:

An excited hoarse voice, a shriek, a peal of screaming laughter, the flash of shirttails, a tousled brown head—Ethel! Her face is at one moment

a picture of utter guilelessness and at the next alive with mischief . . .
The 49ers didn't have to search very far to find in Ethel a heart of gold.

Ethel was smart and clever—her letters to family and friends were always lively and well written—but she was never considered an intellectual heavyweight. She had a native aversion to introspection and embraced her mother's religious teachings apparently without question. And that maternal influence was strong: Inside the Greenwich home's library stood a font of holy water and several praying chairs. Ann would drive into town every morning for 7:00 a.m. mass at St. Mary's Roman Catholic Church on Greenwich Avenue, towing each child with her as soon as they turned four years old. Every day she and the children said a special prayer that George would convert to Catholicism. Ethel's lifelong religiosity was rooted in "saying grace before every meal, of wearing a silver rosary every waking and sleeping moment, of attending mass daily no matter how late she had come home the night before."

But Ethel's faith was borne of more than just ritual. Ann routinely invited clergymen and educators to visit the home and gather in the ornate library—its ceiling-high shelves lined with books—and lead informal discussions on matters of religion. While hardly intellectual debates, the discussions covered a broad range of topics and lent an air of sophistication to the otherwise rough-edged home.

Still, many who grew up with Ethel in Greenwich remembered her and her brothers as irresponsible, unruly, even arrogant. Tales of the Skakel kids running amok became the stuff of local legend. The boys had followed in their father's footsteps to become gun fanatics—George was known to always keep a loaded revolver in his bedroom nightstand—and stories were rampant about them shooting up mailboxes and streetlamps around town. "There were some forty-five-caliber bullet holes in some of those mailboxes," childhood friend Ken McDonnell remembered. "They were using big stuff, and there was some retaliation. Some people went up there to the Skakel house and put a few holes in their mailbox."

Then there was the time the brothers decided they wanted to build a bridge across a small lake near their home. Instead of wood and nails for the construction, they used Buicks, driving at least a half-dozen cars into the lake hood-to-trunk, so that the boys could walk across the roofs and get from one side of the lake to the other. "All those cars ended up accordion-pleated in the water," Pan Jacob, a childhood friend of Ethel's, later recalled. "And that was considered lots of fun by them. No one in the house said, 'What a horrible thing to do!' It was just 'Isn't this fun? Isn't this amusing? Those naughty boys!' There was no punishment."

Pan blamed the parents for a lack of discipline. "The Skakel kids weren't spoiled so much as they were deprived. They had money but they didn't have anything else. There was no structure." She once said,

> *Most families have a way of doing things, a pattern of behavior. There was no pattern at Lake Avenue. It was an abstract painting as opposed to a formal painting, more surreal than Rembrandt; a Jackson Pollock world where everything was exploding, where there was no cohesiveness. The Skakel house had a sadness about it. It didn't have a core. The family had no established roots. We all felt insecure. I don't think they did. In fact, they were a mass of insecurity.*

But while some people remembered the family as unstable, others remembered it as a riotous good time—including Jim Skakel, Ethel's brother. "Our parents weren't strict, but we didn't do anything too ridiculous, either," he said. "There wasn't any pressure. The philosophy was 'Enjoy yourself.'" The animals, the parties—all of it made for outrageously wild tales. And Ethel, if not disciplined at home, was certainly self-disciplined. She had a natural competitive edge to ensure she succeeded at anything physical she tried. When she was introduced to horses at a young age, she immediately took to riding and quickly excelled at competing. She'd don her jodhpurs, top coat, riding hat, and crop and spend most afternoons after school with her rotating cast of horses: There was Smoky Joe, who was black with white socks, and whom her father bought for $800; Guamada, a chestnut mare working hunter that cost $1,500; and Beau Mischief, a dark bay that she owned when she left for college. On weekends, she'd show the animals.

National Velvet, the movie starring a young Elizabeth Taylor and her horse, was Ethel's favorite. "She took to riding the way she took to touch football with the Kennedys," said Ethel's friend Billy Steinkraus, who went on to ride with the US Olympic riding team. Ethel was so consumed by her horses that she had neither the time nor attention span to chase boys like her friends. In fact, she didn't seem to have much interest in exploring her approaching womanhood at all. If she had a date in high school, her childhood friends couldn't remember it. In April 1936, Ethel got her first mention and photo in the *New York Times* when a picture of her, her brothers George and Rushton, and sisters Pat and Georgeann appeared with the caption: "Five Members of One Family Ride in Same Horse Show." It would be the first of hundreds of mentions in our nation's paper of record.

As each child got old enough to drive, they were given a new car—and each earned their own lead-foot reputation with the Greenwich Police Department. Friends remembered the police chief routinely stationing an officer at the end of the family's driveway, hoping to nail them for speeding before they even reached the public roadway. Access to cars prompted the boys to play a game they called "King of the Castle," in which one would climb on top of the car's roof while another drove it recklessly around town in search of low-hanging tree branches. The goal: to knock the roof-rider from the moving vehicle to the ground.

When Ethel came of age, she got a spiffy red convertible. Oppenheimer wrote:

> *Ethel drove recklessly and at high speeds, sometimes at night with her lights off. Once, coming back from a horse show, she drove her car off the road and through the woods as a shortcut home. One year, she had a car without a reverse gear and everywhere she went she caused a traffic jam and hot tempers if she had to back up, which she found hysterical. Ethel or her passengers would push the car backward.*

While the kids raised hell around town, father George continued amassing a fortune. Great Lakes Coal and Coke began in 1919 when Skakel launched the business with Walter Gramm to buy coal wholesale and distribute it to retailers. Within a few years, the company expanded its interest to petroleum coke—a byproduct of the oil-refining process.

While the market crash crippled much of the nation, Great Lakes flourished, opening an office in New York City and marketing petroleum coke as a solid fuel for domestic and industrial heating. Soon, George expanded into the international market, setting up sales offices in Germany and Japan, among other countries. Eventually, Oppenheimer reported, 65 percent of the company's income would be derived from foreign sales.

George was forever looking for ways to expand, and he was shrewdly entrepreneurial. He saw that electrochemical and electrometallurgical industries had been purifying the petroleum coke that they used in their plants, and he figured that his company could take over that process at plants situated close to the refineries. "It could sell the purified product at higher prices than the raw material, and the industries, relieved of the calcining burden, would be happy to pay them," David wrote. The first calcining plant opened in 1935 at Port Arthur, Texas, and was a huge success. More plants followed in Illinois, California, and Wyoming, and George's grand idea ended up making him millions of dollars. It was a long-term moneymaker, too: Calcined petroleum coke is a key ingredient in producing aluminum, and George's company had a near monopoly on supplying it to the growing aviation industry. The nation struggled, but not the Skakels: George was one of about two dozen known millionaires in America in the early 1930s.

"In judging other men, my father's standard was *when* those men made their fortune, not how *big* it was," Jim Skakel, Ethel's brother, would later say. "He was always proud he made his money in the Depression, the *worst* of the Depression."

As World War II got under way, George partnered up with an army colonel with shipping connections. George bought several tramp steamers, a type of merchant ship, which he named after his daughters. The *Ethel Skakel*, the *Patricia Skakel*, and the *Ann Skakel* had hefty government contracts that George's army buddy, Alfred Parry, helped procure. Great Lakes Carbon owned 75 percent of the shipping company, and Parry got 25 percent for running the business. Once the war ended, George sold off his two remaining boats—one had been sunk by a German U-boat in the war—and he got out of the shipping business.

Despite this high-profile wealth, George's name rarely made the papers. Unlike Joe Kennedy, who courted the press, George was wary of it. As the company grew, George refused repeated requests from the likes of *Fortune* magazine and the *Wall Street Journal* to interview him for profiles. "Whenever a colleague would advise him to talk to a journalist to get free publicity, George would scoff," Oppenheimer wrote. "His philosophy was, 'You can't quote silence.'"

Back at home, Ann Skakel was a study in contradictions when it came to her wealth. On one hand, she let the kids chase each other, spraying carbonated soda all over the house—drenching the drapes and carpet—without a thought about the cost. Ethel once rode her horse straight through the front door and out through the back, and Ann is said to have shrugged it off. And yet, Ann had a cheap streak. She once decided that soda was costing her too much (the kids, after all, didn't just drink the stuff), and she had heard that private schools were given a discount from the distributor. "So she telephoned the distributor, informing them that the big house on Simmons Lake was a school and could she have the discount, please?" author Lester David wrote. "She could and she did for a number of months, until the distributor found out and politely but firmly refused to grant the discount any more."

4

MANHATTANVILLE

THE NUNS AT MANHATTANVILLE HAD ENCOUNTERED PLENTY OF PRECO-
cious young women over the years, but none was quite like Ethel Skakel—
especially when she joined forces with her roommate, Jean Kennedy. Just
as the high jinks in the Skakel home lent to local folklore, so, too, did
Ethel's pranks at the pious college.

Once, the girls wondered aloud what the nuns wore to sleep. Ethel
decided there was only one way to find out, so she pulled the fire alarm,
and the nuns scurried into the halls in their nightgowns. Another time,
after being snubbed by an Irish boy showing his horse at a New York
horse show, Ethel snuck into the stables and painted the boy's horse green
with vegetable dye, in honor of his Irish roots. Then there was the time
Ethel targeted Monsignor Hartigan for arriving on campus in a fancy
new Cadillac. She put a handwritten note in his windshield that read,
"Are the collections good, Father?"

Years later, Ethel would remember one prank above most others.
She and Jean had racked up serious demerits that the nuns tallied in a
dreaded book. Ethel's offenses were many: chewing gum in assembly,
disorder in the tearoom, talking during lunch. She had so many demerits that she was going to be "campused," forced to stay at Manhattanville
while the other girls were free to go to the annual Harvard-Yale football
game.

"This is ridiculous to ground us at this age," Jean complained. "We're
too old to be grounded."

Ethel agreed, recalling that they "took the demerit book and threw it
down the incinerator, and went to the Harvard-Yale game."

Rose Kennedy worried that the high-spirited Ethel was leading Jean down a troubling path, and so she tried to separate the girls. "Mother didn't think we were studying, and Mother thought that Ethel was a bad influence," Jean later recalled. "I had had honors when I graduated from Noroton, and my marks went steadily down. So she put up a wall between us." The divide didn't last, however, and even after Bobby passed up Ethel to date her sister, Ethel still worked her way into the Kennedy clan. In 1946, as Bobby and Pat dated, she went to work on Jack's congressional campaign, ringing doorbells, passing out literature, and telling anyone who would listen just how "terrific" a candidate John F. Kennedy was. "We'd drive up to Boston and lick stamps," Ethel recalled. "I thought, this is so exciting! We went house to house and talked to people. And why they would listen to a 17-year-old who knew nothing, I have no idea. But it was a great experience. It was a room full of people who I had never rubbed elbows with before."

Ethel had never paid much attention to politics before she was drawn in by Jean's enthusiasm. In fact, her parents were conservative Republicans. Her father considered Franklin D. Roosevelt an enemy because of the president's plan to impose new regulations on big business. "George hated Roosevelt," Jay Mayhew, Great Lakes' chief geologist and George's longtime friend, would later say. "He felt that Roosevelt would run the country into the ground. He felt Roosevelt could have become a dictator." Asked years later whether she had any consciousness of their political beliefs growing up, Ethel replied, "None whatsoever."

Still, Ethel worked doggedly for Jack's campaign, scurrying to sometimes six or seven neighborhood parties a day, serving cookies and pouring coffee and handing out brochures. She found the whole process invigorating, and after the campaign ended, returned to college a fervent believer in the Kennedy cause. She even wrote a college thesis on Kennedy's book *Why England Slept* and peppered in enough firsthand research to earn an A.

After graduation, she toured Europe with Jean and Eunice and, upon her return, decided to enroll at Columbia University for graduate work. By then, Bobby was ready to settle down. Though he was the seventh born to Rose and Joe, he planned to be the first married—and he hoped to raise a family bigger than his own.

5

BOBBY'S WIFE

FACED WITH A CHOICE BETWEEN BEING BOBBY'S WIFE AND BECOMING A nun, Ethel took the secular path and never looked back. Despite how different their personalities were, Ethel seemed the perfect match for Bobby, according to just about everyone who knew them. Bobby was the son that came after four straight daughters, and he wouldn't get another brother for seven long years. He looked up to Joe Jr. and Jack, just as Ted would look up to him. Art Buchwald, the *Washington Post* humorist who became close friends with Bobby and Ethel, said that Bobby had an inferiority complex. "He just couldn't live up to his brothers," Buchwald said. "And he was caught in the middle there. I don't think he got as much attention as the other kids. Therefore, he was always shy and always unsure of himself." That changed, Buchwald said, when Bobby met Ethel. "Ethel was the one that changed him and gave him complete loyalty and ego building."

The two announced their engagement at a lunch gathering at the Skakel home in early 1950. "Ethel was head-over-heels in love with Bobby. That's all she talked about and wanted," said Ann Maric O'Hagan Murphy, a friend. "She couldn't wait for the weekends so she could see Bobby. As soon as she started going with him, it was *Bobby, Bobby, Bobby*; it was *Kennedy, Kennedy, Kennedy*—and not so much Skakel anymore."

Her engagement ring was a showstopper, a beautiful marquise diamond that Ethel had selected from a huge tray of rings from Cartier's that Bobby had delivered to Rambleside. The engagement made Bobby's hometown paper, the *Boston Globe*, May 28, 1950, with a story that declared the union the "ideal romance." A photo of Ethel's young, fresh face, with a button nose and large teeth accentuated by her thin upper lip, accompanied the inside-page story. "The difficulty in writing about Miss Skakel, a tiny brunette with large brown eyes, is that everyone makes the identical comments," wrote Mary Cremmen in May 1950. "Each person to whom I spoke mentioned her excellent swimming ability, the many blue ribbons she had won for horsemanship at Madison Square Garden, and then shifted to her personality." Among the descriptions: charming, vivacious, and unaffected.

Bobby and Ethel's impending wedding was the talk of Greenwich. Every hotel room in town was booked. The Skakels and Kennedys separately would have spared no expense, and united, they hosted one of the most lavish events Greenwich had ever seen. This, even as the two families predictably butted heads—reportedly because the Skakels refused to invite Joe and Rose to stay at Rambleside for the festivities, forcing the elder Kennedys to find a hotel room. But whatever tensions there were, the families buried them for the big day. The ceremony was held at the ornate St. Mary's Church, where Ann went to daily mass. Inside, the stone building was filled with white peonies, regal lilies, and dogwood. Jack was Bobby's best man; Teddy was one of the many ushers. (Ethel would later recall he had twenty-one.) Pat Skakel Cuffe, once Bobby's girlfriend, was matron of honor; Little Ann, Ethel's youngest sister, was maid of honor. As Ethel readied to walk down the aisle, the church filled with the tenor singing of Michael O'Higgins, a vocalist from the Royal Irish Academy of music who was flown from Dublin for the affair.

The twenty-two-year-old bride looked lovely in a modest white satin gown with a bateau neckline and a fitted bodice. Her long veil was double tulle attached to a cap of Point Venise lace, and she had a simple, single strand of pearls on her neck. In her hands, a bouquet of stephanotis, eucharis lilies, and lilies of the valley. "There were fountains of champagne," Ethel remembered. "Lots of dancing, lots of dogs all over everything." The reception was at the Skakels' opulent home, transformed to accommodate some six hundred guests. It was there that Bobby swept Ethel onto the dance floor. Soon, Jack cut in, and after a few spins, Ted approached to have his turn with the bride. But by then, Joe had grown impatient, so he walked out and elbowed his way in front of Ted to dance with his first daughter-in-law.

Ethel was the first Kennedy wife of the new generation, and she immersed herself completely in the role. After the wedding she and Bobby flew to Hawaii to start their three-month honeymoon. They stayed in the most lavish suites money could buy in plush resort hotels on Waikiki Beach and Maui. Each day, the bridal suite was filled with fresh, fragrant orchids. Once they were done strolling the beaches and lounging beneath the coconut trees, they flew to Los Angeles and bought a convertible to drive across the country. It was "just will of the wisp," Ethel would later say. "We'd go to Montana, and then we'd go to a southern state. We went wherever we had friends."

Bobby was in his last year studying at the University of Virginia School of Law—itself a storied institution, founded as part of Thomas Jefferson's famed "academical village" in 1819—and Ethel settled in as a homemaker. She was, by all accounts, horrible at it. Her children would later remember her trying to fry a banana in petroleum jelly. This was one challenge she didn't feel like rising to meet, so she hired a cook; from then on in their marriage, she cooked only in emergencies.

Unlike some of the later Kennedy unions, Ethel and Bobby truly seemed to enjoy spending their leisure time together, often walking hand-in-hand to morning mass at Holy Comforter, a small Roman Catholic church near campus, and later to the Farmington Country Club to battle on the tennis court until it was time for dinner. The new wife wanted her marriage to be a partnership, so she set out to support Bobby in whatever goals he set for himself. When Bobby would give a speech, Ethel would be there to listen. When he began making court appearances, she attended as many as she could. "I like to see Bobby in action," she once said. Even after she began having children, she would take all but the youngest with her to watch their father at work.

Bobby's work ethic was stellar and his goals lofty. He was elected president of the Student Legal Forum, which invited big names to campus to lead discussions on the issues of the day. Bobby at times would turn to Joe for help in recruiting national figures, and when the father and son worked together, the sessions were packed. "He was careful to choose them from all shades of political and social opinion," author Lester David wrote. Among the guests: liberal Supreme Court Justice William O. Douglas, Republican Senator Joseph McCarthy, and Thurman Arnold, President Franklin Roosevelt's assistant attorney general, known for his trust-busting campaign. But it was Bobby's invitation to Ralph Bunche that would expand Ethel's horizons. Bunche, a United Nations official, was the first African American to win a Nobel Peace Prize. He accepted the invitation to speak on the condition that he be allowed to speak to an integrated crowd—a tricky request in Charlottesville, Virginia, where the law called for separation of races in all public places. The request naturally incensed the segregationists in the small Southern town, but Bobby pleaded Bunche's case. He argued the case to University President Colgate Darden by pointing to a Supreme Court decision based in Texas that decided that any educational event at any law school in the country must be desegregated. Darden agreed. "When, at long last, Dr. Bunche arrived at Cabell Hall, it was filled to capacity," US Attorney General Eric Holder would tell a group of students graduating from the UVA law school in 2011. "And, for the first time in history, nearly a third of the seats were taken by African Americans."

Bunche's impact on the young Kennedy couple wouldn't end there. Because of the angry threats lobbed at the doctor, Bobby and Ethel decided the safest place for him to stay would be their home. "He was so charming and non-complaining," Ethel later recalled, "but they did throw things at our house all night long. It was so unthinkable and outrageous. You got a little taste of what black people in our country had to go through at that time."

Joseph McCarthy's visit was almost as upsetting to the liberals on campus. The Wisconsin senator was gaining national attention with his allegations that members of the Communist Party had infiltrated the government in high places. He tossed around words like "treason," "espionage," and "corruption." The Skakels had long been anti-Communist and idolized McCarthy as soon as he entered the scene. Ethel's sister Pat had even lectured to students that "Christians should work as hard for Christianity as Communists were working for communism," and she and her brother George Jr. would intercept and toss out literature and pamphlets they deemed too left-leaning. When Bobby invited McCarthy in the fall of 1950, Ethel was thrilled, and friends said she began planning her most lavish party yet.

Years later, when asked if she truly had worried about the "Communist threat," Ethel didn't hesitate: "Yes, I did," she said. "Especially growing up in a Republican atmosphere, they were always talking about the Communists." McCarthy had been a personal friend, too, having dated two Kennedy girls, Pat and Eunice. Bobby later would join McCarthy's Senate Subcommittee on Investigations, and then he would leave when he determined that McCarthy's allegations were overblown and his tactics questionable. He left McCarthy's orbit before McCarthy completely self-destructed, but their association would be an embarrassment for the rest of Bobby's life. In the mid-1960s, he told writer Peter Maas that, "at the time, I thought there was a serious internal security threat to the United States . . . and Joe McCarthy seemed to be the only one who was doing anything about it." Bobby paused, and concluded, "I was wrong."

In his work for the UVA Student Legal Forum, Bobby sometimes drew his speakers from a little closer to home. Joe was invited, as was Jack, who was about to launch his first senatorial campaign. His forum speech went well, but the visit caused some tension with Ethel, who, in a flurry of uncharacteristic domesticity, had readied a room for Jack in the couple's modest Charlottesville home and had overseen the preparation of an elaborate dinner in his honor. Jack arrived at dinner late, and when he finally appeared, he wasn't alone. With him was a French girl dressed in a short, tight skirt, tight top, and platform heels. Jack announced he'd be staying at a hotel rather than with his brother. Ethel fumed. "You know I told you I was fixing up the guest room for you. I had flowers in the room and everything!" she complained.

While Jack's sexual appetite was well known and eventually well documented, Bobby's wasn't as voracious, and certainly wasn't as visible. Before marrying Ethel, he had fallen in love with a beautiful British actress named Joan Winmill, whom he'd met on a visit to London in 1948, not long after Kathleen's death. While there, he had attended a play called *The Chiltern Hundreds*, about a beautiful young American millionairess who—in defiance of her Catholic family—marries the Protestant son of an English Earl. It was transparently based on Kathleen's story, and twenty-seven-year-old Winmill played the lead, which was based on her. The two began a love affair. Bobby had stood at a crossroads, torn between two women who represented two entirely different paths in life, and he'd chosen exuberant, energetic Ethel. After marriage, Bobby, like his brothers, may have had affairs outside of marriage. Over the years, a long list of alleged conquests has surfaced. Some of the names seem plausible—Marilyn Monroe, for example—and others less so, but if Ethel knew about any such dalliances, she has never acknowledged them.

From the beginning of their marriage, Bobby seemed utterly devoted to his wife, and she invested everything into his career and happiness. In June 1951, as Bobby graduated middle of his class with a mediocre grade-point average of 2.54, Ethel was about to make him a very happy husband indeed: She was ready to give birth to their first child.

6

FIRST BIRTHS, FIRST DEATHS

WHILE THE COUPLE WAS THRILLED TO BE THE FIRST TO MAKE ROSE AND Joe grandparents, Ethel was less stoked about the physical symptoms of pregnancy. She was used to running around and being active—and, with later pregnancies, she'd make headlines for doing just that—but this first experience was uncomfortable and, even worse, limiting. The nausea, the physical twinges and heartburn—all of it prompted Ethel to stop the tennis playing and the swimming and instead act, as biographer Jerry Oppenheimer put it, "like a patient preparing for major surgery." Sue Drake, a friend of Ethel's, recalled that the mom-to-be was sick and miserable initially. "She was basically terrified by the whole thing," Drake said. "She wanted to do what was right, but she was scared." It didn't help that the baby hung on a good two weeks past Ethel's due date.

Bobby and Ethel had moved into a Rambleside guesthouse in the summer of 1951 to await the birth. One night as they watched television with the family in the sitting room, Ethel let out a scream. Bobby rushed his twenty-three-year-old wife to Greenwich Hospital and called on trusted Nurse Hennessey to help.

"He called me and said, 'Ethel has gone to the hospital, and the doctor is kind of worried. . . . Will you come down? Will you fly right down?'" Hennessey hesitated. She didn't like to fly at all, but she refused to fly alone, so Bobby flew up, met her at the airport, and boarded with her on a return flight, and the two arrived in Greenwich to be by Ethel's side.

On July 4th Ethel gave birth to a healthy daughter they named Kathleen, after Bobby's late sister, Kick. Senator Joseph McCarthy—for whom Bobby was still working—would be the child's godfather. Hennessey, who would attend the birth of all of Ethel's eleven children, recalled that the young mother was anxious and depressed after the birth. "Ethel had a lot of problems," the nurse later said. "I wouldn't call it a nervous breakdown. I would say it was exaggerated anxiety. It was a very difficult, quite hard delivery for Ethel and she was suffering when I got there." Physically, it had been a grueling delivery, one that would leave Ethel aching for days with an internal injury caused by the baby being so big—likely in part because it was overdue—inside of Ethel's petite frame. It didn't help Ethel's mental state that she had trouble nursing Kathleen and had to bottle feed her instead, Hennessey said.

As happens with many new moms, the expected feelings of motherly love and joy didn't immediately wash over Ethel, and some of her recent worries bubbled to the surface. She told Hennessey that she'd been lonely in the little house in Charlottesville, where Bobby studied all the time and she mostly had superficial friends. "With her old friends she could discuss intimate things," Hennessey later said. "In Charlottesville, Ethel didn't have that luxury. She didn't have her mother or father or an aunt or an old friend to help her. She felt she had been thrown into pregnancy far away from home." And now that the baby was born, she worried about the family's next step. "Nothing in her life was settled and that bothered her," Hennessey said. "She was concerned that she didn't have her own home with Bobby to go back to. She didn't feel it was natural going back to her parents' house."

It was a rare, unguarded moment for Ethel, who usually put on a happy front for others, and this instance of atypical vulnerability wasn't shared with the rest of the family—possibly not even Bobby, Hennessey said. When Ethel finally left the hospital for Rambleside two weeks after giving birth, she immediately ordered a dozen red roses for Rose Kennedy, starting a tradition that she'd keep for ten more births—a tribute to the family matriarch and Ethel's acknowledged role model. Hennessey moved into a guesthouse with the baby, and every morning, she'd bring Kathleen to Ethel in the main house, where the new mom stayed with Bobby. The proud father seemed thrilled to have a girl because he could cuddle her. "Little boys are different," Hennessey remembered him saying. "You can love a little girl."

That summer, Ethel was active again. Returning to Hyannis Port, she and Bobby swam, sailed, and took long walks along the beach. But Bobby was still weighing his next career move, and he was gone for long stints at his father's behest while he sorted out the future. Bobby debated joining a law firm in New York, but public service had been hammered into him so much as a young man that entering private practice would have been a betrayal of the family ethos. He decided to put his connections to use: Senator McCarthy helped him get his first job with the Department of Justice's Internal Security Division, where Bobby would earn $4,200 a year investigating records kept by suspected spies. Ethel was thrilled that they'd be able to settle down, especially as she learned in the fall of 1951 that she was already pregnant again. But the flirtation with stability would be short-lived. Jack was going to run for the Senate in 1952, and he tapped Bobby to be his campaign manager. Bobby had worked for the Justice Department for just three months. "It was a major decision," Ethel recalled. "He felt he was just starting out his own career and he had to put it on the back burner. It was a big sacrifice."

Ethel already had tasted Kennedy campaigning during Jack's congressional bid, but now, as a wife and full-fledged member of the family, she would be expected to play a much more visible role. She joined Rose and Jack's sisters in hosting the famous tea parties and remained front and center as the summer waned, even as her stomach ballooned in the later months of her pregnancy.

Privately, Ethel worried about her unborn baby. Her sister Georgeann, also pregnant, had been stricken with rubella—German measles—which was known to affect fetuses in utero. Fear plagued Georgeann's pregnancy, and unfortunately, Alexandra was born blind and deaf, with profound developmental disabilities. She labored to breathe and eventually was placed in a home for the terminally ill. Ethel prayed on her rosary that her own unborn child wasn't affected, as she had been in contact with Georgeann when the vicious illness developed. Her worries proved unfounded: on September 24, 1952, Ethel gave birth to a healthy boy that Bobby chose to name Joe, after his departed older brother.

"All of her prayers had worked," Hennessey later said, providing a clue to understanding her and Ethel's basic affinity. "As soon as she was told the baby was fine, she visibly relaxed." It was not the only good news the Kennedys enjoyed that fall: in November, Jack won election to the Senate.

—◦—

By the time she was married, Ethel had parted ways with her Republican upbringing so much that she would later wince when admitting that her parents weren't "bedrock Democrats." "I just totally put the Republican part behind me," she later said. The Skakels took notice, she added with an eye roll: "I think they thought I was a little Communist." The political divide eventually translated into a personal one, family members told Oppenheimer. Though the two families were seemingly similar on paper—large, Irish Catholic, rich—theirs was a clash of personalities. The Kennedys saw the Skakels as obscene and boorish; the Skakels saw the Kennedys as amoral hypocrites. Ethel's mother, Big Ann, found it especially offensive that Joe engaged in such flagrant affairs, and she lost respect for Rose because of how much she tolerated his behavior. Neither Ann nor George cared much whether Jack won his Senate seat, nor were they impressed with the publicity Ethel was getting for helping the campaign. "The only talk about the Kennedys was the jokes the Skakels made about them," said Virginia Skakel, who married Ethel's brother Jim in 1952. "There was no closeness between the two families at all."

Once, after the Senate campaign, Ethel's brother George Jr. sailed with Jack in a race off Martha's Vineyard. Jack barked at him to adjust the sheets, but George Jr. was sure that if he followed the instructions, they'd lose the race. "Look, Jack," he shot back, "are you going to keep screaming at me to trim this sail when I know damned well better than you do how it ought to be trimmed?" Jack yelled at him to "shut the hell up and do as you're told!" An insulted George Jr. flipped Jack the bird, jumped into the water, and swam two miles back to shore, leaving the senator without a crew.

The two families clashed when it came to money as well. Though Big Ann was always on the lookout for a bargain, she was not cheap, and she'd raised her children without any concept of budgeting. Once, when told that her checking account was overdrawn, Ethel said naively, "It can't be. I still have some checks left." This caused some friction and prompted Rose to try to convince Ethel's parents to help reel in their daughter's shopping sprees, but Big Ann wasn't interested in passing along the message. "If Bobby can't treat Ethel in the manner to which she's accustomed, we'll just take her back," she said, later adding, "I thought you Kennedys had nothing but money."

Rose would tactfully try to rein in her daughter-in-law. Once, she wrote her a letter: "Bobby took me to the top floor of your house the other evening and I noticed a Jaeger-LeCoultre clock in one of the maid's rooms," she began, noting that the fancy clocks sold for "$50 or $60 in Switzerland." "It is very easy to get a good electric clock for $4.95 and this would be most suitable for the maid's room."

Joe wasn't as delicate. At a family gathering, he barked that all of the children were spending well beyond their means, except for Joan and Ted. "No one appears to have the slightest concern for how much they spend," Joe said. Then he zeroed in on Bobby's wife. "Ethel, you are the worst," he said. "There isn't the slightest indication that you have any idea what you spend all your money on. Bills come in from all over the country for every conceivable item. It is utterly ridiculous to display such disregard for money."

"Dad, I think you have made your point," Bobby interjected just as Ethel, red-faced and tearful, ran from the room. Bobby chased after her. After a few moments, they reemerged. "Ethel, don't worry," Jack said. "We've come to the conclusion that the only solution is to have Dad work harder."

Bobby knew it was time for him to work harder, too. After Jack's election, he again needed a job, and he again turned to Senator McCarthy for help. McCarthy had been made chairman of the Permanent Subcommittee on Investigations of the Senate Government Operations Committee, more commonly called the McCarthy Committee. Bobby didn't land the high-profile job he wanted—McCarthy had already promised it to Roy Cohn and Bobby still didn't have a lot of post-graduate experience—but he was offered a job to be the committee general counsel's assistant. McCarthy said Bobby could move up as he gained experience. After conferring with his father, Bobby took the gig, which paid just ninety-five dollars a week. It didn't last long. By November 1953, after a public confrontation with Roy Cohn, McCarthy's right-hand man, Bobby had resigned and taken a job assisting his father on a presidential committee on government reform.

Ethel was sent to Washington to go house hunting, and she eventually found a furnished four-bedroom detached home—one of the few in Georgetown—near the entrance of Dumbarton Oaks. It was outside of the $500-a-month limit Bobby had set for Ethel, but she managed to charm the owner into dropping the rent. Finally, after more than two years of bouncing between her parents' home and her in-laws, Ethel had an address she could call her own. Soon, she'd begin filling it with more children. On January 17, 1954, Ethel gave birth to the couple's second son, Robert Francis Kennedy Jr. David Anthony followed on June 15 the next year.

Four months after David was born, tragedy struck the Skakel family. George and Big Ann had just thrown an anniversary party for their youngest daughter at Rambleside and were headed to California, where George had been shifting gears from petroleum coke to real-estate development. George loved to fly but wasn't crazy about commercial flights, so he began buying surplus military aircraft from the government, which he'd then have converted for civilian use. He and Ann would set off on a whim, and access became a perk of working for Great Lakes Carbon. "George Skakel was quite fond of the old bomber, but others found the plane uncomfortable," Oppenheimer wrote. "Passengers were forced to sit in the bomb-bay section and had to crawl on their bellies to get from one end of the ship to other. And a few had recently questioned its safety." Some said they smelled the sickly stench of fuel inside the plane, but when they alerted the pilot, he shrugged off the concerns.

On October 3, 1955, Skakel's plane exploded in the air over Oklahoma. He and Ann were killed instantly, as were two others flying with them. Georgeann, Ethel's oldest sister, learned the news when Ann's social secretary called her in the morning and asked, "What's all this nonsense I hear about your parents being dead?" The news had been splashed across the *Greenwich Time* as the front-page banner headline: "Mr., Mrs. Skakel, 2 Pilots Die in Plane Crash . . . Exploded in Mid Air over Oklahoma; Were Flying to Coast on Business Trip."

For years, Ethel would refuse to talk about her parents' death. In 2012, after her daughter Rory, by then an Emmy-winning and Oscar-nominated documentary filmmaker, asked to make a movie about her mother, Ethel opened up just slightly. "It was hard on everybody. It was," Ethel said somberly about her parents' deaths. Bobby—once again managing his brother Jack's senatorial campaign—was supportive, she said. "I remember he was campaigning and I really felt it would be good to be with him, and, God love him, he got off the train and drove home. He had to drive all the way through the night, and he did it."

As hundreds of people filled St. Mary's on October 7 for the funeral, Ethel arrived with Bobby. Virginia Skakel remembered hugging her sister-in-law. "There were no tears from her, or from any of them," she recalled. "Instead of crying, they laughed. It was their way of coping. It was the only way they could cope."

It was the first of many tragedies that Ethel would experience, and she handled it the only way she knew how: with prayer and deflection. "She does go to mass every day," her eldest daughter Kathleen would later say, "and you always see her holding the rosary, but she certainly doesn't talk about it and she doesn't discuss it and she doesn't reflect on it. She wanted a lot of people around and, I would say, not solitude. I think that's how she got through a lot of the really, really tough things."

While Rose's faith provided a framework within which she could ruminate quietly over her losses, Ethel's faith seems to have been more reflexive, its consolations more automatic. Rather than providing a vocabulary for the process of grief, as it had for Rose, Ethel's faith *replaced* grief. Those she lost were in heaven. God had a plan. That was the beginning, middle, and end of the story.

The deaths of George and Big Ann put an end to the madcap era of Rambleside. None of the children wanted the sprawling estate, and it sat on the market for five long years until it finally sold for $350,000. For Ethel, there would be no point in mourning its loss. She and Bobby were about to create their own magical kingdom for their kids on a similar estate near Washington.

7

HICKORY HILL

WHEN ETHEL AND BOBBY FIRST SPIED HICKORY HILL—THE ESTATE that would forever be linked to their legacy—it actually belonged to Jack and Jackie. The Georgian spread, which they bought for about $125,000 from the family of a late Supreme Court justice, stretched across six acres of beautifully landscaped grounds across the Potomac River from Washington. It was Jack and Jackie's first time owning a home, and Jackie was hard at work designing and overseeing the renovation of a nursery for the baby, expected in September of 1956. However, after the little girl was delivered, stillborn, by cesarean section in August, Jackie couldn't bear to stay in the McLean home anymore, so she and Jack sold it to Bobby and Ethel, who found it ideal to accommodate their fast-growing family. It was a beautiful, thirteen-bedroom, thirteen-bath estate of white brick with roots in the Civil War era—George Brinton McClellan, the general in charge of the Union Army during the war's early years, made the home his headquarters. Like Rambleside, it was known for its trees—this time, hickories rather than elms—though it was far less opulent than Ethel's childhood home.

She and Bobby bought it in 1956 and moved in with the children—which by now also included No. 5: a daughter named Courtney, born September 9, 1956. Ethel found out she was pregnant again just months after the family settled into the house. Michael was born February 27, 1958. After Michael, Ethel actually managed a nine-month rest before conceiving again.

Bobby's prestige was steadily growing, first prompted by his head butting with Roy Cohn in the 1954 Army–McCarthy hearings. Cohn was the man whom McCarthy had hired as chief committee counsel to the Subcommittee on Investigations—the job Bobby had wanted. But as McCarthyism gained steam, the senator's targets had widened to include many government agencies, universities, the defense industry, and the United Nations. His critics were hesitant to speak out for fear they'd be labeled Communists, an association that could cost them their jobs and livelihoods. McCarthy finally made a critical miscalculation when he launched a two-month investigation into Communist infiltration of the army. The assault backfired, incurring the wrath of not only army brass but also President Dwight D. Eisenhower, who'd devoted his life to the institution. The hearings that followed were televised and riveted the nation, and Bobby joined in, feeding questions to Senator Henry "Scoop" Jackson of Washington and snickering as Jackson ripped apart McCarthy and Cohn. As Evan Thomas wrote in *Robert Kennedy: His Life*:

> *During a recess, Cohn stormed across the hearing room to Kennedy and threatened to "get" Senator Jackson. "You can't get away with it, Cohn," Kennedy snarled. The conversation rapidly deteriorated. "Do you want to fight right here?" Cohn demanded. He started to swing at Kennedy, but aides pulled them apart. With a tight smile, Kennedy turned away. The papers found sport the next morning: the headline in the* New York Daily News *was "Cohn, Kennedy Near Blows in 'Hate' Clash."*

The year after the hearings, Bobby became chief counsel of the Senate Permanent Subcommittee on Investigations. With McCarthy's Communist hunts no longer en vogue, Bobby turned his attention to organized crime, working with the federal Bureau of Narcotics for a crash course in mobsters. He seemed fascinated by this lawless underworld. Here he was, the only Kennedy son so straight-laced that he was actually able to cash in on a $1,000 reward his father offered for not drinking or smoking until age twenty-one, joyriding with cops at night to learn about the dark forces that secretly ran the city. Once, a drunk in a bar recognized

Bobby's photo from the McCarthy hearings and called him a "rich kid" and hurled insults at his father. Mel Finkelstein, a police photographer for the tabloids, was certain the drunk would slaughter Bobby in a fight, but as the man turned around, Bobby swung and caught him in the face, breaking his nose.

Soon, Bobby was zeroing in on the Teamsters Union. In 1957 an Associated Press story headlined "Senate Probers Link Rackets to Teamsters Union" laid out the latest allegations: "Senate investigators said today they will use secretly recorded gangster conversations and testimony from prostitutes, gamblers and others to show whether some West Coast officials of the Teamsters Union had ties with the underworld." Bobby, by then a part of the Senate Rackets Investigating Committee, and its chairman, Senator John McClellan, were named in one newspaper report after another as the allegations surfaced: A Portland racketeer "spilled like Niagara Falls to a special Senate committee" that he was used as a front man to open up "gambling joints, houses of prostitution, punchboard operations and the like in Portland."

Among Bobby's targets: Teamsters president Dave Beck and vice president Jimmy Hoffa. It was harrowing work that earned Bobby plenty of enemies. The year before, syndicated labor columnist Victor Riesel had been attacked an hour after finishing a radio broadcast that assailed the leadership of a Long Island local of the International Union of Operating Engineers. A man emerged from the shadows and threw acid in Riesel's eyes, leaving the columnist blinded for life. Once Bobby's sights were turned on the Teamsters, he got an anonymous threat that the next victims of an acid attack would be his children. Unnerved, Ethel forbade the children to leave school at the end of the day with their classmates. Instead, they sat in the principal's office until their mother came to pick them up in person. There's no evidence, however, that Ethel even considered asking Bobby to back off for the sake of the family. In fact, quite the opposite.

"I think her inner Skakel came out and she was emboldened," son Chris would say years later, "and I think that helped my father through that difficult time."

Ethel became a regular fixture at many of Bobby's racketeering hearings, often bringing the older kids with her. "I think it might've been a little over their heads, but it gave them a taste of what their daddy did," Ethel said later.

Sometimes she'd lead the youngsters in a cheer inside the car as they drove past Hoffa's Washington headquarters. "What's up there?" she'd ask, to which her children would reply, "The Teamsters Union!"

"And what do they do there?"

"Work overtime to keep Jimmy Hoffa out of jail!"

"And?" Ethel would prod.

"Which is where he belongs!" the children would squeal.

On September 8, 1959, when Ethel delivered Mary Kerry, who would go by her middle name, the family was gearing up for Jack's presidential run. Three days after the birth, Bobby resigned from the Senate Rackets Committee. He and Ethel dove into the campaign without hesitation, leaving the children with nannies as they stumped nationwide. Later, daughter Kathleen—who turned nine the year of the election—said that she remembered 1960 mostly for "daddy's absence." He'd be gone for months-long stretches at a time, particularly during the hotly contested West Virginia primary, where each of the Kennedy wives was flown in to help. In September, Ethel headed to Chicago with her sister-in-law Joan. In three days, the two women attended well over a dozen rallies, meetings, and teas in private homes, primarily with women voters. The children sometimes joined the campaign, wearing special outfits and slapping "Nixon" stickers on stop signs to create a "Stop Nixon" message. "[Bobby] really wanted the children with him, so whenever we could, the children campaigned, too, and I think the children really loved it," Ethel said.

In July, *Boston Globe* reporter Thomas Winship wrote a whimsical story describing the circuslike atmosphere that six of the youngsters created as Jack officially became the Democratic nominee in Los Angeles. "Kids spilling cokes on their pretty dresses and blue top coats, empty paper bags and broken balloons under the chairs," Winship described. "Louella [*sic*] Hennessey had her hands full but her calm smiling face belied it. Somehow the kids never strayed very far from her." Three of the children had Brownie cameras in tow, though they seemed too distracted by all the balloons floating toward the ceiling to use them.

Ethel, while uncomfortable with public speaking, filled the role whenever it was asked of her. She and Bobby appeared on *The Tonight Show* with host Jack Paar, who jokingly introduced Mrs. Kennedy as "this lovely little girl here, the mother of seven children, who has given birth to her own precinct."

"Do you have any news for us?" Paar prodded.

Ethel, catching the pregnancy innuendo, laughed. "No, I don't!"

Asked what her children thought of the campaign, she quickly replied, "Mostly they think it's taking an awfully long time for Uncle Jack to become president." The audience laughed.

It was a grueling pace, but when the votes were counted, everyone was too excited to be exhausted, Ethel later recalled. The family gathered at the Hyannis Port house for a portrait. "Nobody looked tired in the photograph," Ethel reflected. "I was just so full of joy knowing that the rest of the world would now know how great Jack was."

The newly elected Jack needed someone in the cabinet he could trust absolutely, and over Bobby's initial objections—and after Adlai Stevenson and Connecticut governor Abe Ribicoff both turned the position down—he appointed his little brother to the post of attorney general. Predictable charges of nepotism followed, but Bobby was easily confirmed.

The energetic faces of the "New Frontier" were enormously popular, especially when any of the kids were part of the equation. Seven-year-old Bobby Jr. once visited Uncle Jack at the White House bearing a gift: a wriggling salamander. A news photographer captured an image of a bemused Jack watching as Bobby made a home for the lizard in a vase. The accompanying story was appropriately perplexed: "There was this salamander named Shadrach presented to the President of the United States today, and the question is what does he do with it?"

Bobby Jr. had found the creature in his back yard, which was hardly a surprise. Much like the Rambleside of Ethel's childhood, Hickory Hill was like an unregulated zoo, with ponies, horses, goats, pigs, cows, and chickens. Ethel once brought home a seal. "He had to be fed fish every day but he didn't like the eyes, so there were always hundreds of eyes all around," Ethel later recalled. "Ugh. That we could've done without." (The seal eventually was donated to the Washington Zoo after pushing Kathleen into the pool.) Ethel said the animals helped make Hickory Hill magical. "You'd be walking up to the front door and a herd of horses would come galloping by," she said. "It was kind of unusual."

Ethel also would host pet contests—sometimes for the best, sometimes for the most bizarre—and the Kennedy children, taking after their competitive mother, played to win. A supposed conflict of interest arose for family friend and humorist Art Buchwald, who was asked to help judge one of the contests. He later defended his calls in a tongue-in-cheek piece he wrote in the *Boston Globe* under the headline "Judge Stays Impartial under Terrific Pressure." "Then we got to the most unusual pet class," Buchwald wrote. "This was a tough one, because one of the Kennedy children brought in either a large lizard or a small alligator. My 8-year-old daughter had entered a hamster and I was in a tough spot. Mrs. Kennedy kept tugging my arm and my daughter kept tugging my shirt. I decided that there was a tie for first place."

Ethel became a regular fixture in newspapers' society sections, and the parties she threw at Hickory Hill surpassed the legends created at Rambleside. The press labeled her "Washington's No. 1 Hostess" and filled their pages with tales of raucous poolside antics. Guests in fancy attire were routinely tossed into the pool in a rite of passage that came to be called "dunking." The water capers climaxed in June 1962 at a party for Ethel and Bobby's twelfth wedding anniversary, which was attended by some three hundred guests. Ethel laid some wooden planks across the pool and put a table and some chairs on top of the makeshift bridge. She and astronaut John Glenn tiptoed out and sat at the precariously positioned table, which predictably lurched, tossing Ethel into the water. Arthur M. Schlesinger—a Harvard historian, speechwriter, and special assistant to the president—plunged in next. "We changed our clothes and the party went pleasantly on," Schlesinger recounted.

Rose was said to disapprove of Ethel's wild parties. "Rose Kennedy thought Ethel's parties were outrageously overdone," Barbara Gibson, Rose's secretary, said years later. Certainly Rose, who esteemed civility and formality—some of her fondest memories being of parties at the

English court when her husband was ambassador—would have preferred parties more reflective of the dignity of her sons' offices.

The parties usually featured live music that blared well into the morning hours. Though Hickory Hill was spread across six acres, the tunes wafted into neighbors' homes. Some took advantage of the entertainment. "At 3 o'clock in the morning, with all that wonderful Lester Lanin music coming in our windows, we got up and danced in our bare feet right in our bedroom," one neighbor said.

Others weren't as embracing. At one party, the orchestra leader kept bellowing over a loudspeaker, "Any more requests?"

A neighbor called back, "How about a little more peace and quiet!"

Ethel transferred more than just Rambleside's parties to Hickory Hill, however. She also introduced monthly seminars to discuss a variety of issues, much as Big Ann had done in the stately library of the Greenwich home. Sometimes those invited were deep thinkers. Many were politicians. The gatherings, dubbed "Hickory Hill University," were also influenced by Bobby's Student Legal Forum days, and sometimes the "classes" were held at other locations, though the Hickory Hill University moniker remained. Usually twenty people attended the seminars, including some of Bobby's cabinet colleagues. One regular recalled Ethel attempting an intellectual battle with British philosopher A. J. Ayer, challenging him to explain why he rejected metaphysics. When Ayer asked Ethel to define the term, she hesitated, and then said, "I mean whether conceptions like truth and virtue and beauty have any meaning." And the debate ensued.

Ethel's childhood prankster ways never left her, and as her husband ascended politically in Washington, she earned the reputation of a cutup. General Maxwell Taylor, then chairman of the Joint Chiefs of Staff, arrived at an early 1963 party in his honor to find a life-size dummy hanging from a tree by a parachute harness. Ethel had hoped it would make Taylor, who had parachuted into Normandy on D-Day, feel more "at home." She once sprayed a young member of a European royal family with shaving cream. Another time, she used live bullfrogs as centerpieces for a St. Patrick's Day dinner party. The antics earned her the nickname of America's new "knacky baby" in London, where she once arrived at a party with a suitcase and disappeared to change into a rhinestone-studded black shift that was far shorter than most dresses Ethel tended to wear. The risqué gesture was calculated, on her part, to lighten the mood. Ethel declared, "Everybody was talking about Vietnam and I thought we all needed a change of pace!"

8

A TIDAL WAVE

ON FRIDAY, NOVEMBER 22, 1963, AS ETHEL AND BOBBY ENTERTAINED guests poolside at Hickory Hill, the telephone rang. Ethel pulled away from her hosting duties to answer it and was surprised to hear J. Edgar Hoover on the line, as the FBI director had never called the house before. Director Hoover and Bobby had a fraught and complicated relationship. While Bobby, as attorney general, was nominally the FBI director's boss, the de facto power that Hoover wielded was unprecedented for a non-elected official. The files he hoarded—containing scandalous personal information on major Washington and Hollywood figures—served to ensure his position and influence. Throughout the Kennedy administration, Hoover had periodically and with great relish contacted the attorney general to let him know about some damaging new piece of information he possessed, usually about JFK's prodigious sex life. It was always couched in courtesy, but the meaning of these calls, if oblique, was unmistakable: Hoover had a lot of dirt, and he was not to be messed with.

For his part, Bobby chafed against the bullying and resented the fawning that Hoover seemed to expect as a matter of course. He also had more substantial problems with the director: for example, Bobby wanted to wage a war on organized crime, while Hoover steadfastly denied the existence of the Mafia. Their relationship was one of distance and ornate courtesy, punctuated by overt clashes. Ethel, naturally, shared her husband's antipathy: She once left a note in the FBI's suggestion box helpfully proposing that the agency find a new director.

Bobby took the phone call from Hoover. After a beat, he put his hand across his mouth. "Jack's been shot!" he said. Ethel ran to him and wrapped her arms around his waist to support him, as she would over the dark months to come.

Just as she had when her parents died, Ethel held fast to her faith. When nostalgia arose, she would say that Jack was in heaven, looking over the family. "*That's* the wife of the Attorney General speaking," Bobby icily replied. He wasn't as comforted by his faith, and he struggled with this latest loss—the third of his siblings to die, and the one with whom he was closest. While the rest of the family gathered as usual at Hyannis Port for Thanksgiving dinner the week after Jack's funeral, Bobby chose to stay away and instead spend the holiday with Ethel and the children at Hickory Hill. Bobby swallowed his tears, trying to abide by the family dictum "Kennedys don't cry."

"It was like a tidal wave of grief," Ethel recalled of Jack's death. "To see this vibrant man with all his character and sense of fun and wonderful judgment, it was lost. Everyone was devastated." Ethel didn't know how to reach Bobby. "It was like [he] had lost both arms," she said. "It was six months of just blackness."

"Daddy became much more withdrawn after Jack died," said Kathleen, recalling her father spending more time alone reading poetry and the Bible. "I think that he tried to really feel the pain. He said, 'I'm going to dwell in the pain, and I'm going to understand that something terrible has happened.'"

—◆—

Ethel gently pushed her husband back into the world—encouraging him to go to New York, for example, to represent the family at a ceremony to change the name of New York International Airport to John F. Kennedy International Airport—and, eventually, his friends credited her for keeping him from drowning in his grief. In 1964, after months of reflecting on God and loss and his own mortality, and after seeing his little brother, Ted, nearly killed in a plane crash, Bobby refocused and set his sights on a US Senate seat in New York. If he succeeded, he'd be joining Ted, who'd first won a seat in the assembly four years earlier and was running his first reelection campaign. Though Ted would be confined to a hospital bed for much of the campaign recuperating from a badly injured back from the plane wreck, he was staying in the race, with wife Joan making appearances for him.

Bobby obviously couldn't run where he'd long lived in Massachusetts—Ted already possessed a Massachusetts Senate seat, and not even the Kennedys had the chutzpah necessary to claim both—and by moving to Long Island, he faced predictable backlash for being a fair-weather resident and carpetbagger. Bobby responded with a pledge: "Whether I win or lose this election, I'm going to stay in the state of New York." Despite the controversy, he was given rock-star treatment as he campaigned, stirring up scenes of frenzy everywhere he went. Women left lipstick on his face, and his campaign convertible was showered with confetti and rice as he drove down the street. "Three times, while standing in the car to shake hands, he was almost pulled over backwards," wrote the Associated Press's Relman Morin from the campaign trail. "After that, one aide grabbed his belt and another a leg to keep him upright."

On November 3, 1964, he won, though not by as much as he had hoped. While Lyndon Johnson carried the state by an overwhelming 2.7 million votes in the presidential contest, Bobby won by only 700,000.

Bobby's transition to the New York political scene was pretty transparent: Ethel and the children were moving back to Hickory Hill by January, and by 1966 Bobby's name was being floated as a possible challenger to Lyndon B. Johnson for the presidency. Asked about one poll that showed voters would prefer Bobby on the Democratic ticket in 1968 by 51 percent to President Johnson's 49 percent, Bobby said he wouldn't be a candidate "under any foreseeable circumstances."

9

RUN, BOBBY, RUN

WHILE MOST PEOPLE BELIEVED THAT BOBBY SAW THE SENATE AS A stepping-stone to the Oval Office, he insisted, almost until he declared his candidacy, that he did not. On January 4, 1965—the same day he was sworn in as the junior senator from New York—he playfully declared to the press, "I have absolutely no Presidential ambitions." A Cheshire cat smile appeared on his face. "And neither does my wife—*EthelBird.*"

However kittenish he might've been in acknowledging his own deep-seated ambitions, Bobby was also a realist who had trouble imagining a viable run for the Democratic nomination. Though Johnson was deeply unpopular and Bobby felt that LBJ's policy on Vietnam was catastrophically wrong, Bobby knew that the odds were against a successful bid to replace a sitting president on the 1968 Democratic ticket. Whatever Johnson's dismal public approval ratings, in the sixties the nominee for president was decided by the party officials who controlled the delegates; with only fourteen primaries, the public's voice in the decision was somewhat muted. And even a weakened Johnson was still the most gifted political dealmaker of his generation, and he could be expected to fight effectively for his own interests.

Further, Kennedy circle heavyweights like Teddy Kennedy and Ted Sorensen argued against his running: They reminded Bobby of the potential to split and weaken the party by challenging the presumptive nominee. They also argued that Bobby would be seen as a selfish spoiler, chasing the presidency to expiate grief over his brother, or simply because he believed it was due him by dynastic right.

As of the mid-1960s, however, Bobby still had time to decide. In the meantime, he was a senator. While he and Ethel bought a five-room apartment on the east side of New York City, in the United Nations Towers, they spent little time there. The majority of their time was spent at Hickory Hill, and Ethel's life continued largely as before: overseeing a rowdy brood of children, throwing raucous parties, and serving as Bobby's cheerleader, confidante, and comfort. Parties during that time included a 1966 gala thrown in honor of Ambassador-at-large W. Averell Harriman's seventy-fifth birthday, where Peter Duchin's orchestra provided the evening's entertainment. The next year, only a few months after the premature birth of Douglas Harriman Kennedy—child number ten—Ethel and Bobby celebrated their seventeenth wedding anniversary with marathon festivities.

Beginning on Embassy Row, the progressive party eventually made its way to Hickory Hill, where three film projectors showed quick-cut footage on the walls of the empty swimming pool; the Duchin orchestra was again the accompaniment, until three o'clock in the morning, when a jukebox took its place. The party was still going in the morning, when Ethel served breakfast for those assembled before leading the entire sleepless crew to mass for Douglas's christening.

The Senate years were not all fun for Ethel. In September of 1966, her beloved older brother, George Jr., died when a small plane, piloted by an off-duty Air Force Master Sergeant and carrying George and three friends, botched a tight canyon landing and crashed at a remote ranch in the Idaho wilderness. George had lived a flamboyantly dangerous and hedonistic lifestyle—his funeral would be attended by several of his blonde, blue-eyed mistresses, known to family and friends as the Swedish Girls. His death as a heedless adventurer, crashing in a plane loaded down with guns and liquor for a twenty-person hunting expedition, was completely in character for George Jr. His adoring younger sister was devastated. Ethel dutifully attended the funerals of not only her brother but of another of the passengers, CIA official and RFK's friend Dean Markham.

According to friend Sarah Davis, Ethel handled her brother's death "with incredible grace and incredible bravery. She never got maudlin or dramatic. She never shed tears that anyone saw. She dealt with it by ignoring it." This stoic approach to death—the approach she took with her parents and her brother, and which she would later take to the deaths of her husband and two of her sons—is jarring in the hypertherapeutic era. Though professional grief counselors preach that there's no wrong way to grieve, there's something in Ethel's approach to bereavement that strikes the contemporary observer as obtuse. But for a woman who survived so much, perhaps a little obtuseness is excusable. There's a certain depth of loss where the fact of surviving it is more important than how it was survived.

———

As 1968 arrived, Bobby began reflecting with more urgency on whether to enter the presidential contest. His most enthusiastic cheerleader was Ethel, who in January got the kids to hang a "Run, Bobby, Run" banner out a bedroom window at Hickory Hill. At a January dinner Bobby worried that a presidential run would "go a long way toward proving everything that everybody who doesn't like me has said about me . . . that I'm just a selfish, ambitious little SOB that can't wait to get his hands on the White House."

Ethel piped up: "You're always talking as though people don't like you. People do like you, and you've got to realize that."

At a February meeting at Hickory Hill where RFK weighed a run with friends, aides, and allies, Ethel's advice was direct and unequivocal: "Run. You'll beat him. Run. Do it." One of the meeting participants remarked that, since Ethel had spoken, the debate was over. Bobby insisted that it wasn't Ethel's decision, though he was clearly buoyed by her confidence.

One concern on most everybody's mind—which Ethel never outwardly acknowledged—was Bobby's physical safety should he seek the presidency. Jackie Kennedy gave her blessing directly to Bobby but later shared her true feelings with Arthur Schlesinger Jr.: "Do you know what I think will happen to Bobby? The same thing that happened to Jack," she said. "There is so much hatred in this country, and more people hate Bobby than hated Jack . . ." The fear that Bobby—like his brother—would be cut down by an assassin was very real, and it was shared by many in the Kennedy family and entourage.

Blackmail was also a worry, though not one that Bobby ever openly acknowledged. President Johnson, with the help of a very eager FBI chief J. Edgar Hoover, had been gathering dirt on the Kennedys since Jack's administration. LBJ was in possession of untold amounts of damaging information: on Bobby and Jack's Cuba plots, on the brothers' sexual escapades, on the little known fact that, as attorney general, Bobby had authorized wiretaps on Martin Luther King and others in the civil rights movement. Some in his circle worried that a ruthless LBJ wouldn't hesitate to release information to capsize the campaign of a man with whom there was such long-standing mutual enmity.

But the voices urging him to run gained volume, and, as 1968 progressed, events made his decision easier. In February, a massive uprising by the Viet Cong—the Tet offensive—caught US forces in Vietnam flat-footed and gave Bobby more evidence that the war was a strategic and moral quagmire. And Minnesota senator Eugene McCarthy entered the race and proved with a strong showing in New Hampshire that Johnson was not invulnerable. On March 16, 1968, Bobby Kennedy announced his candidacy.

He stood in the US Capitol, at the same podium where his brother had started his campaign a little more than eight years before. Ethel and nine of their ten children sat in the front row. Ethel's adoring attention was only interrupted by hopeless attempts to corral the rowdier children. Kerry, then eight years old, raced around the Senate chambers. Four-year-old Christopher kicked a reporter in the shin; Matthew Maxwell wrestled with him.

"I do not run for the Presidency merely to oppose any man but to propose new policies," Bobby said in his Boston-tinged monotone. "I run because I am convinced that this country is on a perilous course and because I have such strong feelings about what must be done." He vowed to end the bloodshed both in Vietnam and in our cities at home, and to "close the gaps between black and white, rich and poor, young and old, in this country and around the world."

The initial response was rapturous—for Bobby and for Ethel. "If Ethel Kennedy becomes First Lady," Paul Healy wrote in the *New York Daily News*, "the White House will have the swingingest First Family since Teddy Roosevelt's day." The day after the announcement, Bobby spoke to crowds of fifteen thousand and seventeen thousand screaming supporters at Kansas State University and the University of Kansas, respectively. The Kennedy camp was reassured by the excitement he had generated even in the heartland: The people at the Kansas rallies weren't radical rabble-rousers, but clean-cut Middle Americans. "This is Kansas, fucking Kansas!" *Look* photographer Stanley Tretick exclaimed at one of the deafening Kansas events. "He's going all the fucking way!"

The nomination still wasn't a sure thing. More than half of the delegates were controlled by the South, where Bobby was hated for his pro–civil rights stance, or by party bosses beholden to Big Labor, whom he'd antagonized as head of the rackets committee, as attorney general, and as a senator. He had no particular liking for or rapport with the business community. And among the politically motivated student movements, support for Eugene McCarthy was strong; many young people saw in Bobby an opportunistic spoiler. He somehow had to create, in the words of Evan Thomas, a "coalition of the have-nots," while simultaneously wooing any party boss he could get under his tent.

Ethel was, as ever, Bobby's most avid supporter. She was with him as often as she could be for the campaign, and various minders looked after the younger Kennedy children at Hickory Hill. Kathleen and Joe, sixteen and fifteen, respectively, were both away at boarding schools, and the five youngest children, from one-year-old Douglas to ten-year-old Michael, were the charges of two nurses and a secretary. But Bobby Jr., fifteen, David, twelve, and Courtney, eleven, were less supervised. Ethel hired a handsome twenty-one-year-old named Bob Galland to look after them. Galland was a college dropout, but a devout Catholic; as a former Boy Scout, Ethel reasoned he could be their instructor in camping and sailing. He discovered soon after taking the job that he was more of a live-in nanny. He also discovered that, though often far away, Ethel had very specific ideas of how the children were to spend their time.

"One of her rules was, 'You will watch the six-o'clock news every night because your father might be on,'" said Galland. "We did that religiously. They'd get real excited to see their parents. There was a lot of elation—'Yea, there's Dad! This is great!'" The fact that she and Bobby were so often in the media was important to Ethel, and she kept a wary eye on the press. After Washington newspaper columnist Richard Harwood accused Bobby of being a "demagogue," Ethel responded by approaching him on the campaign plane, crumpling up the offending newspaper, and throwing it in his face. When Ethel was campaigning in Indiana, a tongue-tied local TV reporter asked her about Bobby's reputation among fellow senators as "worthless." The reporter had meant to say "ruthless," which would have been bad enough; "worthless" was beyond the pale. Ethel's eyes took on a reptilian hardness. "I would use 'brilliant' to describe him myself because that's what he is," she hissed and then walked away.

Just two weeks after Bobby announced his candidacy, Johnson revealed to the nation that he wouldn't be seeking reelection. Bobby was shocked. "Well, he didn't deserve to be president anyway," Ethel said to a near-catatonic Bobby, who'd gathered his advisers at the New York apartment. Bobby was quiet, his eyes glued to the television coverage. Ethel brought out the Scotch.

A few days later, on April 3, LBJ reluctantly received Bobby at the White House and assured him of his neutrality in the upcoming presidential contest. Both men knew he was lying. After Bobby left, Johnson met with Vice President Hubert Humphrey and pledged his behind-the-scenes backing. He also met that day with Eugene McCarthy, who'd won the Wisconsin primary on April 2. When Robert Kennedy's name came up, a silent LBJ "drew the side of his hand across his throat."

——

The next day, April 4, on his way to a campaign appearance in inner-city Indianapolis, Bobby was informed that Martin Luther King Jr. had been shot in Memphis. By the time his plane had landed, it was confirmed that King was dead.

King's assassination sparked riots in dozens of urban areas throughout the nation, including Baltimore; Chicago; Washington, DC; Louisville; and Kansas City. Fearing the same thing in Indianapolis, the police chief advised strongly against Bobby making his appearance. Ethel begged him to skip it as well. Bobby sent her back to the hotel and made his way to the rally with a handful of campaign workers. His police escort peeled off and abandoned him as soon as he entered the ghetto. The message from the local authorities was clear: You're on your own.

It was dark when Bobby arrived at the rally site—a vacant lot surrounded by tenements. He climbed onto the bed of a pickup truck, declined the speech his campaign had written for him, and removed from the pocket of his overcoat his own hastily scrawled remarks. It was then that he informed the crowd that Martin Luther King Jr. was dead.

Those assembled gasped in unison. Anguished shouts—moans, really—of "No! No!" rose from the audience. After a few seconds, the initial clamor died. Bobby continued:

> For those of you who are black and are tempted to be filled with hatred and distrust at the injustice of such an act, against all white people, I can only say that I feel in my own heart the same kind of feeling. I had a member of my family killed, but he was killed by a white man. But we have to make an effort in the United States, we have to make an effort to understand, to go beyond these rather difficult times.
>
> My favorite poet was Aeschylus. He wrote: "In our sleep, pain which cannot forget falls drop by drop upon the heart until, in our own despair, against our will, comes wisdom through the awful grace of God."
>
> What we need in the United States is not division; what we need in the United States is not hatred; what we need in the United States is not violence or lawlessness; but love and wisdom, and compassion toward one another, and a feeling of justice toward those who still suffer within our country, whether they be white or they be black . . .

Riots broke out in 110 cities nationwide that night. Thirty-nine people died in the violence, and more than 2,500 were injured. Indianapolis was one of the few major metropolitan areas that remained peaceful.

A few days later, Ethel flew with Bobby to Atlanta, where they attended King's funeral service. There, she did her best to comfort King's widow, Coretta. Though mere acquaintances, "we embraced each other," Mrs. King reported. "It was a natural reaction from her to me, and I had that kind of warm feeling about her as a woman who reached out to me."

Bobby won the Indiana primary on May 7. Early returns showed that minorities were turning out in large numbers for Kennedy. "Don't you just wish that everyone was black?" Ethel asked, with her patented unfiltered honesty. Her frankness, spontaneity, and sense of the absurd were often buoying on an exhausting campaign. "Kennedy's mood, often irascible, improved when Ethel was on the plane," Bobby Kennedy biographer Evan Thomas noted.

On a campaign train in Colorado (following a decisive primary win on May 14 in Nebraska), Ethel arranged a surprise for Fred Dutton, Bobby's right-hand man. As the train arrived in tiny Julesburg—Dutton's birthplace—Ethel produced signs created by her and some of the women on the campaign. "Make Fred, Not War," read one. "Fred Dutton's Brother for Attorney General," read another. Ethel had made "Dutton Buttons" and Bobby held up a sign reading "Sock It to 'Em, Freddy!" RFK led the puzzled crowd in a "We want Fred!" chant, and Ethel forced Dutton to deliver a speech imitating Bobby's stock phrasing and sharp Boston accent.

In addition to her importance within the campaign, Ethel played her part in maintaining the family-centric Kennedy image. "I plan to remain active in my husband's campaign [but] I want to spend at least three or four days a week at home with my kids," she said. In early May, Washington columnist Maxine Cheshire reported that Ethel was pregnant with her eleventh child. In Davenport, Iowa, she played up her image as mother hen and homemaker. "I try to keep our family life happy and easygoing so [Bobby] doesn't have to worry," she said. "It's important for him to know the children are well."

But with both parents gone so much, not all was well at Hickory Hill. David in particular was beginning to cause trouble with increasing frequency. Neighbors complained that their homes were being vandalized, that firecrackers were being thrown at their houses and damaging their mailboxes. One particularly aggrieved neighbor, Jack Kopson, fired a shotgun near David's feet late one April night in an attempt to scare the boy off of his property. In early May, shortly before the Indiana primary,

David and a classmate were picked up by the police for throwing a rock through the windshield of a passing motorist. The driver was unhurt and agreed to drop the charges on the conditions that the Kennedys pay for the damage and that they deal seriously with their son's behavior. They came through on the first condition.

It does not seem, however, that Bobby and Ethel confronted David in any serious way. "David was chided and ridiculed by the Senator and Mrs. Kennedy, but not for what he did," recalled Bob Galland. They "felt he was stupid to get caught. I think the Senator took Dave aside and they had a chat . . . but that was it." The situation concerned Bobby, at least, more than Galland perceived. He spoke to child psychiatrist Robert Coles about what might have motivated twelve-year-old David to throw rocks at a car's windshield. Because he wanted to hit someone, Coles responded. It was not to be the end of David's difficulties.

10

A TREMENDOUS AMOUNT OF PRESENCE

Bobby lost Oregon. There was almost no minority population in the state, and both the Teamsters and the state's large progun hunting population—alarmed by Bobby's advocacy of gun control—were well organized. Bobby was never able to gain any traction and lost to McCarthy by six points, 44.7 percent to 38.8 percent. It marked the first time one of Joe Kennedy's sons had ever lost an election, and it stung. The campaign had left him exhausted, his face haggard, his voice shot. Each night at dinner, Ethel counted out a dozen or so pills for Bobby to take—mostly vitamins—and he was receiving a large B12 shot every other day.

Despite the Oregon setback and his exhaustion, he and Ethel were hopeful for his success in California. On May 29, the day after the Oregon primary, Bobby arrived in LA and toured majority black and Mexican neighborhoods in the back of a convertible. The crowds were ferocious in their enthusiasm: They tore at his shirt, shredding it, his cufflinks a memory. He lost his shoes. With the crowd's adoration, his weariness lifted. More than once, he turned to Fred Dutton and said, "These are my people."

"He was being truthful," Evan Thomas wrote. "There had not been since Lincoln, nor has there ever been again, a white national politician so embraced by people of color."

Ethel had Bob Galland bring six of the children to be with their parents for primary night. On May 30, Galland and David, Kerry, Michael, Courtney, Christopher, and Max flew from Washington to LAX, where

Ethel met them and got them situated in a three-bedroom bungalow at the Beverly Hills Hotel. After a surprisingly bland debate with McCarthy on June 1 in San Francisco, Bobby returned to LA and managed to spend half the day with Ethel and the kids at Disneyland. While you couldn't say he stepped away from the campaign—the press was with them every step of the way—the hours with his family would, in retrospect, seem precious. "The kids were constantly badgered by the press" that day, remembered Galland. "Cameras in their faces, microphones in their faces. The photographers would be walking backward taking pictures and the kids would run ahead and get down on hands and knees so a guy walking backward would stumble and fall over them. Ethel got a kick out of it."

The last day of the California campaign—June 3—was grueling for both Bobby and Ethel. They traveled from Los Angeles to a rally in San Francisco, then back south to San Diego and Long Beach—more than a thousand miles. At the rally in San Francisco's Chinatown, a cluster of firecrackers exploded near Ethel and Bobby's open convertible. The crowd tensed, fearing gunfire. Ethel crouched into the backseat, clearly frightened. Bobby remained standing, seemingly unafraid.

That night, Bobby, Ethel, and the six kids stayed at the Malibu beach house of film director John Frankenheimer. They relaxed together that night and spent the morning of the primary at the beach. When David became caught in the cold, crashing Pacific waves, Bobby went in after him. Both were rolled by the surf as Bobby, clutching his son, regained his footing and emerged onto the beach. He had an abrasion over his right eyebrow and David in his arms.

—✦—

That evening, not long after Bobby had arrived at Room 516 of the Ambassador Hotel to await the returns from the primary, he learned that he'd already won the South Dakota primary that day with a full 50 percent of the vote. The Royal Suite was filled with family, campaign advisers, celebrities, and a few handpicked members of the press. Ethel arrived in her orange and white minidress and entertained the crew—who'd been drinking for hours—as they waited for the California returns. The four older children who'd come out to LA spent a few hours in the suite but, tired from their day at the beach, returned to the Beverly Hills Hotel with Bob Galland around 10:30. Shortly before midnight, with the networks projecting Bobby beating McCarthy with 50 percent of the vote, Bobby and Ethel decided to head down to the Ambassador ballroom to declare victory.

The ballroom had been packed for hours with enthusiastic supporters, who exploded into cheers when Bobby and Ethel appeared. Bobby stood at a podium, crushed in among a throng of supporters, Ethel at his right shoulder, beaming.

He thanked various campaign workers, and his sisters and mother, and jokingly his dog, Freckles. "I'm not doing this in the order of importance but I do want to thank my wife, Ethel, as well," he added with a sheepish laugh. She giggled good-naturedly beside him and the crowd cheered.

He urged those listening to help end the violence and strife that so characterized the late 1960s. "We are a great country, an unselfish country, and a compassionate country," he said. "So my thanks to all of you, and now it's on to Chicago, and let's win there."

Bobby left the podium and was led by a maître d' through the dense crowd into a back corridor near the kitchen, where he started shaking the hands of excited members of the kitchen staff. Having become separated from Ethel, he turned to look for her, at which point Sirhan Sirhan, a mentally ill, unemployed young man—who blamed Bobby for the troubles of the Palestinian people—stepped from the shadows with a snub-nosed .22 caliber pistol and opened fire. His first shot entered Bobby's head just behind the right ear. The assailant then emptied his pistol around the room. Bobby covered his face with his hands and fell backward onto the cement floor.

Bill Barry, Bobby's bodyguard, tackled Sirhan and a struggle involving several people ensued. Ethel broke free from where she'd been pulled to safety and rushed to Bobby's side. Kneeling beside him, she stroked his face. He handled a rosary that a busboy had placed in his hands. "Is everybody else all right?" Bobby whispered.

Reporting on the victory festivities live for Mutual News, Andrew West reported what he saw as it happened. What he said about Ethel, as the chaotic scene unfolded in front of him, is revealing. "Ethel Kennedy is standing by," West reported. "She is calm. She is raising her hand high to motion people back. She's attempting to get calm. A woman . . . with a tremendous amount of presence. A tremendous amount of presence."

She motioned for a hovering cameraman to stop shooting, but he crassly shot back, "This is history, lady." Ethel somehow maintained her composure in the madness. Five other people had been hit by Sirhan's bullets—a forty-three-year-old campaign worker who had been friends with the Kennedys; two newsmen, one of whom was just nineteen years old; a seventeen-year-old campaign worker; and a forty-three-year-old political activist who was actually supporting Bobby's opponent, Eugene McCarthy.

Two medics arrived and began to lift Bobby onto the stretcher. "Gently, gently," Ethel said. Bobby, in obvious pain, cried, "Oh, no, no, don't," before slipping into unconsciousness.

All of Bobby's children were asleep by the time he was shot, except for one. At the Beverly Hills Hotel bungalow, David—about ten days shy of his thirteenth birthday—sat quietly watching television with Bob Galland when, in front of his eyes, his father was gunned down. According to Galland, "he said something like, 'Oh, man, it's over . . . they got him, too.'"

Over the next twenty-six hours, except for the hours he spent in surgery, Ethel would not leave Bobby's side: in the ambulance on the way to Los Angeles' Central Receiving Hospital, where doctors attempted to assess his condition and where he received absolution and last rites from a priest; or through his transfer to Good Samaritan Hospital a couple of hours later. She left his side only when he was wheeled into surgery. Surgeons tried to remove two bullets—one lodged in the midline of the brain, the other in the back of the neck. Ethel sat in a tiny room near the surgery unit for nearly four hours as doctors tried to save his life. When Bobby was finally wheeled to the recovery room, Ethel climbed onto a surgical table and lay next to him.

Years later, daughter Kerry—eight at the time of her father's death—would still fight tears as she described how she learned of the shooting. She'd gone to bed with her siblings back in the hotel room, then woke up at four or five o'clock in the morning and turned on the television to watch cartoons. "And the news just kept coming across about Daddy," she said through tears.

After the surgery, Bobby showed no brain function but was breathing on his own. Throughout the night and the next day, Kennedys began arriving. As Bobby faded in intensive care, a calm but purposeful Ethel led the discussion of his funeral arrangements.

On June 6, 1968, at 1:44 a.m., nearly twenty-six hours after he was shot, Robert Francis Kennedy was pronounced dead.

Robert Kennedy's body lay in state in St. Patrick's Cathedral in New York City for two nights and a day. Mourners lined up for twenty-five blocks to walk past his coffin and pay their respects. Ethel went over arrangements for his funeral mass, which she insisted would differ in tone from the solemn ceremonies surrounding Jack's death in 1963. "If there's one thing about our faith," she told one of the priests, "it's our belief that this is the beginning of eternal life and not the end of life. I want this mass to be as joyous as it possibly can be." With her fellow mourners, too, she wore a brave face and did her best to enforce good cheer. Greeting a weeping friend in the days before the funeral, she said, "Don't cry now. We'll all have a good cry later."

On Saturday afternoon, after the funeral mass—at which Teddy memorably eulogized him as "a good and decent man, who saw wrong and tried to right it, saw suffering and tried to heal it, saw war and tried to stop it"—Bobby's body was carried by a twenty-one-car funeral train from New York to Washington, a 226-mile stretch of tracks lined with hundreds of thousands—perhaps a million—of mourners, members of the general public who stood along the tracks in the June heat to pay their respects.

Bobby's casket was in the final car, where Ethel spent the first part of the trip alone with him. "It was the only moment, then or since, that I saw her cry," said RFK aide Carter Burden, who glimpsed Ethel with the coffin. "She sat there, immensely still, and hunched over in a plain, straight-backed chair. She had a rosary in her hands, and her head was resting against the casket."

It was not a posture she allowed herself for very long. She grabbed her eldest son, Joe, and walked through all twenty cars in the stifling heat, thanking people for coming, seeing how they were holding up, hugging, laughing, kissing friends on the cheek. She greeted nearly every one of the train's 1,100 passengers.

It was just before 9:30 p.m. that his funeral train arrived in Washington. Ethel rode with Bobby's coffin in the hearse as it was taken to Arlington National Cemetery, the motorcade passing tens of thousands of people along the route. She stood on the hillside at Arlington as Bobby's coffin was conveyed to his burial plot, only feet from where Jack was buried. A priest said a prayer, and the flag on the casket was folded and presented to Ethel. She and Teddy knelt and kissed the casket before it was lowered, at 11:34 p.m., into the ground.

11

STILL HERSELF

IF THE YEAR THAT FOLLOWED BOBBY'S DEATH WAS DIFFICULT FOR Ethel, she did everything in her power to conceal it. The concessions she did make to grief were strangely formal: For the year after his death, she observed the old-fashioned convention of wearing only black and white; and there were no public events at Hickory Hill until May of 1969, when she held a charity pet show. But in general, she made a concerted effort to carry on as before Bobby had died. Friends were constantly around, and Ethel stayed active with tennis and swimming. The children were expected to carry through on plans they made before their father's death—Kathleen, for example, continued with her plan to work for the summer on a Native American Indian reservation in Arizona. Ethel also traveled by herself and with the kids on a few occasions.

She took a short trip to Aristotle Onassis's private Greek island, Skorpios, in August, and met up again with Jackie and Ari in Nassau in early 1969. She took the kids on skiing trips that winter. She poured significant energy into raising money: $10 million for the Robert Francis Kennedy Memorial Foundation, and another $3.5 million to settle Bobby's campaign debt. She remained as rambunctious as ever until the middle of October, when she experienced labor pains two months prematurely. She endured bed rest (reading, watching TV, being visited by her kids—even planning Thanksgiving) until December 12, when Rory, her last child, was delivered via C-section.

"Ethel Year After: Still Herself," read the headline on Betty Flynn's May 1969 *Boston Globe* article. "Ethel is the same person she was before

Bobby's death," an "intimate friend" is quoted as saying. "And her house is run the same way, almost as if he wasn't gone."

Even in a resolutely light and sunny piece, however, a "frequent visitor to Hickory Hill" said, "I am afraid to see Ethel's face in repose. With the kids around and all her friends, she does fine. . . . When things quiet down, you can see the sorrow there." And indeed, Ethel's anguish, no matter how well submerged, found its way out in other ways.

In February of 1969, a Gallup Poll named Ethel the most admired woman in America. ("I got it because of my cooking," she quipped.) Still, "Ethel's mood swept from deep private despair to manic irritability to frenetic highs of ceaseless activity," author Laurence Leamer wrote. The children saw some of her mood swings, but more of it was taken out on the help. The turnover for maids and cooks and other household staff at Hickory Hill was remarkable and it was the rare exception that stayed more than a few months.

Money was also a source of tension at Hickory Hill. Ethel's riotous spending—on food, on clothing, on *everything*—continued at its usual pace, and she became well known in Washington as perennially delinquent on bills. She most often had outstanding bills sent to the Kennedys' New York office for payment, where Stephen Smith—Jean's husband and administrator of the family fortune—tried in vain to curtail Ethel's spending. He pleaded with her, asked for intervention from other Kennedys, even threatened to cut her off. Nothing worked. More than a decade after Joe had first hectored her about her wastefulness, it remained an issue.

And it wasn't just Ethel's spending that created so much expense for the Kennedys. Increasingly, Ethel's brood was incurring damages. A rowdy bunch, they destroyed condos in Aspen during ski vacations, becoming so notorious in the town that Ethel took to using an alias when trying to secure lodging for their visits.

Ethel struggled to keep her children in line. Her three eldest boys, in particular, gave her trouble. In Hyannis Port, Joe II and Bobby Jr., often with the help of David and cousins Chris Lawford and Bobby Shriver, created havoc all over town. "They untied boats from the docks and took perverse pleasure in seeing them lying beached at high tide," Laurence Leamer wrote. "They sent water balloons soaring high into the sky, landing on the top of moving automobiles, preferably police cruisers. On the Fourth of July the youths were accused of knocking on the door of an eighty-two-year-old neighbor, and when the old woman opened the door they threw lit firecrackers into the house."

Unfortunately, the boys did not restrict their shenanigans to mere pranks. In the summer of 1970, Bobby Jr. and Bobby Shriver were arrested for pot possession. In Nantucket, Joe II took his little brother David and David's girlfriend, Pam Kelley, for a joyride in a friend's Jeep. Spinning the vehicle in circles, Joe lost control and crashed in a ditch. He and David escaped with minor injuries, but Pam Kelley was paralyzed from the neck down. Bobby Jr. and David's drug use grew to include heroin, and while Bobby was able to pull himself together enough to attend Harvard, David became increasingly alienated from the family as he struggled with addiction. He would die of an overdose in 1984, his body discovered in a Palm Beach hotel room. He'd been in town to visit Rose.

There were a number of men in Ethel's life in the decades after Bobby died. Through the late sixties and seventies, she was most frequently seen with singer Andy Williams, who had been friends with Bobby as well. It's a matter of some debate whether their relationship was romantic—some sources report them holding hands at charity events while others dismiss the idea out of hand—but he was clearly the main gentleman in her life. There would be others throughout the seventies and eighties: Warren Rogers of *Look* magazine, liberal New York attorney William vanden Heuvel, even sportscaster Frank Gifford. But Ethel never remarried. After all, none of the men was Bobby Kennedy.

Years later, her children appreciated the way in which Ethel had formed them. "There have been so many times in my life," Rory told Courtney in her 2011 documentary, *Ethel*, "where people have said, 'I want to introduce Robert Kennedy's daughter—'"

"It makes me so mad!" Courtney interrupted. "What about the one who delivered us, and carried us for nine months, and then has been with us for the last forty years?"

However hidden her grief over Bobby, Ethel worked through it on her own terms and raised her children the best she could. The paces that she put herself through to keep Bobby's legacy alive in the years just after his death—raising money for the grape pickers of California, sitting on the board of the Bedford-Stuyvesant Redevelopment Corporation, campaigning for Democratic politicians throughout the country—became causes dear to her own heart. And that passion was transmitted to her children. Ethel became an activist in her own right, with her own moral authority, and remains so to this day.

Though David's story would end tragically—and another son, Michael, would die in a skiing accident in 1998, at the age of thirty-nine—Ethel's children have, for the most part, thrived and joyfully carried forward their parents' ideals. Kathleen Kennedy Townsend became an attorney, author, and the first female lieutenant governor of Maryland. Kerry Kennedy has worked in the human rights movement for decades and in 1988 established the Robert F. Kennedy Center for Human Rights. Both Kathleen and Kerry share their mother's Catholicism, and they work for reform within the Church. Joe Kennedy II served as the congressional representative for Massachusetts' eighth district from 1987 to 1989, and afterward he went to work for a charity providing heating oil to low-income families. Bobby Kennedy Jr. became an environmentalist, author, and radio host.

Ethel herself avoids the media spotlight and denies requests for interviews. It's telling that the only person for whom she has been willing to make an exception was her daughter, Rory, whose loving documentary portrait, *Ethel*, was released by HBO Films in 2012. When asked why she agreed to sit for an interview after so many years, her answer was simple and pointed: "Because it was Rory who asked."

PART III
Jackie

1

BLACK JACK AND JANET

JACKIE BOUVIER ADORED HER FATHER. AND HER FATHER, JOHN VERNOU Bouvier III, had much to commend him.

Dashingly handsome in the Clark Gable mold, his year-round tan and Byronic charisma earned him the nickname Black Jack. He doted over his daughters, Jackie especially, and was irresistible to scores of women, his wife Janet occasionally among them. He and his family split their time between Park Avenue and East Hampton. He was athletic, impeccably dressed, rakishly charming—and rich.

Well, he *had* been rich. Black Jack's father, Major John Vernou Bouvier Jr., was a former trial lawyer who enjoyed living well—first off of his wife Maude Sergeant's family fortune, later off a sizable inheritance from his uncle. Black Jack used some of this family money to make a chunk of his own as a stockbroker. But less than a year and a half into his marriage to Janet Norton Lee, in October of 1929—only three months after Jackie was born—the stock market collapsed, commencing the Great Depression and the rapid decimation of Black Jack's personal fortune. His father's fortune never recovered either, though that didn't stop "The Major," as he liked to be called, from maintaining his extravagant lifestyle.

Though Black Jack borrowed (and borrowed some more) to keep his family living in style, his financial instability provided an ominous hum beneath Jackie's early life. According to Jackie biographer Sarah Bradford, it would give "Jackie and her younger sister, Lee, a sense of insecurity and fear of poverty that was to last almost all their lives."

Like Black Jack, Jackie's mother, Janet, came from a wealthy Wall Street family. But that's where their similarities ended. Janet was a more formal, inhibited, and brittle person. Sixteen years younger than Black Jack, the petite, fine-featured, dark-eyed brunette was barely twenty-one when they were married in July of 1928, much to the dismay of both families. While Janet's mother and father disapproved of the union—they thought Black Jack an adventurer and a cad—their authority was diminished in Janet's eyes: They had already very ably modeled a loveless marriage and were living apart by the time Janet and Black Jack wed.

Just over a year after the East Hampton wedding—on July 28, 1929—Jacqueline Bouvier was born. Her sister, Caroline Lee Bouvier, forever known as Lee, was born four years later.

Black Jack may well have been broke, but his marriage to Janet kept the natural consequences of this at bay, at least for a while. They lived rent-free in an eleven-room duplex at 740 Park Avenue—Janet's father built and owned the building—and rented an East Hampton cottage every summer. Jackie's early life revolved around Central Park, East Hampton, and horses. Janet was herself an accomplished equestrian, and Jackie was put on a horse as early as age two. She was competing in equestrian events by the time she was five.

Jackie and Lee would both cherish memories of their childhood summers in East Hampton, and Jackie would recall her parents, from the era of her early childhood, as a very glamorous couple. But cracks were already beginning to show in their marriage, which by the time Jackie was age seven was on a clear downward trajectory. Black Jack was a compulsive and quite open—to the point of viciousness—philanderer, and as the 1930s progressed, debts began closing in from several sides: the estate of his great uncle, his father-in-law, the Internal Revenue Service. Black Jack was clearly the scoundrel in the relationship: A photo of him holding a mistress's hand while standing next to his wife appeared in the *New York Daily News*, much to Janet's humiliation. Just as clearly, Jackie and Lee preferred his company to their mother's. Janet deeply resented this. A neurasthenic woman with a nasty temper, she occasionally hit the girls, which only reinforced Black Jack's position as the preferred parent.

In a 2013 interview, Lee, her childhood wounds vivid after decades, spoke bitterly of her mother's "almost irrational social climbing" and glowingly of Black Jack. "He was a wonderful man," she said. "He had such funny idiosyncrasies, like always wearing his black patent evening shoes with his swimming trunks. One thing which infuriates me is how he's always labeled the drunk black prince. He was never drunk with me, though I'm sure he sometimes drank, due to my mother's constant nagging. You would, and I would."

In September 1936, Janet asked for a six-month trial separation, and Black Jack moved into the Westbury Hotel. Despite a brief réchauffé in East Hampton the next summer, the marriage never recovered. Thereafter, the split was deeply acrimonious, and once Janet filed for divorce in 1940, very public. The *New York Daily Mirror* reported on the divorce, publishing details of Black Jack's extramarital dalliances, along with photographs. "There was such relentless bitterness on both sides," Lee said. "Jackie was really fortunate to have or acquire the ability to tune out, which she always kept."

Very early on, Jackie became the master of appearing serene no matter what roiled inside of her. But such a nasty and public divorce must have left a mark. "It was like for the years from ten to twenty never hearing anything [from your parents] except how awful the other one was," according to Lee. It's easy to see, in Jackie's later life, the effects of Black Jack and Janet's tabloid divorce. It's in the fierce approach she took to guarding the privacy of herself, her family, and their legacy. It's in her lifelong caginess with the media. And it's in her absolute insistence, wherever possible, on controlling the narrative. She sought out journalists who would be pliable to her will, such as Theodore White, who dutifully printed the Camelot myth that she pretty much invented in the week after Jack's death.

She also fought with journalists—most notably William Manchester, author of a book on her late husband titled *The Death of a President*—who wanted to print things of which she did not approve, regardless of their veracity. And she became famous for excommunicating intimates and employees who committed the sin of writing or talking about their time with her family, no matter how benign their accounts. (Maud Shaw, Caroline and John Jr.'s beloved governess, was to learn this very suddenly after Jackie discovered that she'd secured a book deal.) These are but a few of the examples of the lasting sting of Jackie's early public humiliation.

In the midst of all this family strife, Jackie attended to the business of growing up. She was, despite whatever sorrows she was repressing, a charismatic, bright, and mischievous child. In 1935 she began attending the Chapin School for Girls—Miss Chapin's—in New York. It was there that she made several lifelong friends, including Nancy Tuckerman, who would go on to attend high school at Miss Porter's with Jackie and become the White House social secretary under President Kennedy; she would remain Jackie's confidante until the end of her life.

Jackie was soon known at Miss Chapin's for her intelligence and restlessness. In *America's Queen: The Life of Jacqueline Kennedy Onassis*, biographer Sarah Bradford notes:

Jackie was already a rebel, unsubdued by the discipline at Miss Chapin's. She was brighter than most of her classmates and would get through her work quickly, then was left with nothing to do but doodle and daydream. All the teachers, interviewed by Mary Van Rensselaer Thayer twenty years later, remembered her for her beauty and, above all, her mischief. "She was the prettiest little girl," recalled a Miss Affleck, "very clever, very artistic, and full of the devil."

Outside of school, Jackie's joys were books and horses. She shirked naps by reading *Robin Hood*, *The Jungle Book*, and *Gone With the Wind* on her bedroom windowsill. Balancing her mischievousness was a retiring bookishness, and throughout her life the world of literature would offer her a quiet and a nourishment she couldn't find anywhere else.

Throughout the late 1930s and early 1940s, Jackie was winning blue ribbons at equestrian events in the Hamptons. By June 1940, when her parents' divorce became final, she'd developed a special kinship with one of Janet's horses: Danseuse, whom Jackie nicknamed Donny. Despite his increasingly limited resources (he'd had to move out of the Westbury and into a smaller apartment on East 74th Street), Black Jack paid for the horse to be stabled at Durland's livery on West 66th Street, enabling Jackie to ride in Central Park.

In June 1942, Janet remarried. Jackie and Lee's new stepfather was the "dull" (Lee's adjective) and extraordinarily wealthy Hugh D. Auchincloss II, known to all as Hughdie. Hughdie was the heir to the Standard Oil fortune, with palatial homes in McLean, Virginia (just outside of DC) and Newport, Rhode Island. Gore Vidal, whose mother had earlier been married to Hughdie, portrayed him as a bit of a dope in his memoir, *Palimpsest*. "My amiable, long-suffering stepfather," Vidal called him, "known as Hughdie or, more often, poor Hughdie." He credited Hughdie with making him "permanently susceptible to the charms of the born bore." Hughdie and Janet's son, Jamie, held a more moderate view. He told Sarah Bradford, "He was a kind man and he was a gentle man but he was a man who stayed in the nineteenth century in many ways." He was never a match for the fierce-tempered Janet, who generally ran the show, with his acquiescence.

Hammersmith Farm, Hughdie's Newport "cottage," was a twenty-eight-room nineteenth-century behemoth. "A house more Victorian or stranger you cannot imagine," according to Lee. "Oh, I longed to go back, to be with my father." ("There was the ocean," Lee said. "But naturally my sister claimed the room overlooking Narragansett Bay, where all the boats passed out. All I could see from my window was the cows named Caroline and Jacqueline.") Lee's description was apt: originally built by Hughdie's great-grandfather, the furnishings were heavy and somewhat eerie: the "deck room" featured "dark, musty upholstery, bear-, tiger-, and leopard-skin rugs and, hanging from the ceiling, a stuffed pelican caught by [Hughdie's] grandfather around the turn of the century." It wasn't all gloom and doom, though: Jackie enjoyed the gardens (laid out by Frederick Law Olmsted, famous for designing Central Park) and the view of the sea. Jackie did not share her sister's feelings about Hammersmith Farm, having by all accounts loved spending her summers on its ninety acres with her dogs, her horses, and the aforementioned cattle.

Similarly, Jackie quickly fell in love with Merrywood, situated on the Potomac River in McLean, Virginia, a "large brick neo-Georgian house" overlooking "the lawn and the woods beyond the lawn and the milk-chocolate-brown Potomac River far below." Jackie also made a deep connection with her stepbrother, Hugh D. Auchincloss III, known as Yusha, the eldest son from Hughdie's first marriage. Only two years older than Jackie, the fourteen-year-old Yusha was quite taken with his stepsister-to-be when they first met in December 1941 on a sightseeing trip to Washington. They shared a bookishness, an inquisitiveness, and a fascination with history. Snippets from their later correspondence give great insight into Jackie's sweetness, her sly wit, and her curiosity about the larger world. "I always love it so at Merrywood," she would later write to him. "So peaceful—with the river and the dogs—and listening to the Victrola. I will never know which I love best—Hammersmith with its green fields and summer winds—or Merrywood in the snow—with the river and those great steep hills."

Jackie did her best to become integrated into the new family. "Jackie never once spoke of step-this or half-that," a cousin told Sarah Bradford. "To Jackie they were all her brothers and sisters." Though she was bored by Hughdie, she recognized his essential kindliness and what his wealth meant for her, Janet, and Lee; and though she disliked her mother's rigidity and temper, Jackie appreciated more and more, as she got older, how much Janet sacrificed for the sake of her girls—from braving the world as a divorcée in the 1930s to marrying for money in the 1940s.

Janet's remarriage must have been a huge blow to Black Jack. The hypersolvency of her new husband aside, the union greatly decreased the amount of time Black Jack was able to spend with his daughters. The only sustained time they spent with him was every August in East Hampton, and holidays were now split with his ex-wife. "I think he counted on us so much," Lee said. "We were his *raison d'être*—sports, perhaps, came next and the stock market after that. But we always came first. I think the big responsibility we felt was ours. Mainly because he was so alone and counted on us totally."

In 1944 Jackie and her horse Danseuse won shows in East Hampton, Southampton, Bridgehampton, and Smithfield, an extraordinary accomplishment at any age, much less fifteen. That fall, Jackie entered Miss Porter's boarding school in Farmington, Connecticut, for three years of college prep. It took only a little pleading with her grandfather, The Major, for him to agree to have Danseuse stabled in Farmington so that Jackie could ride him while away at the homogeneous WASP enclave.

According to historian Barbara Perry, Miss Porter's "had begun to concentrate on academics, rather than 'finishing' young women, but the norms continued to emphasize elite manners." There Jackie continued her interest in drawing and poetry and became more interested in art history, French, and literature. She connected to Wordsworth, Chekhov, and of course Byron, "the prototype of the dangerous, risk-taking, heart-breaking men she was drawn to." Her father visited frequently on the weekends, raising eyebrows every time he zoomed up in his Mercury convertible.

———

"What we liked to do was run around and shake our behinds at him because he was an absolute lecher, absolute ravening, ravenous lecher," remembered one of Jackie's schoolmates, Ellen "Puffin" Gates. "And Jackie, of course, knew it, and it amused her, but I don't think she was aware—she might have been, she didn't miss anything—of the extent to which we were teasing her father and making fun of him. . . . This man was decidedly repulsive. He came through as this sort of cartoon example of a dirty old man."

During the week, however, Jackie split her devotion between her studies, Danseuse, and her friends. And throughout, the Miss Porter's ethos was inculcating something just as important. Wrote journalist Evgenia Peretz:

> *From its very start, in 1843, Miss Porter's has been committed not just to the old-fashioned values of charm, grace, and loyalty but to another, unspoken value as well: the ability to tough it out. Deeply ingrained in the school's DNA, it makes the school a kind of upper-class, social Outward Bound. Throughout its history, Miss Porter's has tested girls' personal fortitude in a variety of ways: through academic rigor, strict rules, and rituals designed to produce anxiety and intimidate. Whatever their problems, Miss Porter's girls were expected to buck up, not to go crying home to Daddy.*

This toughness was something that Jackie would have occasion to rely on in her adult life, time and again. Through a philandering husband, a challenging set of in-laws, an intrusive press, and many tragedies large and small, Jackie maintained a regal stillness, an impenetrability, a quiet but powerful resolve.

At Miss Porter's, her childhood strain of mischievousness didn't disappear; it simply matured. "She really had a very dirty sense of humor," Puffin Gates told Sarah Bradford. "I had more fun with Jackie than almost anybody because of that streak in her which was so naughty and irreverent about almost everything." She took up smoking, which was to be a lifelong habit, and wrote hectoring letters to Lee. (One advised her twelve-year-old sister that smoking would help her lose weight.) She graduated in 1947, a month shy of her eighteenth birthday, with an A-minus average, the Maria McKinney Memorial Award for Excellence in Literature, and the ambition to "never be a housewife."

That summer, a Hearst columnist pronounced her "Deb of the Year." The Auchinclosses threw two events for her society debut; Black Jack was invited to neither. It was during this summer, according to Barbara Perry, that Jackie began affecting the "breathy, cooing tone" that would characterize her speech as first lady. Her self-possession and charisma around men were becoming evident, as well. "I remember that talking with her was very different," remembered writer George Plimpton. "She sort of enveloped you—rare for someone of that age to be able to learn how to. She had a wonderful way of looking at you and enveloping you with this gaze." Plimpton would not be the last man to find Jackie utterly bewitching—and she was about to spend four years refining, among other things, her feminine magnetism. That autumn she was to take her poise and self-possession to Vassar College in Poughkeepsie, New York.

2

THAT DAMN VASSAR

"I SPENT TWO YEARS AT VASSAR," JACKIE WROTE IN 1951, "AND CANNOT quite decide whether I liked it or not."

Situated on one thousand acres outside of Poughkeepsie, New York, Vassar College was one of the "Seven Sisters," a group of elite, progressive, all-women's colleges that included Smith, Mount Holyoke, and Wellesley. Its remote location and lack of young men would come to bother Jackie, but perhaps its biggest deficiency, as she would later see it, was that it was not Paris. She would not end up finishing at Vassar, but the two years she spent there were none the less formative. It was where she became interested in journalism, where her appreciation of art and literature deepened, and where she started dating. More importantly, it was where she realized that she was not content with the limits of her sheltered world.

Jackie arrived at Vassar in the fall of 1947 preceded by the buzz conferred upon her as "Debutante of the Year," which she seems to have considered a dubious honor. "I knew about her Deb of the Year title, but I don't remember her ever bringing it up," Charlotte Curtis told Jackie biographer C. David Heymann. "I think it rather embarrassed her." Curtis lived next door to Jackie in Main Hall with Selwa Showker (later Selwa Roosevelt), who also characterized Jackie as modest. Both mentioned her beauty, but both also stressed her intellect, and something else—a curiosity about other cultures and varieties of experience.

"She was intellectually very curious," Roosevelt said.

She constantly asked me about my family. I was of Lebanese extraction and had grown up in a small town in Tennessee. These aspects of my life fascinated Jackie. She wanted to know all about how my father stowed away on a boat as a young boy to come to America. She wanted to know about Lebanon. I had pictures of my family in my room and Jackie would scrutinize the faces and ask questions about various members of the family, almost like a reporter gathering material for a story. She had a way of focusing on a person that left one dazzled; it was most flattering.

In addition, Jackie did not lack for classroom stimulation. She enjoyed her classes in studio art, art history, and English—she enjoyed her Shakespeare class especially. Her roommate Edna Harrison took Spanish with her and remembered that she had a particular gift for languages. "I was struggling like mad," she told Sarah Bradford. "She whizzed through the class, she got all A's and she was just trying to coach me through it." This was on top of her extracurriculars, which included drama and the college newspaper.

It was at Vassar that she began dating, and the Deb of the Year had no shortage of suitors. Her stepbrother Yusha, an upperclassman at Yale, would set her up with friends from various Ivy League schools. "It was a transitory period of her life," Yusha later said. "She liked playing the field, meeting a variety of types—varsity swimmers at Yale, Harvard pre-med candidates, up-and-coming New York lawyers and stockbrokers." Whether that list represents a "variety" in any meaningful sense is debatable, but it is true that she refused to settle on any one man to date seriously. Instead she seemed to approach dating as a sort of rehearsal, a way of honing her skills with the opposite sex.

"Jackie was learning the American geisha technique of attracting or, rather, not frightening men," wrote Sarah Bradford. "Clever women of the time learned to conceal their intelligence. 'I remember a man telling Jackie he was afraid he was going to fail his exams,' [classmate] Zup Campbell James said, 'and Jackie saying cooingly, "I have that problem too," knowing that she had succeeded.' It was a technique she honed to perfection." She certainly didn't take any of these men very seriously, referring to them as "beetle-browed bores," emphatically not marriage material. A member of the family who would later host Jackie during her year in Paris would observe, "She couldn't tolerate weak men. If she didn't esteem and admire a man, if she didn't look up to him, she dropped him immediately."

Despite the light touch she brought to her collegiate dating life, it seems clear that the prospect of losing her disturbed Black Jack. "I suppose it won't be long until I lose you to some funny looking 'gink,'" he wrote to her, "who you think is wonderful because he is so romantic looking in the evening and wears his mother's pearl earrings for dress-shirt buttons, because he loves her so." After she'd begun skipping weekends with him to stay at Yale, his letters dispensed with the jovial tone. "A woman can have wealth and beauty and brains, but without a reputation she has nothing," he wrote in one deeply felt, sincerely sexist missive.

Edna Harrison, who would occasionally accompany Jackie home for the weekend, remembered, "If I was dressed up and ready to go out on time, [Black Jack] said, 'Oh, you should never be ready on time, that's just ridiculous, you should always make a young man wait!' He always said, 'Play the game.'" His advice to Jackie and Lee was even more direct. "You just remember, Jacqueline, All Men Are Rats. Don't trust any of them," Lee remembers him saying. "I guess he felt it was his obligation to warn us," she added.

—•—

Losing Jackie to some "gink" was only one source of anxiety for Black Jack at that time. In January of 1948, his father, The Major, died of prostate cancer. His "last will and testament contained some unpleasant surprises, particularly for Black Jack who received no inheritance whatsoever, his accrued loans cancelling his share of the estate." Most of what little was left went to Black Jack's twin sisters, Maude and Michelle. Wrangling over the management of that money, as well as the investiture of the measly three-thousand-dollar trusts left for Jackie and Lee, created a great deal of stress and fallout. The turmoil was not only within the languishing Bouvier clan, but between Black Jack and Janet as well. "The precipitate decline of the Bouviers' fortunes provided Jackie with an illustration—if she needed one—of the precarious nature of family prosperity and the importance of money in the social equation," wrote Sarah Bradford. "For her, the Bouviers were now history."

Her father's struggles led him to rely more on, and be more demanding of, his daughters' affection. It's perhaps no surprise then that, in the summer of 1948, instead of spending July and August with her father as she normally did, Jackie took a seven-week trip to Europe—her first. Taken with the children of some of Janet and Hughdie's friends, and chaperoned by one of Jackie's old Latin teachers, the whirlwind trip included stops in Provence, the Riviera, Switzerland, Italy, London (where she met one of her heroes, Winston Churchill), and most importantly, Paris, where she was able to meet up with Yusha and which she described as filled with "glamour, glitter and rush." "I've had a glimpse," she wrote her mother. "Next time I want to soak it all up."

That school year, she discovered that Smith College had a yearlong program at the Sorbonne in Paris. Accepted by the program, she left on August 23, 1949, for Paris and what she would later call "the high point of my life, my happiest and most carefree year."

The first month of her trip was spent in the south of France, in an intensive French course at the University of Grenoble. She and the members of her program lived with a French family and spoke no English. In October, it was off to Paris, and the Sorbonne. Though most American students lived together in Reid Hall, Jackie chose instead to live with a family of French aristocrats, the de Rentys, which included Claude de Renty, a daughter Jackie's age. The two were to become lifelong friends. Though her hostess, Guyot de Renty, was indeed a countess, this status did not necessarily translate into the creature comforts to which Jackie was accustomed. "Like most French residences, the Avenue Mozart apartment had no central heating," Countess de Renty remembered. "During the winter months Jacqueline did her homework in bed wrapped like a mummy in scarf, mittens, sweater and earmuffs. There was a single antique tin tub for all seven of us, but hot water was rare." Further, in 1949 there were still many postwar shortages of basic groceries like sugar and coffee. Jackie "was fearless, a trooper in the truest sense of the word."

Nor did her Spartan living arrangements stop Jackie from enjoying all the culture that Paris had to offer. "The most wonderful thing here is all the theaters and operas and ballets and how easy they are to get to," she wrote to Yusha. "You could go out every night all winter and still not have seen everything that is playing." Over the Christmas break, she visited London and stayed with one of Black Jack's former mistresses, Ann Plugge.* Jackie also used the break to travel through Austria and Germany. Having felt on her previous European trip that "it was just too luxurious and we just didn't see anything," this time she traveled "on second- and third-class trains, sitting up all night talking to people and hearing their stories."

By the time she returned to Paris, she was planning even broader tours in Europe. ("Don't you ever intend to come home?" Black Jack wrote plaintively.) Further, she had decided that she did not want to return to Vassar, much to Black Jack's dismay. "You may hate the thought of going back to that damn Vassar, as you call it," he wrote. "But perhaps going back as a senior, and one who can relate all her travels, you may not find it half as bad as you think."

By the spring, Jackie had established herself, with the help of friends like Claude and the Compte Paul de Ganay, a charming French aristocrat, as something of a society party girl. She attended soirees at the home of writer Louise de Vilmorin, the mother of a Vassar classmate who was known for parties where you could spot everyone from Orson Welles and Rita Hayworth to Jean Cocteau, Max Ophuls, and Jean Anouilh.

Jackie finished her Sorbonne exams by the middle of June but hung around for the summer, enjoying Paris and taking excursions all over France and England with Yusha, Claude, and others from their set. She finished off her summer by spending August in Ireland and Scotland with Yusha. "Jackie's favorite activity was to stop to talk to strangers, whether shopkeepers, pub crawlers, tinkers, tramps or farmers," Yusha said. "She was endlessly fascinated by ordinary people and the stories they had to tell."

The two sailed back to New York together aboard the French liner *Liberté*. Black Jack met them at the dock. To compound the heartbreak of her decision not to return to nearby Vassar, Jackie stayed with her father only two days before rushing home to Merrywood, where she would

---

* Ann had left Black Jack and reconciled with her husband in the spring of 1943 and had given birth to twins in November of 1944; Jackie wrote Black Jack from London expressing her conviction that the twins were his. He agreed, replying, "You are dead right about the Plugge twins."

live while she completed her college education at George Washington University in Washington, DC. Transferring her credits from Vassar, she enrolled as a senior and majored in French literature.

Her courses included journalism and creative writing. "She was an extremely intelligent young woman, but she also possessed a brilliant imagination," one of her teachers would later recall. "This was coupled with a genuine talent for the craft of writing. She had a gift as a writer and might have become prominent in her own right as a writer had she followed another path. . . . She didn't need to take my classes."

Even so, winning the 16th Annual *Vogue* Prix de Paris was by no means a sure thing. The competition required the completion of several sections, including "an autobiography; technical papers on modeling, fashions for coeds, beauty treatments, and the marketing of a perfume; a plan for how to teach women about men's clothing; a proposal for a complete issue of *Vogue*; and an essay on 'People I Wish I Had Known.'" She spent most of the second semester of her senior year hard at work on the assignment. The prize itself was a yearlong stint at *Vogue*—six months apiece at its New York and Paris offices.

"As to physical appearance," she wrote in her autobiographical essay, "I am tall, 5'7", with brown hair, a square face and eyes so unfortunately far apart that it takes three weeks to have a pair of glasses made with a bridge wide enough to fit over my nose. I do not have a sensational figure but can look slim if I pick the right clothes." As for the historical figures she wished she had known, Jackie chose three artists: poet Charles Baudelaire; poet, playwright, and all-around wit Oscar Wilde; and Russian ballet impresario Sergei Diaghilev. Jackie wrote that Wilde and Baudelaire were both "poets and idealists who could paint their sinfulness with beauty and still believe in something higher." In Diaghilev she saw a synthesizer of Eastern and Western artistic traditions, and a tireless perfectionist.

The late spring of 1951 was a heady time for young Jackie. On April 25 she was informed that she had been chosen as a finalist for the prize; a few days after her final exams in May, she received notice that she had beaten out 1,280 applicants from 225 colleges to win the 1951 Prix de Paris. She was in New York the next Monday morning to sign with *Vogue* and pose for studio portraits, which would be reproduced in the August issue. Then, on June 7, she set sail for Europe yet again—this time with Lee, who had graduated from Miss Porter's that spring. The trip was a graduation present from Janet and Hughdie. The sisters would visit London, Madrid, Provence, Venice, and Florence. They later collected their memories, along with photographs, poems, and drawings, in a book called *One Special Summer* and presented it as a gift to Janet. The whirlwind trip was, for Jackie, a final taste of childhood before starting her career at *Vogue* that fall.

Just a few days before she left for Europe, in early June 1951, she accepted a dinner invitation at the home of family friend and Washington columnist Charlie Bartlett. There, Bartlett and his wife introduced Jackie to another friend of theirs: the thirty-four-year-old Democratic congressman from Massachusetts, John Fitzgerald Kennedy.

"After the dinner, why, I walked her out to her car," Charlie Bartlett remembered. "And Jack Kennedy came sort of tailing after, and he was muttering shyly about, 'Shall we go someplace and have a drink?' And Jackie at that stage noticed in the back seat that some man had—a young friend, had been walking along the street and he'd gotten in her car, and crawled into the back seat and was waiting there. So she was forced to tell the Senator that she couldn't join him for a drink." That night Jack and Jackie went their separate ways and she, a few days later, left for Europe with Lee.

By the next January, Jackie would be back in the States and, having turned down the *Vogue* job, be working a newspaper job in Washington. She would also be engaged to a tall, handsome young man with money and a promising future—a man named John Husted, Jr.

3

THE CAREER WOMAN AND THE
DISTINGUISHED GENTLEMAN

W‌HY JACKIE EVENTUALLY TURNED DOWN THE PRIX DE PARIS, SOMETHING
for which she'd worked so hard and which seemed so in line with her interests, is something of a mystery. Historians and biographers offer several
theories. Barbara Perry lists some possibilities: "Perhaps her mother and
stepfather feared that she would fall back under the spell of Black Jack
during the prize's six-month stint in New York. Or they may have been
concerned that she would become an expatriate if she moved to Paris for
another long stay. Janet might have believed that her daughter . . . was falling behind in the 'race' to find a suitable mate . . ." Sarah Bradford quotes a
source as saying that Jackie started the job at *Vogue*'s New York offices but
didn't even last the morning: An encounter with a flamboyantly gay staff
member convinced Jackie that *Vogue* was no place to find a husband.

Instead, Jackie headed back to McLean, and the Auchinclosses. Eager
to establish an income and a life beyond Merrywood, and interested in
a career in writing, she used Auchincloss connections to secure an interview at the *Washington Times-Herald*. Starting with secretarial duties, she
quickly agitated for a more substantial role at the paper. After much back
and forth with the editor-in-chief, who worried that she was just marking time until the inevitable marriage proposal, she acquired the position
of "Inquiring Photographer." Jackie, trained in the use of a professional-
quality camera, hit the streets asking citizens (and sometimes, members
of Congress) their opinions on questions that she devised.

"You could make the column about anything you wanted to," she said. "So I'd find a bunch of rough, salty characters and ask them about a prize-fighter just so I could capture how they talked."

More often than examining boxing, questions she asked seemed designed to playfully engage the age-old battle of the sexes. "Do you think a wife should let her husband think he's smarter than she is?" she asked. "When did you discover that women are not the weaker sex?" "Are wives a luxury or a necessity?" She'd ask young women if they'd rather be "an old man's darling or a young man's slave?" It was not just her own family history that made her desperate to secure a fortune; every element in her milieu was urging marriage. The subject was undoubtedly on her mind. Which was only appropriate: By the time she took on her "Inquiring Photographer" job, she was engaged to be married.

There are differing accounts of when Jackie met and began a serious relationship with John Husted Jr., but we know that she accepted his proposal of marriage around Christmas, 1951. Husted was "tall, well-built, urbane, very handsome in a WASPish way," said Mary de Limur Weinmann, who claimed to have introduced them in late 1951. A Yale-educated Wall Street investment banker, he seems to have fallen decisively for her, but the engagement was not to last very long. In mid-March, Husted visited Merrywood. When Jackie dropped him off at the airport, she silently took off the engagement ring and deposited it in the pocket of Husted's suit jacket. "She didn't say much and neither did I," Husted would remember. "There wasn't much you could say."

A few factors contributed to the brevity of the engagement. Janet, having herself been disastrously married to an urbane, Yale-educated Wall Street man, was not in favor of the union. And Jackie confided her fears to friends that being married to an investment banker would be boring. But the biggest force that eclipsed John Husted was Jack Kennedy, the thirty-four-year-old senatorial candidate she'd met at Charlie Bartlett's the previous summer. He'd found his way back onto Jackie's radar.

Jack Kennedy was born in 1917, Joe and Rose's second child. Growing up between Brookline and Hyannis Port, he enjoyed the intellectually and physically vigorous family life insisted on by his parents. As a boy he learned to sail and took part in the family's famous touch-football games, known for their fierce, rough-and-tumble competitiveness. And the Kennedy family dinner table was always a place for spirited debates regarding the issues of the day. (Jackie would observe of the Kennedy dinner table: "If you didn't get on the offensive, they'd have you on the defensive all night.")

He was a bright, precocious child, and he attended some of the nation's top schools: Boston Latin, Choate, Harvard. But he was never that great of a student. His consistently mediocre academic performance could be attributed to an intellect that was in need of constant stimulation. Another factor was almost certainly his poor health.

Chronically ill, Jack Kennedy was in and out of hospitals and clinics throughout his life, where doctors treated symptoms while attempting to diagnose the shifting constellation of his underlying ailments: gastroenterological problems, a serious adrenal deficiency called Addison's disease, a degenerative back condition. Staying healthy would remain difficult as treatments for one condition would aggravate another. For example, steroids prescribed for digestive problems may have triggered his Addison's disease and caused osteoporosis in his spine. His digestive problems kept him rail thin throughout his childhood and early manhood, and they gave him a gangly, sometimes gaunt appearance as he grew to just over six feet tall.

His back problems were exacerbated by the PT 109 incident. After returning from the war and spending much time dealing with stomach, back, and adrenal problems, Jack turned his attention to politics. In 1946 he campaigned for, and with the help of his father's millions won, a seat as representative from Massachusetts. Though his record as a congressman was unexceptional, he was popular in his district and was reelected twice. Almost as soon as he took office in the House, he began eyeing the Senate, and he ran for the Senate in 1952. He was assured of victory by his own star power and his father's considerably deep pockets.

JFK was an incredibly handsome and charismatic young man. The history books bulge with friends and acquaintances trying to define what made him so personally magnetic. American composer and conductor

Leonard Bernstein, who socialized with both Jack and Jackie during their White House years, put it this way: "A remarkable combination of informality and stateliness—that's not precisely the word—casualness and majesty.... It's a funny thing: he could say, 'Pass the salt,' and I was deeply touched. It's that quality he had which I am still hard-put to define ... the thing that made him precious, beyond calculation."

By the time Jackie met him, John F. Kennedy was one of the most sought-after men on the East Coast, a junior congressman with an eye on a Senate seat. She was to fall for his many virtues, and in time come to learn about the darker components of his complex personality.

4

A SPORADIC COURTSHIP, A CELEBRITY WEDDING

THOUGH WE KNOW THAT JACKIE AND LEE VISITED THE KENNEDYS IN Palm Beach in late 1951—around the time she was to become unenthusiastically engaged to John Husted—both Jackie and JFK would mark another dinner at Charlie Bartlett's house, on May 8, 1952, as when they started dating.

In many ways, they were well matched. Their similarities gave each an amount of instant understanding of the other, while their differences added frisson. Both came from at least ostensibly wealthy Catholic families, in which the charming, philandering fathers were beloved by the children. Both also had complicated and ambivalent relationships with their mothers.

But where Jack Kennedy's family, though dysfunctional in its own way, was strong and tightly knit, Jackie had seen hers fragment bitterly before she was even ten years old. And where a crowded, competitive childhood and a burgeoning political career had inured Jack to a great deal of clamor and bustle, Jackie's disposition was more retiring and contemplative. Barbara Perry catalogs the differences that made them, in some ways, a genuinely odd couple:

> *He had no facility for languages; she was multilingual. . . . He cared not a whit for fashion, including his own; she was the queen of couture. . . . He was allergic to horses and dogs; she had grown up surrounded by equine and canine pets. He had never owned a home and had no interest in or*

taste for decorating; she had a natural eye for the finest decorative arts.
His idea of the perfect night out was to see a movie Western and grab
a hamburger and malt; she loved the ballet, opera, and symphony and
maintained her taste for French cuisine and wine. . . .

To these differences, there were strong and compensating similarities:
Each had a sly, wicked sense of humor and tremendous personal magnetism. But perhaps what matched them most was that they shared a wry,
stoic demeanor. The violence of war, the premature deaths of his brother
Joe and sister Kick, and his own precarious health had bred in Jack a
fatalistic streak. For Jackie, the very public and humiliating disintegration
of her family had forged her implacable poise.

Lem Billings, Jack's lifelong best friend and the consummate Kennedy insider, felt he understood their bond, saying: "He saw her as a kindred spirit. They both had taken circumstances that weren't the best in the
world when they were younger and learned to *make themselves up* as they
went along. They were both actors," he added, "and I think they appreciated each other's performances. . . . Both of them had the ability to make
you feel that there was no place on earth you'd rather be than sitting there
in intimate conversation with them."

Jack and Jackie's dating life was relatively conventional for the time.
They played parlor games at the Bartletts', went to the movies (Jackie
gamely went to the Westerns), and double-dated with Bobby and Ethel. It
was a sporadic courtship: Running for the Senate, Jack was frequently out
of town. "He'd call me from some oyster bar up on the Cape with a great
clinking of coins, to ask me out to the movies the following Wednesday,"
Jackie remembered.

Certainly he appreciated her exceptional book smarts. Both were avid
readers of history and poetry. She took part in his intellectual and professional life, editing his senatorial position papers and translating books for
him on Southeast Asia from the original French.

In the summer of 1952, Jack invited Jackie to the Hyannis Port compound, where the Kennedys were welcoming, but formidable. "How can
I explain these people?" she would later write. "They were like carbonated
water, and other families might be flat." Leisure time with the Kennedys

was highly energized. A parlor game could become a debate on current events, which could continue through one of their strenuous touch-football games. They sailed, they played tennis, they swam, they played golf—all of it as competitive as their dinner-table conversations.

Jack's sisters, Eunice, Pat, and Jean, joined by irrepressible sister-in-law Ethel, were just as competitive as the men, and during that summer they subjected Jackie to something like a sorority hazing. Jackie called them the "Rah Rah Girls" and told Lee that, "when they have nothing else to do, they run in place. Other times they fall all over each other like a pack of gorillas." They made fun of her cooing lilt and her delicate manners, calling her "The Deb."

Whatever the sisters thought, the patriarch, Joe Kennedy, loved her. "Joe Kennedy not only condoned the marriage," Lem Billings said. "He ordained it. 'A politician has to have a wife,' he said, 'and a Catholic politician has to have a Catholic wife. She should have class. Jackie probably has more class than any girl we've ever seen around here.'" She was, in Joe's eyes, the perfect package: well-spoken, photogenic, and poised—and tough enough to handle marriage to Jack.

Jack also dutifully presented himself to the Auchinclosses. "I remember the first time Jackie asked Jack to Merrywood, to pick her up for some dinner," Lee remembered. "You couldn't mention the word 'Democrat' in my stepfather's house or even presence—nor in my father's for that matter—and I felt Jack was in for a rough ride. But he was a senator, so he already had a kind of authority as well as a dazzling personality. He won them over pretty quickly."

Jack Kennedy was without a doubt reluctant to marry. He enjoyed life as the dashing, rich, young Capitol Hill playboy, and his compulsive womanizing would have made the idea of "settling down" unattractive, if not downright disturbing. But Jack was no fool, and he knew that a wife would be a necessity if he aspired to higher office. And whatever mixed feelings Jack had at the prospect of marriage, Jackie had clearly captured his imagination. "He really brightened when she appeared," said Chuck Spalding, one of Jack's oldest friends. "You could see it in his eyes; he'd follow her around the room watching to see what she'd do next. Jackie *interested* him, which was not true of many women."

For her part, Jackie went in with an awareness of some of the challenges that would face her and Jack as a married couple. She knew that he had troubles with his back and stomach. "The year before we were married, when he'd take me out, half the time it was on crutches," she later said. "You know, when I went to watch him campaign, before we were married, he was on crutches. I can remember him on crutches more than not." And she had heard rumors of his womanizing. But it's hard to imagine, given her relationship with her father, that she'd have found anything irregular or unforgivable about that. "She wasn't sexually attracted to men unless they were dangerous like old Black Jack," Spalding posited. "It was one of those terribly obvious Freudian situations."

The importance of the Kennedy fortune in Jackie's calculus should not be downplayed. She saw what happened as the Bouvier family fortune declined, and she experienced a new level of lush living after her mother married Hughdie. But while Hughdie's biological children were given enormous trusts, no such provisions were made for her or Lee. If she wanted her own fortune, she'd have to marry into it. Though Jackie Bouvier was gaga over Jack, as Sarah Bradford wrote, "she would never have married a poor Jack Kennedy."

While Jackie continued her work at the *Washington Times-Herald*, she was ready for a change. In the spring of 1953, she headed to London to cover the coronation of Queen Elizabeth II. The stories, sketches, and photos she filed showed her creativity. A telegram from Jack in America read, "Articles excellent but you are missed. Love, Jack." When she returned, Jack gave Jackie a two-carat diamond-and-emerald engagement ring. The engagement hit the papers in June 1953, and *Life* magazine wrote a cover story on the couple later that summer.

The wedding was, at Joe's direction, a star-studded media event: Fourteen hundred invitations were sent and a crowd of three thousand showed up to spectate on September 12 at St. Mary's Catholic Church in Newport. Jackie wore the rosepoint lace veil that Janet's mother and Janet had both worn for their weddings. While Jackie would have preferred to wear a more contemporary wedding dress, she acceded to the wishes of Jack, who had asked her to wear "something traditional and old-fashioned." Her mother and father-in-law also argued for something frillier than Jackie wanted. "Joe reportedly was particularly pleased at the potential political capital to be earned by Janet Auchincloss's commissioning of her African-American seamstress, Ann Lowe, to create the gown." For Joe, using Lowe rather than a French designer, for example, added a humble and progressive touch that would play well with the public.

One shadow fell over the otherwise joyous occasion. On the morning of the ceremony, Black Jack was found in his hotel room, too drunk to stand up unassisted, much less walk his eldest daughter down the aisle, as he had hoped. Over the weeks preceding, he had conscientiously sobered up. He donned a special rubber suit and ran around the Central Park reservoir to slim down for the big day. But when he arrived in Newport, he barely had time to see Jackie before Janet made it plain that he was not welcome.

"He was on his best behavior," remembered Gore Vidal. (Vidal's mother had been married to Hughdie before Janet; he and Jackie shared half-siblings.) "But, inspired by who knows what furies, Janet decided that although she could not bar him from the church, she could disinvite him from the reception. . . . Janet ordered Mike [Canfield, Lee's husband] to go to Black Jack and tell him he was not to come to the wedding reception. Black Jack went straight to the bar."

"The only time I ever saw him really drunk was at Jackie's wedding," Lee remembered. "My mother refused to let him come to the family dinner the night before. So he went to his hotel and drank from misery and loneliness. It was clear in the morning that he was in no state to do anything, and I remember my mother screaming with joy, 'Hughdie, Hughdie, now you can give Jackie away.' During the wedding party I had to get him onto a plane back to New York. . . . It was a nightmare."

Jackie betrayed none of her heartbreak during the ceremony or the reception, held at Hammersmith Farm. A *Life* magazine photographer apparently caught photos of Jackie impishly blowing smoke rings; Jack spent their two-week Acapulco honeymoon worrying they'd be published.

The couple stayed in a villa set into a cliff overlooking the sea. "This is the most beautiful place you've ever seen—Jack adores it too," Jackie wrote to Rose and Joe. Jack "is absolutely HELPLESS—which is such fun—because he doesn't speak a word of Spanish." As the help didn't speak English, Jackie did all the translating. The maids found Jack "beguiling and are convinced we are NOT MARRIED!" She wrote about their water-skiing and deep-sea fishing adventures and rhapsodized about married life. "I want to tell you how perfect it is being married," she wrote. "And how unbelievably heavenly Jack is." For his part, Jack wired his parents that "at last I know the true meaning of rapture. Jackie is enshrined forever in my heart. Thanks mom and dad for making me worthy of her."

Enshrined she may well have been, but Jack had no intention of putting a stop to his womanizing. As early as a couple of weeks into their marriage, he was making excuses to get away from Jackie and flirting with any attractive woman who came his way. Jack's compulsive skirt chasing revealed a darker side of what was, in other ways, a genuinely heroic character.

5

JACK'S DARK SIDE

NOT EVERY WOMAN WAS VULNERABLE TO JACK KENNEDY'S CHARMS— only those attracted to good looks, extreme wealth, animal magnetism, intelligence, and wit.

"I had designs on John F. Kennedy," Pulitzer Prize–winning author Margaret Coit admitted in a 1966 oral history. "Everybody in Massachusetts did. He was the golden boy, the most eligible bachelor in New England." In the spring of 1953, research for her biography of financier/philanthropist Bernard Baruch took her to Washington and gave Coit an excellent excuse to introduce herself to JFK. Her account of that meeting, and a subsequent date, is at times unpleasant to read, but it offers a succinct glimpse into Kennedy's womanizing. This compulsive, reckless, at times cruel aspect of his personality, so difficult to reconcile with his many virtues, is something anyone who reads about JFK or Jackie has to wrestle with. And Jackie's response to it says much about her strength, her grit, and the way in which her childhood prepared her (as much as any woman could be prepared) to be married to such a man.

That spring of 1953—the same spring he became engaged to Jackie— was a difficult time healthwise for Jack, and the exhaustion brought on by his poor health was noticeable to Coit. When she first met him, Coit's "overwhelming impression was of something gray," she remembered. "His eyes were gray, and his suit was gray and his hair was gray at that time. His lips were gray, and his skin had a grayish tinge. His eyeballs were very, very white. He had very piercing eyes, and a hard, harsh kind of voice, small stubby fingered hands."

After the interview in Kennedy's Senate office, he invited her to a party at his Georgetown home. At that party Coit, a Republican, ran into a guilty-looking Richard Nixon: "I gave a gulp, and he gave a gulp. He said, 'I won't tell on you if you don't tell on me.'" At the end of the party, most of which he spent talking in a corner with Senator Stuart Symington, JFK finally approached Coit and suggested a date in the immediate future. A few days later, she agreed to drop by his Senate office at four o'clock in the afternoon.

There, she found him hard at work on Senate business, correspondence, and signing "glamour-boy pictures of himself—hundreds of them." Coit sat on the sofa and perused his bookshelves while he conducted phone business and signed letters in the sweltering, non-air-conditioned office. Finally, after over an hour, he finished his work for the day. He joined her on the couch, and she was impressed by how dangerously exhausted he suddenly seemed. "He just looked more gray than ever, and his eyes were closed," she recalled. "I thought he was going to faint, and I was so scared I didn't know what to do. It was late. Everybody had gone home."

The two agreed that Jack was too tired for a date that night, but he rallied to give her a ride home. Grabbing his crutches, JFK escorted Coit to his car, "a little open topless convertible, absolutely all jammed up, and dented, and marked," and drove her to her rooming house in Southeast Washington.

"Where I made my mistake," Coit said, "was inviting him in."

He threw himself down on the sofa. It seemed all right to me. Then he tried to drag me down beside him. So I struggled, and I said, 'Wait a minute. I made up my mind that I was not going to kiss you on the first date.' He said, 'This isn't a first date. We have been making eyes at each other three times now.' Then he lunged for me . . . I began to cry. . . . I rose and got up to get a glass of water. He watched me. 'You have pretty legs,' he said. . . . 'Well, you are not bad looking for a senator,' I said, thinking that was what he wanted. He looked very rueful. Then he sprang up. He grabbed me. . . . 'Don't,' I said. 'Don't be so grabby. This is only our first date. We've got plenty of time.' He lifted his head and his gray eyes just drilled into mine. 'But I can't wait, you see, I'm going to grab everything I want. You see, I haven't any time.'

It's an incredibly bald statement on his part that provides a great deal of insight on the existential panic that lay behind Kennedy's aggressive womanizing. He was a man who, throughout his life, had good reason to believe he wouldn't live much longer. Besides his health problems and the dire prognostications he'd beaten back time and again, here was a man who, at war, had seen lives ended in an instant. The loss of his brother and sister had shown him in very intimate terms how capricious, sudden, and permanent death was. He wanted to "grab everything" as a way of assuaging a profound panic, of asserting life in the face of death.

This panic did not bring out the best in Jack, at least not where women were concerned. "He was so cold," Coit continued,

It was as if he had shifted gears. We had been talking about books and ideas. . . . He had seen me as a mind; and now he saw me just as something female. He couldn't fit the two together, and it was as if he were two parts. It was the cold machine-like quality that scared me so . . .

Looking back on the incident more than ten years later, Coit would say that "he frightened me more than the facts warranted." Nevertheless, she added, "I was afraid he would [call me], and I got out of Washington as soon as I could because I didn't know what to do about it. I didn't quite know how to cope. I went home."

Besides his fatalism and sense of mortality, Jack's promiscuity can be attributed to how he was raised. He grew up in a home where his father chased women fairly openly while his mother, for the most part, tacitly accepted it. But the simplest reason may be one of the more compelling: Jack was rich, and Jack was handsome, and women were readily available to him. Certainly at that time—and maybe at all times—that was all the license a man like Jack Kennedy needed.

Jackie would never know about all of Jack's conquests, but throughout their life together she'd learn of enough of them to be shocked and hurt. She tried to be philosophical. "I don't think there are any men who are faithful to their wives," she said. "Men are such a combination of good and evil." But according to Robert Dallek, one of Jack's friends remembered that "after the first year they were together, Jackie was wandering around looking like the survivor of an airplane crash."

6

THE SENATOR'S WIFE

JACKIE RETURNED FROM HER HONEYMOON TO A NEW ROLE: SENATOR'S wife. Right away she got a crash course in Massachusetts politics.

"I was taken immediately to Boston to be registered as a Democrat by Patsy Mulkern, who was called 'the China Doll,' because he was a prize fighter once," Jackie later remembered. "And he took me all up and down that street, and told me that 'duking' means shaking hands, and things. And then there was another man with 'Onions' Burke named 'Juicy' Grenara. Well, I mean those names just fascinated me so. You know, to sort of see that world, and then we'd go have dinner at the Ritz."

It was a new world for her, and one which offered little time to sit still.

"It just seems it was suitcases [and] moving," she said of the first year of their marriage. They rented in Georgetown from January to June and then spent the summer living at Merrywood during the week and escaping to Cape Cod on the weekends as much as they could. In the fall they lived in Massachusetts—at Hyannis or Jack's tiny apartment in Boston. "It was terrifically nomadic. . . . Such a pace, when I think of how little we were alone, or always moving."

The novelty of the nomadic lifestyle was fleeting, and that they were so rarely alone frustrated Jackie. She learned, very early in their marriage, that Jack for the most part preferred the company of men. One pillar of his personal cadre was Paul "Red" Fay, a skipper in the same PT squadron during the war. The second leg of their honeymoon was spent with Fay and his wife in Beverly Hills and San Francisco, where Jackie found herself sharing Jack with his old naval buddy. While Jack and Fay attended a 49ers game, Fay's wife drove Jackie around the Bay Area, showing her the sights. And once they were back in the east, Jack's closest friend since his Choate days, LeMoyne "Lem" Billings, became "a nearly permanent houseguest, along with his large poodle."

She also had to share Jack with his large and boisterous family. Having never known much in the way of discipline, either with regard to their behavior or in relation to money, the Kennedys took a great deal of getting used to. In Palm Beach over Christmas, 1953, Jackie gave Jack a very expensive oil painting set. "Almost immediately, all the Kennedys descended upon it," Lem Billings remembered, "squeezing paint out of the tubes, grabbing brushes, competing to see who could produce the greatest number of paintings in the least amount of time. . . . Jackie was stunned. She stood there with her mouth hanging open, ready to explode."

It took time for Jackie to find the right posture toward the Kennedy family ethos. While the Kennedy men instantly adored her, the hazing she'd endured at the hands of the women had done nothing to thaw them to her. "I don't think she ever felt comfortable with the sisters," Doris Kearns Goodwin said. "They were fiercely competitive women and she wasn't like that—she didn't want to play touch football." Not only did she not fit into the culture of Rose, Eunice, Pat, Jean, and of course Ethel; as the shiny new darling of the men, she was competition, provoking envy in Rose and the girls. Nurturing a young marriage was difficult when Jackie had to compete for attention with so many of Jack's constituencies.

After Jack's death, Jackie would put a better face on it. "So he loved the Irish, he loved his family, he loved people like you," she told Arthur Schlesinger Jr. in her 1966 oral history. "He loved me and my sister in the world that had nothing to do with politics. . . . He loved us all. And you know, I don't feel any jealousy." At the time, though, it hurt. In addition to their rarely being alone together, Jack was frequently away during the first part of their marriage, criss-crossing the country to introduce himself to the electorate, traveling around Massachusetts on Senate business, or working long hours in Washington. "I was alone almost every weekend," she later said. "It was all wrong. Politics was sort of my enemy and we had no home life whatsoever."

The alacrity with which Jack returned to womanizing after their wedding also surprised and wounded Jackie. Lem Billings remembered that

Jackie wasn't "prepared for the humiliation she would suffer when she found herself stranded at parties while Jack would suddenly disappear with some pretty young girl."

Without a place to call her own, and feeling lonely without much focused attention from her husband, Jackie found ways to keep herself busy and distracted. When volunteering with other Senate wives, who were mostly much older than she (she was twenty-two when Jack joined the Senate), proved less than stimulating, she took classes in US history at Georgetown University's School of Foreign Service. She tried, somewhat hopelessly, to learn housekeeping and cooking from her maid, and, with greater success, to improve Jack's wardrobe. She took JFK, a notably slovenly dresser since his youth, and remade him into the stylish, effortlessly elegant man that history remembers. "After their marriage his suits fit perfectly, were conservatively cut and pressed," remembered Evelyn Lincoln, who would remain his secretary until his death. Jackie transformed him "from a fumbling person who couldn't tie his own tie, and it was always too long, to an immaculate dresser."

Jackie also helped Jack in the political arena, not just by attending the usual speeches, rallies, and receptions, but by improving the mechanics of his public speaking. According to Jackie biographer C. David Heymann:

> *[Jack] tended to talk on and on, usually much too quickly, never knowing when to take a breath or how to make a point. His voice was rasping and high-pitched. Drawing on her theater training at Miss Porter's and her natural bent for the dramatic, Jackie slowed him down, helped him modulate his voice and give clearer expression to his thoughts. . . . She taught him the benefits of body language and trained him to harness his overabundant energy.*

Beyond the stresses of politics, Jack's family, and his absences, the early years of their marriage were further complicated by Jack's health problems. His 1947 diagnosis of Addison's disease explained a lot of his digestive and immune problems but did nothing to ease the steady recurrence of medical complaints. Kennedy biographer Robert Dallek wrote: "He consulted an ear, nose and throat specialist about his headaches, took medication and applied heat fifteen minutes a day to ease his stomach troubles, consulted urologists about his bladder and prostate discomfort, had DOCA pellets implanted and took daily oral doses of cortisone to control his Addison's disease, and struggled unsuccessfully to find relief from his back miseries."

His back pain, by the beginning of 1954, "had become almost unbearable," Dallek continued. "X rays showed that the fifth lumbar vertebra had collapsed, most likely a consequence of the cortico steroids he was taking for the Addison's disease. He could not bend down to pull a sock on his left foot and he had to climb and descend stairs sideways." In August, a team of physicians explained that a complicated surgery could offer the hope of relief, but that the risks of a fatal infection—especially for a patient with Addison's disease—were substantial.

"Jack was determined to have the operation," Rose Kennedy later said. "He told his father that even if the risks were fifty-fifty, he would rather be dead than spend the rest of his life hobbling on crutches and paralyzed by pain."

On October 21, a metal plate was inserted into Jack's back to stabilize the lumbar spine. In the aftermath, a urinary tract infection nearly killed him. After he sank into a coma, a priest administered the last rites—not for the first or the last time in JFK's short life. By mid-November, he was off the critical list, but he remained very ill.

"Jackie was magnificent with him," remembered Charlie Bartlett.

She had this almost uncanny ability to rise to the occasion. She sat with him for hours, held his hand, mopped his brow, fed him, helped him in and out of bed, put on his socks and slippers for him, entertained him by reading aloud and reciting poems she knew by heart, bought him silly little gadgets and toys to make him laugh, played checkers, Categories and Twenty Questions with him . . . Anything to distract him from the pain.

It's not outlandish to imagine Jackie relishing the chance to spend so much time with Jack, largely removed from the frustrations of their Washington life—or the opportunity to prove to him that she had the toughness requisite for success as a Kennedy.

After a few months, Jack was able to beat back the infection, but he required another operation in February to remove the plate, which doctors feared had itself become infected. He was discharged within three weeks but was forced to spend his Palm Beach recovery time on his stomach: The operation left him with a "huge, open, oozing, very sickly-looking hole in the middle of his back," according to Florida senator and JFK intimate George Smathers. "I realized then that I'd misjudged Jackie," he added. "Anybody who could look at that festering wound day after day and go through all that agony with her husband had to have backbone." Her devotion and toughness in the face of Jack's illness earned her respect from Jack's mother and sisters.

She'd later refer to early 1955 as "the winter of [Jack's] back," so much did his struggle define that period for her. Looking to occupy his mind during his long and painful convalescence, and hoping to boost his name recognition and credibility as a leader in the event of a presidential run, Jack wrote *Profiles in Courage*, a study of moments of political courage in US history. The book, which would win the Pulitzer Prize, had many helpers. Robert Dallek wrote that "Jack did more on the book than some later critics believed, but less than the term *author* normally connotes." Dallek calls the book "more the work of a 'committee' than of any one person." Jackie was certainly part of that committee, editing and critiquing along the way as Jack and Kennedy aide Ted Sorensen, as well as Georgetown history professor Jules Davids and other academics, hammered out drafts. Jack dedicated the book to Jackie, "whose help during all the days of my convalescence I cannot ever adequately acknowledge."

As Jack's recovery hit its stride, the idea of a permanent home for them became more important to Jackie. In October they closed on Hickory Hill, a large, Georgian-Colonial estate in McLean, Virginia, only a couple of miles from Merrywood. "I thought it would be a place where he could rest on weekends the year where he would be recovering from his back," Jackie later said. She set about making the house comfortable for them and the children they hoped to have. Jackie was pregnant, and she was planning a nursery when she miscarried in mid-1955. She also broke her ankle in a touch football game at Hyannis Port that November.

Meanwhile, Hickory Hill was not panning out as she had hoped. Speaking engagements had Jack gone every weekend, and it was too far outside of Washington to offer him much relaxation during the week. Her ankle injury, plus the hour commute time from McLean to Washington, meant more isolation for Jackie. During this time and through the end of 1959, Jack kept a suite on the eighth floor of Washington's Mayflower Hotel, where he entertained his sexual conquests. She most likely did not know about the extent of his philandering; she just knew that he was absent.

New Year's 1956 brought great news, though: Jackie was again pregnant. She spent much of the year transforming the house at Hickory Hill, paying special attention to the nursery. In August, seven months pregnant and in the midst of a heat wave, Jackie accompanied Jack to Chicago for the Democratic National Convention. There, despite feeling weak, she attended rallies, speeches, breakfasts, lunches, and dinners. At the convention, where the Democratic party again nominated Adlai Stevenson for president, Jack made a sudden, failed last-minute play for the vice presidential nomination. (It would go to the somewhat less glamorous Estes Kefauver.) It was perhaps here that Jackie's impatience with the press first began to show. After being pursued across the convention floor for a quote by journalist Maxine Cheshire, the very pregnant Jackie "hiked up her dress and broke into a run."

After the convention, both Jackie and Jack returned to the East Coast exhausted. Jackie headed to Newport to relax in the lead up to her delivery date. Jack departed for France to spend time at his father's rented villa on the Riviera before heading on a Mediterranean cruise with George Smathers and several women. As far as Jackie knew, Jack was relaxing with his dad and a couple of friends in the south of France, and nothing more. JFK's main mistress at the time—a tall blonde socialite who referred to herself as "Pooh"—joined them for the voyage.

Jack was enjoying himself enough that it didn't occur to him to return home when he was notified that Jackie had delivered a stillborn baby girl, via Caesarean section, following an internal hemorrhage on August 23. It was a particularly horrid example of the way his decency so often deserted him when it came to the women in his life—especially his wife. Jackie, unconscious during the Caesarean, was informed of the child's death by Bobby, who was sitting at her bedside when she awoke. Jack didn't speak directly to Jackie until he reached Genoa on August 26, and he flew home two days later. Only after Smathers warned him that a divorce would destroy Jack's presidential ambitions did he agree to cut short his vacation and return to the States.

In a letter to Rose shortly afterward, Jackie practiced her bittersweet stoicism. "Everything is getting better now—and the bad time seems far behind. All I can think of is what a close shave it was and how lucky I am to be able to have more children," she wrote. "Everything else fades into unimportance." It's not hard to see the sadness behind her brave face. "Don't worry," she wrote. "I'll make you a grandmother yet!"

Having built a nursery at Hickory Hill and invested the home with so much expectant joy, Jackie now associated the house with loss. She later said plainly, "I didn't want to live there any more." They sold Hickory Hill to Bobby and Ethel for $125,000, the same price they originally paid for it, and rented a house in Georgetown, on P Street. In March, she found out that she was once again pregnant; buoyed by the news, the couple again sought out a permanent home, and they finally settled on a Federal-era house at 3307 N Street NW in Georgetown. Built in 1812, the three-story redbrick house gave Jackie a broad canvas on which to practice what was becoming a passion of hers: redecoration.

"I remember that when she got the N Street house, it was going to be just right—it was going to be absolutely marvelous," remembered Jackie's mother, Janet.

> *It was a house with a lot of feeling about it and a lot of charm, but she did that living room, the double living room downstairs, over at least three times within the first four months they were there. I remember you could go there one day and there would be two beautiful needlepoint rugs, one in the little front drawing room and one in the back one towards the garden. The next week they would both be gone. They would have been sent on trial. Not only that, but the curtains were apt to be red chintz one week . . .*

Decoration was, like many of Jackie's other passions, an expensive one. Her ability to spend huge sums of money—on couture, on decor, on food—annoyed Jack and his family. While there were arguments and confrontations about Jackie's spending throughout the years, it seems that the mode Jack adopted was one of bemused resignation. George Smathers quipped, "They had an entirely average marriage—she spent and he seethed."

Jackie's mother, Janet, told an amusing, and revealing, story from that period:

> We were having dinner there one night and Jack didn't get home until quite late, after we had finished dinner. He was having dinner on a tray. At that moment the room was entirely beige: the walls had been repainted a week or so before, and the furniture had all been upholstered in soft beige, and there was a vicuna rug over the sofa . . . And let's see—rugs, curtains, upholstery, everything, was suddenly turned lovely different shades of beige. I knew how wildly expensive it is to paint things and upholster things and have curtains made, but I can remember Jack just saying to me, "Mrs. Auchincloss, do you think we're prisoners of beige?"

Nesting in preparation for the baby had done much for her morale, but Jackie suffered another blow in August when her father died of liver cancer. Years of drinking had taken their toll. Jackie took charge of his obituary and funeral arrangements while Lee and her husband, Michael Canfield, flew in from Italy. On August 6, after a funeral attended by fewer than two dozen mourners (many of them Black Jack's mistresses), John Vernou Bouvier III was laid to rest near St. Philomena's in East Hampton, where he'd married Janet almost thirty years before. Buried next to his mother, father, and brother, his casket was covered with yellow daisies and cornflower, Jackie's favorites.

In losing her conflicted, charismatic father, Jackie's world had undergone a seismic shift—John F. Kennedy was now the titanic male figure in her life. Black Jack Bouvier had provided Jackie with her first and most influential picture of what a man was. Joined in Jackie's mind with so much love, affection, and nurturing, her father's example provided the foundation for her most basic, unexamined ideas of what a man could and should be. In a sense, Black Jack had prepared Jackie to fall in love with a man like John F. Kennedy. In JFK she'd found a man with the same dangerous attractiveness, the sense of insouciant fun, the jet-set good looks and lavish lifestyle. She'd also found a man who, like her father, was incapable of being faithful.

Her world would change again only four months later, when she gave birth to Caroline Bouvier Kennedy, named after Jackie's sister, in New York.

7

THE CAMPAIGNER

CAROLINE, BORN VIA CAESAREAN THE DAY AFTER THANKSGIVING 1957, was a healthy girl: six pounds, seven ounces, "as robust as a sumo wrestler," JFK proudly said. The expectant father had been waiting nervously outside the delivery room in New York's Lying-In Hospital when he was notified that mother and child had come through the delivery with flying colors.

For Jack, the relief was intense. After Jackie's two failed pregnancies, he feared they might never produce children, a failure which in the fecund Kennedy family would have carried a stigma. "I will always remember the sweet expression on his face and the way he smiled," Janet would remember. "He just looked radiant when he heard that all was well." When Jackie awakened, Jack was at her bedside, happily holding Caroline. Jack "was more emotional about Caroline's birth than he was about anything else," noted Lem Billings, "and I had seen him respond to a hell of a lot of emotional occasions over the years."

The new family returned to their N Street house, along with Maud Shaw, the short, matronly, gray-haired British nurse they'd hired to help care for Caroline. Fifty-four years old when the Kennedys took her on, and a well-traveled, experienced nurse, she would stay with the Kennedys through the White House years and become an important figure in Caroline's early life. Shaw was only one member of the household staff on whom Jackie, weakened by the Caesarean operation, depended. There was cook Pearl Nelson, who prepared all their meals; Jack's valet, George Thomas; driver Muggsy O'Leary; and Jackie's personal maid, Providencia "Provi" Paredes, not to mention other maids to attend to chores in the now larger household.

As her health improved, Jackie returned to her passion for decoration, enjoyed Caroline's infanthood, and re-connected with her husband. While he hadn't curtailed his womanizing, he and Jackie enjoyed more of a home life together during this time. Jackie also begrudgingly came to accept that, as part of a very public political family, she would have to make some concessions to a press that was constantly curious about them. She appeared with Lee in a fashion layout for *Ladies' Home Journal* in December 1957. The accompanying article quoted her as saying—apparently with a straight face—that "I don't like to buy a lot of clothes and have my closets full. A suit, a good little black dress with sleeves and a short evening dress—that's all you need for travel." Jack even convinced her, despite her reservations, to allow *Life* magazine to publish photographs of baby Caroline. (Part of the convincing included a trip to Paris in the summer of 1958.)

Jackie also solidified her importance as a campaigner for Jack during his 1958 reelection campaign for Senate. As soon as she was well enough—and back from Paris—Jackie put in campaign appearances around Massachusetts. Apart from the tea parties that Rose and Ethel pioneered, she was a draw unto herself, and her skills with foreign languages were particularly helpful in multiethnic pockets of the state. She spoke to the Francophones in Worcester and the Italian Americans in Boston. An Italian ward politician in Boston said, "When Jackie opened her mouth and introduced herself in Italian, fluent Italian . . . all pandemonium broke loose. . . . I think her talk is actually what cemented the relationship between Senator Kennedy and the Italian-Americans in the district." Jack himself called her "simply invaluable. In French speaking areas of the state, she is able to converse easily with them, and everyone seems to like her." Jack handily won reelection, with 73.2 percent of the popular vote.

Jack's campaign for the 1960 presidential nomination had, in actuality, already begun, and Jackie's life from 1958 through the 1960 election was one long campaign. In October 1959, the couple was invited to campaign in Louisiana by a local political maven named Edmund Reggie. (Reggie's daughter, Victoria, would become Ted Kennedy's second wife almost thirty-five years later.) At Lafayette's Queen of the Rice Festival, Jackie whipped the crowd into a frenzy simply by speaking French.

"Bonjour, mes amis," she cooed.

Reggie recalled: "You could just hear the screaming. . . . It was just unbelievable, the applause, the shouting." She went on, in French, to call Louisiana "the beautiful part of France." "When the couple rode at the head of the parade afterward," Sarah Bradford wrote, "the screaming of the crowds was deafening; women ran out of the crowd to speak to Jackie in French." Jack seemed to be appreciative of what his wife offered on the campaign trail. On the way to the airport, Reggie reported, the Kennedys "were just like little lovebirds . . . almost to the point of embarrassment on my part."

Though hindsight has conferred upon his presidency a sheen of youthful and vital inevitability, Jack's nomination and eventual victory were far from a sure thing. The press and the public worried about Jack's youth—he would be the youngest president ever to take office, if elected—and his unexceptional record as a legislator. Further, our country had never had a Catholic president, and there was real concern, and not just on the fringe, that a Catholic president would be a puppet of the Vatican. No matter how much money his father sank into the campaign—and he would sink millions—Jack had to get out and convince the electorate—which meant a long and hard-fought campaign.

For Jackie, this meant an engagement with her old enemy: politics. Not only did campaigning and senatorial work take Jack away from her, she also disliked so much about the aesthetics of politics: the rowdiness of the crowds, the insincere hand-shaking and back-slapping, the two-faced interactions that occurred throughout political life, even among nominal allies. She disliked the cynicism and the enemies lists and the pandering to the lowest common denominator. She hated the unsettled, peripatetic life that politics so often engendered.

But she was no shrinking violet, nor was she deluded about the life and the family into which she'd chosen to marry. On January 2, 1960, Jack announced his campaign for the presidency, which found her becoming a player in Jack's political life. Not only did she come to realize her own strengths as a campaigner, Jack and his political apparatus came to see the qualities that made her so valuable. Barbara Perry notes that this was part of a historic shift that took place during the 1960 election. Where first ladies (and aspiring first ladies) had not previously played much of a part in presidential campaigns, "candidates' spouses in the 1960 election (including Mesdames Kennedy, Johnson, Humphrey, Nixon, and Lodge) set precedents for active participation in their husbands' campaigns, which helped define the prominent political role of modern first ladies in the late twentieth century."

Jackie had a star power of her own. Men wanted to be around her for obvious reasons, but Jackie was also a great draw to women, who loved her graceful manner and the understated elegance of her wardrobe. She was a greatly aspirational figure—women wanted to be like her—and this gave her a great deal of power when it came to getting out the female vote. This was most visible in her launching the "Calling for Kennedy" week in October, during which women supporting Kennedy would poll their friends on the most important issues of the day and "answer any questions they may have about my husband." It was explicitly to gather women's ideas on matters of policy, but the effort, which according to Jackie brought in thousands of responses from women all over the country, doubled neatly as a get-out-the-vote initiative in the last weeks before the election. The female vote was not a trivial matter, and the Kennedy campaign knew it: In 1960 "there were over three million more voting-age women than men," Kennedy family biographer Laurence Leamer noted, "and Jack's success or failure would inevitably rest in part on how well he did with women voters."

According to several in the Kennedy circle, though, what Jack valued most in Jackie was her tremendous gift for sizing people up. Arthur Schlesinger recalled that "underneath a veil of lovely inconsequence, she concealed tremendous awareness, an all-seeing eye and a ruthless judgment." John Kenneth Galbraith praised her "judgment of people," which was "something on which I think JFK depended." He goes on:

> He tended to take people at their face value, she looked at them much more scrupulously to see what they were up to, to distinguish between those who had something from those who were promoting themselves. . . . For all the people that I have known, she had the shrewdest eye for a phony or somebody who was engaged in self-advancement, and she didn't conceal it.

Jackie's power on the trail was somewhat diluted by a curtailed campaigning schedule. That spring she found out that she was again pregnant, and, having lost two previous pregnancies, neither she nor Jack wanted her to risk overexertion. And the campaign trail was a wearying slog: "About the fifth day out," she'd later say, "it's just sheer exhaustion." She wasn't present in Los Angeles when Jack accepted his party's nomination in July, staying in Hyannis Port with Caroline, but she stayed active in campaigning on the road, at least intermittently, until September. Even after she mostly eliminated her campaign travels, she wrote a weekly column called "Campaign Wife," which the DNC syndicated to newspapers around the country. When Jackie's habit of wearing French couture became a point of controversy—she should be wearing American designers, critics said—Jackie was able to respond in her column. "All the talk over what I wear and how I fix my hair has amused me and puzzled me. What does my hairdo have to do with my husband's ability to be President?" Jackie knew quite well what an asset she was to her husband's campaign, but she was all too happy to feign irrelevancy when such criticisms arose.

The Kennedy family spent the night of the election ("the longest night in history," Jackie later called it) in Hyannis Port, huddled around a portable television watching the returns. Though initial returns were promising, the numbers grew closer and closer throughout the night. Jackie went to bed at 11:30, with Nixon pulling even, and Jack followed at 3:00 a.m. Though the Secret Service quietly created a security perimeter around the Hyannis compound at 5:45 a.m., it wasn't until 9:30 the next morning that Jack could be sure of his victory. The margin was shockingly small: Though Kennedy had won "303 electoral votes to Nixon's 219, his popular margin was a scant 118,574 out of 68,837,000 votes cast." It wasn't the narrowest victory in presidential history, but it was close.

Just weeks later, on November 27, Jackie gave birth to John Fitzgerald Kennedy Jr. Almost a month premature, he spent the first five days of his life in an incubator, fighting off a respiratory infection while his mother, exhausted from another Caesarean and the campaign hangover, recovered in bed. The two were not released from the hospital until December 9, the same day Jackie was scheduled to be given a tour of the White House by outgoing First Lady Mamie Eisenhower. Jackie's doctor permitted the tour only on the condition that she be in a wheelchair, but when she arrived at the White House, none was waiting. Mrs. Eisenhower had stipulated to White House chief usher J. B. West that one could be available, but "behind a door somewhere, out of sight," only available should Mrs. Kennedy request it. Jackie later admitted to West that she'd been too cowed by Mamie to ask, and the ninety-minute tour of her soon-to-be home, daunting to someone in the best of health, left her pale and in great pain and resulted, she later told friends, in a "two-hour crying jag." Jackie immediately headed to Palm Beach, where she'd spend the next two weeks in bed.

"The month after the baby's birth had been the opposite of recuperation," she'd later write to Rose:

I was ill and recuperating in the room I shared with dear Jack. He was writing his inaugural speech in the room; I remember the yellow pages being strewn all around. . . . Then Pierre Salinger or someone would come in the room and have conferences with Jack, so I'd go sit in the bathroom 'till it was over. . . . I didn't come to meals—I couldn't hold any food down.

Laura Bergquist, a writer for *Look* magazine, came to interview the first-lady-to-be about which first lady she admired most. Too sick to attend the interview herself, Jackie convinced Jack to answer in her place. "I said Mrs. Truman . . ." Jackie wrote to Rose. "She kept her family together in the White House . . . under the bright hot heat of the lime-light that suddenly hits a president. She kept her own values as before. That is what I wanted to do more than anything. I didn't want to go into coal mines ([like] Mrs. Roosevelt) or be a symbol of elegance ([like] Dolly Madison). I just wanted to have a normal life for Jack and the children and me. And even if lots of beautiful things happened there later . . . my first fight was to fight for a sane and normal life for my babies and their father."

Jackie used this time of convalescence to begin researching the history of the White House, the restoration of which she was already beginning to envision. "I felt," she later wrote, "the President's house should stand for—in every field—what Jack always stood for: excellence."

"From her bed [Jackie] is trying to plan the moving of her young family into the White House—and gather her strength to start out there," Rose wrote in her diary at the time. "She has strong feelings about many facets of her new life. She has sent for all books and magazine articles of the White House in the past, from the Library of Congress." Jackie was interested in improving the White House's decor, but she was also a woman keen to find out how other families survived in such unique circumstances. It was imperative to her that growing up in the White House not warp, spoil, or confuse her children. In the midst of all the commotion, Jackie enjoyed the company of Caroline's cat, Tom Kitten. Unfortunately, JFK was allergic to cats, and after Jack started sneezing, the cat was consigned to the basement.

A pressing issue, as the inauguration approached, was who would design Jackie's clothes. The clamor over her (and her mother-in-law's) preference for French styles had never entirely died down, and there was pressure from several quarters for her to buy only American-designed and -made clothes. The perfect compromise was found in designer Oleg Cassini, a Palm Beach golfing buddy of Joe Kennedy's and a naturalized White Russian aristocrat. Jackie presented him with sketches from a variety of American designers and he designed and constructed clothes for her specifically. Cassini later insisted that the role of style icon did not interest her; nevertheless, their partnership would help define women's fashion in the 1960s.

"The common misconception about her is that she wanted to become a fashion trendsetter," he said. "Nothing could be further from the truth. Jackie basically had her own carefully directed style. She dressed for herself. She wanted to be noticed, not copied. But it was clear from the beginning that anybody with Jackie's exotic beauty and high visibility was bound to have a profound influence on fashion." (The designer Halston claimed that Jackie wearing a leopard-skin coat had single-handedly put the animal on the endangered species list.)

Jackie knew that press interest in what she wore—and every other facet of her life—would only intensify. As she assembled her own White House staff, she knew that the press secretary would be a critical position.

Pamela Turnure was a counterintuitive and, it turned out, inspired choice for the role. Only twenty-three years old, her sole work experience had been as a receptionist in JFK's Senate office. (She had also been—and would continue to occasionally be—his lover. While it doesn't seem likely that Jackie knew about it, she may well have.) Soft spoken, pretty, and unfailingly polite, she would prove herself perfectly able in carrying out Jackie's policy of dealing with the press.

"You will be there as a buffer," Jackie informed Turnure in a memo. "My press relations will be minimum information given with maximum politeness." While she had been willing to be somewhat open with the press as a way of getting her husband elected, she hoped that now that she was the first lady, she'd be able to assert her own boundaries and enforce them with her own staff. "I won't give any interviews, pose for photographs, etc., for the next four years," the memo continued. "Pierre [Salinger, JFK's press secretary] will bring in *Life* and *Look* or Stan [Tretick] a couple of times a year and we'll have an ok on it." Jackie would respond to press inquiries about the White House restoration project and State dinners, bu   ⁀ns about it. Everything else—from the way she wore her hair to   ᵇ⁀ children—was entirely off-limits.

C   ᵣr Jackie's East Wing staff was Tish Baldridg   n with the energy of a dervish. She was a littl⁄   ᵈ also been educated at Miss Porter's and Va⁄   t US embassies in Rome and Paris. Tish was p⁄   ᵗer came to find her surfeit of energy exhaust- iⁿᵍ⁄   with her knowledge of Washington's players, made her ѕ⟋_   ⟋d fit: She would play an important role during the first part of Jack's ᵗₑ_m.

Jackie's convalescence continued. On the second Sunday in December, Jackie was still too ill to attend mass with Jack, but she and Caroline walked him to the gate of the Palm Beach compound, where a group of well-wishers had gathered, hoping to catch of a glimpse of the next first family. She saw him into his waiting car and waved to the crowd before taking Caroline back inside.

She'd saved her husband's life with that simple appearance. Parked nearby was a seventy-three-year-old man named Richard Pavlick, who carried seven sticks of dynamite and a conviction that he'd be seen as a hero for assassinating the president-elect. Seeing Jackie and Caroline made him hesitate. "I did not wish to hurt her or the children," he later told the Secret Service. "I decided to get him at the church or someplace later." The Secret Service, having intercepted letters Pavlick had written in which he threatened to turn himself into a "human bomb," arrested him four days later.

As her strength improved, she took short walks and engaged in light physical activity. On January 16, not yet fully recovered, she nevertheless returned to Georgetown to prepare for her husband's inauguration as president of the United States.

Before Jackie and her staff could dig in for the challenging transition to life in the White House, she first had to survive the inauguration. Though a celebration in many respects, the occasion was—for a media-wary woman not yet wholly recovered from a C-section and experiencing some post-partum depression—daunting, nerve-wracking, and exhausting. "[It] was not a happy time in my life that it looks like in all the pictures," she admitted over a decade later. That she carried it off with the appearance of sincere enjoyment is a tribute to her fortitude, her stoicism, and her unfailing sense of decorum.

At 10:40 a.m. on January 20, 1961, Jack Kennedy had already attended mass and was dressed and ready to go despite having gotten home just before dawn. The night before, he and Jackie had attended the pre-inaugural concert, which featured performances by everyone from Frank Sinatra to Harry Belafonte, Ella Fitzgerald to Ethel Merman, Bette Davis to Sir Laurence Olivier. An exhausted Jackie had been driven home before midnight while Jack partied with the A-list at a dinner thrown by his father. Inauguration morning, the presidential limousine arrived and took them to the White House, where they endured a chilly tea with the Eisenhowers, the Johnsons, and the Nixons. (Pat Nixon, who sat next to Jackie at the tea, basically pretended Jackie wasn't there.)

A few days before, a snowstorm had dropped eight inches of snow on Washington, and the inauguration day was frigid and windy. Jackie's discomfort in the cold wasn't visible to those who saw her at the ceremony, where her simple yet striking outfit—a Cassini-designed fawn-colored wool coat with matching pillbox hat—made the rest of the crowd look dowdy. After Jack's swearing in, they returned to the White House to watch the inaugural parade. She lasted less than an hour on the frigid outdoor viewing stand before she had to excuse herself for a nap. She was so exhausted that she couldn't even come down for the family reception later that afternoon, where, wrote Laurence Leamer, "the Kennedys, Fitzgeralds, and Bouviers eyed each other like hostile clans until the liquor and the forced proximity drew them together." ("Jesus Christ," Joe Kennedy was heard muttering, "I didn't know Jackie had so many goddamned relatives.") She stayed upstairs in bed with a heating pad stuffed under her back.

No doubt buoyed by the Dexedrine administered by Jack's personal physician, she again managed to appear—at ten-thirty that night, stunning in a self-designed white, silver, diamante-studded ballgown—for the first of five inaugural balls. Sources differ on how many of the balls she was able to make it to, but it was no more than three.* She was driven back to the White House while Jack partied late into the night.

"I missed all the gala things I would so have loved to share with Jack . . . with everyone who was going to be in the New Frontier. . . . I always wished I could have participated in those first shining moments with him. But at least, I thought, I had given him John, the son he longed for so much. . . . Anyway," she concluded, "I don't think I disgraced Jack in that time—as when there is an occasion, one rises to it."

---

* There's an amusing lack of agreement: Leamer and Heymann say she left after the third, Perry and Bradford agree that she only endured two, and Jackie herself, in her 1973 letter to Rose, would recall that she attended only one.

8

THE QUEEN OF THE RESTORATION

WHEN JACKIE FLEW BACK TO WASHINGTON IN MID-JANUARY, SHE LEFT the children in Palm Beach, watched over by Maud Shaw and Secret Service Agent Clint Hill. As they wouldn't be returning until February 4, Jackie had two weeks after the inauguration to recover her health and spirits, and to prepare for her family's life in the White House. "My first impression of Mrs. Kennedy was, to be perfectly frank, that here is a young woman who has a lot to learn about an institution like this," admitted Isaac Avery, the White House carpenter who started in 1930 and would serve six presidential administrations before his death in 1967. "But she learned it rapidly and gracefully."

When the Kennedys moved in, the White House was, in the words of Sarah Bradford, "a gaunt, unloved mansion." "I can recall," wrote columnist and frequent Kennedy guest Joe Alsop, "the peculiar combination of vomit green and rose pink that Mrs. Eisenhower had chosen for her bedroom and bathroom." Worse, Jackie's toilet didn't flush and her shower didn't work. Public drinking fountains were built into the halls of the third-floor guest rooms. The room where the Eisenhowers ate dinner on trays featured twin portholes built into the wall, which concealed his and hers television sets. (The two preferred to eat together, while watching separate television shows.)

According to White House chief usher J. B. West, "there was not a kitchen or a dining room on the second floor in the family quarters. As a matter of fact, when the Eisenhowers were there, if they wanted to eat upstairs, they ate off trays in front of the television set." (Or sets, as it were.)

During the Truman administration, parts of the White House were found to be structurally unsound. According to Barbara Perry, "Because the process of gutting and reconstructing the White House interior was so expensive ($5.76 million), period antiques were beyond the government's budget. In any case, Truman was not a connoisseur of antique furnishings and thought them impractical for the high-traffic state rooms." The Eisenhowers had made their own changes as they entered it in 1952.

"It was filled with a lot of reproduction furniture which was not to Mrs. Kennedy's liking," J. B. West explained. The Eisenhowers hadn't felt the need for bookshelves or wastebaskets.

Jack and Jackie, the first president and first lady of a new generation, and having young children, would have made striking changes to the White House, even if Jackie had not set herself to the restoration. The alterations Jackie requested for their second-floor living quarters were unprecedented. Avery remembered that when the Kennedys moved in,

for the first time we were faced with the necessity of providing for a family with small children. . . . Immediate changes had to be made in the House to accommodate the children particularly, and the convenience of Mrs. Kennedy in looking after them. Bedrooms were to be altered, dining rooms to be altered, playrooms to be supplied, and nursery school equipment to be installed.

Jackie had spent much of the interregnum thinking about making the White House comfortable for Jack and the kids, and she coordinated with J. B. West to see that her designs were implemented to her satisfaction. She worked with the decorator who had helped her with her N Street home, Sister Parish, to produce the look she was hoping to achieve. "Mrs. Kennedy came in frequently to keep herself informed as to how much progress we were making," Avery said. "She had a habit of writing little notes, and she would also pick up the phone and call you. Usually, if it was not quite satisfactory, you'd get the note. If she was quite happy, you'd get the phone call."

The "little notes" to which Avery referred were Jackie's famously numerous and exacting memos. J. B. West wrote that "Jackie's wish, murmured with a 'Do you think . . .' or 'Could you please . . .' was as good as a command. When she told you to jump, you jumped."

Between the paces she put West, Avery, and Sister Parish through, she burned through the entire $50,000 allocation for White House redecoration in two weeks—on the residence alone. But her ambitions went far beyond the presidential family residence. "When I learned I would be living in the White House how could I help but think of restoring as much of its past as possible," Jackie wrote in 1963. "It would have seemed criminal of me not to—and I cared terribly about it. Here is a house that all Americans love and almost revere—and practically nothing in it earlier than 1948."

"We've got a lot of work ahead," she told J. B. West. "I want to make this into a grand house!" She had to find a way, without spending her own money, to make the White House the kind of place in which she wanted to live, and a place that Americans would be proud of. "I know we're out of money, Mr. West," Jackie said. "But never mind! We're going to find some way to get real antiques into this house." She told *Time* magazine at the time, "I would write 50 letters to 50 museum curators if I could bring Andrew Jackson's inkwell home." Europe had shown Jackie how a nation's history and artistic traditions could be emblems of its greatness. She imagined how the White House could provide an image, in microcosm, of America's depth, beauty, and history. She saw the potency of placing such strong, resonant history and imagery in the very seat of American power. And she saw the importance of placing her husband's New Frontier in the tradition of American progress.

"I knew funds would be needed and that one could not possibly ask Congress for them," she wrote in 1963. "So the obvious solution was a committee. It had to be fairly small to start with as we had to work hard and together and the task seemed Herculean—if not impossible." She told *Life* magazine correspondent Hugh Sidey, "It would be a sacrilege merely to *redecorate*—a word I hate. It must be *restored*, and that has nothing to do with decoration. That is a question of scholarship."

To this end, she created the Fine Arts Committee for the White House. Unveiled on February 23, its purpose was, she said, to locate "authentic furniture of the date of the building of the White House and the raising of funds to purchase this furniture as gifts for the White House." She used her family and society connections, and no small amount of charm, to recruit scholars and curators, as well as wealthy, powerful, and like-minded people to participate.

One of her most important recruits was Henry F. du Pont, whom she chose to chair the committee. The eighty-year-old du Pont was one of the nation's foremost connoisseurs of early decorative American art, and he had turned his own home, Winterthur, into a museum. The 175-room mansion, situated on a thousand Delaware acres, was the nation's finest collection of Americana. Jackie needed his expertise, his connections— and his collection.

Jackie and du Pont peopled her committee with seven women and four men with "extensive curatorial and/or collecting experience." Among them: Sister Parish, the decorator that Jackie used on N Street; David Finley, former director of the National Gallery of Art; and Mrs. Albert Lasker, a collector of French art and trustee of the Museum of Modern Art. For all their expertise, the value of most committee members was in their connections and their ability to wrest from those connections money and donations. (One of Jackie's masterstrokes was to have the White House declared a national museum; thereafter, donations of art and furniture were tax deductible.) The true academic core of the committee belonged, in true Washington fashion, to a subcommittee dubbed the Fine Arts Advisory Committee, which consisted of sixteen museum curators and two scholars. The Advisory Committee produced a paper arguing for an expansive view of the restoration: "To furnish the White House uniformly in the eighteenth century style current when it was built would give a static even monotonous air to a house whose history is by no means finished. . . . It will therefore be necessary to be eclectic."

This pronouncement fit well into Jackie's plans. While *restoration* is an indisputably accurate term for what she did to many of the rooms in the White House, the work of the committee also simply gave her and her decorators unparalleled access to the sort of antiques she coveted for the *redecoration* of the rest of it, whatever term she chose to use. That's not to detract from the amazing restorative work she did bring to 1600 Pennsylvania Avenue. "Without question," Barbara Perry wrote, "she redecorated all of the White House rooms, and some she restored to particular historical eras through furniture, wall, floor, and window treatments, and lighting. The Blue Room took on the air of its Monroe-period, Francophilic incarnation; the Red Room depicted early nineteenth-century Franco-American Empire; the Green Room displayed Federal-era furniture; the Treaty Room and the Lincoln Bedroom exhibited Victorian decor (Mrs. Kennedy's least favorite style but one she felt compelled to represent); the East Room and State Dining Room preserved many of the 1902 McKim elements."

The three biggest players in her restoration effort turned out to be du Pont, Parish, and a French decorator named Stephane Boudin, each with expertise, reputation, and ego to match. The three were often at cross-purposes, and Jackie was to use every ounce of her charm, diplomacy, and cunning to keep them in detente, if not harmony. Jackie had a great working relationship with Sister Parish, but "her classic country, chintz-laden interiors were simply not suited to the stately public rooms of the White House," Perry wrote. "Consequently, her work was primarily confined to the second-floor hallways and family quarters. . . ." Du Pont, as the nation's foremost expert on US decorative arts, was invaluable, but Jackie's tastes tended to run more toward the Continental than his. Enter Boudin, who'd decorated stately homes (including for the Duke and Duchess of Windsor) throughout England: He stood in as proxy for Jackie's tastes. Where most rooms ended up displaying a combination of Boudin's and du Pont's influences (one usually dominant), Parish's designs, except for the Yellow Oval Room, were mostly redone by the end of 1963.

By the time JFK's administration ended—early, tragically—in November 1963, the White House decor had been transformed by Jackie's savvy mix of advocacy, politicking, and simple hard work. Her more lasting contribution was to create the official methods and safeguards to ensure that the White House will always remain a showplace and repository for all that is finest in America's decorative tradition, a house of which all Americans can be proud. She also started a restoration movement, according to Corinne "Lindy" Boggs, a Democratic party power player and friend of both JFK and Jackie. Boggs praised "the inspiration that

[Jackie] was to so many remarkable restorations, rehabilitations, renovations of historic buildings and places, sites, [when] she made the White House a little museum. And she certainly encouraged the uplift and the renovation of thousands of buildings all over this country."

Ethel and Bobby beam on their wedding day, June 17, 1950, in Greenwich, Connecticut. Hundreds of guests flooded the town for the extravagant affair. Ethel, then twenty-two years old, wore a gown created by noted New York City fashion designer Mamie Conti. ASSOCIATED PRESS

Jackie poses in her Ann Lowe–designed gown at Hammersmith Farm on her wedding day: September 12, 1953.
TONI FRISSELL/PUBLIC DOMAIN

Jackie poses for photographer Jacques Lowe in the summer of 1960 in Hyannis Port. The First Lady had stopped campaigning because of her pregnancy. Lowe titled the image "Yellow Dress."
JACQUES LOWE/ COURTESY OF GANNETT NEWS SERVICE

Joan Kennedy, nicknamed "The Dish" for her stunning looks by her brother-in-law Jack Kennedy, models an Oleg Cassini gown at a Catholic charity benefit in Boston, April 7, 1962. ASSOCIATED PRESS

Jack, Jackie, John Jr., and Caroline leave Easter services in Palm Beach on April 14, 1963.
CECIL STOUGHTON/PUBLIC DOMAIN

The first family poses for a portrait on the porch in Hyannis Port on August 4, 1962.
CECIL STOUGHTON/PUBLIC DOMAIN

Jackie stands next to Lyndon Johnson as he takes the oath of office following Jack's assassination, November 22, 1963. CECIL STOUGHTON/PUBLIC DOMAIN

Holding her childrens' hands, Jackie walks down the steps of the United States Capitol on the day of JFK's funeral, November 25, 1963. She is followed by RFK and his sister, Pat Kennedy Lawford. ABBIE ROWE/PUBLIC DOMAIN

Rose Kennedy in 1967.
© 1967 CBS TELEVISION/PUBLIC DOMAIN

Ted, Rose, and Joe Kennedy make their first public statement in the aftermath of RFK's assassination in Hyannis Port on June 15, 1968.

Rose appears with Dinah Shore on *Dinah's Place*, 1972.

After Bobby's death, Ethel dedicated her remaining years to preserving his legacy and continuing his causes. Here, Ethel sits next to the 2003 Robert F. Kennedy Human Rights Awards, which were awarded to three people from the Coalition of Immokalee Workers on Capitol Hill on November 20, 2003.

MATTHEW CAVANAUGH/GANNETT NEWS SERVICE

Vicki Kennedy attends the signing of President Obama's health care bill, which many consider the culmination of her late husband Ted's legacy, at the White House in March 2010.

PETE SOUZA/WHITE HOUSE

Vicki Kennedy attends the groundbreaking ceremonies for the Edward M. Kennedy Institute for the United States Senate in Boston on April 8, 2011. Edward Kennedy Jr., Ted and Joan's oldest son, looks on.

9

LIFE AT THE WHITE HOUSE, AND AWAY

JACKIE WAS JUST FINISHING IMPROVEMENTS TO THE LIVING QUARTERS, and her restoration plans were still in their infancy, when Caroline and John arrived at the White House on February 4, 1961. To welcome three-year-old Caroline and two-month-old John to their new home, one of the White House gardeners fashioned a life-size snowman at the edge of the driveway.

As the Kennedy family moved into the nation's best-known address, Jackie was more concerned than ever about maintaining their privacy. For Caroline, one of the most recognized children on the planet, Jackie's worries were especially acute. "She is going to have to go to school," Jackie said in an April interview. "And if she is in the papers all the time, that will affect her little classmates, and they will treat her differently." Once, in Hyannis Port, Caroline wandered into the frame while *Look* photographer Stanley Tretick was photographing Eunice Kennedy Shriver's children. Quickly he caught several playful photos of Caroline horsing around with her cousins. Laura Bergquist showed them to JFK on Tretick's behalf; Jack loved them. But Jackie vetoed his approval of their publication. "It is partly because [the pictures] are so good I must sadly tell you I just can't give you permission to publish them," Jackie wrote to Bergquist, cushioning the rejection in praise. "Caroline was being recognized wherever she went. That is a strange enough thing to get used to at any age—but pretty sad when one is only three. Every article just increases interest in her—her little friends and cousins see it and mention it to her and it is all bad for her."

In fact, the most powerful man on earth had to subvert his wife in order to get any pictures of the children published. "Some of the most enduring images of the Kennedy years—'John John' peeking out from underneath his father's desk, Caroline eating chocolate in Evelyn Lincoln's office—were organized by their father while Jackie was out of town," historian Sally Bedell Smith wrote. It never failed to irritate the first lady.

Certainly, Jackie's own painful memories of being teased when her divorcing parents were in the newspaper must have had something to do with her extreme wariness of the press and her children. But Jackie also was determined that her children be raised to be polite, levelheaded, civilized people, and she worried about the power of attention—even or especially positive attention—to warp and spoil a child.

Her children were always to address adults formally (Maud Shaw would always be "Miss Shaw" to them), and pleases and thank yous were strictly enforced. Jackie herself always addressed the children in an adult manner, never talking down to them. On the other hand, she was hardly the distant, formal mother typical of a woman of her class. "She usually had her youngsters in tow," said James Ketchum of the White House Curator's Office. "Mrs. Kennedy had the kids more than Miss Shaw, which was a great shock to me."

When they lived in Georgetown, Caroline had attended a playgroup, which several of the mothers took turns hosting. Once in the White House, one of the ways that Jackie was able to maintain Caroline's privacy was to request that the playgroup meet at the White House exclusively. The playgroup was run cooperatively—the parents all contributed toward expenses—and by the fall it had blossomed into a nursery school, with two teachers, a playground on the South Lawn, and a schoolroom in the sunny third-floor solarium. By the fall of 1962, the nursery school had grown to twenty four- and five-year-old students (many of them children of administration officials) and included a kindergarten.

Meanwhile, Jackie adjusted grudgingly to her role as first lady, skipping out on as many official responsibilities as she could. "Jackie was not ready to spend her days observing the abominable rituals delegated to the first lady," wrote Laurence Leamer. "Attending luncheons with the wives of senators and representatives, meeting ambassadors' wives from obscure nations, promoting one charity or cause after another, mouthing banal comments. She had almost as many excuses as she had invitations, and she avoided all but the most public and important functions."

Luckily, she had many women who were able to take her place on short notice. Tish Baldridge and Pamela Turnure took to referring to Lady Bird Johnson as "Saint Bird"; in Jackie's first year at the White House, she asked Lady Bird to cover for her more than fifty times. Janet Auchincloss, Rose, Ethel, JFK's sisters—all were pressed into service at some point during the Kennedy administration, most more than once. Jackie's absence wasn't always a last-minute cancellation. The truth is that she spent as much time away from the White House as she did living there, "mostly alone or with the children at Glen Ora or Hyannis Port, or on overseas trips with Lee," wrote Sarah Bradford. Nancy Tuckerman remembered Jackie being gone—usually in the country—from Thursday to Monday or Tuesday.

Glen Ora was a seven-bedroom country house situated on four hundred verdant acres just over an hour's drive outside of Washington in Middleburg, Virginia. Jackie had convinced Jack to rent the retreat before they'd even moved into the White House (she rejected Camp David out of hand, sight unseen) as a place for them to get away on the weekends. In truth it was of limited interest to Jack, who was allergic to horses, loved the ocean, and preferred to be around more people than just his immediate family in his downtime. But it was a place where Jackie could escape a White House that she sometimes found oppressive, where she and her children could get exercise in the fresh air and ride without constant fear of the press or much need for close Secret Service protection. Middleburg's remoteness was appealing to Jackie for another reason: It was unattractive to journalists. "Middleburg was just plain boring," wrote Secret Service Agent Clint Hill. "It was small, rural, and quiet. Nightlife was non-existent. Outside of monitoring the infrequent comings and goings of the Kennedys and their visitors, there was nothing to do, and nowhere else to go. The press hated Middleburg."

Though the home was only a rental, Jackie and Sister Parish redecorated it from top to bottom. The two spent ten thousand dollars on everything from furniture to wallpaper to rugs. Jack was enraged at the expense but lived with it. Not only was Glen Ora a concession on behalf of Jackie's happiness; her absence removed a level of stress from his compulsive philandering, which, though restricted mostly to the White House, was no less feverish than before.

The fact of JFK's compulsive—indeed pathological—womanizing is now widely accepted by historians, no matter how well the press's code of silence protected him at the time. "Kennedy had affairs with several women" while in the White House, wrote Robert Dallek, "including Pamela Turnure, Jackie's press secretary; Mary Pinchot Meyer, Ben Bradlee's sister-in-law; two White House secretaries playfully dubbed Fiddle and Faddle; Judith Campbell Exner, whose connections to mob figures like Sam Giancana made her the object of FBI scrutiny; and Mimi Beardsley, a 'tall, slender, beautiful' nineteen-year-old college sophomore and White House intern. . . . There were also Hollywood stars and starlets and call girls paid by Dave Powers . . ."

An entire enabling apparatus composed of aides and Secret Service agents protected the president's ready access to these women. Secret Service Agent Larry Newman ruefully remembered: "You were on the most elite assignment in the Secret Service, and you were there watching an elevator door because the president was inside with two hookers. It just didn't compute. Your neighbors and everybody thought you were risking your life, and you were actually out there to see that he's not disturbed while he's having an interlude in the shower with two gals from Twelfth Avenue."*

Though Jackie seems to have had few illusions about Jack's behavior, it still hurt and angered her. Though in the abstract she had a Continental acceptance of a "man's nature," and though her childhood with Black Jack had normalized a certain amount of infidelity, Jack's continual need for so many fresh conquests was humiliating. Friends report that as late as 1958—five years into their marriage—she still wondered if she could bear to be married to such an unfaithful man. By the White House years, it seems that her attitude had hardened into one of resignation. Her outward

---

* Newman also remembered joking with his colleagues about which one of them would testify on Capitol Hill if and when "the president received harm or was killed in the room by these two women." (Sabato, *The Kennedy Half-Century* , ch. 6)

response was generally one of bitter aplomb, as when she was showing a Parisian journalist around the White House. As they passed the secretary known as "Fiddle," Jackie casually mentioned in French, "And there is the woman that my husband is supposed to be sleeping with." (The journalist was apparently taken aback. "What is going on here?" he asked one of Pierre Salinger's aides.)

Jack's behavior is less a reflection of a loveless marriage than it is symptomatic of a man with a profoundly stunted capacity for intimacy with a woman. "I think that Jack in his way was enormously proud of Jackie," Charlie Bartlett would later say. "I think he really adored her in his way. But it was in his way. It wasn't exactly what Jackie needed. I think she needed a warmer, cozier husband, more constant. Jack was difficult, easily bored, and he liked to be amused—not what she needed."

Jack and Jackie's relationship was, to understate it by a great deal, complicated. Part of the enduring fascination with them both lies in our attempts to reconcile so much that is seemingly irreconcilable: his genuine heroism with his patently despicable personal behavior; Jackie's intelligence and strength of character with her maddening willingness to take his abuse; our knowledge of the pain she must have felt with her adoring, nearly hagiographic, and apparently sincere memories of their married life. Through these contradictions, the Kennedys remain a puzzle, one with which we never tire of playing, no matter how impossible the solution.

—◦—

When both were at the White House, the Kennedys took genuine pleasure in entertaining company; Jackie would often organize small dinner parties in their second-floor residence. "[Jack] never wanted to have the people in the evening that he worked with in the daytime," she later remembered. "And I'd often say . . . 'Why don't we have Ethel and Bobby for dinner?' because I thought Ethel's feelings might be getting hurt. But he never wanted to see Bobby, and Bobby didn't want to come either, because they'd worked all day. So you'd have people who were rather relaxing. You'd have Charlie Bartlett and the Bradlees a lot. It was sort of light."

Sometimes the parties were larger, "a mixture of cabinet and friends from New York, and young people." Jackie remembered:

I worked so hard on those parties because I felt once we were in the White House, I felt that I could get out, and I just can't tell you how oppressive the strain of the White House can be. I could go out . . . but Jack couldn't get out. So I used to try to make these parties to bring gay, and new people, and music, and make it happy nights. And did he love them. Just walked around, puffing his cigar . . .

"Best parties I've ever attended," Arthur Schlesinger Jr. recalled. "The greatest girls, the nicest times. Everyone was so much better than normal. Everyone was the gayest and the prettiest and the nicest."

One of Jackie's great achievements as first lady was to prove equally as adept at entertaining in an official capacity as when she hosted their private soirees. She and her staff changed the complexion of state dinners, bringing glamour and vibrance to what had been very dull affairs. "They set a feeling of warmth and ease in all their entertaining which was very catching," remembered Tish Baldridge. "Formerly guests would come to the White House in fear and trembling; it is an austere place. . . . But immediately, with the Kennedys, the whole atmosphere changed. Their guests were at ease and found it was a good party and lots of attractive people and pretty surroundings." At Jackie's direction, Jack's state dinners were the first where smoking was permitted and hard alcohol available. Jackie eschewed the long, U-shaped table in favor of several smaller round tables, a move considered revolutionary at the time, and, whenever possible, she got rid of reception lines in favor of free-form mingling.

This convivial atmosphere made the White House a much more pleasant place for the new group of visitors Jackie brought there. Part of her crusade to make the White House a "grand house" was to bring in as many great artists, dancers, and musicians as she could. She arranged a performance of scenes from Shakespeare in the East Room for Sudanese president Ferik Ibrahim Abboud and a concert by virtuoso cellist Pablo Casals for the governor of Puerto Rico. Margot Fonteyn and Rudolf Nureyev performed ballet at a state dinner for French Minister of Culture André Malraux, where the guest list included Tennessee Williams, Saul Bellow, Elia Kazan, Geraldine Page, Archibald MacLeish, Andrew Wyeth, and Arthur Miller. It was through Malraux that Jackie was eventually able to have the *Mona Lisa* brought to the United States, where it was displayed in the National Gallery—perhaps the strongest testament to her powers of persuasion.

For the first time, a state dinner was held away from the White House when Jackie and her staff painstakingly planned a state dinner at George Washington's residence, Mt. Vernon, for Pakistani president Ayub Khan. Jackie had been impressed when, during a state visit she and Jack made to France, President Charles de Gaulle held a dinner for them at Versailles. She wanted to bring some of that grandeur, some of that pride of history, to US state dinners, and thought Mt. Vernon, on the banks of the Potomac, would be a perfect choice. It would be the task of others to implement her grand vision—often with great difficulty.

"A logistical nightmare," remembered Clint Hill. "One of the worst headaches that any office ever had to contend with," Tish Baldridge agreed.

The dinner, held on July 11, 1961, went off without a hitch. But it required the mobilization of a virtual army to realize. Jackie's vision for the evening required the cooperation of several organizations, "including Tish Baldridge's staff, the office of the Military Aide to the President, the National Park Service, the State Department, the White House usher's office, the Mount Vernon Ladies' Association, the Secret Service, and Rene Verdon, the White House chef," according to Hill.

Baldridge explained:

We had to have [the Marine Band] lining the drive coming up from the pier to the house. We had to have the National Symphony Orchestra and build them a special stage. Before and after dinner we had to worry about the acoustics. We had to worry about feeding the musicians—getting them out there and feeding them; worry about portable johns, where to hide them in the bushes so it wouldn't ruin Mt. Vernon. . . . We worried about the weather. I gave orders to my whole staff to pray. . . . We prayed for six months solidly and it worked! They

*sprayed. It was a terribly buggy summer and they sprayed three times
that day against bugs and mosquitos . . .*

The 137 guests traveled from Washington to Mt. Vernon on the
Potomac via four boats, among them a PT boat and the Kennedy family
yacht, the *Honey Fitz*. After a tour of the home, the guests were treated to
a Revolutionary War re-enactment. "It just so happened that the sixty or
so members of the press corps were right in the line of fire," Hill remembered. "Even though the guns were loaded with blanks, the noise and
smoke were realistic, causing more than a few members of the press to
jump at the sudden gunshots. When I saw the smile on [Jackie's] face, I
had little doubt that placement of the press . . . was all part of her master
plan."

The event's unqualified success once again showed Jack how valuable Jackie could be. She spent most of the evening in conversation with
the guest of honor, President Ayub Khan; the two hit it off. Both shared
a passion for horses, and Jackie, with her native curiosity about life in
other parts of the world, was fascinated by Khan's stories of life in Pakistan. Khan offered an open invitation for the president and first lady to
visit him in Pakistan. It was an invitation that Jackie, at least, would later
accept.

—⁓—

John F. Kennedy assumed the presidency at the height of the Cold War,
and his management of international conflicts and tensions—both his
triumphs and his missteps—characterized his term in office as much
as his response to the civil rights movement at home. Jacqueline Kennedy's star power and charm often helped ease tense relations, or at least
enforced a cordiality, in JFK's relationships with many foreign leaders.
Her glamour also provided good press when his approval ratings might
be low. Never was Jackie on prouder display, or playing more to her
advantages, than on state visits abroad. And she was abroad a lot: her
official and "semi-official" trips took her to eleven countries: Canada,
France, Austria, England, Greece, Venezuela, Columbia, the Vatican,
India, Pakistan, and Mexico.

The importance of the Kennedys' first official trip, to Canada in May of 1961, was heightened by its proximity to the Bay of Pigs disaster, which had happened only a month before.

It was Eisenhower who initially signed off on the CIA's plan to train a group of 1,400 Cuban exiles for a sneak invasion to overthrow Fidel Castro. But Kennedy willingly went along with the scheme, even if, as many later claimed, he was misled by CIA and military advisers, who convinced him that the small commando unit, if able to reach the mainland, would spark a popular uprising. In truth, Castro was relatively popular with his people, and no such uprising was likely to occur. And the invasion, such as it was, was a complete and utter failure.

Early on the morning of Monday, April 17, 1961, the Cuban exile commandos landed on the south coast of Cuba. By Tuesday midnight, Jack was being informed that the operation had been botched and that the only choice now was to rescue as many exiles as possible. (The Soviets had known of the invasion for a week, it turned out. The CIA knew they knew but did not stop the invasion, nor did they inform Kennedy.) United States forces managed to rescue only 14 men; 1,189 surrendered to Castro's forces. It was a military disaster, a diplomatic disaster, and a public relations disaster.

It also shook Jack's confidence. "Within the privacy of his office," Dave Powers remembered, "he made no effort to hide the distress and guilt he felt." On April 19, Jackie told Rose that Jack "had practically been in tears. . . . She had never seen him so depressed except once at the time of his operation." The same day, Pierre Salinger found Kennedy crying in his bedroom. Kennedy took full responsibility for the incident; his credibility, both at home and abroad, was wounded.

With the embarrassment fresh on their minds, President Kennedy and others in his administration were understandably nervous when he and Jackie made their official visit to Canada the next month. How relieved he was when they arrived in Ottawa and the streets from the airport to the governor-general's residence were lined with cheering crowds. It didn't matter that the crowds—chanting "Jack-ie! Jack-ie!" —were more excited to see his wife than they were to see him. It mattered that the welcome was warm.

Jackie similarly eased Jack's passage when they visited Paris at the beginning of June. The scene along the streets was nearly identical to their Canadian reception— "Vive Jacqui! Vive Jacqui!" Jackie's celebrity so outshone JFK's that, taking the podium after a press luncheon, he began by famously saying, "I do not think it altogether inappropriate to introduce myself. I am the man who accompanied Jacqueline Kennedy to Paris. And I have enjoyed it." The crowd went wild.

Just as important, Jackie's charm warmed relations between leaders. On the Paris trip, the notoriously difficult de Gaulle came away impressed with Jack's intelligence and gravitas. This impression was no doubt helped by the way that Jackie mesmerized him with her flawless French and knowledge of French history that, according to de Gaulle, was superior to most French women's. "Thanks in large part to Jackie Kennedy at her prettiest," *Time* magazine reported, "Kennedy charmed the old soldier into unprecedented flattering toasts and warm gestures of friendship."

In Vienna, immediately afterward, it could be said that Jackie salvaged the trip from utter ruin.

Jack had high hopes for Vienna, where he was to meet Soviet leader Nikita Khrushchev. Barely six weeks removed from the Bay of Pigs debacle, the Soviet Union and the United States faced even larger tensions over the status of divided Berlin and the ever-present threat of nuclear war. Kennedy came hoping to effect a detente by building a rapport with Khrushchev. It wasn't to be. At the talks Khrushchev hammered away at Kennedy, threatening war over the divided city, uninterested in the easing of tensions that Kennedy came to Vienna seeking. "If you want war," Khrushchev said, "that is your problem."

"He savaged me," admitted a shaken JFK to a reporter for the *New York Times*. British Prime Minister Harold Macmillan observed that, in meeting Khrushchev, "for the first time in his life Kennedy met a man who was impervious to his charm." "I think [Jack] was quite depressed after that visit," Jackie would remember. "I think he'd gone there expecting to be depressed, but I think it was so much worse than he thought."

Khrushchev may have been immune to JFK's charm, but he wasn't immune to Jackie's. Photos from the visit show him grinning like a schoolboy at Jackie, and she would remember how expertly she disarmed him at an official dinner. "I'd just read *The Sabres of Paradise* by Lesley Blanch, which is all about the Ukraine in the 19th century . . . and [Khrushchev] said something about 'Oh yes, the Ukraine has—now we have more teachers there per something, or more wheat.' And I said, 'Oh, Mr. Chairman President, don't bore me with that...' —and then he'd laugh."

She also impressed Khrushchev with her knowledge of the names of the dogs in the Russian space program, and she playfully asked him to send her one of their puppies. "And by God, we were back in Washington about two months later, and two absolutely sweating, ashen-faced Russians came staggering into the Oval Room with the ambassador carrying this poor terrified puppy who'd obviously never been out of a laboratory ..." It is an odd illustration of international relations, where a leader can threaten his enemy's country with nuclear annihilation in one instant, and give his enemy's wife a puppy in the next. But Jackie—with her ability to envelop a man, make him feel important, and impress without intimidating him—made such exchanges unremarkable.

Jackie would travel farther abroad without JFK, often in the company of her sister, Lee. Though Jackie and Lee's relationship remained incredibly complex—a mixture of devotion and singular mutual understanding with great resentment, competitiveness, and jealousy—their time of greatest closeness was during Jack's presidency. Lee lived primarily in London with her second husband, Polish Prince Stanislas "Stas" Radziwill, but the two sisters were able to spend time together, as when Jack and Jackie went to London following the Vienna summit. Together with Lee, Jackie made a triumphant "semi-official" visit to India and Pakistan in the spring of 1962.

From the moment Jackie stepped off the plane in New Delhi to a roaring crowd of three thousand, she was an object of adoration and fascination, to the populace and the leaders. Sometimes, as many as 100,000 people would line the roadways as her motorcade flew by. "Every move, every comment, every event, every outfit on her 16,000 mile voyage appeared in journalistic photographs and narratives," wrote Barbara Perry. She enchanted Indian Prime Minister Jawaharlal Nehru, and Pakistani President Ayub Khan, already a friend from his lavish Mt. Vernon state dinner, presented Jackie with a horse, an exquisite bay gelding named

Sardar that Jackie had shipped back to the United States to ride around Glen Ora and, later, Camp David. On these and other trips, Jackie represented the United States with great poise and sophistication, burnishing not only her own image, but lending reflected glory to her husband's administration.

10

PATRICK

EARLY IN 1963, JACKIE DISCOVERED SHE WAS AGAIN PREGNANT. IN March the White House announced that Jackie was expecting in September and would be reducing her travels and the performance of her duties as first lady. Until June she maintained her normal stateside schedule of short weeks at the White House and Thursday through Sunday at Glen Ora, coordinating everything from the details of state dinners to the final stages of her restoration project from wherever she was. Having lost two pregnancies, Jackie and Jack both wanted to err on the side of caution. That spring, Tish Baldridge, burnt out from the pace of life in the White House, and tired from trying to spur Jackie to more public involvement, amicably resigned, taking a job at the Kennedy-owned Chicago Merchandise Mart. She was replaced by one of Jackie's oldest friends, Nancy Tuckerman. "Tucky" and Jackie had known each other since Miss Chapin's, and their working relationship would prove so harmonious that Tuckerman would remain her personal assistant for the next thirty-one years, until Jackie's death.

Throughout that year, Jack kept his frenetic pace, traveling to Germany, Ireland, England, and Italy and throughout the United States. In June, Jackie stationed herself for the remainder of her pregnancy at a house they rented on Squaw Island, not far from Hyannis Port, and thereafter Jack only saw his family on weekends. Jackie continued to make plans and write memos from her Cape Cod hideaway, instructing Nancy Tuckerman on every detail of the planned state visit of the king and queen of Afghanistan on September 5. She painted and read and luxuriated in the ocean air. She prepared scrapbooks containing photos and memories of her life with Jack, to present to him in recognition of their upcoming tenth wedding anniversary. Before they could celebrate, however, Jackie's pregnancy would end suddenly and tragically.

On August 7, just as Jackie was returning from Caroline's riding lesson, she began to experience intense labor pains. Five weeks premature, she was immediately taken by helicopter to nearby Otis Air Force base, where a ten-room hospital wing had been on standby for just such an emergency. The president left Washington immediately but arrived after his second son, Patrick Bouvier Kennedy, had already been delivered. The four-pound, one-ounce boy, delivered by Caesarean section, was baptized right away and placed in an incubator. Jackie never held Patrick, as he was considered too fragile to remove from the apparatus. He was diagnosed with hyaline membrane disease, a malformation of the lungs, and it was decided that he should be moved to Children's Medical Center in Boston. Jack flew to Boston and kept vigil at the hospital. But the child was simply too small, too premature, the state of his lungs too grave. Despite the medical team's best efforts, Patrick died early on the morning of August 9.

Jackie was awoken at six-thirty that morning and told the news by her doctor. "She was devastated," remembered Clint Hill, the Secret Service agent who stood watch at her door that morning. "It was heartbreaking to see her in such emotional pain." Jack made it back to Otis and cried at her bedside. The next day, Jackie was too ill to attend Patrick's small funeral in Boston, officiated by Cardinal Cushing and attended by Jack, Lee Radziwill, and Jackie's half-brother and half-sister, Jamie and Janet Auchincloss. Jack placed a St. Christopher medal in the child's tiny coffin. On Sunday, August 11, he brought Caroline and John to see their mother, still hospitalized at Otis, "which seemed to boost Mrs. Kennedy's spirits more than anything." On Tuesday he returned to Washington to resume his presidential duties.

A week after the birth, Jack was with Jackie as she was released from the hospital. It was here that people close to the couple really started to notice a difference in their relationship. "With press photographers snapping away, President and Mrs. Kennedy emerged from the hospital hand in hand," Hill remembered. "It was a small gesture, but quite significant to those of us who were around them all the time." The couple normally avoided physical affection in public; the death of their son had cracked something open in them.

Jackie and the children remained at the Cape for the rest of the summer, and Jack came up when he could. A devastated Jackie spent much of her time at the Squaw Island house secluded in her room. She ventured out occasionally to play with the children, but it was clear to those around her that she was suffering. Jack spent more time with the children when he was up from Washington; whether he was spurred to greater closeness by his loss or covering for a less-present Jackie is hard to tell. The two put on brave faces for the low-key celebration of their tenth anniversary at Hammersmith Farm. Jackie presented Jack with the scrapbooks she'd spent the summer making, as well as a gold St. Christopher's medal to replace the one he'd buried with Patrick. JFK simply gave her a catalogue from a New York antiques dealer and told her to pick whatever she wanted. Those in attendance again remarked how close they seemed, how warm their relationship had become.

It was around this time that Jack decided that Jackie might benefit from some travel abroad. Lee spoke to her friend and sometimes lover, a Greek shipping magnate, about Jackie's situation. He immediately invited both Jackie and Lee to visit him on his yacht in the Greek Isles. And so, with Kennedy's blessing, Jackie and Lee spent two weeks relaxing aboard the *Christina*, the yacht owned by Aristotle Onassis.

11

DALLAS

It was only a three-day trip, but the stakes were high.

Not long after a revitalized Jackie returned from her Greek vacation, Jack asked her to accompany him on an official visit to Dallas later in November. Whether out of gratitude for sending her to Greece or out of some newfound devotion, Jackie was excited to go. She knew that Jack would need her star power, there more than ever. The civil rights legislation that Jack was trying to push through Congress had made an enemy of many Southern states, and the vitriol against Jack was as strong in Texas as anywhere else in the South. Further, the Democratic Party within Texas had split into squabbling factions, and Jack needed the state unified—and behind him—if he was to carry the electoral college in 1964. He was joined by native Texans Lyndon and Lady Bird Johnson in an effort to win Texan affection.

They were relieved by the warmth of their reception in San Antonio and Houston, where Jackie got to speak Spanish to the meeting of the League of United Latin American Citizens. Her Spanish was halting, but, predictably, the crowd went wild. The next morning, in Ft. Worth, Jackie was twenty minutes late to the Chamber of Commerce breakfast, but when she appeared, the ovation she received prompted Kennedy to begin his speech by saying, "Two years ago I introduced myself in Paris by saying that I was the man who had accompanied Mrs. Kennedy to Paris. I am getting somewhat the same sensation as I travel around Texas." As an aside, he added, "Nobody wonders what Lyndon and I wear." The audience ate it up.

After breakfast they made a quick flight to Love Field in Dallas, where they smiled and waved and shook hands with the jubilant throng.

Jackie, flat-out pretty in a pink Chanel suit and matching pink pillbox hat, was given a dozen roses, which she cradled in her lap as the president's motorcade departed for the Dallas Trade Mart, where Jack was to give his luncheon speech. Though it had stormed in Dallas the night before, the day was bright and clear, and the Kennedys, riding with Texas governor John Connally and his wife, Nellie, soaked up the sun in the back of the Lincoln Continental convertible. The Johnsons were in a convertible just behind them. It was to be a relatively quick drive—seven miles from the airport to the Trade Mart.

As they approached downtown Dallas, the adoring crowds thickened. "Mr. President," Mrs. Connally shouted over the sound of the cheering spectators, "You certainly can't say that Dallas doesn't love you."

Then Jackie heard what sounded like a motorcycle backfiring. Turning to look at her husband, she saw that his hands were at his throat; he was trying to slump forward, but, as it turned out, a brace he was wearing for that perennial bad back held him erect. It was then that the final shot hit its mark. Jackie watched the right side of his head explode.

Secret Service Agent Clint Hill had started running toward the president's car as soon as he saw Kennedy's hands at his throat. He was close enough when the headshot came that his clothes, face, and hair were covered in a haze of blood and brain tissue. As he reached the car, a terrified Jackie was crawling onto the trunk of the moving car.

"She was reaching for something," Hill wrote. "She was reaching for a piece of the president's head."

He pushed Jackie back into the back seat, where Jack fell into her lap. "My God! They have shot his head off!" she cried. The back seat of the convertible was an abattoir: blood, brain matter, and skull fragments were everywhere. Governor Connally had been wounded as well, though not fatally. Hill wedged his body above Jackie to shield her from any further bullets as the car accelerated up Elm Street.

She cradled Jack's head. "Jack," she said. "Jack, what have they done to you?" Four minutes later they arrived at Parkland Memorial Hospital, where Jack would be declared dead at 1:00 p.m., thirty minutes after bullets struck him in Dealey Plaza.

These details have been played and replayed a thousand times: the pandemonium outside of Parkland Hospital and the controlled chaos inside; the surgeons attempting interventions they knew were hopeless; Jackie's refusal to leave the hospital—and then Texas—without her husband's body. One moment, though, shows Jackie in microcosm.

As the Lincoln convertible arrived at the hospital, Agent Hill tried to get Jackie and the president out of the back seat. But Jackie wouldn't budge. She remained crouched over Jack's destroyed head, covering his wounds from the gaze of onlookers and a press that was already arriving. Hill pleaded with her to let go, and he presently realized that she didn't want anyone to see Jack so injured, so vulnerable. He took off his suit coat and draped it over Jack's head.

"She still hadn't said a word, but as soon as my coat was covering the president, she released her grip."

It was now Jackie's job to control, as best she could, what the world saw of Jack, and what would remain hidden.

12

AFTERMATH

A week after the assassination, a stunned Jackie summoned journalist Theodore White to Hyannis Port, where she was marking a stunned Thanksgiving with her stunned in-laws.

"She and I spoke for nearly four hours," he told C. David Heymann.

> *She regurgitated many of the details of the assassination. She remembered the pink-rose rings on the inside of the President's skull after the top had been blown off. 'The inside of his head was so beautiful,' she said. 'I tried to hold the top of his head down, so more brains wouldn't spill out. But I knew that he was dead.' . . . From the moment of the assassination, people were trying to get her to change her clothes, eradicate all signs of the crime. She didn't want them to forget. Her only solace was that he hadn't suffered. He had a 'very neat' expression on his face after he was hit . . .*

Jackie hadn't asked White to Hyannis Port so she could go over details of the assassination, though she would go over the details—with White and with many others—compulsively in the hours, days, and months after JFK's death. She called White to the Kennedy compound to further the burnishing of Jack's mythology, a project she'd begun within hours of his death. It was as if there were two levels of Jackie's consciousness in play simultaneously: a traumatized woman, thunderstruck after witnessing the murder of her husband, stumbling through the denial phase of grief; and a canny image-maker, carefully orchestrating the way the country would remember the tragedy, her husband, and, to a large degree, herself.

She refused to change her clothes. She wanted the world to see the pink suit, stained with her husband's blood and brain matter. "I saw myself in the mirror; my whole face was spattered with blood and hair," she told Theodore White. "I wiped it off with Kleenex . . . then one second later I thought, why did I wash the blood off? I should have left it there, to let them see what they've done. . . . If I'd just had the blood and caked hair when they took the picture . . . I should have kept the blood on."

Sitting in the back of Air Force One by the hastily purchased casket, guarded by Kenneth O'Donnell, Dave Powers, and Lawrence O'Brien, Jackie talked about Abraham Lincoln's funeral, and her need to find "the book" on it. In the face of her horror and disbelief, Jackie oversaw nearly every element of the next few days. "I'm not going to cry until the next three or four days are over," she told Charlie Bartlett.

She gathered tokens to be placed in Jack's coffin, from her first anniversary gift to him of gold cuff links to a sapphire bracelet from Lee to a rosary from Ethel and Bobby. She added three letters to him, as well: from Caroline, John Jr., and herself, expressing, as best they were able, how much they would miss him.

The children had been told, at Jackie's direction, on the night of his assassination. The task fell to Maud Shaw, who told the children that their father had gone to watch over baby Patrick in heaven. Too young to even begin to comprehend what he was being told, John Jr. asked if his father would be taking his airplane with him. Caroline cried and cried.

While the nation—indeed, the world—reeled from JFK's senseless death, the White House filled with mourners. Jack and Jackie's families, the White House staff, friends of the first couple: Many of them would help to carry out her wishes and see that the funeral and surrounding events would be correct. Sargent Shriver, Eunice Kennedy's husband, handled most of the logistics.

Jackie wanted the Black Watch Highlander Regiment, which had performed at the White House the previous week and which Jack had so enjoyed. She also requested an honor guard of thirty cadets from the Military College of Ireland, whom Jack had been impressed with on his recent trip to Ireland. Jackie requested that Bunny Mellon, who had designed the White House rose garden, arrange flowers for the Capitol, the church, and the gravesite. "I don't want the church to look like a funeral," Jackie told her. "I want it like spring. I want it not sad because Jack was not a sad man." Robert McNamara convinced her that the hillside in Arlington National Cemetery would be an appropriate resting place, and it was Jackie's idea that an eternal flame burn at his gravesite.

It was Jackie's idea, too, that the funeral procession should walk the eight blocks from the White House to St. Matthew's Church that Monday morning. "Her face covered by her newly made long black veil, Jackie led the funeral procession, flanked by Teddy and Bobby, with Sarge Shriver and Steve Smith directly behind," wrote Sally Bedell Smith. "Directly behind the horse-drawn caisson, a black riderless steed symbolizing the lost leader pranced and snorted along the route. He was a sixteen-year-old gelding called Black Jack—a spooky coincidence of names Jackie did not know about at the time."

Inside the church, Cardinal Cushing intoned the pontifical requiem mass in Latin. In lieu of a traditional eulogy, and at Jackie's direction, the Reverend Philip Hannan read a collection of Bible verses interspersed with quotations from Jack's speeches. When Hannan read passages from JFK's inaugural address, Jackie broke down and sobbed for the first time in public. Lee gave her a "blue pill" and Clint Hill handed her his handkerchief.

In Arlington, "fifty air force and navy jets (one for each state of the Union) flew overhead in formation, followed by Air Force One, which paid tribute by dipping one wing." Jackie and Bobby together lit the eternal flame. They would return alone together that night near midnight, after receiving heads of state who had come from around the world to mourn, to spend some quiet time at the gravesite. Jackie soon had the caskets of her stillborn daughter and Patrick brought from Newport and Brookline, respectively, and buried next to their father.

⌁

While in Hyannis Port, Jackie added the masterstroke in the mythification of her dead husband.

"Only bitter old men write history," she told Theodore White. "Jack's life had more to do with myth, magic, legend, saga, and story than with political theory or political science."

"That's when she came out with her Camelot theory," White later said. "She didn't want Jack to be forgotten, or have his accomplishments cast in an unfavorable light. She wanted him to be remembered as a hero. She reported how at night he would often listen to *Camelot* on their phonograph, and how he personally identified with the words of the last song: 'Don't let it be forgot, that there once was a spot, for one brief shining moment that was known as Camelot.'"

White recognized at the time that the Camelot myth "was a misreading of history, but I was taken with Jackie's ability to frame the tragedy in such human and romantic terms. . . . At that moment she could have sold me anything from an Edsel to the Brooklyn Bridge. Yet all she wanted was for me to hang this *Life* epilogue on the Camelot conceit. It didn't seem like a hell of a lot to ask."

The myth she created would prove remarkably durable.

13

THE MANY LIVES OF JACKIE KENNEDY

At age thirty-four, Jackie feared her life was over. "I don't have much to live for," she admitted in a letter to Nikita Khrushchev written in the week after Jack's death. "But for my husband's dreams." But it wasn't over. She had so much more life—or many more lives—to live.

After a brief period in Averell Harriman's Georgetown home, Jackie moved herself and the children to New York City, which, except for the first couple years of her marriage to Aristotle Onassis, would be her primary home for the rest of her life.

She set herself immediately to memorializing her husband. In December 1964, President Johnson broke ground on the John F. Kennedy Center for the Performing Arts on the banks of the Potomac River in Washington. Jackie was active on the Program Committee of the center, which was tasked with formalizing the center's artistic and cultural mission. She also served, with Lady Bird Johnson and Mamie Eisenhower, as an "honorary chairman" of its Board of Trustees. The Edward Durell Stone–designed building—an elegant, perfectly proportioned horizontal marble matchbox—is one of the most recognizable buildings in the world.

The same can be said of I. M. Pei's design for the John F. Kennedy Presidential Library and Museum, though its road to completion was not as smooth. Jack had wanted his presidential library to be connected to Harvard, his alma mater, and Jackie, with the help of Bobby Kennedy and architect Jack Warnecke (who created the final design of Jack's gravesite in Arlington), acquired a spot for it near Harvard Yard in 1970.

Cambridge residents, fearing additional congestion around the university area, protested. After years of attempting to negotiate with the people of Cambridge, plans to build the JFK Library there were abandoned in 1975.

The library's foundation instead settled on a twelve-acre plot of land near the University of Massachusetts, Boston. Located on Columbia Point, a small peninsula on Dorchester Bay not far from Honey Fitz's Dorchester home, the structure—monolithic, interlocking, geometric figures in glass and poured white concrete—perches on the shore, evoking a giant sailing ship. Jackie was present when it finally opened on October 20, 1979, more than fifteen years after her husband's death. Though the library would not end up situated on the Harvard campus, the university's Graduate School of Public Administration was rededicated, in October 1978, as the John F. Kennedy School of Government. Jackie worked closely with professor and former Kennedy adviser Richard Neustadt in creating a place where students could think imaginatively about aspects of politics and government.

In addition to memorializing Jack's life, Jackie saw it as her mission to protect his legacy. This meant, in the years following his death, tangling with a series of Kennedy friends and associates who decided to write books about their time with him. The children's nanny Maud Shaw, JFK's Navy buddy Red Fay, and Jack and Jackie's mutual friend Ben Bradlee each wrote memoirs that, though largely benign and complimentary, earned them permanent excommunication from Jackie's good graces. Others, such as Arthur Schlesinger, cut material at her request. In each work, she objected not only to any content she found unflattering about her husband, but also any intimate information about the life they shared.

"There won't be one shred of his whole life that the whole world won't know about," Jackie wrote to Schlesinger. "The world has no right to his private life with me—I shared all those rooms with him—not with the Book of the Month readers—I don't want them snooping through those rooms now . . ."

Jackie's largest clash was with a writer that she herself had recruited. Shortly after Jack's death, she and Bobby had asked Wesleyan University Professor William Manchester to write the authoritative account of the assassination. He spent three years—and his life savings—producing the eight-hundred-page manuscript. But as *The Death of a President* neared publication, Jackie and Bobby both requested many changes, deletions, and rewrites; when Manchester would not agree to all of the cuts they demanded, Jackie sued him, his publisher, Harper and Row, as well as *Look* magazine, where the book was to be serialized. They eventually settled out of court, with Manchester agreeing to cut certain passages from the book and forego some of the revenues he might otherwise have received from its publication. In the court of public opinion, it was a misstep for Jackie. Many Americans thought less of the former first lady for censoring a professor she herself had commissioned.

Jackie remained close with the Kennedy family after she moved with Caroline and John to New York, but her income from the family fortune decreased greatly. Though the $200,000 a year she received ($150,000 from a Kennedy trust fund and another $50,000 from Bobby) would've sustained most families of three very handsomely, it would not go very far in meeting Jackie's exorbitant needs. Her situation was reminiscent of where her mother had found herself in the late 1930s: with a young family to support and suddenly bereft of a fortune. Jackie had the additional burden of being one of the most recognizable and sought-after people in the world. She wanted privacy for herself and her children, and a large fortune could certainly buy her a great deal of that.

Greek shipping magnate Aristotle Onassis, one of the richest men in the world, could fulfill all those needs. Though the short, stocky, and not conventionally handsome man was in some ways an odd choice for Jackie, he did offer much beyond his wealth. "Jackie and Ari did have a lot in common," Lee later insisted. "They both shared a great love of the sea, they both had a great knowledge and love of Greek mythology . . ." And in some ways he was exactly the type of man that Jackie was programmed to like: in the Joe Kennedy mold, Onassis was powerfully charming and charismatic, a generous friend and hospitable host, a loyal friend and a fun companion. He also had the ability to be ruthless and cruel in personal and business dealings. His positive qualities had made a strong impression on Jackie as far back as her time aboard his yacht in the aftermath of of her son Patrick's death in 1963.

Onassis had been courting Jackie for some time, but her decision to marry him came after Bobby's assassination. The marriage was an attempt by Jackie to escape the grief-filled orbit of the Kennedys; it was also an attempt to make impregnable her family's privacy and financial stability. For the most recognizable woman in the world, a man who owned an airline and a private Greek island was a sensible choice. Their marriage gave her the freedom to travel, live, and spend as she desired.

Onassis was sixty-two years old and Jackie thirty-eight when they married in October of 1968. "He was dynamic, irrational, cruel I suppose," Lee—who had been Onassis's lover during Jack's administration—would later say. "But fascinating." Though the marriage was initially warm, in short order it grew distant and unhappy. After a couple of years, Jackie lived separate from her husband for the majority of the time. Onassis died in 1975 after a long illness. After a court battle with her stepdaughter Christina, Jackie inherited twenty-six million dollars.

Jackie was now independently wealthy and free to live as she chose. She surprised everyone by starting another life as a career woman. She went to work as a book editor, first at Viking and then at Doubleday, bringing the eye for detail—the eye that had transformed the White House and made so many state dinners so memorable—to literature. She was, by all accounts, respected and prolific until her death, from a swiftly moving cancer, in 1994.

She found a longtime companion in Maurice Tempelsman, a wealthy New York diamond merchant, who carefully administered her fortune. Together they shared a luxurious, if low-key, life. She used her name and fame sparingly, appearing as a public figure only rarely, and usually in the name of the preservation of historic buildings, such as Grand Central Station, in her beloved New York City.

Jackie lived to see her children grow into intelligent, attractive, successful adults: John, after a few tries, passed the New York bar exam, but after her death in 1994 he would become more well known as the founder of political magazine *George*, as well as a mainstay on lists of the world's best-looking men, before his own premature death in a 1999 plane crash.

Caroline became a lawyer, author, editor, and mother to three children, upon whom Jackie doted. In November 2013, Caroline became a diplomat, when President Barack Obama appointed her the twenty-ninth US ambassador to Japan.

Jacqueline Kennedy the woman continued long after the death of Jack Kennedy. But the mythic figure we remember today was forged largely in that week in November 1963, when, though a disoriented and grief-stricken widow, she used her own brilliant alchemy to create, with simple words and stark imagery, an enduring, heroic, romantic picture of what our country could be.

PART IV
Joan

1

THE MUSIC

Aтop the stairs, little Patrick Kennedy huddled against the floor. He had to position himself just right—crouched low, his head resting on the carpeted landing—so that he could peer through the railing and see the piano down below without alerting his mother to his presence. He was supposed to be in bed, after all, but the lilting music had lured him down the hall, as it did so many nights, and he held still as he listened to his mother play.

If Joan Kennedy knew that her youngest son had crept from his bedroom and was spying on her overhead, she didn't bust him. Instead, she lost herself in the allegro that flowed from her fingers to the keys. Sometimes it was "Allegro Assai" by Rudolf Baumgartner, or maybe Fritz Reiner's "Molto Allegro." She loved waltzes, too, and Alexis Weissenberg's "Clair de Lune." Years later, she would combine these pieces as a soundtrack to a book she wrote about classical music. But for now, it's the early 1970s, and six-year-old Patrick is defying his bedtime to listen to his mother's music wafting from the living room.

The moment is a sweet respite, Patrick's family is fractured. His father, Edward Kennedy, is the last living son of Rose and Joe, and his mother is a beautiful blonde, arguably the most conventionally attractive of the Kennedy wives. Ethel had the spunk, Jackie the sophistication. But Joan had the looks. Her daughter, Kara, came first in 1960, followed by Edward Jr. in 1961. It took six years and multiple miscarriages before Patrick joined them. And after, Joan and Teddy had tried for more, but there was another miscarriage, and then there were the affairs and a very public accident, and family life in their home on Squaw Island, Massachusetts, felt weighted and heavy. Patrick felt freest as a child listening to his mother play her music; it filled an ever-hollowing home.

"Those are some of my fondest memories as a child, creeping out of my bedroom and sneaking to the top of the stairs and laying on the carpet while I listened to my mom play piano downstairs," Patrick Kennedy says. "I was always hesitant to go down. If I'd gone down just one or two stairs, she would've seen me and known I was out of bed.

"She played throughout my life, obviously, but those are poignant memories."

Virginia Joan Bennett was born September 2, 1936, at New York's Mother Cabrini Hospital. She was named after her mother, Virginia Joan Stead—known to friends as Ginny—but called Joan from birth. Her father, Harry Wiggin Bennett Jr., was an advertising executive whose family first arrived in Massachusetts in the 1600s. He was both Protestant and Republican, but his wife had been raised Catholic, and so their children would be, too. Joan was educated in Catholic schools, much as the Kennedy children were, and attended Manhattanville College, the same that Rose Kennedy attended in the early 1900s and which Eunice and Jean would attend in the 1940s.

Ginny was slender with delicate features set in a round face beneath her light brown hair. She was a solid seamstress who sewed most of the clothes Joan wore to school. Joan recalled her father as tall and handsome, an amiable and charming man whose acting talents landed him roles in neighborhood theater productions.

"My father was an avid amateur actor, and his idea of relaxation was to perform with the local Bronxville theater group, or the Westchester County Players," Joan said. "He often had leading roles, and this normally shy man caught fire when he was inhabiting a character. I remember him as Thomas Becket in T. S. Eliot's *Murder in the Cathedral* when I was about ten."

As was the case with most Bronxville families, Joan's father would commute to Manhattan for work while her mother stayed home. Harry's job was secure enough that the family started out in a four-room apartment in an upper-middle-class neighborhood in Bronxville; before long, they would move into a four-bedroom Mediterranean-style house. It was Joan, her mother, her father, and her sister, Candy, two years Joan's junior. When the girls came home from school, Ginny was always there to greet them. Ginny and her music.

"If the radio wasn't on, Ginny was singing," recalled Joan. "It might be a tune from a Sigmund Romberg operetta (I can still hear her warbling 'My desert is waiting') while she straightened up the living room, or hits from the thirties—her teenage heyday—like Cole Porter's 'Night and Day' or 'Begin the Beguine' as she got dressed to go out in the evening."

Music was such an integral part of the Bennett household that the radio stood in its center, visible to all who walked through the front door. It was a massive console with a turntable on top, and it was almost always on. In the living room was a piano, which Joan began to play before she turned five years old. Harry and Ginny didn't play instruments, but their love of music prompted them to put Joan and Candy in private lessons. Candy lasted about two years, but for Joan, the weekly one-on-one lessons with gray-haired Maud Perry fostered a passion for music that would inform her college studies. Later on it would prove a unique asset as she navigated the demanding role of a politician's wife as an adult.

"The radio and the phonograph were our at-home entertainment," Joan said. "Television didn't appear until I was in high school, when we were one of the first families in the neighborhood to acquire one, a tiny black and white model."

Harry needed the TV to watch the Colgate and Palmolive shampoo and soap ads for work, but it never provided the same backdrop that music did.

"With the television . . . programming was limited, unlike music, which seemed limitless," Joan said.

Joan grew up a daddy's girl. She was the "apple of his eye," she recalled as an adult, and she remembered him fondly as a nice man and a hard worker. When she was twelve, he arranged for her to play on a radio station, WVET in Rochester, that he'd bought with some other World War II veterans. Joan played George Gershwin's "Embraceable You." Harry also took Joan to musicals, her favorite being *South Pacific*.

"When I heard the velvety, operatic voice of Ezio Pinza booming into the theater and wooing Mary Martin with 'Some Enchanted Evening,'" Joan said, "I was hooked."

But family life in the Bennett house wasn't always so idyllic. Ginny was a stiff disciplinarian. "I had Joan and Candy bring the hair brush to me and tell me whether they needed one or two whacks to remember not to do it again," Ginny once told a reporter. She hung the brush on the wall with a big pink ribbon to serve as a reminder for the girls to behave. As an adult, Joan rarely talked about her mother, said friend-turned-author Marcia Chellis. "I sensed that there were unhappy memories she did not care to recall," Chellis said. "I learned why from one of Joan's friends, who told me Joan's mother was an alcoholic."

Some childhood friends remember Harry as a drinker, too; if true, the extent of it is unclear—and apparently never confirmed by Joan. Joan doesn't tend to elaborate in interviews and, in her 1992 book *The Joy of Classical Music*, she talks about only the pleasant, music-centered memories of her childhood.

"Both parents were drinkers, though no one ever mentioned it, ever," said Joseph Livingston, a childhood friend of Candy and Joan's. "It was as if it didn't exist, which is the way it is in many alcoholic families. It doesn't exist."

Childhood friends remember Ginny as icy and judgmental. She seemed capable of instantly deflating Joan with a superficial criticism of her dress choice or hairstyle.

Ted Livingston, Joseph's brother and Joan's boyfriend when the two were in the eleventh grade, said Ginny made him nervous.

"Just her presence in the room made everyone a little uneasy," he said.

Joan came downstairs all smiles, beautiful and wearing a blue knee-length dress and white sweater. Mom followed, also smiling. She seemed jittery, but trying very hard to act casually. Then, just before we left, Ginny said to Joan, "I'm still not sure that that dress is the right color for you, Joan. I think it makes you look, oh I don't know, pale, I guess. You just don't look right." You could just see Joan's happiness just sort of evaporate. She deflated right in front of me. I felt terrible for her.

"It struck me as odd that the girls never referred to their parents as 'Mom' and 'Dad,' it was always 'Harry' and 'Ginny,'" Joseph Livingston said. Explained Joan: "I called them Harry and Ginny—it was what they called each other, and they never suggested I do anything different."

Bronxville was a small community of just a few thousand people, most of whom were white and upper-middle class. "I had as cloistered a background as you can imagine," Joan told a reporter in 1962. "The community is highly restricted and I grew up knowing people pretty much like myself." By the time Joan graduated from high school in June 1954, she'd led a sheltered existence.

That fall, she left her father's home for Manhattanville, which had just recently moved from New York City to a fifteen-acre campus in Purchase, about forty-five minutes north of Manhattan. There, Joan studied for classes taught by nuns and found herself surrounded by friends and would-be suitors. It was a new world for her. In Bronxville, she'd been shy and reserved. She and her sister Candy were opposites in personalities. Candy was bubbly and outgoing, a boisterous cheerleader. Joan was studious—quiet in school, and quick to return home to practice her music and listen to records. She was also self-conscious. In her early teens, she stood a good foot taller than most of the boys in her class, so instead of dancing with them at school functions, she planted herself behind the piano and played for them instead.

"I was a loner," she told Chellis. "I had no friends in high school. Candy was a lot more popular than I was. . . . [She] went out on dates while I went to the library. I was a late bloomer."

In college, without the tumult of an alcoholic home to return to each night, Joan seemed to find new confidence. She was still studious, and that quiet reserve of hers remained. She majored in English with a minor in music, allowing her to bury herself in novels and notes. But she was blossoming, shedding her native reserve and opening up to new friends and experiences. She joined classmates for weekend treks to Yale and other men's colleges and became an adept flirt with the boys from Juilliard and Columbia. In fact, she had so many boyfriends in college that it became the campus joke that she'd surprise everyone and become a nun.

On her days without classes, she got dressed up and mustered the confidence to go on modeling auditions and go-sees with her portfolio in hand. Her father had encouraged the part-time vocation and even pitched her to one of his advertising clients with a proud, "Have I got a girl for you!" Candy Jones, head of one of the country's top modeling agencies and whose husband was Harry Conover, initially rolled her eyes. "How many times have I heard that from a proud father!" she said. "They're all convinced that their little girls are God's gift to the modeling business."

Still, Jones decided to humor Harry and agreed to meet with Joan. Years later, she still remembered being floored by the introduction: Joan, the "golden girl" with a deep tan and long, wheat-colored eyelashes. "She had fine facial bone structure and a strong-looking, glowingly healthy body," Jones recalled, "a refreshing change from the gaunt, emaciated girl, a half step from anemia, we had all been accustomed to seeing at the agency."

Joan was booked by the Conover Agency in New York City and dyed her hair lighter. Her measurements were documented: just shy of 5 feet, 8 inches, 132 pounds with a 36-inch bust, 25-inch waist, and 37-inch hips. Jones noted that Joan "needs brows groomed *slightly*," and that her lipstick shade was too dark. Her only noticeable flaw was a clunky walk that Jones could only describe as a "lope." The agency worked to teach her how to "float a little more instead of putting all her 132 pounds on the floor at one time," Jones said. "She became quite light on her feet."

Joan's first modeling assignment was in a sixty-second, national commercial for Maxwell House coffee, for which she got $2,500. Jones wasn't surprised when the calls kept coming. Joan got jobs in print ads modeling beauty products and foods, as well as other TV spots. "She was one of those rare beauties we got infrequently," Jones said. "I found myself comparing her to an Ingrid Bergman when she was Joan's age."

Years later, Joan remembered the period as an exciting time.

"Television was in its infancy, and I started doing some commercial acting," she said. "I got a taste of show-biz frustration, but I also landed a few jobs."

She did live in-show commercials as the Revlon Hairspray girl on the TV show *The $64,000 Question* before it was engulfed in a cheating scandal.

"I was also one of the gang on 'Coke Time with Eddie Fisher,' a fifteen-minute show," Joan said. "He sang, and during the two or three commercial breaks, a few of us would drink Coke for the camera in our bobby socks, saddle shoes and poodle skirts."

Joan was even supposed to do a Coke-drinking skit with Eddie, but he threw a fit when he realized Joan, at five-foot-eight, was taller than the diminutive crooner by three unacceptable inches.

"Drinking Coke for a national audience isn't exactly singing at the Met, but it had its challenges," Joan said. "The piece of direction I'll always remember is the stern admonition 'Don't you burp, young lady!'"

But, like most of the Manhattanville students, Joan's college agenda was as much on getting her "Mrs. degree" as it was on getting a solid education. Her senior year, she was introduced by Jean Kennedy Smith to the youngest in the Kennedy clan: twenty-five-year-old Edward. The family had donated money for a gymnasium to the college in memory of Kathleen Kennedy, and Jack was scheduled to give a speech at the dedication. At the last minute, there was a change of plans. Recalled Ted:

> It was Jack, not me, who'd originally agreed to give the talk. But when my brother showed up at the apartment and saw me there he said, "Oh! Dad, since Teddy's here, why don't we let him do it? I want to go to the football game." I didn't think it was a terribly good idea. I'd looked forward to seeing that game. Jack held his ground: it was going to be a great game, and he wanted to see it. Our father said, "Fine. Why don't you two work it out?" We worked it out, and Jack went to the football game.

It was a fluke that Ted gave the speech—one that Joan, incidentally, had no interest in hearing. She was writing a term paper and didn't bother attending.

"I was totally unimpressed," she later recalled to an interviewer. She figured the dedication would be "another boring event at the castle with the nuns." Plus, she hated politics—current affairs had been her worst subject in school.

But her roommate of four years, Margot Murray, came back to their room to warn her that she'd likely be missed and get reprimanded by the nuns if she didn't at least swing by to the tea being held afterward. That could mean she'd be ordered to stay on campus, which she couldn't abide.

"Then I couldn't go to Yale the next weekend," Joan said. So Joan hurriedly changed out of her bathrobe and into a dress before hustling to the event. That's where Jean spotted her.

The two women had met once before the previous summer at the Skakel home in Greenwich, where George Jr., Ethel's brother, was having a party.

"I arrived at the party with not one but two dates," Joan recalled. One of the men had previously been engaged to Jean and was a friend of Steve Smith's, Jean's husband. Curious about the woman with two dates, Jean had approached and the women chatted. Now, months later, Jean made the fateful introduction to her "little brother."

"I'll never forget that moment," Joan later said. "I expected to see a small boy. Instead I found myself looking up at somebody 6 feet 2 inches and close to 200 pounds. And, I must say, darn good-looking."

Ted was immediately drawn to Joan. She had all the requisites of a potential mate, and his mother, Rose, had made it clear that her preference was for Teddy to follow in brother Bobby's footsteps by marrying young and having many children. Ted maneuvered to get a ride to the airport from Joan and her roommate that night, allowing him to steal a few extra minutes with the attractive blonde. "I definitely wanted to see more of Joan," Ted wrote decades later in his memoir, *True Compass*.

Joan's sheltered life was about to change.

2

MARRYING THE KENNEDYS

JOAN AND TED'S COURTSHIP WAS AS CHASTE AS THEY COME. WHILE SHE'D had many boyfriends in college, Joan was a good Catholic girl and a virgin. And the Kennedy allure that perhaps worked on other girls wasn't as persuasive with her, in part because she had no idea who the Kennedys were when she and Ted met. "I just took no interest in current events; my lowest grade in college was in current events," Joan later told journalist Lester David. "I had never even heard of the Kennedys."

The two went on several dates, always chaperoned. "I had to be chaperoned everywhere. Nobody slept together. Nobody spent time alone," she said. "You were always in groups—at least if you were a Manhattanville girl."

And Ted treated her as such, despite having a reputation of being less than patient. After all, his nickname was Cadillac Eddie. By the time he met Joan, he was twenty-five and had endured the shocking loss of both his oldest brother and older sister. Another sister had been all but lost to a lobotomy. The mortality check, matched with the freedom that came with being a wealthy trust-fund child, had infused him with an air of recklessness and impatience. Like his brothers, he chased women unabashedly, but Ted's danger lust went beyond skirt chasing. He had a well-known impertinent side and also a lead foot, once outrunning a Virginia police lieutenant in his Oldsmobile convertible.

Ted took Joan out every time he went to New York. Getting to know each other's friends was as important as getting to know each other. One ski trip was a double date with Margot Murray and her boyfriend. With perfect propriety, the girls roomed together and met the boys on the ski slopes.

The two got serious enough by the autumn of 1957 that it was time for Ted to take Joan home to Hyannis Port. Rose was the only family member there, and the three got cozy, eating every meal together. Rose quizzed Joan about her faith, her upbringing, her values, her plans for a family—everything was fair game. "She asked me about Bronxville, about Manhattanville, about the nuns, but mostly we talked about music," Joan later said. "My mother-in-law played the piano very well, and she asked me to play. I had to give a big recital in order to graduate, and I played some of that music, some Brahms, and she played a Chopin etude for me. There was something that first week I met her that really connected. There was so much in common and the nuns and mostly our piano."

Joan loved the Hyannis Port backdrop. She took long walks along the waterfront and enjoyed playing golf with Ted. It was a picturesque setting, and intoxicated by the sun-drenched affluence and windswept coastal grandeur, Joan quickly fell for Ted. He was a catch by all standards—handsome, athletic, ambitious, and from a wealthy family. He was quick-witted and charming, but with a down-to-earth element that was irresistible. He was even known to poke fun at his ever-proper mother, especially when she corrected his grammar.

Joan, too, was exceeding expectations. Rose, still protective of her youngest child, called Manhattanville to check with the headmistress, a longtime family friend, on Joan's grades and reputation—all stellar. So the courtship continued, even without Joan meeting Joe, who was spending the summer vacationing in south France. The couple rarely was alone, but they fit in ski trips and gathered at a house party in Alstead, New Hampshire—Joan's grandparents' home, where the Bennetts vacationed. That visit gave Joan a glimpse of Ted's bold, fun-seeking spontaneity. Once, they went to a square dance together, where there was a caller and a band. Before Joan knew what was happening, Ted was on stage, doing the calling, to everyone's delight. Later during that visit, Joan's mother bought easels for the guests to paint the view from the top of the mountain. They decided to turn it into a contest, and Ted's painting won.

The two quickly were on a fast track for marriage. "I was keen to join my brothers as a married man, a family man," Ted would later recall. "I certainly *wished* to be a family man." He had his mother's approval, at least. She'd worried so much about him settling down that she'd started saying her rosary that he'd meet a nice Catholic girl, settle down, and start a proper family. "Apparently, he had brought other girls home, but she hadn't approved. I guess she said something to Eunice, 'I can't believe *our* luck.' I was a nice Catholic girl with a nice upbringing, upper middle class or upper class, and . . . I was gorgeous," Joan told an interviewer.

There's less arrogance here than it would appear. Joan was told all her life that she was a stunner, and she accepted and enjoyed the advantages her looks gave her. But her adult life revealed time after time that her beauty was a shaky foundation on which to build a sense of self-worth. When she reflects on her youth and marriage, there's a weariness, a sadness to her pat acceptance that she was beautiful. There's also a recognition that her beauty was a dubious virtue that was never enough to hold off her other insecurities. "It was too good to be true, that I was somebody that Teddy could be attracted to, a beautiful young woman, with the other qualifications."

In late summer 1958, Ted proposed to Joan while the two visited Hyannis Port. It was awkward, to say the least.

"What do you think about our getting married?" he asked.

"Well, I guess it's not such a bad idea," Joan answered.

Ted seemed pretty matter-of-fact about the agreement. "What do we do next?" he asked.

That next step was for Joan to finally meet Joe Sr., who had just returned from his vacation in France. Joan recalled it as a formal meeting with her prospective father-in-law, something akin to an interview. Joe sat in a great wing chair with Joan at his feet on an ottoman. "Do you love my son?" he asked. Joan said she did. At the end of the discussion, Joan recalled feeling "terribly relieved. He may have been tough, but he did make you feel at ease." Next, it was Harry Bennett's turn to give his blessing.

"She came home and told me, starry-eyed, two feet off the ground," Harry recalled to a reporter in 1965. "Then Ted called me at the office and made an appointment to come to ask, formally, for my daughter's hand." The conversation was stiff and included chitchat about the weather. "Then he asked the traditional question," Harry said. "It was all a new experience for me so I came back with the traditional reply: I asked him if he

could support my daughter in the manner to which she was accustomed."
This quip—asked of a member of one of the nation's wealthiest and most
powerful families—instantly became family legend.

———

With permission granted, the wedding planning commenced in a flurry.
The couple was to exchange vows just three months after the proposal,
and Ted had been tapped to run his brother Jack's upcoming reelection
campaign in Massachusetts for the US Senate. He and Joan didn't have
much time to spend together before the wedding. They got together once
for a campaigning weekend. It was Joan's first exposure to the political
arena—"I had no idea what I was getting into," she later said—and while
fun, it wasn't really conducive to getting to know each other. They were
usually accompanied by Jack or Ted's sister Eunice as they hit old factory
and fishing towns.

"That was my introduction to politics, the basic grass-roots, press-
the-flesh kind," Joan recalled.

The only other time the couple got together before the wedding was
for an engagement party at the Bennetts' Bronxville home. Ted showed
up late, sneaking into the house through the maid's quarters so as not to
embarrass Ginny.

Ted finally brought Joan a ring his father had bought, in a box that
Ted hadn't yet opened.

It was all moving too quickly for Joan, whose nerves began to rattle
her. It seemed Ted wasn't thrilled about marrying her. He didn't make
time to see her, and when he was out campaigning for his brother, he
always seemed to have an entourage of attractive young women at his
side. While Ted shared his worries with drinking buddies, Joan shared
hers with Harry and Ginny.

"My parents thought it wouldn't hurt to postpone it for a while," Joan
later said. So Harry approached Joe about delaying the wedding until the
following year. Joe was furious at the request and insisted the wedding
proceed on schedule. But not because he worried about his son's tender
heart. The wedding date had already been announced in the papers, so a
retraction would have reflected poorly on the family. The invitations—very

formal, with a script so frilly as to make it illegible—were sent to nearly five hundred guests, and the wedding banns began on Sundays in early November at churches in both Hyannis Port and Charlottesville, where Ted attended law school.

Ted and Joan's wedding events began with a prenuptial dinner on Thursday, November 26, 1958, at the elegant Hotel Pierre. The hotel had opened in 1930—"a place of Champagne bubbles and swing bands," a *New York Times* article later described it—and quickly became "the exclusive province of high society in Depression-era New York." In the decades that followed, the hotel's upper floors became an opulent supper club frequented by figures such as William Vanderbilt and Walter Chrysler. Long after that club disbanded, the roof garden lived on, becoming a popular ballroom that hosted debutante receptions and rehearsal dinners, the attendees of which graced the society pages of the city's newspapers. One hundred and twenty guests attended the Kennedys' prenuptial dinner, where they and the couple dined on smoked salmon, anchovies, deviled eggs, stuffed mushrooms, steak burgers, and heart-shaped ice cream. Atop the tables were cigarettes in glasses for the guests. A professional photographer roamed the event, snapping candids. At Joan's request, the Lester Lanin Orchestra played four straight hours. Noted in all caps on the orchestra's $675 receipt was the direction: PLEASE HAVE THE PIANO TUNED TO 440 INTERNATIONAL PITCH.

The rehearsal dinner was at Le Pavillon Restaurant, where a private room was rented for thirty-two guests. And on Saturday Joan nervously stepped into her stunning, ivory satin dress with a sweetheart neckline and long sleeves. Her chin-length hair was loosely pin-curled and perfect, and from atop her head cascaded a floor-length veil of delicate rose point lace. Candy stood at her side as maid of honor at St. Joseph's Roman Catholic Church in Bronxville; Jack was the best man. Ted's gift to Joan was a clover-shaped pin that had belonged to Rose. Harry gave his daughter away. Ginny got a glimpse of what life would soon be like for Joan when a newspaper photographer snapped her picture at the church as she wore her tea-length, bubble-skirt dress, a fur draped over her shoulders.

But as perfect as the day looked to outsiders, it contained omens. Joan had wanted to be married by John Cavanaugh, the president of Notre Dame, but the Kennedys insisted that they be married instead by Cardinal Francis Spellman, an American archbishop of the Catholic Church. Joan also had wanted an intimate affair for just family and friends. Her father-in-law had other plans. He "wanted to invite every political crony he'd ever met and others he wanted to impress," she said. The couple had been fitted with microphones to provide audio for a wedding video—a gift from a friend of Harry's. Before the ceremony, Jack and Ted seemed to forget they were being recorded, and Jack counseled a nervous Ted that being married didn't mean he had to be faithful. Joan discovered this when she later watched the movie.

Ted's law-school schedule was too demanding for an immediate honeymoon, so they took just three days together initially before returning to Charlottesville so Ted could focus on graduating. The couple accepted an invitation from Lord Beaverbrook to spend their brief honeymoon at his sprawling estate in the Bahamas. Beaverbrook was publisher of the *Daily Express* and other British newspapers, and Ted's father had stayed friendly with him after meeting him in London. The honeymoon invitation, while appreciated, proved to be awkward.

"The truth is that Joan and I hadn't expected to be quite so friendly with him on our honeymoon," Ted wrote.

When we arrived at his estate, he didn't seem to know quite what to do with us. He certainly didn't make himself scarce. We ate every meal together. For him—and therefore for us—that meant a baked potato, and only a baked potato, for lunch. Dinner was not much better. We were served exactly one daiquiri apiece before dinner and then something that was definitely not standout cuisine.

In an effort to give the newlyweds some time alone, Beaverbrook shipped the couple to an isolated island. It sounded romantic, but Joan remembered it as anything but. "We were dumped there for an overnight," she recalled. "It was the worst experience of our life. It was a little cottage, practically a shack, on this tiny island, just sand. We slept on these mats. There were bugs, and it was a nightmare."

The couple returned to Charlottesville, where Joan's life suddenly took a turn for the domestic. "I had to clean house, cook, do the laundry, and I really learned a lot. It was fun—for a while!" she recalled. After Ted graduated law school in June, they took a longer honeymoon—a five-week trip through Chile and Argentina in South America. Joan by then was in the early weeks of her pregnancy. Still, she didn't hesitate when Ted offered to teach her to ski in the Chilean Andes, some of the most challenging skiing country in the world.

"She grew adept in an amazingly short time," Ted wrote. "We trekked on southeastward to Argentina, traveling by riverboat and in the backs of trucks over bumpy roads, and staying at inns that had no heat."

Toward the trip's end, they finally indulged in a beautiful resort in Bariloche, Patagonia. From there, they launched to Buenos Aires before returning home—back to both reality and politics.

As 1959 arrived, plans were under way for Jack's presidential bid. Bobby would run the overall campaign, and Steve Smith would set up the administrative and financial operations. Ted was tapped to be campaign manager for the western states. It was a grueling job—"every state was critical, because Jack's nomination was a long shot," Ted recalled—and so that meant Ted left pregnant Joan alone to stay with her parents in Bronxville.

"Politics took over our lives almost immediately," Joan later said. And having taken over, politics would be the controlling factor for years to come.

3

CAMPAIGNING WITH THE KENNEDYS

Joan gave birth to the couple's first child on February 27, 1960—a daughter they named Kara—Gaelic for "dear little one," which they'd picked out from a book of old Irish names. Ted came home from Wisconsin, a key primary state, and seemed to relish his new role as father. "I have never seen Ted so excited," the new mother wrote to Lord Beaverbrook. "Ted is away all week traveling around Wisconsin, and now West Virginia, making speeches for Jack. He phones home every night and asks, 'How is my daughter?' I love the way he enjoys using those two new words—my daughter!"

Ted made known his dreams of having a big family. By now, Bobby had seven children, and Ted wanted Joan to keep up with Ethel's baby-a-year schedule. "He wants nine," Joan once said. "He says if his mother hadn't had nine, I wouldn't have him."

Joan stayed home with Kara for just six weeks before joining her husband on the campaign trail. Ted was overseeing eleven western states, and Joan was quickly learning that when one Kennedy was campaigning, all Kennedys were expected to join. There were coffee parties, Rotary club lunches, radio interviews, and rallies. Joan later described it as a whirl, rushing from one event to the next and eating whenever food was offered, because they could never be sure when the next offer would come.

"I felt rather like a tourist," Joan said, "entertained, but as though none of what was going on really had anything to do with me. After all, there had never been any talk of Ted going into politics himself. He was still planning on private practice after his graduation from law school."

Since their wedding and Ted's graduation, the couple had largely lived with Joan's in-laws in Hyannis Port and Palm Beach when they weren't staying in hotels and living out of suitcases on the campaign trail. Despite the chaos, Joan was easing into her life as a Kennedy, and she loved her new family. She didn't always feel like she fit in—they were far more competitive than she, and try as she might, she never could get herself too worked up about politics—but she admired Rose and quickly bonded with her sisters-in-law, Ethel and Jackie.

"I never felt any anger of being swallowed up by such a large family, because I saw immediately all the in-laws were individuals in their own right and were respected as such," Joan told a reporter in 1962. "They all have their own interests and social life, and when we all come together, this gives us a lot to talk about."

Joan, nicknamed "Joansie" by the family, was especially embraced by the Kennedy women: "I felt accepted as a little sister almost at once," she said. "When I first learned I was expected to make some public appearances during the president's campaign, I felt totally unprepared. Jackie, who was pregnant, heard me say I didn't have the proper clothes for campaigning, and she insisted on lending me so many of hers. I think that for a girl to lend her clothes to another girl is one of the greatest signs of friendliness there is."

In the spring after Kara's birth, Jackie stepped in to help Joan by renting a house for her and Ted in Georgetown, about two blocks away from Jackie and Jack; Jackie also hired an Irish nanny to help Joan with Kara. Having Jackie keep watch over her made Joan feel like she had an older sister, someone who understood her and helped keep her safe. When Joan went to Washington with her baby, Jackie took them through the house and even stocked it with groceries.

Jack tapped Joan to escort him on one campaign trip to West Virginia, so Jackie lent her clothes and offered suggestions about the role she was to play. "We'd chat, talk about campaigning, and I'd ask her questions and she'd say, 'Seems to me you're doing the right thing,' or she'd make suggestions about how to work the room." Jackie also had an ulterior motive: She wanted to keep Joan close to her husband so that when a photographer inevitably snapped a picture of him alongside an attractive woman, the odds were heightened that the attractive woman was a family member rather than a stranger who could fuel the rumor mill. It was in keeping with the role Joan had been assigned within the family: As the pretty one, most of the jobs she got had more to do with her appearance than her ability.

"I remember [Jackie] saying to me, 'Stay very close to Jack. Just glue yourself to him," Joan recalled. "'Don't let anybody else wiggle in, especially when they're taking those pictures. . . . They'll love meeting you because your name is Kennedy, whereas Jean Smith is Jean Smith even though she's his sister.'"

No one was staying very close to Ted at this time, however. During the campaign, he once flew to Hawaii to meet Peter Lawford and Frank Sinatra for a fund-raiser. Someone spotted him leaving his first-class seat and talking to a European beauty queen who was sitting farther back. Lawford got word and contacted campaign worker Dick Livingston, who was dispatched to meet Ted at the airport. Livingston quietly registered the woman at a hotel away from Ted. "That night Frank is having a dinner party and Teddy hasn't shown up, and Frank is getting pissed," Livingston later recalled. "And finally Teddy arrives with this beauty queen on his arm. I thought Frank was going to get up and whack him, he was so pissed off."

While the press in those days never reported on the Kennedy men's roving ways, rumors inevitably reached the wives. Joan, at least ostensibly, refused to believe them. "She acted like Rose," Chellis recalled. In a sense, Chellis was right: Like Rose, Joan came to some psychological accommodation that allowed her to go on. And like Rose, the exact nature of that accommodation, whether it consisted of denying the truth even to herself or simply deciding to contain it, was not something she revealed to anyone. The difference was that, for Rose, the denial proved sustainable. Joan would not be so lucky.

—⁓—

Just as it's tough to imagine a time of chaste, chaperoned courtship, it seems dated to ponder a political campaign without a professional campaign manager. But in 1960, that was the norm, so the large Kennedy family was dispersed across the country to convince voters that Jack was neither too young nor too Catholic to become president. Joan's first primary state was West Virginia, which was important because it was just 1 percent Catholic. "If Jack could win there, or do well, it would augur well for a national race," Joan said. Joan's job was to "look nice and be friendly," which she seems to have pulled off without much effort. In fact, when she went down to the West Virginia mines with brother-in-law Jack, she "got whistled at by the miners." In the sexism-drenched backdrop of the era, Joan considered it a compliment, and Jack's handlers thought it was great. But, as entertained as Jack was, he didn't like Joan being a distraction, so he became more cautious in his use of her. Joan wrote:

> *It turned into a bit of a joke: when Jack's campaign people sat around talking about "Where can we use the mother?" or "Where do we pull the sister in?" and my name came up, invariably someone would answer with "Joan? She's too beautiful to use." Jack thought it was great, and when he gave everybody souvenirs at the end of the campaign, mine was a cigarette box with those words engraved on it.*

Not that Joan was off the campaigning hook. Gerard Doherty, a thirty-three-year-old state lawmaker who'd become one of Ted's primary political advisers, had seen how quickly voters warmed up to Joan. She was down-to-earth, surprisingly relatable, and candid—sometimes too much so for the Kennedy family. She revealed to a journalist that Jackie wore wigs and that Jack's bad back kept him from lifting his children. The family was upset enough that they asked "Joansie" to backtrack, which she dutifully did. Despite the Kennedys' displeasure with Joan's openness, voters reacted well to her candor, so Doherty put her in heavy rotation.

Joan once joined Ethel on a trip to Chicago where the two spent three days attending a dozen teas, rallies, and meetings, mostly with female voters. Joan was even asked to represent the Kennedy women on a televised program that would have sat her alongside other prominent political women, including Lady Bird Johnson, the wife of Jack's vice presidential nominee, and Muriel Humphrey, wife of perennial Democratic frontrunner Hubert Humphrey. Joan's nerves wouldn't allow it: "I don't know if I'll know what to say," she said, rejecting the request.

When Jack learned he'd won the presidency, Joan and Ted were at his side, along with a big gathering of family and friends who'd converged on the Cape house on November 8, 1960. By the morning after the election, the votes had been tallied. Soon after, Ted and Joan joined Bobby and Ethel for a few days of relaxation in Acapulco. During that trip, Bobby confided in Ted that he wasn't going to seek Jack's vacated Senate seat when it became available in 1962. This put some pressure on Ted to go for the seat. It was important to their father, Joe, to keep it in the family. Jack had been allowed to choose a temporary successor in Benjamin Smith, a Kennedy family friend, and when the special election came in 1962, Ted would have just turned thirty years old—the minimum age to serve as a senator.

With Bobby out—and, in fact, about to be tapped by his president brother to become the US attorney general—that left Ted as the only Kennedy man available to run. Trouble was, Ted didn't know if he wanted to enter into politics. His wife certainly thought his plan was to stick with lawyering. Before Ted lay two distinct paths, and so much of Joan's future would be determined by what he chose. Whereas Ethel and Bobby were a partnership, Joan's role in her marriage was much more passive: Ted made the decisions, and she could only wait and see.

4

CATCHING UP

TED'S DECISION TO RUN FOR JACK'S FORMER SENATE SEAT IN 1962 DID not come easily. If he ran, he'd be vying first against Edward McCormack Jr., the popular attorney general of Massachusetts, who also happened to be the nephew of the Speaker of the US House, John McCormack. And if he bested McCormack, he'd still have to face Republican George C. Lodge, a former political reporter who had just been reappointed by President Kennedy as assistant secretary of labor for international affairs. Lodge was from a prominent political family in New England with a long history of battling the Kennedys in elections. In 1916, George Lodge's grandfather, Henry Cabot Lodge, defeated John F. Fitzgerald for the Massachusetts Senate seat. Thirty-six years later, Henry C. Lodge Jr. was edged out by Jack for the seat. Now, Henry Jr.'s son would try to win it back. Ted knew that both of his opponents would attack his lack of experience and accuse him of coasting on the Kennedy name. If he were to run, he'd need to steel himself for that.

Then there was another matter: the plans he'd made with Joan. While campaigning in the west, the couple had fallen in love with the region. They had briefly moved to San Francisco with Kara and had set their sights on Arizona as a possible home. But with the Massachusetts Senate seat there for the taking, Joe insisted that it was "their turn." And Ted, for all of his dreams of independence, like his brothers before him had trouble turning his back on his father's wishes. Later, he recalled pondering words he'd heard his family say to him when he was a boy:

You can have a serious life or a nonserious life, Teddy. I'll still love you whichever choice you make. But if you decide to have a nonserious life, I won't have much time for you. You make up your own mind. There are too many children here who are doing things that are interesting for me to do much with you.

Ted struggled mightily with the decision. "I'd worshipped my father as a young boy," Ted confided. What son doesn't want to make his father proud? And then there were Ted's brothers, whom he idolized. They were war heroes and public servants—serious-minded winners who didn't seem enticed by the frivolity that often tempted Ted. They certainly had their father's attention, and his respect. Ted wanted those things for himself.

I had been swept up by the dash and nobility of Joe Jr., and admired his wartime self-sacrifice even as I wept over it. Jack and Bobby had been godlike figures to me and my sisters. Now Jack was about to be installed as a world leader, and Bobby had already earned national recognition. . . . I was ready to step into the public arena alongside these men who were my father and brothers. To be of use. And to catch up.

Joan could hardly compete with the lifelong aspirations embedded into a man who, at heart, was in many ways still a boy wanting to please his father. "Ted was the obvious choice [for the Senate seat]" Joan recalled, "so all thoughts of private practice were put on hold—permanently, as it turned out."

As soon as Ted decided to run, their lives seemed to hurtle down this new course. Ted, now twenty-eight years old, felt too green for the seat, so he asked Jack for a role in the administration, padding his resume until the 1962 elections. Cold War tensions were at their highest and Ted claimed he was "passionately . . . interested in arms control." But Jack shrugged off the suggestion, telling Ted he'd do more good working his tail off in Massachusetts. But first—the president announced as though a light bulb went off in his head—Ted should go to Africa.

"Yes. Go [to Africa] and see what's going on over there. That's a continent that's going to be enormously important," Jack said. "There are all kinds of things happening down in the Congo. This Tshombe's on the loose. And there's this East-West struggle going on in these countries. The Belgian Congo has just obtained its independence from Belgium." Ted remembered stammering a response. There was no time to put together such a trip! But the president had his ways. After making a few phone calls, he found that a group of senators had just two days earlier gone on a fact-finding tour of West Africa. If Ted left that night, he could catch up with them. So just like that, Ted packed his bags and left his wife and daughter for a four-week trip, on the advice of his brother, meant to shore up his credentials.

Within a week, Joan was house hunting in Boston alone so that she, Ted, and Kara could move there, as the president had suggested. Joan found the family a small apartment on a top floor in Louisburg Square on Beacon Hill, in one of the city's most elite neighborhoods. It was a gorgeous brick building, built in the 1830s, which had served as home to such famous names as William Dean Howells, the former editor of the *Atlantic*, and *Little Women* author Louisa May Alcott. The private square was historically significant to the Kennedys, too: Decades earlier, citizens of Irish descent had protested Ted's grandfather for appointing an Italian American to a post. The mob had shouted, "Remember your own, Honey Fitz. Remember your own!"

Joan, who soon learned she was pregnant with her second child, settled back in Boston and began readying for the race. "This time, we were on our own," Joan said. "Everybody else was down in Washington running the country, so Ted and I started the grassroots round ourselves."

"We went to every little town in Massachusetts. We would go together or we would go separately," Joan said. Ted would hit the big cities, and Joan would go to the smaller towns. "If Ted was in Boston, then I tried to be in Springfield. I met with women's groups and went to many small towns my husband couldn't get to. I used to be at three coffees and three teas in one day." Ted seemed pleased with his popular wife, whose looks were so fetching that the president had nicknamed her "The Dish." Ted told her once that "everyone is curious about what the sister-in-law of the

President looks like and what she wears." About the campaign events, he would proudly announce, "Joansie, you got a crowd."

"It was just a bunch of us kids," she later recalled. "We felt it was us against the world."

Joan's long legs and enticing smile proved useful as always, but so did her piano playing. She and Ted would gather with voters for the typical candidate events—morning coffees, afternoon teas, often attended by one ethnicity at a time—and after the hand shaking and back patting, Ted would give a little pep talk, and Joan would take her place at the piano. "I'd get the hostess to tell me what her favorite songs were . . . they often turned out to be some of those show tunes that came in handy at parties when I was a teenager—and, if I was lucky, everyone would sing along."

Sometimes the crowds were not so adoring, and the ugly side of political life surfaced. Joan, optimistic and trusting to a fault, had to steel herself with her husband now in the public eye. She had of course witnessed Nixon's attacks on her brother-in-law during the presidential campaign, but those lobbed at her husband were just as harsh and hit closer to home. Ted was mostly attacked for his inexperience, as highlighted in particularly vicious language by McCormack during one of two televised debates between the candidates. McCormack said: "I say we need a senator with a conscience, not connections. We need a senator with experience, not arrogance. The office of a United States senator should be merited and not inherited." Joan admitted the insults stung. "Yes, I minded . . . but I tried not to let it upset me, and I tried not to let it show," she said. Getting upset and losing her composure would have put her out of step with the family, so she adopted the same approach that had worked for Rose and Jackie: She ignored the lobs, held her tongue, smiled, and said only the most genteel and quotable things. Sometimes, she would wash those quotes down with a drink.

With one brother-in-law in the Oval Office, another in the cabinet, and her husband vying for the Senate, Joan increasingly found herself the focus of newspaper stories. Invariably focusing first on her looks, the articles usually included staged and smiling photographs of the young mother with her family, which now included a second child, Edward Jr.

Her words were always upbeat, and her interests summed up in good-little-girl sound bites. When a photograph was included of her and Ted together, she often was smiling at him in clearly visible, utter adoration. One AP profile of Joan circulated to newspapers nationwide highlighted several interests that Joan adopted to be closer to Ted: politics, of course, and skiing, and going for long walks outdoors. The article focused on the many hobbies Joan could return to once the election was over: visiting her sister in Texas, scrapbooking, and preparing for Thanksgiving. They were the safe and predictable activities expected of a wholesome, all-American, stand-by-your-man kind of wife.

But Joan's contributions to the campaign were in reality more substantive than that. Each night she'd do her "homework," as she called it, and learned more about local and national politics than she ever thought she could stomach. She rounded up delegates to the Democratic State Convention, and, after a few trial runs alongside Ted, began accepting invitations to speak on her own in public. In fall of 1962, she spoke to a meeting of women at Ohabei Shalom Temple in Brookline with the wives of Ted's rivals. "All the way to Brookline, I practiced saying the name of the temple," Joan told a reporter soon after. "Then at the last minute, I lost my nerve. I skipped the name. I was afraid I'd mispronounce it."

Joan didn't see much of her husband that summer—in mid-July 1961, he left for a month to tour several Latin American countries—but he was home in time for the birth of their first son, Edward Moore Kennedy Jr., in September. Joan told the magazine *Redbook* that she tried to set limits on Ted's time away. She admitted that she didn't see her husband until eleven o'clock most nights but that they put Saturday aside as a day for each other.

If Joan had any misgivings about the part she was to play, she certainly didn't share them with the press.

"My role, as I see it, is to be ready to go anywhere and to accommodate myself to Ted's schedule," she once said, as though relinquishing her personal interests and individuality weren't a surefire way to slowly erode her young marriage. "It's not a difficult role, frankly, because I learned to love campaigning in 1960. I think I've learned a lot about the country, and about politics too." To another reporter, her words rang equally hollow:

"Really, I'm quite fortunate. Most women have no opportunity to learn about their husband's working lives. But when you're in public life, it's not a 9 to 5 job. You bring it home with you."

And in November 1962, Ted brought home a victory.

5

THE SUPPORTIVE WIFE

As ELATED AS TED AND JOAN WERE WITH THE POLITICAL WIN, A CLOUD
had settled over the family. Less than three months after the birth of
Edward Jr.—nicknamed Teddy—Joe Sr. had his stroke. This was particularly hard on Ted, who, as the baby of the family, had a special bond with
his demanding father. It was Ted who located a vascular specialist in Boston and flew him down to Florida to diagnose the elder Kennedy with the
brain hemorrhage that stole Joe's speech.

"My father's illness hit me very hard," Ted later wrote. "He had been
so strong, so vital, so important in all our lives. And finally, for the first
time in my life, the two of us had been together as men, sharing a common purpose. Now that aspect of our relationship was lost to me. It was
almost more than I could bear."

In true Kennedy fashion, however, the family didn't dwell on the tragedy or reflect on it much publicly. Joan, ever the optimist, put on a happy
face for the media and dutifully played the role of supportive wife. And
just as her husband was forever compared to his brothers, Joan would forever be weighed against her iconic sisters-in-law. One newspaper article
began: "In Boston, Mrs. Kennedy isn't Jacqueline. She's Joan, the tall, very
pretty blonde girl who's married to the President's youngest brother." The
writer added, "We went to talk to Joan Kennedy about clothes because we
had heard that she's as elegant as the First Lady."

Ted was enormously popular for a freshman senator, especially one
so young. His name obviously helped, but it was more than that. He was
affable and charismatic. His broad smile and shoulders, along with the
genetic Kennedy good looks, didn't hurt, either. By fall 1963, his Senate

office received five thousand letters a week—"an immense mail for a freshman Senator from a state this size," according to the *Boston Globe*. Ted had been slightly bruised by the battering he took during the election for being the president's brother, so post-election he avoided public appearances with either Jack or Bobby in Washington. As one *Boston Globe* columnist wrote: "He is diligently working to belong, to lighten the presidential shadow beside him and to build a record of his own."

In those early stories, Joan was unfailingly upbeat about every aspect of her woman-behind-the-man position. Ruth Finney, a writer with the *New York World-Telegram and Sun*, captured it perfectly in the top of a 1962 story written just after Ted's election:

> *She's going to be the youngest Senate wife in the history of that august body, but for 26-year-old Mrs. Edward M. Kennedy, the prospect holds no terrors.*
>
> *She's already managed—in the five years since she met Ted Kennedy—to make the transition from non-political, non-athletic debutante and music major to a fully participating member of the country's most game-loving, hard-driving political family. She's sure one more change will be no problem.*
>
> *Senate debates?*
>
> *"You'll find me right there in the gallery looking on. I want to find out about everything."*
>
> *Constituents to be shown around town?*
>
> *"That way I'll get to do some sight-seeing, too!"*
>
> *Sewing for the Red Cross with other Senate wives every Tuesday?*
>
> *"It sounds fine."*

Behind the scenes, the veneer on her seemingly perfect life was starting to chip. Ted was growing more distant, and the always-present rumors about his female companions were steadily growing. In the spring of 1963, Joan, five months pregnant, miscarried for the first time. It had been her third pregnancy, and unlike the first two, she was under far more public scrutiny now that her husband was a senator. The *Boston Globe* carried a short story with the headline: "Joan Kennedy Loses Baby; She's All

Right." Even in the seven-paragraph article, Joan couldn't escape comparisons with her sisters-in-law. The final paragraph referenced Ethel and Jackie's current pregnancies and their respective due dates, almost as if the press were keeping score. A year later, Joan lost another pregnancy, this time in her fourth month. The personal tragedy again became headline fodder for her hometown paper. The baby's remains were flown from Washington to Boston and interred by Cardinal Richard Cushing, Archbishop of Boston, in the Kennedy family plot at Holyhood Cemetery in Brookline.

For Joan, the miscarriages were especially heartbreaking; besides the obvious personal loss, she knew they disappointed her husband. He'd been vocal about his plans for a large family like his own and his brother Bobby's, and Joan couldn't deliver. "We've been married four years and Ted can't understand why we don't have four children," she once said.

"It was discouraging and depressing for Joan not to be able to see her way through her pregnancies like Ethel did," Nurse Hennessey said. "Joan felt she wasn't as healthy as the others because she was unable to carry to full term. The problem lay in a hormonal deficiency, but there was no impairment whatever of physical health."

Each baby lost served as tragic reinforcement of Joan's darkest insecurities. She simply couldn't fulfill the procreative demands made of a Kennedy wife.

～⁓～

That summer at Hyannis Port, Joan detached from the Kennedy clan and spent more time on adjacent Squaw Island, where she and Ted had an oceanfront home. The island took its name from a squaw buried in an unmarked grave at its highest point, and most who summered there were folks of old money looking for some peace and quiet in its secluded embrace. The house had been rejected by Jackie and Jean, Ted's sister, as being too small, but Joan loved the gray-shingled, four-bedroom home. It stood alone on a high bluff and boasted a view of Nantucket Sound from every window. "Teddy's away so much, he told me to decorate it any way I want to," Joan told a reporter at the time. So she got to work: She carpeted the living room in vivid blue, which, set against the warm white walls and ceiling, lent a nautical feel to the space. The huge master bedroom upstairs was decorated with pink carpet and a white velvet chaise, and throughout the house were early American antiques that Joan adored.

Joan had always been closest with Jackie of all the Kennedy wives. The two shared a deep love for the arts, and, unlike the rest of the family, they preferred sneaking away when the touch-football competitions began. Joan said: "Jackie would say, 'They have no idea what we do when we're alone. I know you go over to Squaw Island by yourself and play the piano and I go off alone and paint, and they think we're weird because we're alone. They can't stand to be alone.'" Having found a like-minded introvert among a clan of rowdy competitors, Joan treasured the camaraderie. "In the summers, everybody else in the family would do everything together from morning to night—the touch football, the sailing, the tennis, the waterskiing—all day long they'd play together en masse. [Jackie] was wonderful, she made me feel like it was OK to be myself."

The two would steal away together, a Secret Service man in tow. Joan remembered getting one agent to drive Jackie's speedboat so the two wives could water ski. "She was very very good, and she would go again," Joan reported. "Then the two of us were dropped off a mile away from the harbor and we swam in together. We did this the whole time she was first lady, and almost nobody knew about it."

Soon, everything would change in a way that neither Joan nor the rest of the family could have possibly fathomed. As the summer of 1963 gave way to fall, Ted and Joan were readying to settle into a new, bigger house on 31 Street Northwest. That November, they were coming up on their fifth wedding anniversary, and Joan had planned a special celebratory dinner to mark the event on November 22, a week before the actual anniversary. That morning she was still polishing off her to-do list before heading to Elizabeth Arden's to have her hair styled for the big night. She was there when Jack climbed into the presidential limousine in Dallas, Texas.

Ted was sleepily presiding over the Senate chambers that afternoon. Later, he recalled it'd been a dull day with a routine debate about federal aid to public libraries. At about 1:40 p.m., he heard a shout from the lobby. It had come from someone who'd stopped to read an Associated

Press teletype machine. Ted was summoned over, and he watched as the machine clapped out a bulletin: "My first overwhelming sense was disbelief," Ted would later write. "How could it be true? And then horror, as I stood there listening to the *tick, tick, tick* of the teletype machine. I couldn't hear anything or anyone else. Gradually, I became aware of the voices around me. I heard someone say the president was dead." His thoughts quickly turned to Joan, his sensitive and still-sheltered wife. "She adored Jack. She would be devastated by the news. I asked Milt Gwitzman, my Harvard classmate and an adviser to Jack, to drive me to our Georgetown house. My old Texan friend Claude Hooton, in town to join weekend festivities, rode with us as we sped through traffic lights. . . . We located Joan at her hairdresser getting ready for a weekend with our friends." Ted knew the loss would shatter Joan, but after ensuring she didn't get the news from a stranger or the media, he had White House staffers call her to say he wouldn't be home at all that night. He and his sister Eunice were flying to Hyannis Port to be with their parents.

Candy McMurray, Joan's sister, arrived at Washington National for the party. She called Joan and suggested that she and her husband take the next flight back home to Texas. She assumed Joan would be mired in family responsibilities, but that wasn't the case. Joan was left behind in Washington, her jovial dinner plans shattered. She begged Candy to stay, so the McMurrays took an airport cab to Georgetown, where Joan was in bed, prostrate.

That night, caterers arrived as scheduled with food and drink for the anniversary party. Joan had canceled the event, of course, but the caterers had been booked and paid long before. Ultimately, Joan was grateful: The anniversary feast fed mourners, instead. "People kept drifting in all evening long," she recalled to a reporter in 1970. "We were the closest Kennedys to Washington, with Bobby and Ethel in McLean and the Shrivers in Maryland. Our friends wanted to comfort us and be comforted. I didn't feel as though I could shut myself upstairs in my room and cry." Joan spent the day after the assassination at home, unlike the other Kennedy mothers. As the late historian William Manchester wrote in his 1966 book *The Death of a President*, "Joan found the mere contemplation of violence crippling." She had rarely before faced heartbreak, and to have a family member gunned down, stolen from his wife, his children, the whole country, was too much for kindhearted Joan to bear.

The Kennedys weren't ones to be crippled, however. Life moved on, and Ted swallowed his grief. Joan began to drink hers. Ted didn't seem to notice much at first. He immersed himself in work, the long hours keeping him away from home more than ever. "In the end, the best way to honor Jack's memory was to take up his unfinished work," Ted decided. That meant forging ahead with his 1964 campaign to win his first full term in the Senate.

On June 19, 1964, seven months after his brother's death, Ted boarded a plane in Washington headed to the Democratic State Convention at West Springfield, Massachusetts, where he was to be re-nominated by acclamation for senator. He'd planned to leave earlier in the day, when the weather was clearer, but he was delayed by a Senate vote on civil rights—a groundbreaking anti-discrimination vote on a bill that had prompted the longest continuous debate in Senate history. There were four other occupants on the tardy plane: the pilot, Edwin Zimny, Kennedy aide Edward Moss, US Senator Birch Bayh of Indiana, and his wife, Marvella. Just fifteen miles from its destination, the plane crashed into an apple orchard, its low branches acting "as a knife, slicing open the front of the plane," Ted would recall. "The impact hurled my corkscrewed body forward into the cockpit, directly between the pilot and my friend Ed Moss."

Senator Bayh and his wife pulled themselves out of the wreckage with only cuts, but the pilot was killed on impact. Moss was unresponsive in the cockpit, where he'd been fatally injured. "I tried to get some response from the others in the plane and I could not raise anyone," Senator Bayh told a reporter soon after the wreck. "Ted was crumpled up on the floor. I got out thinking I could get help for him. My wife and I decided to take one more try. I called his name and he answered. I reached my hand through the opening and he grabbed it."

Ted was badly hurt—his back was broken and a lung punctured, and, as he tried to escape the plane for fear the scent of gasoline was forewarning an explosion, he discovered his legs weren't working. The Bayhs courageously helped pull him from the wreckage, leaving him covered with a raincoat in the apple orchard as they rushed, barefoot, to the nearest road to flag down a passing car for help. "Nine cars passed them before one finally stopped," Ted wrote. "A man named Robert Schauer picked up the Bayhs and drove them to his home, where they called for help. Schauer lent them blankets and pillows and returned them to the crash site. Police and an ambulance finally arrived about an hour and a half after Birch had pulled me from the plane."

Joan, who had suffered her second miscarriage not four weeks earlier, was already at the convention when word spread about the crash. She was sped to Cooley Dickinson Hospital in Northampton with Governor Endicott Peabody at her side. When she arrived, reporters were already there, shouting out questions. She replied automatically, armed not with facts or doctors' prognoses, but with little more than hope. "He's going to be fine. He's going to be fine," repeated Joan, hurrying past the crowd with stoic determination. When she reached his room, Ted managed a weak, "Hi, Joansie. Don't worry."

Initially news reports actually downplayed Ted's injuries, seemingly relying on hospital spokesmen who perhaps had been coached. "Kennedy's injuries were not serious. He was semiconscious when brought in. . . . The injuries appeared to be cuts and bruises," the *Boston Globe* reported. In reality, Ted's condition was dire. "My life hung in the balance for a while," he recalled. Several ribs were broken, and Ted underwent transfusions to replace lost blood. Doctors had suctioned away water and air from his chest to keep him from suffocating. In the end, his youth, size, and fitness all worked in his favor, and Ted was given a choice on how to address his badly broken back: He could either have immediate surgery or he could stay in bed, immobilized, for some six months to let the vertebrae attempt to heal on their own. Joe Sr., unable to walk or talk on his own because of his stroke, still managed to make the trip to be at Ted's hospital bed, where he made his preference known: "Whipping his head from side to side, he shouted out, 'Naaaa, naaaa, naaaa!'" Ted recalled. "I understood that Dad was recalling the back operation on Jack that had left him in permanent pain (and no doubt thinking of Rosemary as well). I made a decision that not only honored his wishes, but mine also: I would take the more conservative option of allowing the broken bones and vertebrae to heal naturally." It's remarkable that, even as an adult—a married man and father—Ted still deferred to his ailing father, even in matters of his own health.

Dropping out of the Senate race wasn't an option, so Joan was tapped to do what's expected of Kennedy wives in such a crisis: She was to campaign on Ted's behalf. She would stand in for her injured husband. It would be her finest hour.

6

THE PRETTIEST STAND-IN

"A MAN NEVER HAD A PRETTIER STAND-IN TO OPEN HIS POLITICAL campaign than Sen. Edward M. Kennedy had Monday."

And so began Joan's—actually, Ted's—1964 campaign.

If Joan had entered the Kennedy family as a shy loner—as she'd described herself in high school—she was now unrecognizable, appearing completely at ease while shaking hands and making the small talk that she'd long ago so desperately avoided. In September 1964, still rattled from her husband's near-death experience and the loss of her brother-in-law, she stood before a crowd of four hundred and asked for their signatures of support in Ted's drive for reelection.

"I am no doctor, but I believe that if Ted could be here tonight to see this enthusiastic gathering, it would hasten his recovery by at least a month," she told the friendly crowd. It was the first of many such stops all across the state. Joan tapped the acting experience she'd had in college—those days when she sipped Coca-Cola next to Eddie Fisher—and quelled the stage fright just as she'd done during all of those piano recitals years earlier. "I'd hit a VFW hall in Springfield and relay Ted's greeting from his hospital bed, asking his supporters to keep up the good work. Then I'd read his speech," Joan recalled. "There wasn't much occasion for piano playing on that campaign. . . . Speaking was easier as I got used to it—after all, no one expected me to really deliver the speech the way Ted would have, though I did my best to give it some spin."

Not only did Joan campaign for Ted's Senate seat, but she also took over as a Massachusetts delegate to the Democratic National Convention for her brother-in-law. Bobby, the attorney general, had given up his seat on entering New York's senatorial race, and Joan was chosen as his replacement. Once again, she stole the headlines. How could she not? Few other delegates lent themselves to descriptions such as "lovely" and "radiant." Wrote biographer Adam Clymer:

> *Joan, who had crumpled when Jack died, thrived in this season of adversity. She was needed. Joan went across Massachusetts for Ted. She danced the polka and tried a sentence in Polish in Dorchester, showed home movies of Ted and the children in Lawrence, shook hands and appeared with visitors like [Hubert] Humphrey and [President Lyndon] Johnson. She collected cards pledging to vote for Ted. Thanking one audience for a pile of cards, she said, "The fun part is going back and telling Ted all about it. That's the best medicine, bringing a pile of signatures to Ted."*

Recuperating slowly, Ted spent his downtime in the hospital reading, contemplating, and gathering essays about his father that he later compiled into a book. Joan told a campaign crowd that he had been "a very busy patient," that his recovery was "excellent," and that he remained in "fine spirits." Joan's schedule was on pace, though she managed to maneuver her travels so that she'd never leave her children for more than two days at a time. "Still, I was on the road six days a week," she recalled. It was a grueling pace, one that was rewarded with Ted's easy victory in November. The whole Kennedy clan knew what Joan had done for Ted. At a news conference outside of Ted's hospital room after the election, Bobby stood next to his little brother. Both had won their Senate seats; Bobby stood in a suit while Ted lay in pajamas. Ted made a joke about how Bobby's victory had been narrower than his, to which Bobby shot back, "He's getting awful fresh since he's been in bed and his wife won the campaign for him."

7

"NOBODY, NOTHING"

THOUGH JOAN HAD TRIUMPHED ON THE CAMPAIGN TRAIL, TED REMAINED the always-roving husband. After Jack's death and Ted's brush with his own, his wandering eye became ever more blatant. Joan managed for a long time to plant herself firmly in a state of denial, but the rumors were chipping away at her confidence and sobriety; by the middle of the decade, her footing there was slipping. Not that you could tell by her public appearances: She stayed as busy as ever after the 1964 election, visiting schools for mentally challenged children—the Kennedy family's major charity—and touring hospitals to cheer up soldiers wounded in Vietnam. When Ted buried the hatchet with Ed McCormack—the Senate opponent whose line about how the office "should be merited, not inherited" stung in 1964—Joan provided the musical accompaniment for McCormack's bid for governor. And she was by her husband's side when the John F. Kennedy Federal Building was dedicated in Boston during a solemn ceremony led by Bobby.

In late 1966, she learned she was pregnant again, and this time, she limited her traveling in hopes of avoiding the miscarriages that ended her previous two pregnancies. Well into her third trimester, she had another scare: She, her husband, and their two children were aboard the Kennedy family's New Frontier aircraft, the *Caroline*, when an engine died on takeoff and the pilot was forced to make an emergency landing. "The timing was ironic," a news report declared. "The senator was flying back hurriedly from the Midwest because of a fatal air crash. Ethel Kennedy's brother had just been killed, along with one of the closest clan cronies, Dean Markham." After the landing, Joan caught a commercial flight back to Boston and visited her obstetrician, who said she was fine. Just days later, on July 14, 1967, Joan gave birth to Patrick, her third child. He was baptized by Cardinal Cushing and made his newspaper debut, as most Kennedys did, in the *Boston Globe*.

Joan immersed herself in the role of the glamorous senator's wife so deeply that it became her primary identity, subsuming the woman she'd been before she met him. When she was needed, she filled the role precisely. But being Ted Kennedy's wife meant that a lot of typical needs in life were met, whether you wanted them to be or not. "The house was always full of cooks, baby nurses and staff," she once said. "I felt extra, no good. When I said I didn't want a baby nurse, we had a baby nurse. Everything was done and taken care of and I didn't do it. I was nobody, nothing, not needed."

Behind the scenes, Joan wrestled with Teddy's cheating and reached out to Jackie for advice. "He thinks you're a wonderful wife," said Jackie, who had become closer to Ted since Jack's death. "And you're smart and you're talented and you're a wonderful mother. His mother and father adore you, and the whole family loves you. You're just the perfect wife. But he just has this addiction." Jackie had come to accept this "addiction" in Jack. Joan was far more vulnerable. She began turning to the bottle more and more, and the distance between her and her husband steadily grew. The more women Ted entertained, the more she began to question herself. Joan confided:

> *When one grows up feeling that maybe one is sort of special and hoping that one's husband thinks so, and then suddenly thinking that maybe he doesn't, well, I didn't lose my self-esteem altogether, but it was difficult to hear all the rumors. And I began thinking, well, maybe I'm just not attractive enough or attractive anymore, or whatever, and it was awfully easy to then say, well, after all, if that's the way it is, I might as well have a drink.*

Joan could hardly expect consolation or understanding from Rose, whose own husband's dalliances included well-known affairs with multiple women. In the mid-1960s, after a magazine had reported that Ted was having an affair with a married woman, Rose approached Joan at Palm Beach. "My dear," Rose said, "You can't believe any of these things you are reading. Women chase after politicians." For Rose, to acknowledge and name a thing was to give it power. Her psychological constitution couldn't have differed more sharply from Joan's.

Joan tried to convince herself that the womanizing didn't matter. If Ted strayed, he always came home, after all, and it isn't as though she was the only Kennedy wife to have to deal with an unfaithful husband. "I tried telling myself it didn't matter," she said, "but I couldn't help wondering who might be with him. What hurt most was finding out about someone I knew."

As Joan's self-esteem shrank, so did her skirts. "The only thing I was sure of at that time was that I was a very attractive woman and I had a good figure," Joan later said. Of course she knew: She'd always made news with her looks first—"radiant" was a common description from reporters—but when she started wearing minidresses to formal White House gatherings, the tone changed. "Joan Kennedy wore a glittering silver, six-inches-above-the-knee mini-dress to a White House reception for members of Congress and their spouses last night, where long gowns were informally prescribed. She was the talk of the party," began one United Press International story. "'It hardly covers the subject,' quipped one senator as he watched the attractive, blonde wife of Sen. Edward M. Kennedy go down the receiving line in the Blue Room in the White House."

In 1968 she again was on the campaign trail—this time for Bobby, who was taking his own run at the presidency. Though Ted wasn't immediately in favor of Bobby running—he worried that his brother would fail to take down a sitting president and divide the party, not to mention hurt Bobby's chances in 1972—the family threw their full might behind him as soon as he'd made his decision. Ethel was pregnant with their eleventh child, so when she wasn't traveling, Joan would be "substitute consort." Bobby's theme was Woody Guthrie's "This Land Is Your Land," so whenever a piano was nearby, Joan ably played it for the crowd.

On June 4, 1968, the music stopped. Just minutes after Bobby won the California primary, virtually assuring him the party's nomination, he was gunned down in Los Angeles. Ted had been out campaigning for him that night about four hundred miles away in San Francisco and was one of many nationwide who learned of the shooting from a live newscast of the primary. Ted maneuvered a flight to Los Angeles, and when Bobby's spokesman Frank Mankiewicz spotted him in the hospital, he saw a broken man. "I have never, ever, nor do I expect ever, to see a face in more grief," Mankiewicz later recalled. "It was beyond grief and agony."

When word reached Joan, she again withered. She stood with the family for Bobby's funeral at St. Patrick's Cathedral in New York, and she was aboard the train that carried his body back to Washington—the route of which was flanked by millions of mourners waving flags in an outpouring of shared grief. But Joan was too devastated to attend the burial at Arlington, Chellis wrote. "She disappeared, and no one knew where she had gone."

After another brother died young, political watchers immediately saw the change in Ted. As the months passed after Bobby's death, he seemed to age in years. Reporter Jeremiah V. Murphy wrote of Ted's August visit to the Holy Cross college campus: "He looked slightly heavier, his hair was cut a little longer, and there were lines around his eyes that were not there before June 5." Continued Murphy:

> *Gone, perhaps forever, is the Teddy Kennedy with the quick smile, the funny quips about "Bobby." Gone is the Ted Kennedy who in the company of close friends would imitate the speech-making of the late James Michael Curley. He has been replaced by an older Ted Kennedy, taller and bigger through the shoulders than both his brothers. He is still handsome, but there is tragedy in his eyes.*

This new, darker Ted spent a lot of time at sea and with his mistresses, while Joan spent more and more time drinking. "It wasn't my personality to make a lot of noise, or to yell or scream or do anything," Joan told Chellis. "My personality was more shy and retiring. And so rather than get mad, or ask questions concerning the rumors about Ted and his girl friends, or really stand up for myself at all, it was easier for me to just go and have a few drinks and calm myself down as if I weren't hurt or angry. I didn't know how to deal with it. And unfortunately, I found out that alcohol could sedate me. So I didn't care as much. And things didn't hurt so much."

Neither Joan nor Ted slowed their public appearances in the wake of Bobby's death. Within months, Joan had announced that she'd be campaigning for a Kennedy family friend, US Representative Edward Boland. The *Boston Globe* reported that she was greeted by "a flurry of awed whispers—'She is pretty! She is pretty!'" Not two weeks later, Joan announced she'd campaign for Bayh, too. Whatever grief she felt, she didn't share it with reporters—not that they didn't prod. One reporter asked, "What will your husband be doing now? The whole world is waiting to know." And another: "Won't it be a strain now that the spotlight has shifted onto Ted?" Joan provided vague non-answers to both.

She drank to cope, to numb, to lessen the heartache and the loneliness. "I drank socially at first, and then I began to drink alcoholically," she later said,

> But at the time I didn't know it. No one really ever does know. I mean, sure, once in a while you have too much to drink and you wake up the next morning and you have a hangover and you think, Oh, I'm not going to do that again. And you say something like that and then a week or two goes by and nothing happens, and then you go and you drink too much again. It becomes a pattern that starts to creep up on you.

Joan wasn't a daily drinker but a binge drinker, staying sober for spells and then diving headfirst into days of uncontrolled drunkenness. The family knew she had a problem but considered drinking a personal vice, a weakness, something that she should buck up and take control of. "I tried to talk about it, but I was embarrassed and Ted was embarrassed about it," she said. "Everybody was embarrassed, but nobody would really talk about it."

Still, the couple muddled through, and in spring 1969, Joan finally got welcome news: She was pregnant again. She again planned to take it easy, as she'd done with her third pregnancy, to lessen the risk of miscarriage. She stayed at the couple's Cape house and curtailed her traveling. Now that election season was over, she focused again on her children—Kara, now nine, Teddy Jr., seven, and Patrick, eighteen months. She seemed to bristle when reporters asked about Ted's prospects for a presidential run. "It's too early to predict anything about anyone," she told one reporter. "I can't say I'd urge him to run. . . . Anyway, it's his decision, not mine." It seemed clear that the next few years of Joan's life would be consumed by the new baby and her husband's potential presidential bid.

In a few short months, Ted would make a tragic decision that would forever alter the family's future.

8

CHAPPAQUIDDICK

By July 18, 1969—the day that Ted was flown to Martha's Vineyard to sail in the Edgartown Regatta—speculation was intense that he was destined for the White House. Even the year before, in the wake of Bobby's slaying, party heads had hounded Ted to join the race and fill his brother's shoes; after serious contemplation, Ted decided he was in no condition emotionally, nor was he prepared mentally, for such an enormous challenge. He certainly didn't have Joan's support. To one interviewer after another, she said that she didn't want him to run. Ascension to the country's highest office had ended the lives of her two beloved brothers-in-law and left their wives widows and their thirteen children without fathers. It was a real and ever-present threat and Joan felt it.

Soon after Bobby's death, Ted received one of many ominous letters and notes. It read, "Don't run for President or Vice President or you will be shot dead, too." Another was sent to Ethel, recently widowed, at Hickory Hill: "If Ted runs for Pres. Or VP he will be killed. We hate Kennedys. Stop him." Still, Ted couldn't dodge the wishes of his party— or of voters, almost 80 percent of whom believed he would one day be the Democratic nominee for president. President Richard Nixon, elected in 1968, had almost immediately started tracking Ted's TV airtime, assuming a new Kennedy could be a threat in 1972. A writer observed: "The feeling of momentum was almost palpable; it was as though he were wearing the clothes of Jack and Bobby, fulfilling their destiny, which was now his own."

But on the hot and humid Friday in Martha's Vineyard, Ted could step away from those pressures and enjoy some time on the water.

Afterward, he visited a gathering of Bobby's former "boiler room" staffers, who gathered on nearby Chappaquiddick Island to reminisce about their days working in the windowless nerve center of the short-lived campaign. They were six young women, all single, meeting up at a small house rented by Kennedy cousin Joey Gargan, a regular of the family campaigns. One of the staffers, Mary Jo Kopechne, was a twenty-eight-year-old who had worked for Bobby in his Senate office since 1965; before that, she'd volunteered for Jack's campaign as a college student. She was a loyal worker and serious minded, known for her "convent school" demeanor and her love for the Boston Red Sox. "Politics was her life," said her father, Joseph Kopechne.

Ted wasn't close with the so-called Boiler Room Girls, but he stopped by the gathering to show his continued appreciation for the work they'd done for his brother. At about 11:15 p.m., Ted asked his chauffeur for the car keys, saying he was tired and wanted to go back to his hotel, and drove off with Mary Jo. Later, he said he'd offered her a ride back to Edgartown. He took a wrong turn and plunged into Poucha Pond, his Oldsmobile coming to a rest wheels-up. "The next thing I recall is the movement of Mary Jo next to me," Ted later said in an inquest,

> *the struggling, perhaps hitting or kicking me, and I, at this time, opened my eyes and realized I was upside down, that water was crashing in on me, that it was pitch black. I knew that and I was able to get a half a gulp, I would say, of air before I became completely immersed in the water. I realized that Mary Jo and I had to get out of the car.*

Ted managed to free himself and swim to the surface. He said he dove repeatedly back to the car, calling Mary Jo's name, but he couldn't free her. She died, entombed in the car. The incident was tragic, clearly an accident, but it was Ted's next steps that would forever cast a shadow on his political career. He stumbled back to the rented cottage, passing houses along the way. He didn't stop for help. Once he reached the cottage, he climbed in the back seat of a rental car there and sent for his cousin and a friend, both lawyers. The three said they returned to the pond to try to save Mary Jo but failed. They never stopped for help, and once it was clear that Mary

Jo was gone, Ted dove back into the water and swam all the way to Edgartown. He didn't report the accident until the next morning, after the car had already been discovered by two boys fishing on the bridge.

While the Kennedy machine went to work—family members flew in from all over the country to be by Ted's side and attempt to reinforce his quickly crumbling reputation—Joan was left in the dark. "No one told me anything," she later said,

> *Probably because I was pregnant, I was told to stay upstairs in my bedroom. Downstairs the house was full of people, aides, friends, lawyers. Ted called his girlfriend Helga before he or anyone even told me what was going on. It was the worst experience of my life. I couldn't talk to anyone about it. No one told me anything. I had to stay upstairs, and when I picked up the phone I could hear Ted talking to Helga. Nothing ever seemed the same after that.*

Joan wasn't included in the plan making, but she certainly was included in the plans—as Ted's steadfast, dutiful wife. She would be by Ted's side at Mary Jo's funeral, which meant forgoing the recommended bed rest. A few weeks after the incident, as public opinion about Ted began to dip and an inquest into the wreck neared, Joan had a miscarriage, losing her third baby in six years. She was days shy of her thirty-third birthday. About this time, she also learned that her mother, Ginny, had left for Europe with a friend after her father asked for a divorce. And in November, just months after a tearful Ted broke the news to him about Chappaquiddick, Joseph P. Kennedy, the onetime indomitable patriarch, suffered yet another stroke. On November 18, 1969, he died in his Hyannis Port home with the core of his surviving family keeping watch at his bedside.

It was a period that would have left even the most stoic person in a traumatized daze. But Joan's sensitivity left her especially vulnerable to grief's disorientation, and instead of rallying around her during this period, most of the Kennedy family turned away—reacting with instinctive distaste to basic human frailty and occupied with being "strong" in the face of their own wounds. Years later, Joan would still have trouble talking about Chappaquiddick. "For a few months everyone had to put on this show and then I just didn't care anymore. I just saw no future," she said. "That's when I truly became an alcoholic."

9

"THE BEGINNING OF THE END"

After Chappaquiddick, Ted and Joan's already-rocky union gradually fell apart. "We remained together for many years longer than we were happy, but I don't think either of us seriously considered a divorce for most of those years," Ted would later write. "So many other things were going on in our lives, so many difficulties, so many tragedies, that breaking up our marriage just wasn't on the agenda. The reasons were many: our children, our faith, my career, and perhaps fear of change."

Joan considered Chappaquiddick "the beginning of the end for Ted and me." She could no longer ignore the rumors of womanizing. She was tired of playing the part of the dutiful senator's wife. Still, she remained in the role, even as the distance between her and Ted became insurmountable. "I believe everything Ted said [about Chappaquiddick]," she told one reporter in June 1970. She called her husband "brave" for diving after Kopechne. "I'm lucky he came out of it alive at all," she added. The union was dead, but breaking free of a Kennedy marriage was unthinkable—it hadn't been done before—and Joan probably found it difficult to imagine being a pioneer in that regard. There was so much to lose in leaving Ted, and little reason for Joan to think that the decision would be received with gentleness and understanding by the rest of the clan.

In addition to taking refuge in the bottle, Joan drew some comfort from her music. She started performing in more prestigious venues, such as when she appeared with the Philadelphia Orchestra—a fund-raising benefit for the governor of Pennsylvania, who also happened to play violin. Joan later recalled the audience response as "electric." The performance's success opened new doors for Joan outside of her role as politician's wife and Kennedy; she was hounded by television networks to "repeat the performance on any prime-time spot she chooses." She'd already carved a niche for herself in narration, starting with *Peter and the Wolf*, and now she was being recognized as a talented pianist as well. Her performances gave her focus, and she'd refrain from drinking while rehearsing for them. "It took a lot out of me," she later admitted.

During this period, she attempted a few affairs but found she wasn't as skilled at romantic liaisons as was her husband. She was terribly unhappy, seeking psychiatric help as she tried to begin acknowledging and treating her drinking problem, but nothing worked. Sometimes she'd leave the children with nannies and disappear for a few days, eventually to be fetched by a friend of the family.

"My mom struggled mightily with mental illness and alcoholism," her son Patrick said. "She, like the rest of my family, was enormously impacted by the violent murders of my uncles and the ensuing emotional impact of that trauma. No one knew what post-traumatic stress disorder was when we were growing up. She unfortunately also had mental illness running in her family, and both the biological predisposition and the environmental triggers pushed her into that illness in a very big way.

"I know she didn't choose to suffer in the way that she suffered," he continued. "This disease was something that took over. Because it's so stigmatized and discriminated against, she never got the kind of early active intervention and support that frankly still aren't available to many people."

As the 1972 presidential race neared, the media began their quadrennial speculation about Ted's possible candidacy. As in 1968, Ted was feeling a push from party leaders to consider a run, but Joan denied reports that the "Kennedy family" was pressuring him into the race. "What family?" she asked a reporter in a rare and bold moment of candor. "What's left of the Kennedys? Besides Ted—only women and children. You don't seriously think we want Ted to be President, do you? I never wanted Ted to be President. Never." Ted ultimately decided against it in 1972, saying that the timing felt off. Joan was too unstable, for starters, and the fear of assassination felt all too real. He was not interested in "subjecting my family to fears over my safety . . ." Kennedy told *Look* magazine. He added, "I feel in my gut that it's the wrong time, that it's too early."

It proved the right call. In late 1973 Joan and Ted got news that would level most parents: Teddy Jr. had cancer. The twelve-year-old had been home sick from school with Ted while Joan was off in Europe. As the youngster walked around the house in a bathrobe, Ted noticed a red lump below his right kneecap. "He grudgingly admitted that it hurt a little—which meant, in Kennedy lexicon, that it hurt a lot," Ted later recalled. The concerned father summoned a doctor, and Teddy Jr. was soon diagnosed with bone cancer. He'd have to have his right leg amputated above the knee. Joan flew home to be at her son's side.

While such a tragedy might unite other parents, at least temporarily, Teddy's illness served as a reminder of how much Ted and Joan had grown apart. They had opposite philosophies on how he should be parented during his treatment and recovery.

Joan explained:

Ted would bring in the whole front line of the Washington Redskins and they would slap little Teddy on the shoulders and say, "Tough guy, you're going to do fine." And in the afternoon Ted would parade all these dignitaries and nurses and this stream of people through the room to meet little Teddy. Ted really believed that we can't let the kid have one moment to himself to rest. He should be kept entertained. And this went on until finally about five or six days later little Ted said, "I'm so tired but I can't tell Dad." And so I had to do it.

Ted, reared in Joe's exuberant but unforgiving household, did not appreciate being told to stand down. "Ted got mad at me," Joan said, "and said I was no fun, that I didn't want my son to have a good time. I had to take it. I guarded the door and I was the traffic cop."

With the Kennedy family's vast resources in his corner, Teddy recovered from the illness. By the time he did, his parents were living apart. Joan had been treated in private sanitariums at least three times, and had been fined for drunken driving after crashing into a car near her McLean, Virginia, home. Each time she stole away for treatment, the press seemed ready to remind her that she wouldn't be recovering in private as headlines reported her most mundane activities like attending or not attending social occasions. As Ted briefly pondered a 1976 run for President, word spread that Joan wouldn't campaign for him with the same vigor she'd done in the past. The couple "has reached an agreement that permits her to lead a life of her own and pursue her own interests," wrote reporter Maxine Cheshire, whose byline appeared over dozens of Joan-related stories over the years. Ultimately, Ted decided against running for the same reasons he'd cited in 1972—he had to focus on his family.

In April 1976, Joan's mother, Ginny, was found dead in her apartment in Cocoa Beach, Florida. Joan said she'd died of alcoholism, and it was a wake-up call. "I couldn't help her," she told Chellis. "But I knew I had to do something for my own survival." And so she made a break from her marriage and the life she felt was driving her to drink. She moved from the home she shared with Ted in McLean to a condominium on Beacon Street in Boston. The children would stay with Ted, except for weekend visits from Patrick. This was Joan's chance to walk away from the pressures of being a political wife and to focus on herself.

"I'd been told that an alcoholic by nature starts to blame everything and everybody except himself," she said. "And that's when I knew that I had to get away from there and have some time for myself." She moved into the seven-room condo, walking distance from a bustling stretch of stores, restaurants, and subway stops, and began life on her own for the first time—though her money and her privileges still came from the Kennedys. Joan's looks still made print, though not always in the way they had during her radiant youth. As *Time* magazine wrote, "public life has not been kind to Joan Kennedy. Its wounds can be seen in the puffy eyes, the exaggerated makeup, the tales of alcoholism." Her sobriety yo-yo'd, her ups and downs chronicled every year or so in *McCall's* or *Look* or *People* magazines. Sometimes the public admissions of her disease fueled her shame and drove her back to drink. It seemed she couldn't handle the applause for her stints of publicized sobriety. She relapsed badly a few days after a 1978 *McCall's* story, for example, then regrouped and conquered the bottle again—albeit temporarily.

But as 1980 neared, Joan seemed ready at long last to be by Ted's side for a presidential run. It was unusual for a fractured couple to be campaigning to become the nation's first couple, but their separation had long been publicized. Some of Ted's handlers argued that Joan shouldn't campaign, with one labeling her a loose canon. But her absence would have spoken even louder. "If Joan did not campaign," Chellis wrote, "all the ghosts of Ted's past might rise up to haunt him: a failed marriage, an alcoholic wife, repeated infidelities, Chappaquiddick. But if she did, voters could assume that she and Ted had reconciled and that if Joan could forgive him, so could they." And Joan, an experienced campaigner with more than a little of her own pride invested in Ted's political success, wanted to campaign; it was a chance to refute the image of her as a hopeless drunk, a chance to prove herself once again as invaluable. It was a chance to prove her mettle to Ted, to the nation, and to herself.

She kept up with the grueling pace and stayed strong for her children, who lived in "torture and torment" as the campaign "raised the dual specters of assassination and the 1969 drowning death of Mary Jo Kopechne at Chappaquiddick." She even had her own platform: She announced she'd commit herself to women's equality. This was buoyed by her return to education, as she was on track to receive a Master's in Education from Lesley College the next year.

Ultimately, Ted's personal missteps were too great to convince voters to pick him over Jimmy Carter, and the campaign to oust the sitting president failed. Ted would never again seek the highest office. After reuniting for the campaign, Joan and Ted finally announced plans to call it quits in 1981 after twenty-three years of marriage. For Joan, it was a chance to reinvent herself again. "I'm learning what it is like for a woman to be living alone and handling all her affairs by herself," she said in an interview. "A lot of women out there can identify with the fact I'm learning about money, I'm learning how to wield a vacuum and how to put the garbage out and how to cook, and how to go to the supermarket.

"I've never been doing better in my entire life."

10

STILL A KENNEDY

JOAN'S LIFE AFTER TED HAS BEEN AS STORIED AND VOLATILE AS ANY other divorcée's. Granted, hers has been more in the public eye than most. The Kennedy name, and its associations with a glamorous moment in the national memory, are not easily shaken off and don't disappear with the finalization of a divorce. But her youngest son Patrick says the public quality of Joan's struggle has been more blessing than curse for millions of people. "She didn't pick being a silent warrior for recognition of mental health and addiction, but she was that face for a generation of people who didn't talk about these issues the way they talk about them today," he says. "She knows it's real and she's made a huge difference in so many people's lives who come up to her on a daily basis and thank her for giving them a sense that they weren't alone."

Joan "had a number of good years when she and my dad were separated," he continued. After the divorce, both parents made extra efforts to spend time with each child alone, to make sure they knew how important they were. "My mom took me overseas on a number of trips," Patrick recalls. "She took me to the Holy Land, throughout Israel, to Masada. We went to midnight mass in Bethlehem. We stopped at Rome and went to St. Peter's, visited all the churches. In London, there were more churches and castles." While Ted focused on more physical activities—fishing, camping, and sailing—Joan exposed her children to culture and traveling.

Her valleys have been many. In 1988, with several drunken-driving arrests under her belt already, she crashed her car into a fence and lost her license for forty-five days. Three years later, she was arrested for drinking vodka straight from the bottle while weaving as she drove her car. Then, in the spring of 2005, a passerby spotted a blonde woman sprawled on a sidewalk on Boston's Beacon Street. A streak of blood ran down the woman's face as she tried to hoist herself up. The passerby, Constance Bacon, didn't learn that the woman she was helping was Joan Kennedy until the next day. "She was conscious," Bacon said. "She had just hit her head pretty hard. She knew that she had fallen and tried to get up and she couldn't. So I just waited until the ambulance came. I had no idea who it was, that it was anything special." Though Joan didn't appear drunk to Bacon, family friends told reporters that she tested well above the legal limit and had taken to secretly drinking mouthwash and vanilla extract. Her street fall—which left her with a concussion and broken shoulder—made headlines again, and Patrick, by then a member of the US House of Representatives, decided he'd shelve the United State Senate run he'd been considering so that he could join his siblings in helping their mother. After a brief-but-publicized legal struggle, the children reached an agreement with Joan: Two financial professionals would watch over her estimated $9.5 million in assets while a guardian would monitor her and guide her medical decisions. The agreement stipulated that if Joan abused alcohol or endangered herself again, more control would be shifted away from her. Any rift caused by the legal proceedings had been long repaired by 2009, when Ted Kennedy died of brain cancer in the Hyannis Port home his family had owned since the 1920s. His new wife, Vicki, was by his side, as were his children. Joan quietly attended his funeral, her presence evoking a quarter-century of his life—both the highs of the long-lost Camelot days and the lows of two assassinations, a near-fatal plane crash, a son's battle with cancer, and a political life nearly derailed.

In 2011, her daughter, Kara, died suddenly of a heart attack at age fifty-one while working out in her Washington, DC, gym. She'd survived lung cancer a decade earlier, despite having been initially told that the illness was inoperable. Ted stepped in and helped her find a surgeon, who removed part of her right lung. The surgery was followed by aggressive chemotherapy and radiation that might have weakened her heart.

For Patrick, so much of his childhood was spent watching his mother struggle. It meant she wasn't always there for him and his siblings, despite her best intentions and efforts. "Her disease sidelined her in a pretty fundamental way," he says. "She did everything she could given the cir-cumstances. This is a powerful disease." But whatever weaknesses she had as a mother, she's worked hard to make up for them as a grandmother. "It is great to have a second chance with her, so to speak," says Patrick, who married schoolteacher Amy Petitgout in 2011. Amy had a daughter from a previous marriage, and she and Patrick had two more children, one in 2012 and one in 2013. Stepdaughter Harper is so enamored with Joan that she gave her a treasured gift—her favorite stuffed animal. "I was aghast that she would part with this pink seal," Patrick recalls. "My mom put it right on the top of her bed. She has it there all the time, not just when we come over. It clearly means something to her. Having my mother back to dote on my babies is great, and they love her."

PART V
Vicki

1

A DIFFERENT TYPE

Victoria Reggie was a stunning woman with high cheekbones, an inviting smile, and brown hair. Attractiveness aside, she did not remotely seem like Ted Kennedy's type of woman—at least not the type that Ted had been well known to chase in his decade divorced from Joan. First, Vicki was smart, a successful partner in a Washington law firm. Second, she wasn't a party girl. As a recently divorced mother of two, she was the furthest thing from one. And third, she had no trouble saying "no" to the senator. So when she opened her door and invited him into her home as a dinner guest to celebrate her parents' fortieth wedding anniversary on June 17, 1991, there was no reason to think the two might hit it off.

Vicki had been told the Commander—as her parents had nicknamed Ted—would be bringing a date, but there he stood alone. She teased, "What's wrong? Couldn't you get a date?"

"I thought you'd be my date," Ted responded.

"Dream on, Kennedy," Vicki shot back.

Vicki's mother overheard the dialogue and was horrified. "Oh, don't talk to men that way," she told her daughter, implying she'd never get another man talking like that, Vicki later recalled.

In truth, few women probably did talk to Ted that way. Ted had earned for himself an embarrassing reputation as a drunken, womanizing, out-of-control mess. Gone were the days of the press kindly refraining from writing about Ted's skirt chasing and booze guzzling. His exploits were regular fodder for not just gossip rags but also mainstream press pieces. Gone, too, were his chiseled good looks. There was still the Kennedy glint in Ted's eye, but decades of partying had ravaged his once-handsome face. As Michael Kelly vividly wrote for *GQ* magazine in 1990:

> *Up close, the face is a shock. The skin has gone from red roses to gin blossoms. The tracery of burst capillaries shines faintly through the scaly scarlet patches that cover the bloated, mottled cheeks. The nose that was once straight and narrow is now swollen and bulbous, with open pores and a bump of what looks like scar tissue near the tip. Deep corrugations crease the forehead and angle from the nostrils and the down-turned corners of the mouth. The Chiclet teeth are the color of old piano keys. The eyes have yellowed, too, and they are so bloodshot, it looks as if he's been weeping.*

Just three months before Ted arrived on Vicki's doorstep, he'd hit the town one night with his son Patrick and nephew William Smith Kennedy, and the result had been disastrous: William would be charged with raping a woman he picked up at a bar and took back to Ted's home in Palm Beach, Florida. A criminal investigation—one that would lead to Ted's testimony being aired on national television, and William's ultimate acquittal on the charges—was under way. Ted's approval ratings were abysmal, sinking into the 40s. Not much was going his way. But as Ted chatted with Vicki in her kitchen, where she grilled steaks and cooked vegetables she'd picked from her garden, he felt more relaxed and light-hearted than he had in years.

This wasn't the first time the two had met. In fact, Vicki's family knew the Kennedys well. Edmund Reggie, Vicki's father, had started campaigning for Jack in the mid-1950s, though the first Kennedy he'd met was Bobby, whose serious eyes Edmund remembered. As for the president-to-be, Edmund was an immediate fan. His loyalty began during the Democratic National Convention of 1956, where Illinois governor Adlai Stevenson won the nomination and Jack had lobbied unsuccessfully to win the vice presidential nomination. Edmund, a lawyer by training who by then had become a Louisiana judge, was a delegate. "There was a film made about the Democratic Party, narrated by Jack, who made such a good impression," Edmund later recalled. He was so impressed that he and a colleague decided that they would try to deliver the Louisi-ana delegation to him. "I was really taken with him completely," he said. "When we got back, every member of my family, including my mother's household . . . every meal said the Hail Mary three times a day, praying for [Jack's] success," he said.

Edmund headed up campaigning in his state for Jack in 1960, for Bobby in 1968, and for Ted in 1980. Edmund's wife, Doris, was a party chairwoman who had cast the only Louisiana floor vote for Ted at the 1980 Democratic Convention—the rest went to Jimmy Carter. "I could never vote for anyone but Teddy," she had declared then. Back when Jack won the office, Edmund had considered joining the administration but decided against it because, he said at the time, "I have six children and I have a fairly decent living here."

Victoria, Vicki for short, was one of the six children, raised in the small city of Crowley, Louisiana, population fifteen thousand. The town is a three-hour drive west of New Orleans, and its slogan—"Where Life is Rice and Easy"—was a nod to its nickname, "Rice Capital of America." At one time, the city bustled with rice harvesting and milling—Jack and Jackie attended the town's annual International Rice Festival in 1959; photos of the event show Jack wearing a rice-studded fedora.

Vicki's home was nice, "but it wasn't a sprawling mansion on five acres of land," recalled Harold Gonzales, longtime managing editor of the *Crowley Post Signal*. "And going to parochial schools, you had to wear uniforms, so you couldn't tell her by her clothes, and Vicki didn't wear a bunch of jewelry or have a car. She borrowed a car from her parents, just like the rest of us." Then he said plainly, "if I had a daughter, I'd want her to be just like Vicki Reggie."

Edmund wanted a home that would keep the six children close by keeping them entertained, so he designed a house with a swimming pool, a big lawn for football, and a nineteen-seat, big-screen theater. "There was a jukebox and pool table and pinball machine and in that big movie the-ater with no adults and plenty of popcorn, we thought we were in heaven," Lila Lambert, a high-school friend, told a reporter.

The Reggie family was of Lebanese descent and very religious, espe-cially Edmund's mother, who attended mass and took communion every day. Vicki was raised Roman Catholic, like Ted. But, big families and religious upbringing aside, they seemed more different than alike, with Vicki hailing from a distinctly different era. Twenty-two years Ted's junior, she graduated Notre Dame High School in 1972; by this time Ted had been married to Joan for fourteen years, had three children, and had served in the Senate for a dozen years.

Lillian Campbell, who had been on staff at Notre Dame for twenty-four years, remembered Vicki as "very sweet and very polite and a very smart girl, except that sometimes, she'd say she was sick and want to go home, although I don't think she was sick at all, just bored, but if Mommy and Daddy say it's OK, what can you do?" In the Kennedy household, children didn't take sick days even when they were truly ill. Even Ted has admitted that he never knew just how serious Jack's health problems were while he was alive. "There were conversational boundaries in our family and we respected them," Ted wrote. "It would never have occurred to us to discuss such private things with each other."

Despite some missed classes, Vicki was valedictorian of her class. For a stint, she also regularly donned a Daniel Boone costume as the school's mascot and danced around the cheerleaders during football games. Cheerleader Georgette Johnson recalled, "What I remember about her is not just intelligence, but her warmth and sincerity. She was genuine, not like a smart person who was above you. She was down to earth." Gonzales echoed this: "[She wasn't] bratty smart, if you know what I mean. Vicki has always been a confidante, like an Ann Landers. She has a good ear, a good knack for sitting down and listening. I bet she was the go-between for more little spats to keep the peace in high school than anybody else." Some friends noted that they didn't realize how much richer Vicki's family was until they all got out of school.

Vicki was close with her father, who had a firm handshake and silver, neatly trimmed hair. "In a blue pinstripe suit with pocket hankie, he makes the models in *GQ* look frumpy," wrote reporter Jack Thomas. Edmund's office felt like a memorial to Democratic politics; photos of Adlai Stevenson and most of the Kennedys were on display. One picture showed Jack Kennedy at a Louisiana yam festival in Opelousas, Louisiana. Vicki grew up vaguely aware of these influences in her parents' life, but, like most high-school kids, was more focused on school than her father's friends. After high school, she attended H. Sophie Newcomb Memorial College in New Orleans, graduating as an English major in 1976. That year, she interned in Ted's Senate office, working in the mailroom. She met Ted just once during that job. "I met him for the photo the last day of work," she later told biographer Adam Clymer. "In fact, I've had the picture, it got stuck to the glass. . . . So that's our evidence of it."

Unlike Ted, Vicki's life by no means had been mapped out for her. After college she found herself at a crossroads, feeling dispassionate about what to do next. She fumbled around until she settled on going to graduate school for English, and she made the life-altering decision to ask Gardner B. Taplin, an eighteenth-century British Literature professor, to write a recommendation letter. Taplin was a brilliant man who had once written a book on the life of Victorian poet Elizabeth Barrett Browning. He wore three-piece tweed suits even in the sweltering New Orleans summer, Vicki later recalled. Vicki approached and asked him for his grad-school endorsement. He refused, and she was baffled.

"No?" she asked.

"No, you shouldn't go to graduate school in English," he said.

Vicki stammered. "Why?"

"Are you willing to bask in the reflected light of some man's glory for the rest of your life?" Taplin asked.

I don't know, Vicki thought. *Who you have in mind?* But what she said out loud was, "Why are you asking me that?"

Taplin launched into a talk about Carla Hills, who had been appointed by President Gerald Ford as the first woman to serve as US Secretary of Housing and Urban Development. She was just the third woman in the country's history to hold a cabinet position. Vicki had never heard of her. After schooling Vicki on Hills, Taplin told her that she should set her sights higher: He told her that he envisioned her as a lawyer.

"I'd never considered it," Vicki told a crowd gathered by the Harry Walker Speakers Bureau. "My father was a lawyer. My father was a *judge*. Why hadn't I considered it? I think it was because I was a girl. Really. It just didn't dawn on me. I feel foolish when I say that to you now, but it didn't dawn on me."

With Taplin's encouragement bolstering her ego, Vicki was accepted to Tulane Law School and graduated summa cum laude in 1979. Years later, she would credit that uncomfortably dressed professor with pushing her to be more than she'd ever envisioned and sending her down the path to become a lawyer.

"There is nothing good that happened in my life since then that would've happened without that decision," she said.

Afterward, she moved to Chicago, where she clerked for Judge Robert A. Sprecher in the Seventh Circuit Court of Appeals. After two years, she moved to Washington to join the law firm with which she'd later become partner: Keck, Mahin and Cate, where she specialized in savings and loan matters. Along the way, she married Washington telecommunications attorney Grier Raclin in 1981, with whom she had two children, one boy and one girl. Vicki and Grier divorced after nine years of marriage. Divorce papers showed that they led a comfortable life, if nowhere near as extravagant as the Kennedys were accustomed: Vicki won the couple's Washington home, valued at nearly three quarters of a million dollars. She also got their Nantucket vacation home and about sixty thousand dollars a year in support from her ex.

In June 1991, Vicki was still healing from the divorce when she planned to honor her parents for their anniversary. Everything was to be "very casual," she later recalled. Certainly, she thought nothing of the invitation extended to her father's best friend. Ted had been to her home for dinner before, in fact, and no sparks had flown. Ted later wrote:

> But as much as Vicki and I had seen each other at various events over the years, I think that anniversary dinner party night was the first time I really saw Vicki. I helped her as she took the place setting away for the date I didn't bring, and I hung out with her in the kitchen as she prepared dinner. We shared easy conversations about issues of the day and spent a lot of the evening laughing.

When dinner was over, Ted asked if he could call her for dinner the next night. Vicki said he could, but Ted later learned that after the door closed, she thought, "Did I just say *yes*? Have I lost my mind?" Ted called the next day as promised. It turned out to be one of the first steps on Ted's road to redemption.

2

THE WOMANIZING ENDS

BEFORE VICKI, THE CALIBER OF WOMEN IN TED'S LIFE HAD BEEN SO LOW that Michael Kelly shared this telling anecdote in his *GQ* profile involving an ex-girlfriend in her mid-twenties whom Kelly had interviewed for the story:

> *As the former girlfriend and I were finishing up our talk, she told me of a big party to which she was going that night. "It's going to be reeelly, reeelly great!" she said. "They're going to have these drinks called sharks, which are reeelly, reeelly fun. You have this plastic shark in your glass and you also have a plastic mermaid and you push the shark and the mermaid together and then pour some red stuff over the mermaid that looks like blood."*
>
> *"Grenadine?" I said.*
>
> *"I think so," she said.*
>
> *At what age does it stop being fun and start being hell on earth to spend your evenings with someone who gets reeelly, reeelly excited about novelty cocktails?*

Ted—much later than most men, it must be said—seemed finally to be approaching that age.

Edmund Reggie had considered Ted a best friend since the late 1960s. He had heard the rumors and seen the tabloid covers. While Ted maintained that some of the hell-raiser tales were "so outrageous that I can't imagine how anyone could really believe them," even he acknowledged that others were accurate. In the hard-to-deny category fell early

1990 photographs of Ted having sex on a boat with a much-younger blonde—an exploit so widely publicized that Washington cronies nodded with a smirk to Ted's "position on offshore drilling." Learning that the senator had set his infamous sights on Edmund's daughter could have been upsetting to the judge. Not so, Edmund insisted in an earnest, if unfocused, response to a reporter. "I've known Ted Kennedy a lot of years. . . . When does dating become womanizing? Does he exploit women? I think his record shows just the opposite. I don't know that there's a member of the US Senate who has ever championed the civil rights of women at all levels, married, single, mothers, unwed, wed—I think his record is the best.

"Well, if you look at Ted Kennedy's commitment record as a senator, I don't know of a member of the Senate who's been there thirty years who's more committed to a more definable or predictable position than Ted Kennedy. So he's a person capable of the finest definition of commitment, and marriage is the ultimate commitment. . . ." It sounded as if Reggie were trying to convince himself with his comments; and his nervousness, given Ted's dismal track record in personal relationships with actual women, was justified. But the faith he extended to Ted ended up being well-founded. Vicki found in Ted a capacity for personal commitment that no one before had been able to tap.

At first, Ted and Vicki got together for dinner once or twice a week. Their playful banter continued as the relationship blossomed. One night Ted mentioned that his approval rating had plummeted to 48 percent. Vicki quipped, "That's a relief, because I never go out with anyone whose approval is less than 47." Ted did well when he met Vicki's children, Curran, then eight years old, and Caroline, who was five. Ted, a father figure not only to his own three children but also to more than a dozen nieces and nephews, had long ago perfected the art of teaching children to imitate animal sounds. He used that skill on Curran and Caroline as well, Vicki recalled. "They were a little older than the real animal sounds age, that are good for, like, two, three years old," she said, "but he still came out with them." Ted began keeping up on football and baseball because Curran loved sports, and he sprawled on the living-room floor with Caroline to color pictures.

Those early date nights were often interrupted by one or both of the children calling for "Mom-my." "I remember one night, I said I really apologize. Look, I'm so sorry. It must not be a pleasant dinner for you because I have to run upstairs five times," Vicki recalled. Ted would hear none of it. "He said, 'No, you don't understand, a child calling 'mother' is the most beautiful sound in the world.'"

In mid-August, after the two had been dating just a couple of months, they had their first tiff. Ted had sailed from Hyannis to Nantucket to visit Edmund and Doris Reggie at their second home. Vicki was there visiting, and Ted tried to persuade her to sail back to Hyannis Port. It was hurricane season, however, and Vicki's response was terse: "There is no way."

Kennedy men—for whom physical courage had totemic importance—were not used to having their gutsiness balked at. And they were especially not used to hearing the word "no." "I won't say that I was hurt by Vicki's refusal to trust me at the helm of a fifty-foot boat sailing across open water in the path of a Category 2 hurricane," Ted said. "But I didn't call her for two weeks."

After Labor Day, Vicki finally broke the ice and called him. Ted remembers saying at the end of the conversation, "Well, listen, I was just thinking, uh—I know you don't want to go out a lot because of your children, so, uh—I thought I would come over to your house for dinner." From that point on, Ted spent nearly every dinner at Vicki's house. It was an old-fashioned courtship, both would later say. What they didn't say explicitly was this: For Ted, he began this relationship with Vicki the way he should have with Joan—slowly, spending time to get to know each other before taking the ultimate commitment plunge.

With Joan, the marriage had been too fast, and the couple's time together far too brief. Ted realized this. "We certainly had not spent a lot of time together during our courtship, and we didn't spend the necessary time together in the early years," Ted said. "Almost immediately after the wedding celebrations were over, I plunged back into law school and the moot court competition, my travels, and campaign work for Jack. And so we never benefited from that critical but fleeting interval in which a young husband and wife get to know themselves and each other as a married couple."

Surely it helped that by the time Ted met Vicki, he'd not only played the field but had the field named after him. And his presidential hopes had long ago dissipated. He'd endured heartache and encased himself in frivolity to remove even the possibility of getting close to someone about whom he could care again. With Vicki, he decided to risk getting hurt because she was worth it.

"As the months went on, I realized that I loved this woman very deeply and that my love for her was overcoming all the defenses I'd built up in myself against the potential heartbreak of marrying again," he said. On January 14, 1992, Ted proposed to Vicki during a performance of the opera *La Boheme* at the Metropolitan Opera in New York. She said yes. Just as he'd done some thirty-four years prior, Ted called the father of the woman he loved. This time, he happened to also be calling one of his best friends. Edmund wasn't surprised to get the call. "He said, 'You know, I love Vicki very much and I've asked her to marry me, and I want to ask you and Doris'—and, you know, Ted did it the proper way."

The couple didn't announce the engagement straight away. Instead, they waited several weeks before telling Ted's children. Vicki told her youngsters as well. All the kids were asked not to repeat the news, but Caroline was just six and this was Washington; she shared the secret with a friend in her kindergarten class who in turn told his parents—who happened to work for the *Washington Post*. Soon, reporters descended on Vicki's hometown of Crowley. Residents of the small town were both wary and protective. "If they've come to Crowley looking for dirt on Vicki, they've come to the wrong place, because no one's got anything bad to say about her," said Gonzales, the newspaper editor. "Not that anybody's hiding anything. It's just there's nothing bad about her. But some reporters try to put words in your mouth because they can't believe this good-looking, 38-year-old girl would want to be married to a 60-year-old Teddy Kennedy, with his past."

The word was out, but Ted still hadn't given Vicki a ring. In April, while visiting Ted's sister Pat at a rented house in the US Virgin Islands, Ted placed a ring near a coral head under the water at Buck Island Reef. As he and Vicki snorkeled, he pointed beneath the water for her to look. "So I swam down underwater, and there was this," Vicki said, pointing to the sizeable diamond on her left hand, "sitting on the coral. And I thought the fish was eating something there. Teddy said he was dying. Can you imagine that fish eating the ring before I got to it?"

As storybook a relationship as theirs sounded, there were skeptics in Washington. With Ted's approval rating so low, grumblings had started that Vicki was merely a shrewd attempt on the senator's part to revamp his battered image. Edmund Reggie dismissed the notion. "If anybody were looking to strategize a political campaign, he would do it, I think, using easier methods . . . than committing his whole life to another woman and her children," he said. Reggie joked that no one could know and say, "'Now, Senator, if you marry Vicki, you'll gain 10 points in the polls or 25 points in the polls . . .' I don't think there's any such empirical evidence anywhere in the world, and so, for him to have landed on this idea to have undertaken a lifetime commitment to a woman without some kind of empirical evidence falls of its own weight, and it's ludicrous."

Vicki knew there were skeptics but shrugged them off. "I knew I was right," she later said. "I knew the man."

The two were married in a private ceremony at Ted's house in McLean on July 3, 1992, with just their immediate families present. Ted gave his new bride an oil painting he'd done of daffodils as a nod to a William Wordsworth poem they had recently read together.

The union did boost Ted in the polls, incidentally. And, as it turned out, he needed all the help he could get.

3

BATTLING ROMNEY

For decades, Ted Kennedy's name on the Massachusetts ballot seemed enough to guarantee his victory. Though the nation's Democrats had decided resoundingly in 1980 that they didn't want a Kennedy presidency, Ted's victory for the Senate in his home state time and again was a given. Until 1994. By then, his reputation as a womanizer and drunk had reduced him to a national joke and paved the way for his first real opponent in years: Mitt Romney, a wealthy forty-seven-year-old businessman making his first foray into politics. The son of former Michigan governor and onetime presidential candidate George Romney, Mitt had what Ted seemed to be lacking: He was a pious family man, raising five sons with Ann, his wife of twenty-five years. He'd complained so much about the bad example Kennedy was setting that one morning, in the summer of 1993, Ann finally turned to him and said, "If you don't stand up and do something about it, then, you know, shut up and stop bothering me."

In traditionally Democrat country, Republican Mitt "was positioning himself as a moderate, almost an apolitical candidate," Ted later wrote. "He was pro-choice, he declared. But efficiency was what he really had to sell: sleeves-rolled-up, businesslike efficiency, to replace the senior senator's outdated ways." It was to be an expensive race: Ted would take out a two-million-dollar loan against his Virginia home and spend more than six million dollars on the campaign. By Labor Day, a *Boston Globe* poll found Mitt and Ted in a virtual tie. Ted realized he was no shoo-in for the post he'd held for thirty-two years, and his campaign strategy had to be updated. In a move that highlighted just how different Ted's union with Vicki was compared with his first marriage to Joan, Ted asked Vicki for advice. She was not just a helper in his campaign, showing her pretty face and reading his speeches; she was a collaborator. When Mitt touted in ads that he'd created thousands of jobs, Vicki suggested to Ted and his campaign managers that they look closely at Mitt's business record. She knew from her work as a bank lawyer that venture capitalists sometimes cut payrolls, "that there would be a lot of downsizing . . . a lot of restructuring of debts and that sort of thing." At first, her suggestion didn't seem to sink in with the advisers, so she even circled back to it to make sure it had registered. It did, and the campaign hired The Investigative Group, Inc., a detective firm, to probe Mitt's company Bain Capital. The firm uncovered slashed jobs, wages, and benefits at a Bain-bought factory in Indiana, helping to bolster Ted's campaign.

With Vicki at his side—as well as a few longtime aides, some of whom were resurrected from retirement to help—Ted was having fun campaigning. A *Boston Globe* story in June described him as "energized" and "feisty." Taking issue with a *Boston Globe* column that questioned whether Kennedy's charisma had waned after three decades in office, Kennedy pointed to his Senate committee's passage of the nation's most comprehensive health care reform measure and asked a campaign crowd, "Do I still have my charisma?"

Vicki went after women voters with vigor (or "vigah," as the Kennedys would say). While Joan had hosted countless teas and spoken to women's gatherings, Vicki was targeting a new woman—not just the stay-at-home mom who influenced her husband's vote, but the working mom who balanced her professional world with her family and cared deeply about her community and its policies. "She was a natural," Ted would recall. "As women in that group have since told me, she was one of them, swapping stories of working motherhood. . . . She listened to the stories of women who have since been her very good friends." But Ted wasn't the young candidate representing the New Frontier anymore, and Vicki wasn't automatically hounded and adored the way that Joan had once been. In fact, plenty of young voters had no idea who Ted was. Some, when asked if they'd like to meet Mrs. Kennedy, replied, "No, thank you!" So Vicki would politely ask them for their vote anyway and move along.

With Mitt gaining on Ted in the polls, the senator beefed up his television commercials. Some had more bite than any he'd run previously. Ted liked to point out that in thirty-two years in politics, he'd never referred to his opponent by name. But this campaign, Ted called Mitt out, attacking his business practices and highlighting his campaign missteps. Vicki helped make that call: "It was important to talk about his opponent's record," she told Clymer, "because his opponent was running on his record. I mean, he put that in play. He said, 'I'm a business man. I've done this, therefore I'm qualified to be your U.S. Senator.'"

For one commercial, Ted donned a white lab coat for a health care–related commercial. Vicki saw him and nixed it. The press reported that she thought the coat made Ted look fat, but, in reality, she said he simply didn't look like himself. "It doesn't ring true to me," she said. "It looked like a costume as opposed to what he really was doing." With Vicki's Lebanese ancestry, Ted was able to reach out to a new ethnicity as well. One Lebanese grandmother pulled Vicki aside and quizzed her about Ted: "So, honey, is he good to you?" "Do you love him?" "Does he eat Lebanese food?" Vicki said yes to all three, and the woman said, "OK, honey, I'm gonna vote for him for the first time in my life."

While Joan had always infused Ted's campaigns with classical music, Vicki's tastes could lean decidedly more contemporary. At an Aerosmith fund-raiser for Ted, the senator relied on his wife while writing a speech that managed to weave in several Aerosmith song references. The *Boston Globe* story reported a few of them, including how Ted "said he needed the help of Aerosmith because he wanted to 'Walk This Way' down to Washington."

Mitt Romney failed to resonate with voters, and Ted proved impossible to beat. On Election Day, Ted won his seat by a margin of 58 percent to Mitt's 41 percent. Later, as he and Vicki celebrated with friends and family, Ted shrugged off the toasts and congratulations being offered him and began, "Well, this victory really isn't about me. It's about my family, and it's about the people of Massachusetts and their residual goodwill that goes all the way back to Grampa's day—"

Vicki cut him off. "Please excuse my language, but BULLSHIT! This is just ridiculous!"

As Ted stared at her, she continued: "You know, Teddy, if you had lost, it would've been *you* that lost. It wouldn't have been your family that lost. *You* would've lost. You *won. You* won! Not your family. *You.*"

4

NEW KIND OF KENNEDY

As Vicki's life intertwined with Ted's, she became a new kind of Kennedy wife. She was his sounding board on the issues, and he respected her opinion and her input. Finally, being married to a Kennedy man wasn't about just propping up his values and ambitions, but about joining forces and tackling matters as a team. "I was involved in every issue that mattered in the life of our country," Vicki later recalled. "And I was lucky enough to be involved in those issues with the love of my life." Ted even respected Vicki enough to float the idea of her someday becoming a senator—a suggestion she quickly dismissed.

Their life together made fewer headlines than Ted's life with Joan had. Surely, Ted's abdication of the pursuit of the presidency helped, as did Vicki's reluctance to talk to most reporters. They still occasionally made a Splash together—Splash being the Portuguese water dog that the couple adopted and that would soon become a fixture on Capitol Hill by Ted's side. Ted and Vicki in 2006 wrote a children's book from Splash's point of view called *My Senator and Me: A Dog's-Eye View of Washington, D.C.* And their names were frequently listed among other hobnobbers at galas and musical performances and other tie-requiring shindigs. Every year they threw theme parties for family and friends, at which Ted and Vicki would don costumes. At Ted's sixty-fifth birthday party, the theme was "the ocean." Ted dressed as Ponce de Leon, and Vicki as the fountain of youth, a playfully self-aware reference to their age difference. At another party—for his staff at Christmas—Vicki dressed as Anastasia to Ted's Rasputin.

Vicki had a profoundly positive impact on Ted, far beyond merely repairing his reputation. After hearing him warbling at a holiday party one year, Vicki gave him voice lessons as a Christmas present. The result was a deep bass so surprising that radio talk-show host Upton Bell said he worried that playing it might cause people to drive off the road. "He's obviously been practicing," Bell said after playing Ted's rendition of the Tennessee Ernie Ford classic "Sixteen Tons." Ted also credited Vicki for helping him shrink his waistline. While stumping for John Kerry in 2004, he dropped forty pounds, "revealing the trademark Kennedy chiseled features and a much trimmer physique." Asked how he dropped the weight, Kennedy replied, "Vicki, Vicki, Vicki."

Vicki would provide Ted strength in 1995 when his beloved mother Rose died at 104 years old. He'd been the Kennedy child with wit and self-deprecation enough to needle his mother when she became too demanding, and Rose had proved herself more than capable of needling back. He described a framed note from "Mother" that had long been hanging on his office wall, in which she reacted to a comment he'd once made to a reporter. "Dear Teddy," Rose had written. "I just saw a story in which you said: 'If I was President . . .' You should have said, 'If I were President . . .' which is correct because it is a condition contrary to fact."

The memory got a laugh from the mourners, and Ted's tone turned more serious: "Mother always thought her children should strive for the highest place. But inside the family, with love and laughter, she knew how to put each of us in our place. She was ambitious not only for our success, but for our souls."

Ted continued to play a father-figure role in the lives of his nieces and nephews, and Vicki would be his backbone as he watched tragedy beset the next generation. Michael Kennedy, Ethel's sixth child and Ted's 1994 reelection campaign manager, died in a skiing accident in 1997. A year and half later, in the summer of 1999, while piloting a Piper single-engine plane to Hyannis Port to attend the wedding of Rory, Ethel's youngest, John F. Kennedy Jr. crashed into the ocean, killing him, his wife, Carolyn Bessette Kennedy, and his sister-in-law, Lauren Bessette. It was a devastating blow to Ted, who was very close with his nephew.

John Jr. had the best Kennedy qualities—the looks, the smarts, the discipline, and the zest for life. Ted had stayed close with Jackie through the years, and he had loved her dearly. "She was always there for our family in her special way," he would say in his eulogy for her in 1994, after she succumbed to lung cancer. "She was a blessing to us and to the nation—and a lesson to the world on how to do things right, how to be a mother, how to appreciate history, how to be courageous. No one else looked like her, spoke like her, wrote like her, or was so original in the way she did things." After Jackie's death, Ted felt even more protective of her two children. John Jr. had always been seen as heir to Jack's throne, and, thanks to Jackie's grounding influence, not just by birthright.

When John Jr. introduced his uncle Teddy at the 1988 Democratic National Convention in Atlanta, he eloquently and unwaveringly called a generation to public service and was rewarded with a lengthy standing ovation. Though John Jr. never ran for office, he was an important behind-the-scenes player, throwing his name and money behind Democratic causes and candidates. Now another Kennedy had been taken in his prime, and Ted was heartbroken.

With Vicki and her father, Edmund, looking on in the Church of St. Thomas More, Ted eulogized his nephew in a stirring tribute a week after the plane went down. "From the first day of his life, John seemed to belong not only to our family, but to the American family. The whole world knew his name before he did," Ted said. Sadly, Ted was becoming way too good at these eulogies. "He had a legacy, and he learned to treasure it. He was part of a legend, and he learned to live with it. Above all, Jackie gave him a place to be himself, to grow up, to laugh and cry, to dream and strive on his own. John learned that lesson well. He had amazing grace. He accepted who he was, but he cared more about what he could and should become. He saw things that could be lost in the glare of the spotlight. And he could laugh at the absurdity of too much pomp and circumstance."

Finally, in a somber nod to the many tragedies that had come before, Ted ended by paraphrasing a Yeats poem about a man who died young. "We dared to think, in that other Irish phrase, that this John Kennedy would live to comb gray hair. . . . But like his father, he had every gift but length of years."

Three years later, Ted was sitting in a doctor's office with his daughter, Kara, at Johns Hopkins Hospital. Kara, then age forty-two, had recently seen a doctor for a routine visit and been sidelined with a shocking diagnosis of lung cancer. Ted had insisted on procuring for her the best possible medical team for another opinion. The news was grim. Not only did she have cancer, it was inoperable, and she had less than a year to live. As he had done with his son, Teddy, the senator went on the offensive. Rejecting the prognosis, he thanked the doctor and left, and then he went to work. "We were told that every doctor we would consult would say the same thing, and I recall saying, 'Fine. I just want to hear every one of them say it,'" Ted recalled. He didn't rest until he found a surgeon who agreed to operate, removing a portion of Kara's right lung in January 2003.

After the surgery, Ted and Vicki took Kara to her chemotherapy treatments in Washington in the morning. When Ted had to leave for Senate work, Vicki would stay behind. Seven years after Kara's aggressive treatment, Ted reported that she was a cancer-free and active mother of two. (Kara would later die of a sudden heart attack in 2011, nine years after her cancer diagnosis. Some oncologists would speculate that the aggressive treatment that spared her from the cancer—and prolonged her life—might have weakened her heart.)

Ted and Vicki didn't know it at the time, but the battle they faced with Kara's illness was an overture for an even more dire diagnosis they'd receive a decade later. Again their mantra would be, "One step at a time."

5

TIME TO SAIL

MAY 17, 2008, STARTED OUT AS A PICTURE-PERFECT DAY. THE WEATHER was ideal—warm but not hot, with a crisp breeze—for Vicki and Ted to take the boat out for the first sail of the year. Ted was still keyed up from the day before, when he felt so "on" that he'd set aside his prepared remarks and spoken from his heart at a ribbon cutting for a learning center at New Bedford Whaling National Historical Park. As he and Vicki geared up for the day's sail, they did the mundane things that couples do on lovely mornings together: They had coffee, read the newspapers, talked about family matters. Before breakfast, Ted thought he'd take the dogs for a walk. He never made it outside. As Ted walked past the grand piano that had once belonged to his mother, he felt disoriented. He moved toward the door to get outside for some air, but he couldn't go any farther. In a haze, he lowered himself into a chair and lost consciousness.

Judy Campbell, Ted and Vicki's household assistant, spotted him and called out for Vicki. Judy called 911, then Ted's Boston physician, as Vicki cradled her husband's head and kissed his cheek. "You're going to be okay," she whispered.

In truth, Vicki had no idea if he'd be okay. She had no idea what was happening at all. "I just knew it was something very serious, something grave," she later recalled. Ted was first taken by medics to a local hospital, and then transported via medevac to Boston for tests. The initial diagnoses batted around were so wildly varied that Vicki couldn't keep up. "I went from concern to fear to terror to uncertainty," Vicki said. As Ted slowly regained consciousness, doctors said they thought he'd had a generalized seizure, but they didn't know what had caused it or whether others might follow. Finally, they had a tentative diagnosis: Ted might have a brain tumor.

"By the end of that day, it was like, you know what? Prove it to me," Vicki would later say. "Enough already. I've had a terrible day. Prove it to me. And I wasn't in denial, but I wasn't in acceptance, either. I just wanted them to show us. And they did."

The following Monday, a biopsy confirmed the diagnosis of a malignant glioma in the left parietal lobe. "Vicki and I privately were told that the prognosis was bleak—a few months at most," Ted said. Most diagnoses of the sort are: Only 30 percent of people with the condition are still alive two years after the diagnosis; just 10 percent of patients may live five years or longer. As with the other cancer diagnoses he'd faced, Ted refused to accept defeat. Neither did Vicki. Make no mistake, she would later tell an audience of cancer patients and their loved ones, Ted's brain tumor wasn't his alone. "It was our brain tumor," she said. "And that's always how I've described it. It was our brain tumor in every single way."

Almost fifty years after Camelot, the Kennedy name still drew the public's fascination and attracted the media spotlight. Photographers and TV crews were camped out on the hospital lawn, so Vicki orchestrated a photograph with a laughing Ted surrounded by his cheery-looking children to accompany the news of his diagnosis. The upbeat tone was intentional. Ted felt a strong obligation to be a role model, particularly while facing such a terrible diagnosis. He'd endured hard times before, and he'd heard from countless strangers how much his strength had helped them through their own trials, no matter how desperate. If Ted could put a hopeful face on this latest obstacle, maybe he could help someone else live just one happier day, he reasoned. And besides, getting his own cancer diagnosis was nothing compared with having heard the diagnoses of his two children. "His perspective was that it was so much worse when it's your child," Vicki said. "He could take it. He was going to be a role model for others. He wasn't putting on a happy face; he understood himself and what he needed to do to stay ahead of the darkness, as he put it."

For Ted, dodging the darkness meant sailing. He and Vicki missed out on that sail May 17, so when they returned from the hospital, they hopped aboard their schooner *Mya* and went to sea. "Everything seemed back to normal, except for the crowd of cameramen and reporters who awaited us onshore," Ted said.

Back at the homestead, Ted summoned a doctor friend to recruit the nation's best medical experts to draw up the battle plans. The result was an extraordinary display of Ted's power and wealth: More than a dozen experts from at least six academic centers heeded the invitation, the *New York Times* reported. Some of the doctors flew to Boston for an in-person meeting May 30; others requested test results and medical records so that they could participate by phone. In the meeting, the experts weighed Ted's options: surgery, radiation, and chemotherapy, according to Dr. Raymond Sawaya, a nationally renowned neurosurgeon who was part of the meeting. Ted said he wanted to be "prudently aggressive" and to make the process as helpful to others as possible.

"If I can show that there is hope for me, perhaps I can give hope to all those who face this kind of disease," he said. But while they aimed to stay optimistic, they were far from naive about it, Vicki said. They understood the gravity of the diagnosis, and Ted quickly got his affairs in order—legal, legislative, financial, and spiritual. That preparation allowed them to both live in the present and to focus on some goals Ted had set.

"We had an unspoken pact between us that we would not grieve until it was time to grieve," she said. "We weren't going to ruin the time we had, which we hoped was going to be a very long time, that we weren't going to ruin it by talking about what-ifs. We weren't going to spend our time dying. We were going to spend our time living, and we did that and it was magnificent."

Ted's first goal was to make it to the Democratic National Convention in August 2008, where he hoped to speak. It was just three months away, which until recently would have seemed like no time at all. But when faced with a terminal disease, it was a lofty goal indeed. Ted wanted to sway the odds in his favor. His team of medical experts had been divided on whether he should undergo surgery to remove as much of the tumor as possible. Most were strongly in favor of it, but two of the doctors balked "because the cancer was not a discrete nodule, but was spread over a large area, making it unlikely that most of it could be removed," wrote Dr. Lawrence Altman for the *Times*. "Chances for success are somewhat proportional to the amount of tumor removed, although experts disagree about precisely how much visible tumor must be removed for the best chances."

Ted opted for surgery. It lasted a grueling three and a half hours, and part of it was performed while Ted was conscious so that doctors could test his neurological function. As neurologist Vivek Deshmukh described to *Newsweek*, Ted likely would have been put to sleep to have his skin incised, some bone removed, and the protective layer of the brain cut open. "But once you've started removing the tumor, the brain itself is not a pain-sensitive structure. That's when you have the patient awake," he said. As the surgeon removes the growth, he constantly asks the patient questions and has the patient perform activities, such as raising an arm or moving a leg. Ted likely didn't feel pain, but he might have felt "some manipulation up there," Deshmukh said.* After Ted's surgery was over, doctors told reporters it'd been a success. Similarly, Vicki e-mailed upbeat notes relaying the positive news to the family.

For the next six weeks, Vicki and Ted drove from Hyannis Port to Boston—a three-hour drive round-trip—five days a week for radiation and chemotherapy treatments. From the outset, Vicki embraced her role as caregiver. Ted had always praised her strength in crises, and she stayed strong in his presence. Sometimes, when the weight of it all got too heavy, she'd slip into the shower and dissolve into tears. But when she would reemerge, she'd again play the role of protector. "He needed me to be his advocate, and I took the role willingly," she said. "He could be the happy lion, and I was the fierce lioness."

That didn't mean her wishes always beat out Ted's. Just before the Independence Day recess, the Senate had a vote on a bill to cut Medicare reimbursement rates. Democrats had fallen a single vote short of the sixty needed to prevent the cut. Ted and Vicki were driving to Boston for treatment when he read the news in the paper. "Medicare is in jeopardy!" he declared in the car. He was consumed by guilt. "I would've been the one vote," he said. "I need to get back to Washington."

_____

* Though Deshmukh didn't treat Ted, he was intimately familiar with brain surgery: He'd performed surgery two years prior on another senator, Senator Tim Johnson of South Dakota, who had required emergency surgery after a brain hemorrhage.

Vicki balked. "You can't go back to Washington," she insisted. "You just had brain surgery."

Ted wouldn't be swayed. The guilt was too much. He'd been away getting treatment, unable to vote, and that single vote had hurt a cause he'd fought for for much of his Senate career—health care. So, just four weeks after his surgery, he orchestrated his return to the Senate.

"It was a secret little background thing that no one knew about, except the majority leader and Teddy, who was absolutely determined," Vicki said.

The vote was called again, and as the roll got under way—the senators' "aye" and "nay" responses going down on record for a second time—Ted appeared in the chamber. Applause erupted. Vicki, who was watching from the gallery, began to weep. The ovation was thundering. "Immediately, the roll call came to a pause, as the cheers for Mr. Kennedy drowned out all other sound," one reporter wrote. Not only did Ted's single vote reverse the Medicare cut, but nine Republicans changed sides. The final tally was sixty-nine to thirty, giving the Democrats a veto-proof majority. Senator Kay Bailey, a Texas Republican, was disappointed in the vote, but not in Ted's appearance. "There wasn't a person in the room or in the gallery who wasn't thrilled to see Senator Kennedy back, looking so good," she said.

Buoyed by that triumphant return to the Senate, Ted and Vicki refocused on his convention goal. Ted called his friend, political adviser Bob Shrum, for help. Shrum had been Ted's speechwriter for years, and he'd worked with eight Democratic presidential candidates (none of whom won). Despite his egg on the Oval Office efforts, Shrum was respected as a political wordsmith. He'd helped write Ted's well-received concession speech at the 1980 Democratic Convention. ("For all those whose cares have been our concern, the work goes on, the cause endures, the hope still lives, and the dream shall never die.") Vicki and Bob became Ted's sounding board as he secretly worked to craft what they knew would likely be his last convention speech. "I knew essentially what I wanted to say at the outset, and Bob and Vicki and I have a synergistic way of working together," Ted said.

For Vicki, the convention goal was invigorating. Every morning, she and Ted would start work at ten o'clock in a secret practice space they'd set up inside the Cape Cod house. They weren't sure what kind of tele-prompter setup would work best for Ted, so they rotated positioning it from front and to the sides before deciding that he could follow the text best when it was in front of him. On August 24, the day before the convention, they boarded a chartered jet for Denver, the convention site, with family and friends and Ted's internist. After settling into an apartment they'd rented in Denver, Ted began practicing his speech again with a teleprompter. A minute in, he had to stop. A sharp pain stabbed his left side.

"You know, I really don't feel well," he said. He was taken to a hospital, where he got a maddening diagnosis. After prevailing against brain surgery and chemotherapy and radiation, Ted's big night was being threatened by a kidney stone. Vicki, who had fought so long to be stoic for her husband, burst into tears as doctors readied to give him potent pain medication.

There's little worse than seeing someone you deeply love in physical agony. But Vicki knew that this could be Ted's final public appearance. She knew that Ted's mental clarity was essential to his accomplishing what had become an important goal for both of them: his speaking at the convention. She knew that his ability to make choices for himself was one of the last things Ted had.

"If you give him pain medicine, then you will have made the decision for him about speaking tonight," she cried. "You can't take away his ability to make this decision for himself. He's worked too hard for this night."

Doctors assured her that the first dose would have left Ted's bloodstream before his speech, so they administered it. A few hours later, a nurse gave another dose—unwelcome news for the concerned wife. "Vicki, shall we say, remonstrated with her," Ted recalled.

Drowsy in his hospital bed, Ted looked up at his wife. "What do you think?" he asked.

"You can just go out and wave," she said. "Just go out there with the family and wave."

Ted wouldn't admit defeat. He couldn't do it. He hadn't flown all the way to Denver after working all those weeks on perfecting a speech to be felled by a lousy kidney stone. No, he would speak. Kennedys don't cry and Kennedys don't let pain sideline them and Kennedys rise to the occasion, no matter how they're feeling. Shrum cut Ted's planned remarks in half—and, as a just-in-case, cut another version even further to just four lines. Ted would have to play by ear which version he felt up to tackling in front of the crowd.

About ninety minutes before the convention was to start, Ted awoke from his drug-induced sleep and decided to test his ability to walk. He made it just a few steps before needing to rest again. Vicki was anxious and exhausted, having been up all night. Soon, the crew was getting him ready to go, and before Ted knew it, his niece Caroline Kennedy was introducing him to the crowd. With Vicki looking on, he basked in the applause of the cheering delegates, and she knew exactly what he meant when he said, "Nothing, nothing was going to keep me away from this special gathering tonight."

After he finished, he didn't want to leave the stage, much less leave the party. His doctors urged him to return to the hospital, but Ted was high on adrenaline. "They liked my speech!" Vicki recalled him saying. The next morning, he was still floating.

With the convention goal reached, Ted and Vicki mapped out his next target: returning to the Senate. It would have special significance, as one of the doctors who had early on provided a bleak prognosis for Ted had assured him that he would never be well enough to go back. Go home, the doctor had said, and love your wife, be with your children.

"It's sayonara, baby, it's all over," Vicki recalled as the doctor's attitude, which "didn't sit well with Teddy." Returning to his office in the Senate would be symbolic of Ted's refusal to accept the defeatist prediction of a gloomy doctor. The Senate had been a second home to him. Family mementos adorned his office walls—family photos, Jack's military dog tags, a framed letter from a very young Jack to Rose, in which the president-to-be asked to be Ted's godfather. Ted's mahogany desk had once been Jack's, and Ted's name was inscribed in a drawer below his brother's. A few days after Barack Obama was elected president, Ted made his Senate return. With Vicki by his side—as well as his dogs, Splash and Sunny— he beamed as he told reporters that he was ready to fight for health care reform. Vicki was touched by the support Ted received from his colleagues. A banner reading "Welcome Back Senator!" hung in the Russell

Caucus Room, and a group of a hundred or so office aides and committee staffers discussed the upcoming agenda while eating Legal Sea Foods—a Massachusetts favorite.

Ted's voice trembled slightly as he spoke and his walk was a tad shaky, so he steadied himself with his father's cane—the same cane the senator had used in 1964 while recovering from the plane crash that nearly took his life. Vicki, too, provided extra support. She later remembered the day with a smile: "You've never seen . . . a senator so happy to be caught by a gaggle of reporters."

6

TO THE GRAVE

And so the days became weeks and the weeks became months and the months became what those first doctors could have never predicted: a year. Vicki knew those precious extra days together were a gift, and, even as her husband slowly began to lose his strength, she felt blessed. They had the resources to move their boat to Florida and transition there in the winter so Ted could recuperate in warmth. He'd set his sights on a new goal: attending Barack Obama's inauguration in January 2009. In true Ted fashion, he began planning in earnest, having a staffer map out exactly how many steps it would take to walk to the Capitol on his own.

While in Florida, he and Vicki adopted a third Portuguese water dog. Captain Courageous, nicknamed "Cappy," joined Splash and Sunny. One day, one of the dogs made a mess inside the house, and Vicki's stoicism eroded. She crumbled into tears. Ted pulled her head to his shoulder and soothed her. "There I was caring for him, and the roles were totally reversed," she told a reporter. "And there he was comforting me. . . . And this was going to be OK. It was all going to be OK."

Ted powered through to the inauguration in January and celebrated his February birthday a couple of weeks late at the Kennedy Center in Washington. Bill Cosby hosted the star-studded event, with guests such as Lauren Bacall, Bernadette Peters, James Taylor, and John Williams. Even President Obama joined in, appearing on stage at the end of the gala to lead the crowd in "Happy Birthday." Ted even threw out the first pitch at opening day for the Boston Red Sox. He flubbed on his first attempt, grounding the ball before it reached Hall of Famer Jim Rice. Ted, of course, asked for another throw. This time, the ball reached Rice before it kissed the ground. (Afterward, Ted beamed to his grandsons: "I was gonna stay out there all day until Jim Rice caught it without a hop. That's what we Kennedys do—we stay at it until we get it right!") And throughout it all, Ted kept sailing into the summer. He'd grab Splash and board *Mya* and hit the waters, the wind in his hair. "Sailing, for me, has always been a metaphor for life," he later said. That became truer than ever during his illness: If he could still sail, he knew he was not yet beaten.

But Ted had one final project to finish. In the early 2000s he'd embarked on a five-year oral-history project that had stirred up a lot of memories, both from his political and personal lives. With those recollections fresh in mind, he decided to write his memoirs. Vicki again was his sounding board. She was amazed by the meticulous notes and journals he had kept for more than fifty years of his life. He even had a diary from his First Communion—which was with the pope—which he had dictated to his nanny. Ted's sensitively written family history, called *True Compass*, would be his final word to the world, though he would never see a finished copy. His publisher's delivery of manuscripts came to the doorstep August 25, 2009, the same day Ted would take his last breath, with much of his family by his side in the beautiful, twenty-one-room home that Joe and Rose had bought in 1926—eighty-three years, nine children, thirty grandchildren, and three presidential campaigns prior.

Cancer ravages the body; it's a difficult death to witness, which Vicki alluded to when speaking in 2013 to a gathering at the University of California-San Francisco. But she refused to dwell on the ugly side. The fifteen months she had with Ted after his diagnosis were nothing short of a blessing, she said. "That was the greatest gift of my life. It was the greatest privilege of my life," she said. "Don't get me wrong, no one wishes for a diagnosis of a glioblastoma. But once I knew that was the hand we were dealt, I would have chosen to live life exactly, in every single way, the way we lived it."

—◆—

Ted was laid to rest August 30, 2009, in a solemn Roman Catholic mass led by President Obama. The two days prior, an estimated fifty thousand people had crowded the John F. Kennedy Presidential Library and

Museum in Dorchester, where Ted's body lay in repose. The morning of the mass, Obama visited Vicki privately, walking across the street from his hotel to offer condolences. More than fifteen hundred people attended the formal service, including three former presidents—Presidents George W. Bush, Jimmy Carter, and Bill Clinton—at the towering and ornate Basilica of Our Lady of Perpetual Help in Boston. Reporters with the *Washington Post* painted the somber scene: "Bells began to toll at 10:45 a.m. as the motorcade arrived and, a few minutes later, Kennedy's casket was taken from the hearse. Vicki Kennedy and other family members stood vigil, water rolling off their umbrellas, as the casket was carried up the steep steps into the church."

There was a day in 1963 when Jackie Kennedy faced the world without Jack. And there was a day in 1968 when Ethel had ten children, an eleventh on the way, and had to walk forward without Bobby by her side. The next year, Rose returned to an empty house in Hyannis Port after burying her husband near their first home in Brookline. Even Joan had to go about the task of inventing a new life in Boston after her marriage to Teddy ended. Now Vicki found herself where each of the others had stood: staring into the future, her husband gone, memories to fortify her, and their shared ideals to carry forward.

—◆—

These five women—The Kennedy Wives—lived twentieth-century US history. Their experiences of wealth and power, love, loss, and tragedy occurred at such a heightened level that it's tempting to see them as mythic, almost archetypal creatures. But Rose, Ethel, Jackie, Joan, and Vicki were and are stubbornly fleshy in their humanity, and they give all of us, men and women, powerful examples of what everyday strength, resilience, and grace can look like. It's because of their refusal to ossify into sterile sainthood that they will always fascinate—and always inspire.

ACKNOWLEDGMENTS

THE AUTHORS WISH TO THANK JANE DYSTEL FOR HER ADVOCACY AND guidance throughout every stage of this project. Many thanks also to the staff of the John F. Kennedy Presidential Library and Museum, in particular Stacey Chandler, Laurie Austin, and Michael Desmond, who were never less than helpful, hospitable, kind, and encouraging. Our sincere gratitude to Patrick Kennedy for being so generous with his time and his memories. Thanks to everyone at Lyons Press, especially Meredith Dias. And a special thanks to Jon Sternfeld, whose editorial acuity improved our manuscript beyond the telling.

Amber Hunt would like to thank Elijah Van Benschoten, whose support and encouragement can't be overstated. Without him, I'd be a mess. Thanks also to my family, especially Missy, who's there for me every single day that I need her. I learned while researching this book that my grandmother Betty Jo Hunt was quite the Kennedy fan. I know she would've been the first to pre-order. To Randy Essex and Mark Wert, I send my gratitude and sympathy, as they're the latest in a series of newspaper editors to tolerate my torment. And, lastly, I have to thank my coauthor, David Batcher, who signed up only to help research but instantly became a full-fledged partner. I always knew he'd write a book someday. I never envisioned that my name would appear next to his. I'm honored.

David Batcher would like to thank his family, who could have been forgiven for giving up on him years ago. Many thanks to the 612 Crew, especially Andrew Furber and Jesse Murray, for their flexibility and support during the writing of this book. Thanks also to the many kind colleagues and customers at Dunn Brothers Coffee, whose enthusiasm was a buoy throughout. Thanks also to Toni Nelson and Sarah Jeffrey, who kept listening even though Kennedys were all he could talk about. Finally, thanks to Amber Hunt for her friendship, her example, and her trust.

ENDNOTES

PART I: ROSE

1. FROM THE CRADLE

2. *284 Bostonians would die:* Leamer, *Kennedy Women*, p. 29.

2. BETWEEN JOE AND HONEY FITZ

4. *"was loud, brash, unrestrained":* Nasaw, *Patriarch*, ch. 2.

4. *"Mother had a limited capacity for":* ibid.

4. *"I've been in the limelight since":* Perry, *Rose Kennedy*, p. 12.

5. *"As motherhood is the greatest . . . perhaps for future generations":* "Being a Mother," Box 4, RFKP.

5. *Instead, she took classes at the Sacred Heart Convent:* Perry, *Rose Kennedy*, p. 20.

6. *The Kennedys and the Fitzgeralds:* ibid., p. 19.

6. *"He was a very good baseball player . . . a very good polite Catholic":* ibid.

6. *"It took teamwork and conspiracy . . . father was aware of":* ibid.

6. *"for what Rose presumed was a brief vacation":* ibid., p. 20.

6. *"toward the end of that summer, it was decided":* Kennedy, *Times to Remember*, p. 31.

7. *all the while keeping Joe's photo on her:* Perry, *Rose Kennedy*, p. 23.

7. *"Rose's gender clearly fettered her education . . . Catholic finishing schools":* ibid., p. 31.

8. *Joe graduated from Harvard in June 1912 and . . . East Boston bank his father had founded:* ibid., p. 41.

8. *"At Harvard and after graduation, Joe":* Nasaw, *Patriarch*, ch. 3.

8. *Fitz had no choice but to drop out of the race:* Perry, *Rose Kennedy*, p. 41.

8. *"I had read all these books about your heart . . . no two ways about it":* ibid.

9. *At the end of October, they returned:* ibid., p. 44.

3. NINE LITTLE HELPLESS INFANTS

10. *"They did come rather rapidly . . . a good many of them":* CBS News broadcast, October 31, 1967, Box 12, RFKP.

10. *"When I look back now . . . morally and physically perfect":* Perry, *Rose Kennedy*, p. 44.

10. *"It was a nice old wooden-frame house . . . trees lining the sidewalks":* John F. Kennedy Library Foundation, *Rose Kennedy's Family Album*, p. 38.

10. *they employed a housekeeper who cooked:* Perry, *Rose Kennedy*, p. 45.

11. *"I conceived the idea of having":* CBS News broadcast, October 31, 1967, Box 12, RFKP.

11. *"I used to weigh them every week":* Perry, *Rose Kennedy*, p. 49.

11. *"When I got to England I showed . . . couldn't possibly keep track of all of them":* CBS News broadcast, October 31, 1967, Box 12, RFKP.

12. *"Joseph P. Kennedy was not a shipbuilder . . ."* Nasaw, *Patriarch*, ch. 4.

12. *Kennedy quietly formed a privately held company:* Nasaw, *Patriarch*, ch. 4.

12. *"I ran the house. I ran the children":* Perry, *Rose Kennedy*, p. 56.

12. *"You never heard a cross word . . . trusted one another and that's it":* ibid., p. 54.

13. *His wife, Mary, similarly became Rose's closest friend:* Nasaw, *Patriarch*, ch. 4, 5.

13. *"In addition to maids, cooks, and nurses":* Perry, *Rose Kennedy*, p. 58.

13. *"I thought that was a terrible waste of money":* Nasaw, *Patriarch*, ch. 6.

13. *"Gee, you're a great mother to go away":* ibid.

13. *"He was a very active, very lively":* John F. Kennedy Library Foundation, *Rose Kennedy's Family Album*, p. 68.

14. *"In looking over my old diary":* Rose to JFK, November 10, 1962, Box 57, RFKP.

14. *Rose had originally wanted to send her boys to Catholic schools:* Perry, *Rose Kennedy*, p. 57.

14. *Though her teacher, Margaret McQuaid, was delighted:* Leamer, *Kennedy Women*, p. 163.

14. *"As time went on, I realized she was slow . . .":* Diary notes, undated, Box 13, RFKP.

14. *"I was puzzled by what this might mean":* Diary notes, undated, Box 13, RFKP.

15. *"were told that she was a little slow":* ibid.

15. *"Would it be possible for Jack . . . do all we can to help her":* Rose to Mr. Steele, January 10, 1934, Box 12, RFKP.

15. *the females were being forcibly sterilized:* Leamer, *Kennedy Women*, p. 164.

16. *"to see what methods the nurse is using":* Diary notes, July 27, 1971, Box 5, RFKP.

4. LEAVING BOSTON

17. *"was the disciplinarian . . . banishments to the closet":* Perry, *Rose Kennedy*, p. 71.

17. *"He would sweep them into his arms . . . they would have conversations":* Nasaw, *Patriarch*, ch. 6.

17. *"Rose touched her children . . . excesses of affection":* Leamer, *Kennedy Women*, p. 153.

18. *The sole exception was Rosemary:* ibid., p. 191.

18. *"great warmth . . . didn't want her around much":* Notes on an interview with Lem Billings, April 1, 1972, author unknown, Box 12, RFKP.

18. *"She was a great believer . . . you ought to try them":* Perry, *Rose Kennedy*, p. 75.

18. *Unfortunately, Joe's escalating involvement:* ibid., p. 67.

19. *"He was interested not in making artful":* Nasaw, *Patriarch*, ch. 6.

19. *"Up to age six, [the children] ate an hour earlier":* Perry, *Rose Kennedy*, p. 69.

20. *"posted articles or documents":* ibid.

20. *"if they didn't pay attention one Sunday":* Leamer, *Kennedy Women*, p. 154.

20. *"It was really quite a lot of fun . . . diplomatic and government discussions":* Hennesey, JFK Oral History #1, pp. 2–3.

20. *"My mother was more articulate":* Perry, *Rose Kennedy*, p. 74.

21. *"The fact has come to my attention . . . demonstrating the different forms":* Rose to George St. John, September 6, 1932, Box 12, RFKP.

21. *"I understood from Jack's letter":* Rose to George St. John, undated, Box 12, RFKP. (Sadly, Rose's papers contain no mention of the results of the subsequent "investigation.")

21. *He called Rose "our Pied Piper into . . . headlines the next":* Perry, *Rose Kennedy*, p. 71.

21. *He bought the mansion, a white Spanish-style:* Leamer, *Kennedy Women*, p. 191.

22. *"the most ably administered New Deal":* Nasaw, *Patriarch*, ch. 12.

22. *"I started going to Europe":* Perry, *Rose Kennedy*, pp.82–83.
23. *She went to Europe at least seventeen times:* Leamer, *Kennedy Women*, pp.187–88.
23. *In Moscow, they visited Lenin's tomb . . . fired her curiosity:* Perry, *Rose Kennedy*, p. 90.
23. *Roosevelt appointed Joe as the United States Ambassador:* ibid., p. 94.

5. AMBASSADRESS

24. *There, Rose thought she fit in:* Hennessey, JFK Oral History #1, pp. 1–2.
24. *"Her doctor called me and said":* Hennessey, JFK Oral History #2, pp. 2–3.
24. *That evening, when Joe visited Rose:* Hennessey, JFK Oral History #2, pp. 2–3.
24. *She agreed, and would remain:* Perry, *Rose Kennedy*, p. 98.
24. *"I wondered why she did that . . . twelve of us to move":* Hennessey, JFK Oral History #2, p. 3.
25. *"Almost invariably they have been":* Nasaw, *Patriarch*, ch. 15.
25. *Joe Jr. and Jack, both at Harvard:* Perry, *Rose Kennedy*, p.97; Leamer, *Kennedy Women*, p. 241.
26. *"I have a beautiful blue silk room . . . never saw one in my life":* Nasaw, *Patriarch*, ch. 15; Leamer, *Kennedy Women*, p. 241.
26. *When Joe Jr. arrived in June:* John F. Kennedy Library Foundation, *Rose Kennedy's Family Album*, p. 201.
26. *"Rose, this is a helluva":* Leamer, *Kennedy Women*, p. 243.
26. *"one of the most fabulous":* ibid.
26. *She threw society debuts for Rosemary:* John F. Kennedy Library Foundation, *Rose Kennedy's Family Album*, p. 201.
27. *She and Joe went to Ascot:* Leamer, *Kennedy Women*, p. 247.
27. *She was informed that a tiara:* Nasaw, *Patriarch*, ch. 15.
27. *"Disciplined, stoical, eternally gracious . . . deeply ingrained habits":* Leamer, *Kennedy Women*, p. 248.
28. *"You have worked very hard":* Perry, *Rose Kennedy*, p. 137.
28. *he traveled to Romania, Russia, Turkey:* John F. Kennedy Library Foundation, *Rose Kennedy's Family Album*, p. 203.
28. *"Try as he might":* Nasaw, *Patriarch*, ch. 19.
28–29. *Later that month, Joe Jr. sailed:* John F. Kennedy Library Foundation, *Rose Kennedy's Family Album*, p. 203.
29. *She was doing so well at the Montessori school:* Nasaw, *Patriarch*, ch. 21.
29. *"We expected to get married . . . He was a pilot ":* Hennessey, JFK Oral History #2, pp. 3–4.

6. ROSEMARY

30. *"Democracy is finished in England . . . may be here, too":* Perry, *Rose Kennedy*, p. 158.
30. *"in such a desultory":* Nasaw, *Patriarch*, ch. 27.
30. *The press savaged him:* ibid., ch. 27, 28.
31. *"I am relieved too . . . no longer a necessity":* Perry, *Rose Kennedy*, p. 159.
31. *Jack was ordered to report:* Nasaw, *Patriarch*, ch. 28.
31. *She was placed in St. Gertrude's School:* ibid.

31. *"In the year or so following":* ibid.

32. *Both Joe and Rose were becoming convinced:* ibid.

32. *Moniz received a Nobel Prize:* Perry, *Rose Kennedy,* pp. 164–65.

32. *Sometime in November, apparently without the approval:* ibid., p. 165.

32. *Rose and the children wouldn't visit her there either:* Nasaw, *Patriarch,* ch. 28.

33. *"It was then we decided":* Diary Notes on Rosemary, Box 13, RFKP.

33. *"The operation eliminated":* Nasaw, *Patriarch,* ch. 28.

33. *"I will never forgive Joe . . . bitter towards him about":* Perry, *Rose Kennedy,* p. 166.

7. THE MARCHIONESS AND THE WAR HEROES

34. *"I can see improvement . . . typographical":* Perry, *Rose Kennedy,* p. 170.

35. *"It was easy. They cut my PT boat":* Dallek, *Unfinished Life,* pp. 95–99.

35. *"We are more proud and thankful":* Perry, *Rose Kennedy,* p. 173.

35. *After a brief visit in Hyannis Port:* Leamer, *Kennedy Women,* p. 353.

36. *Stationed in Cornwall, he received:* Perry, *Rose Kennedy,* p. 173.

36. *"jitter-bugging, gin rummy":* Leamer, *Kennedy Women,* p. 344.

36. *He was widely considered . . . upon his father's death:* ibid., p. 262.

36. *But Kick argued that she couldn't . . . unacceptable husband for her daughter:* Perry, *Rose Kennedy,* p. 175.

37. *He was told he'd need surgery:* Nasaw, *Patriarch,* ch. 29.

37. *"The mere feel of his coat . . . he was really there" . . . "elf" was home safe:* Perry, *Rose Kennedy,* p.174.

37. *"As far as I'm concerned, I'll gamble":* Nasaw, *Patriarch,* ch. 29.

37. *Rose wrote in her diary that:* ibid.

37. *She made herself so sick:* Perry, *Rose Kennedy,* p. 176.

37. *"Religion is everything to us":* Nasaw, *Patriarch,* ch. 29.

37. *"The power of silence is":* Perry, *Rose Kennedy,* p. 177.

37. *Billy Hartington was called into active . . . missions for the invading Allies:* Nasaw, *Patriarch,* ch. 29.

38. *"However, that is all over now":* Perry, *Rose Kennedy,* p. 178.

38. *"No doubt you are surprised":* Nasaw, *Patriarch,* ch. 29.

38. *His mission was to get the bomber:* ibid.

38. *"Dad's face was twisted . . . dissolution into sobs":* Kennedy, *True Compass,* pp. 85–86.

38. *"There were no tears":* Kennedy, *Times to Remember,* p. 301.

39. *"I realized what a wonderful man he was":* Perry, *Rose Kennedy,* p. 182.

39. *"With her supreme faith":* Nasaw, *Patriarch,* ch. 30.

39. *"crippled and mentally deficient children":* Perry, *Rose Kennedy,* p. 184.

40. *"It is beautiful here beyond words":* Perry, *Rose Kennedy,* p.190.

40. *Joe was the only Kennedy who attended:* ibid., pp.192–93.

40–41. *"I heard the grandfather clock . . . suited to one another":* Rose, diary entry, June 24, 1962, Box 4, RFKP.

8. ACCOLADES, WEDDINGS, BIRTHS, VICTORIES

42. *"In spite of his age":* Leamer, *Kennedy Women,* p. 414; Perry, *Rose Kennedy,* p. 197.

43. *Joe Kennedy, as was his wont:* Perry, *Rose Kennedy,* p. 198.

43. *The fact that handsome JFK sometimes appeared:* ibid., p. 199.

43. *"Certainly I can appreciate . . . I lost one son" . . . left the stage in tears:* Leamer, *Kennedy Women*, p. 423.

43. *"those damn tea parties":* Perry, *Rose Kennedy*, p. 203.

44. *"I felt rather like a man":* Dallek, *Unfinished Life*, p. 174.

44. *Somehow Rose also found:* Perry, *Rose Kennedy*, pp. 204–9.

44. *they wed in April of 1954 and Pat gave:* Leamer, *Kennedy Women*, pp. 447–50; Perry, *Rose Kennedy*, p. 213.

44. *The same year, Rose took the chance:* Perry, *Rose Kennedy*, p. 213.

44. *Though Rose was initially unimpressed:* ibid., pp. 220–23.

45. *"Sometimes a mother finds . . . answer to that child's problems":* ibid., p. 212.

45. *just an effective presentation:* Dallek, *Unfinished Life*, p. 250.

45. *"They just* stared *at us":* Kennedy, *Historic Conversations*, First Conversation.

46. *Kennedys are "all over the state . . . different places at the same time":* Dallek, *Unfinished Life*, p. 250.

46. *By the time Jack was elected:* Leamer, *Kennedy Women*, p. 508.

9. THE FIRST MOTHER

47. *"To Mother—With Thanks":* Perry, *Rose Kennedy*, p. 245.

47–48. *"After my hair had been set . . . gave a laugh and out I went":* Rose's diary, January 5, 1961, Box 4, RFKP.

48. *"wanted to start his four years . . . to Almighty God." She didn't approach . . . informal winter bundling:* Perry, *Rose Kennedy*, p. 249.

48. *"we were left out of":* ibid.

48. *More than twenty years later:* Leamer, *Kennedy Women*, p. 516.

48. *"I was overwhelmed . . . approached my 71st birthday":* Perry, *Rose Kennedy*, p. 259.

48. *"He really didn't want her . . . and he let her":* "Billings notes, Friday April 1, 1972." Author unknown, Box 12, RFKP.

49. *"I wonder to myself":* Perry, *Rose Kennedy*, p. 254.

49. *Afterward, she joined Joe:* ibid., p. 255.

49. *The Kennedys gathered for their:* Nasaw, *Patriarch*, ch. 39.

49. *"Jack gets a great kick out of seeing Ted dance":* Perry, *Rose Kennedy*, p. 258.

49. *She objected to there:* Nasaw, *Patriarch*, ch. 39.

49. *He "is not at all himself":* ibid.

49. *Others at the Thanksgiving dinner noticed:* ibid.

50. *After several weeks, he returned:* ibid.; Perry, *Rose Kennedy*, pp. 260–61.

50. *Every evening, they quietly:* Nasaw, *Patriarch*, ch. 40.

50. *"My impression . . . was very content":* Perry, *Rose Kennedy*, p. 263.

51. *"She was awfully good . . . gone so many years ago":* Leamer, *Kennedy Women*, p. 551.

51. *"This is the way . . . so every one will understand":* Rose to Bobby, July 10, 1962, Box 58, RFKP.

51. *"I am trying to rest":* Rose to JBK, November 1, 1962, Box 14, RFKP.

51. *"Mrs. Kennedy changed a great deal . . . left her conscience intact":* Leamer, *Kennedy Women*, pp. 555–56.

52. *She also discouraged their publicizing:* Rose to Bobby, April 29, 1963, Box 58, RFKP.
52. *Jackie left the day of:* Perry, *Rose Kennedy*, p. 274.
52. *"Don't worry . . . You'll see.":* Leamer, *Kennedy Women*, p. 593.

10. "WE ALL SHALL BE HAPPY TOGETHER"

53. *She put on a coat:* Perry, *Rose Kennedy*, p. 276.
53. *"We talked about Jack":* Smith, *Grace and Power*, p. 446.
53. *Joe sobbed:* Nasaw, *Patriarch*, ch. 40.
53. *"What do people expect . . . weep in a corner":* Smith, *Grace and Power*, p. 447.
54. *She flew back to Hyannis Port:* Perry, *Rose Kennedy*, p. 277.
54. *"I am not going to be licked":* ibid., p. 278.
54. *"every place I went the French . . . floods of tears again":* ibid., p. 280.
54. *"I think all of the Kennedys . . . getting out of hand":* Cavanaugh, JFK Library Oral History Program, p. 20.
55. *"I guess the only reason . . . more of us than there is trouble":* Perry, *Rose Kennedy*, p. 283.
55. *The lobotomy was not revealed:* ibid., p. 268.
56. *"Well, you see the answer to that . . . a retarded child":* ibid., p. 269.
56. *This summer camp grew throughout:* Leamer, *Kennedy Women*, p. 572.
56. *The Joseph P. Kennedy Jr. Foundation:* Perry, *Rose Kennedy*, pp. 288–89.
57. *She was, alone among the Kennedy:* ibid., pp. 293–94; Leamer, *Kennedy Women*, p. 627.
57. *A televised news bulletin informed:* Leamer, *Kennedy Women*, p. 633.
57. *The assassin, a confused, unemployed:* Thomas, *Robert Kennedy*, ch. 21.
57. *"It's Bobby! It's Bobby!":* Perry, *Rose Kennedy*, p. 294.
57. *With no children present to be strong:* Perry, *Rose Kennedy*, p. 295.
57. *Later that morning, a photographer saw:* Thomas, *Robert Kennedy*, ch. 21.
58. *"It seemed impossible . . . at home or on his trips":* "Diary Notes on Robert Kennedy," Box 13, RFKP.
58. *"I take renewed strength and":* "Notes on Faith," Box 14, RFKP.
58. *"all of you who offered your prayers . . . it will strengthen and fortify":* "Remarks to the Nation", June 15, 1968, Box 13, RFKP.

11. ON DESTINY

60. *"has taken three stalwart":* "On Destiny," Fall 1968, Box 4, RFKP.
60. *"Our family was the perfect family":* ibid.
61. *That Sunday, the Chappaquiddick incident got more space:* Clymer, *Edward M. Kennedy: A Biography*, p. 145.
61. *"unlike himself . . . disturbed":* Perry, *Rose Kennedy*, p. 306.
61–62. *"Dad, I'm in some trouble":* Canellos, *Last Lion*, p. 177.
62. *Joseph Patrick Kennedy Sr.:* Perry, *Rose Kennedy*, p. 308.
62. *"Several people enclosed a . . . 'The poor . . . help them.'":* "1969 Following Joseph P. Kennedy's death," Box 4, RFKP.
62. *"She sent a letter which quite overwhelmed me":* "She sent a letter," Box 4, RFKP.
63. *"Otherwise, they were more or less surrounded":* "February 1970," Box 4, RFKP.
63. *In July 1970 she flew:* Perry, *Rose Kennedy*, pp. 314–15.

63. *"one of the proudest and happiest"*: ibid., p. 313.
63. *"It seems the longer . . . 'Skippy, Skippy!'"*: Sister Mary Charles to Rose, October 14, 1971, Box 57, RFKP.
63–64. *"I try to give her little . . . with care and concern"*: Sister Mary Charles to Rose, June 21, 1973, Box 57, RFKP.
64. *"she was progressing quite . . . try to accept God's will"*: Rose to Father Robert Kroll, May 1, 1972, Box 57, RFKP.
64. *"I do sense and I do believe . . . has been her gift"*: "Rosemary" Box 13, RFKP.
64. *Published in 1974,* Times to Remember *. . . Joseph P. Kennedy Jr. Foundation:* Perry, *Rose Kennedy,* pp. 321–22.
65. *Exhausted by years:* ibid., p. 326.
65. *Only speaking with great difficulty:* ibid., p. 331.
65. *Her gravestone, fittingly simple:* ibid., p. 332.

PART II: ETHEL

1. A LOVE STORY, WITH DETOURS

68. *Ethel would later say it:* Kennedy, *Ethel,* HBO, 2012
69. *"soft and refined":* Oppenheimer, *The Other Mrs. Kennedy,* p. 142.
69. *"Ouch . . . That was a black":* Kennedy, *Ethel,* HBO, 2012.
69. *Pat would later refuse to answer:* David, *Ethel,* p. 40.
69. *"but he never knew . . . to talk or even think about it":* ibid., p. 40.
69. *"She talks and talks":* ibid., p. 69.
69. *"How can I fight God?":* Taraborrelli, *Jackie, Ethel, Joan,* p. 40.

2. THE RISE OF THE SKAKELS

70. *She had been raised:* David, *Ethel,* p. 6.
70. *His mother, Grace Mary Jordan . . . didn't care much for Catholics or Jews:* Oppenheimer, *The Other Mrs. Kennedy,* p. 6.
70. *"Skakel's temperament was volatile":* ibid.
70. *"Though sweet, refined, petite":* ibid.
70. *As a young man, George:* Munk, Nina, "Greenwich's Outrageous Fortune," *Vanity Fair,* July 2006.
71. *His wealth insulated his:* Taraborrelli, *Jackie, Ethel, Joan,* p. 38.
71. *Ann was a tad taller than George:* ibid.
71. *As latecomers to faith tend to be":* Oppenheimer, *The Other Mrs. Kennedy,* p. 18.
71. *"It was a very religious . . . strong religion in her":* ibid., p. 19.
71. *"He was rarely around":* ibid.
71. *Like Curt Skakel, Brannack:* ibid.
71. *They moved into a house:* ibid.
71. *In all, she had seven children:* ibid., p. 21.
72. *"It was a fabulous place":* David, *Ethel,* p. 15.
72. *"The parties were always impressive":* Taraborrelli, *Jackie, Ethel, Joan,* p.
72. *Potential business partners:* Oppenheimer, *The Other Mrs. Kennedy,* p. 50.

72. *"My father practically never . . . a personal, beautiful thing, in their eyes":* ibid., pp. 50–51.

72–73. *"the parties literally every day . . . we started drinking ":* ibid., p. 50.

73. *George and Ann weren't much:* ibid., pp. 49–51.

73. *The boys enrolled in Canterbury:* ibid., p. 52.

73. *Jack, who received "poor" and "fair":* Canterbury School report card, JFK library, www.jfklibrary.org/Asset-Viewer/r7CyCR4RYUyeJmYMQdtowQ.aspx.

73. *the rowdy Skakel boys:* Oppenheimer, *The Other Mrs. Kennedy,* p. 52.

73. *Eventually, the clan headed:* Taraborrelli, *Jackie, Ethel, Joan,* p. 38.

73. *There, George bought a twenty-five-room:* Munk, Nina, "Greenwich's Outrageous Fortune."

73. *"featured hand-painted chinoiserie":* Oppenheimer, *The Other Mrs. Kennedy,* p. 63.

73. *The library measured almost:* ibid.

74. *Outside the main house:* Munk, Nina, "Greenwich's Outrageous Fortune."

74. *He paid Simmons's widow less:* David, *Ethel,* p. 16.

74. *For another forty thousand dollars, George:* Oppenheimer, *The Other Mrs. Kennedy,* p. 63.

74. *Ann would adopt:* David, *Ethel,* p. 3.

3. THE GIRL WITH THE RED CONVERTIBLE

75. *"Dinner was at 7:15 . . . going to have supper at 5 or 10":* Kennedy, *Ethel,* HBO, 2012.

75. *"Every morning at college . . . I wasn't a very deep thinker":* ibid.

75–76. *"An excited hoarse voice":* David, *Ethel,* p. 36.

76. *Ann would drive into town:* ibid., p. 19

76. *"saying grace before every meal":* ibid., p. 20.

76. *Ann routinely invited clergymen:* ibid.

76. *George was known to always:* Oppenheimer, *The Other Mrs. Kennedy,* p. 29.

76. *"There were some forty-five-caliber bullet holes . . . a few holes in their mailbox":* ibid., p. 89.

77. *"All those cars ended up . . . was no punishment.":* ibid., p. 88.

77. *"The Skakel kids weren't . . . were a mass of insecurity":* ibid., p. 86.

77. *"Our parents weren't strict . . . philosophy was 'Enjoy yourself.'":* ibid., p. 88.

77. *There was Smoky Joe:* David, *Ethel,* p. 27.

77. *On weekends, she'd:* Oppenheimer, *The Other Mrs. Kennedy,* p. 82.

77–78. *"She took to riding":* ibid.

78. *If she had a date in:* David, *Ethel,* p. 30.

78. *Five Members of One Family:* Oppenheimer, *The Other Mrs. Kennedy,* p. 83.

78. *The goal: to knock the:* David, *Ethel,* p. 7.

78. *"Ethel drove recklessly and at high":* Oppenheimer, *The Other Mrs. Kennedy,* p. 87.

79. *While the market crash crippled:* David, *Ethel,* p. 13.

79. *Eventually . . . 65 percent:* Oppenheimer, *The Other Mrs. Kennedy,* p. 45.

79. *"It could sell the purified":* David, *Ethel,* p. 14.

79. *More plants followed in Illinois:* ibid.

79. *Calcined petroleum coke is a key ingredient:* Oppenheimer, *The Other Mrs. Kennedy,* p. 44.

79. *George was one of about two dozen:* ibid.
79. *"In judging other men . . . the worst of the Depression":* ibid.
79. *Once the war ended, George:* ibid., pp. 94–95.
80. *"Whenever a colleague . . . 'You can't quote silence.'":* ibid., p. 44.
80. *"So she telephoned the distributor . . . refused to grant the discount any more":* David, *Ethel,* p. 22.

4. MANHATTANVILLE

81. *Once, the girls wondered aloud . . . nuns scurried into the halls in their nightgowns:* Leamer, *Kennedy Women,* p. 389.
81. *Another time, after being snubbed:* ibid., p. 390.
81. *"Are the collections good":* ibid.
81. *"This is ridiculous . . . too old to be grounded":* ibid., p. 389.
81. *"took the demerit book":* Kennedy, *Ethel,* HBO, 2012.
82. *"Mother didn't think we were . . . put up a wall between us":* Leamer, *Kennedy Women,* p. 390.
82. *"We'd drive up to Boston . . . had never rubbed elbows with before":* Kennedy, *Ethel,* HBO, 2012.
82. *"George hated Roosevelt . . . could have become a dictator":* Oppenheimer, *The Other Mrs. Kennedy,* pp. 45–46.
82. *"None whatsoever":* Kennedy, *Ethel,* HBO, 2012.
82. *Still, Ethel worked doggedly for Jack's:* David, *Ethel,* p. 43.
82. *She even wrote a college thesis:* ibid., p. 44.
82. *After graduation, she toured Europe:* Cremmen, Mary, "Ideal Romance Culminates June 17 for Bob Kennedy," *Boston Globe,* May 28, 1950.

5. BOBBY'S WIFE

83. *"He just couldn't live up . . . gave him complete loyalty and ego building":* Buchwald, Art, recorded interview by Roberta Greene, March 12, 1969, John F. Kennedy Library Oral History Program.
83. *"Ethel was head-over-heels in love . . . not so much Skakel anymore":* Oppenheimer, *The Other Mrs. Kennedy,* p. 144.
83. *Her engagement ring was a showstopper:* ibid., p. 166.
83. *The engagement made Bobby's:* Cremmen, Mary, "Ideal Romance Culminates June 17 for Bob Kennedy," *Boston Globe,* May 28, 1950.
84. *"The difficulty in writing about Miss Skakel . . . shifted to her personality":* ibid.
84. *The Skakels and Kennedys:* David, *Ethel,* p. 48.
84. *reportedly because the Skakels refused:* Oppenheimer, *The Other Mrs. Kennedy,* pp. 167–68.
84. *Ethel would later recall:* Kennedy, *Ethel,* HBO, 2012.
84. *Pat Skakel Cuffe:* David, *Ethel,* pp. 47–48.
84. *As Ethel readied to walk:* ibid., p. 48.
84. *Her long veil was double tulle . . . lilies of the valley:* "Robert Francis Kennedy Weds Miss Ethel Skakel in Greenwich, Conn.," *Boston Globe,* June 18, 1950.
84. *"There were fountains of champagne":* Kennedy, *Ethel,* HBO, 2012.

84. *But by then, Joe had grown impatient:* David, *Ethel*, p. 48.

85. *They stayed in the most . . . suite was filled with fresh, fragrant orchids:* Oppenheimer, *The Other Mrs. Kennedy*, p. 171.

85. *"just will of the wisp . . . wherever we had friends":* Kennedy, *Ethel,* HBO, 2012.

85. *Her children would later remember:* ibid.

85. *This was one challenge:* David, *Ethel*, p. 50.

85. *Ethel and Bobby truly seemed:* Oppenheimer, *The Other Mrs. Kennedy*, p. 173.

85. *and later to the Farmington Country:* David, *Ethel*, p. 50.

85. *I like to see Bobby in":* ibid., p. 51.

85–86. *"He was careful to choose":* ibid.

86. *liberal Supreme Court Justice:* ibid.

86. *"When, at long last . . . third of the seats were taken by African Americans":* Holder, Eric, "Attorney General Eric Holder speaks at the University of Virginia law school commencement," May 22, 2011, www.justice.gov/iso/opa/ag/speeches/2011/ag-speech-110522.html.

86. *"He was so charming . . . had to go through at that time":* Kennedy, *Ethel*, HBO, 2012.

86. *He tossed around words:* David, *Ethel*, p. 53.

86. *"Christians should work":* Oppenheimer, *The Other Mrs. Kennedy*, p. 183.

87. *"Yes, I did . . . always talking about the Communists":* Kennedy, *Ethel*, HBO, 2012.

87. *McCarthy had been:* ibid.

87. *Bobby later would join McCarthy's:* Kennedy, Robert bio, JFK Library, www.jfklibrary.org/JFK/The-Kennedy-Family/Robert-F-Kennedy.aspx.

87. *"at the time, I thought there was . . . I was wrong":* Thomas, *Robert Kennedy*, ch. 2.

87. *You know I told you . . . flowers in the room and everything":* Oppenheimer, *The Other Mrs. Kennedy*, p. 182.

87. *While there, he attended a play:* Thomas, *Robert Kennedy*, ch. 2.

88. *Bobby had stood at a crossroads, torn between:* Leamer, *Kennedy Men*, ch. 13.

88. *Some of the names seem plausible:* ibid., ch. 26.

88. *She was ready to give:* Oppenheimer, *The Other Mrs. Kennedy*, p. 185.

6. FIRST BIRTHS, FIRST DEATHS

89. *"like a patient preparing for":* Oppenheimer, *The Other Mrs. Kennedy*, p. 186.

89. *"She was basically terrified . . . she was scared":* ibid.

89. *It didn't help:* ibid.

89. *"He called me and said, 'Ethel has gone to the hospital . . . fly right down?'" . . . two arrived in Greenwich to be by Ethel's side:* Donovan, Luella Hennessey, JFK oral history, http://archive1.jfklibrary.org/JFKOH/Hennessey-Donovan,%20Luella/JFKOH-LHD-02/JFKOH-LHD-02-TR.pdf.

90. *On July 4th Ethel gave:* Oppenheimer, *The Other Mrs. Kennedy*, p. 186.

90. *Senator Joseph McCarthy—for whom:* David, *Ethel*, p. 55.

90. *"Ethel had a lot of problems . . . suffering when I got there":* Oppenheimer, *The Other Mrs. Kennedy*, p. 187.

90. *It didn't help Ethel's mental:* ibid., p. 186.

90. *"With her old friends . . . back to her parents' house ":* ibid., p. 187.

90. *When Ethel finally left:* ibid., p. 188.

91. *"Little boys are different . . . can love a little girl":* ibid.

91. *Returning to Hyannis Port:* David, *Ethel*, p. 55.

91. *He decided to put his connections:* ibid., p. 56.

91. *Ethel was thrilled:* Oppenheimer, *The Other Mrs. Kennedy*, p. 190.

91. *"It was a major decision . . . a big sacrifice":* Kennedy, *Ethel*, HBO, 2012.

91. *She labored to breathe:* Oppenheimer, *The Other Mrs. Kennedy*, pp. 191–93.

91. *Her worries proved unfounded:* ibid., p. 194.

92. *"All of her prayers . . . she visibly relaxed":* ibid.

92. *"bedrock Democrats":* Kennedy, *Ethel*, HBO, 2012.

92. *"I just totally put the Republican . . . thought I was a little Communist":* ibid.

92. *The Kennedys saw the Skakels as obscene:* Oppenheimer, *The Other Mrs. Kennedy*, p. 196.

92. *"The only talk about the Kennedys . . . no closeness between the two families at all":* ibid., p. 195.

92. *"Look, Jack" . . . An insulted George Jr. . . . without a crew:* David, *Ethel*, pp. 8–9; Oppenheimer, *The Other Mrs. Kennedy*, p. 196.

93. *"It can't be. I still have":* Oppenheimer, *The Other Mrs. Kennedy*, p. 197.

93. *"If Bobby can't treat Ethel":* ibid.

93. *"Bobby took me to the top floor . . . suitable for the maid's room":* Kennedy, Rose to Ethel Kennedy, November 17, 1959, Box 14, RFKP.

93. *"No one appears to have . . . disregard for money":* Leamer, *Kennedy Women*, p. 481.

93. *"Dad, I think you have . . . have Dad work harder":* ibid.

93. *After conferring with his father:* Oppenheimer, *The Other Mrs. Kennedy*, p. 207.

94. *By November 1953:* Thomas, *Robert Kennedy*, ch. 2.

94. *It was outside of the $500-a-month:* Oppenheimer, *The Other Mrs. Kennedy*, p. 209.

94. *"George Skakel was quite fond . . . questioned its safety" . . . Some said they smelled . . . shrugged off the concerns :* ibid., pp. 227–28.

94. *"what's all this nonsense I hear":* ibid., p. 228.

95. *"It was hard on everybody . . . he did it":* Kennedy, *Ethel*, HBO, 2012.

95. *"There were no tears . . . only way they could cope":* Oppenheimer, *The Other Mrs. Kennedy*, p. 233.

95. *"She does go to Mass . . . really tough things":* Kennedy, *Ethel*, HBO, 2012.

95. *None of the children wanted the sprawling:* Oppenheimer, *The Other Mrs. Kennedy*, p. 235.

7. HICKORY HILL

96. *The Georgian estate, which they:* Associated Press, "Kennedy Purchases $125,000 Estate for Virginia Residence," *Boston Globe*, June 2, 1955.

96. *It was a beautiful, thirteen-bedroom:* Oppenheimer, p. 241; John F. Kennedy Presidential Library and Museum, "Ethel Skakel Kennedy," www.jfklibrary.org/JFK/The-Kennedy-Family/Ethel-Skakel-Kennedy.aspx.

96. *George Brinton McClellan :* David, *Ethel*, p. 88.

97. *"During a recess, Cohn stormed across":* Thomas, *Robert Kennedy*, p. 66.

97. *With McCarthy's Communist hunts:* ibid., p. 70

98. *Bobby swung and caught him in the face:* ibid., p. 71

98. *"Senate investigators said today they":* Associated Press, "Senate Probers Link Rackets to Teamsters Union," *Boston Globe*, February 24, 1957.

98. *A Portland racketeer:* Kraslow, David, "Racketeers Tried to Rule City," *Boston Globe*, February 28, 1957.

98. *A man emerged from the shadows:* Van Gelder, Lawrence, "Victor Riesel, 81, Columnist Blinded by Acid Attack, Dies," *New York Times*, January 5, 1995.

98. *Once Bobby's sights were turned:* Kennedy, *Ethel*, HBO, 2012.

98. *Instead, they sat in the principal's:* ibid.

98. *"I think her inner Skakel came":* Leamer, *Kennedy Women*, p. 506.

98–99. *"I think it might've been a":* Kennedy, *Ethel*, HBO, 2012.

99. *"What's up there? . . . where he belongs!" the children would squeal:* Oppenheimer, *The Other Mrs. Kennedy*, pp. 258–59.

99. *Later, daughter Kathleen:* Kennedy, *Ethel*, HBO, 2012.

99. *In three days, the two women:* Leamer, *Kennedy Women*, p. 506.

99. *"[Bobby] really wanted the children":* Kennedy, *Ethel*, HBO, 2012.

99–100. *Three of the children had Brownie:* Winship, Thomas, "It's Just Like Circus to Kennedy Youngsters," *Boston Globe*, July 14, 1960.

100. *"This lovely little girl":* Kennedy, *Ethel*, HBO, 2012.

100. *Nobody looked tired in the . . . know how great Jack was":* Kennedy, *Ethel*, HBO, 2012.

100. *Predictable charges of nepotism:* Dallek, *Unfinished Life*, pp.316–19

100. *"There was this salamander named":* "Nephew Hands President a Slippery Issue," *Boston Globe*, March 12, 1961.

100–101. *"He had to be fed fish . . . kind of unusual":* Kennedy, *Ethel*, HBO, 2012.

101. *"Then we got to the . . . a tie for first place":* Buchwald, Art, "Judge Stays Impartial under Terrific Pressure," *Boston Globe*, May 27, 1965.

101. *"We changed our clothes and the":* Schlesinger, *A Thousand Days*, p. 591.

101. *"Rose Kennedy thought Ethel's parties":* Taraborrelli, *Jackie, Ethel, Joan*, p. 105.

102. *"At 3 o'clock in the morning":* McCardle, Dorothy, "Mystery Follows Dunking Party on Hickory Hill," *Boston Globe*, July 8, 1962.

102. *"Any more . . . little more peace and quiet":* ibid.

102. *"I mean whether conceptions":* David, *Ethel*, pp. 90–91.

102. *General Maxwell Taylor, then:* Oppenheimer, *The Other Mrs. Kennedy*, p. 328.

102. *Ethel had hoped:* David, *Ethel*, p. 74.

103. *"Everybody was talking about Vietnam":* ibid.

8. A TIDAL WAVE

104. *On Friday, November 22, 1963, as . . . never called the house before:* David, *Ethel*, p. 164.

104. *for example, Bobby wanted to wage:* Thomas, *Robert Kennedy*, ch. 5.

104. *Ethel, naturally, shared her:* Kennedy, *Ethel*, HBO, 2012.

104. *After a beat, he put his hand . . . dark months to come:* David, *Ethel*, p. 164.

105. *"That's the wife of ":* Oppenheimer, *The Other Mrs. Kennedy*, p. 356.

105. *While the rest of the family gathered:* ibid.

105. *"It was like a tidal wave . . . six months of just blackness":* Kennedy, *Ethel*, HBO, 2012.

105. *"Daddy became more withdrawn":* Kennedy, *Ethel*, HBO, 2012.

105. *his friends credited her:* Oppenheimer, *The Other Mrs. Kennedy*, p. 358.

106. *"Whether I win or lose":* Pelkey, Herbert, "'Win or Lose, I'm Staying in NY,' Says Robert Kennedy," *Boston Globe*, September 6, 1964.

106. *"Three times, while standing . . . to keep him upright":* Morin, Relman, "An Astonishing Human Storm," *Boston Globe*, September 13, 1964.

106. *On November 3, 1964, he . . . won by only 700,000:* Thomas, *Robert Kennedy*, ch. 16.

106. *Ethel and the children were:* Saltonstall, Pat, "It's Back to McLean for RFKs (and Pets)," *Boston Globe*, January 10, 1965.

106. *"Under any foreseeable circumstances":* Glass, Andrew, "RFK Not a Candidate in '68," *Boston Globe*, October 6, 1966.

9. RUN, BOBBY, RUN

107. *"I have absolutely no . . . EthelBird":* Oppenheimer, *The Other Mrs. Kennedy*, p. 373.

107. *And even a weakened:* Thomas, *Robert Kennedy*, ch. 19.

107. *They also argued that Bobby:* ibid.

108. *The party was still going in:* Oppenheimer, *The Other Mrs. Kennedy*, p. 405.

108. *"with incredible grace and incredible bravery":* ibid., p. 390.

109. *"go a long way toward . . . you've got to realize that":* Thomas, *Robert Kennedy*, ch. 19.

109. *Bobby insisted that it:* ibid.

109. *"Do you know what . . . more people hate Bobby than hated Jack":* ibid.

110. *Kerry, then eight years old . . . Matthew Maxwell wrestled with him:* Oppenheimer, *The Other Mrs. Kennedy*, p. 411.

110. *"I do not run for the presidency . . . in this country and around the world":* ibid.

110–11. *"If Ethel Kennedy . . . since Teddy Roosevelt's day":* ibid., p. 413.

111. *"This is Kansas . . . all the fucking way":* Thomas, *Robert Kennedy*, ch. 20.

111. *He somehow had to:* ibid.

111. *But Bobby Jr., fifteen:* Oppenheimer, *The Other Mrs. Kennedy*, p. 421.

111. *"One of her rules was . . . 'Yea, there's Dad! This is great'":* ibid., p. 420.

112. *After Washington newspaper:* Thomas, *Robert Kennedy*, ch. 20.

112. *When Ethel was campaigning . . . then walked away:* Oppenheimer, *The Other Mrs. Kennedy*, p. 419.

112. *"Well, he didn't deserve to be president anyway":* David, *Ethel*, p.176.

112. *When Robert Kennedy's name:* Thomas, *Robert Kennedy*, ch. 20.

113. *"For those of you who are":* ibid.

113. *Riots broke out in 110 cities:* ibid.

113. *"we embraced each other . . . who reached out to me":* Oppenheimer, *The Other Mrs. Kennedy*, p. 417.

114. *"Don't you just wish that everyone was black?":* Thomas, *Robert Kennedy*, ch. 21.

114. *"Kennedy's mood, often":* Thomas, *Robert Kennedy*, ch. 21.

114. *Ethel had made "Dutton Buttons" . . . and sharp Boston accent:* Oppenheimer, *The Other Mrs. Kennedy*, pp. 430–31.

114. *"I plan to remain active":* ibid., p.421.

114. *"I try to keep our family life happy . . . the children are well"*: ibid., p. 421.
115. *"David was chided and . . . but that was it"*: ibid., pp. 422–23.
115. *Because he wanted:* Thomas, *Robert Kennedy*, ch. 21.

10. A TREMENDOUS AMOUNT OF PRESENCE

116. *Bobby was never able:* Thomas, *Robert Kennedy*, ch. 20.
116. *Each night at dinner:* ibid., ch. 21.
116. *"These are my people":* ibid.
116. *"He was being truthful . . . embraced by people of color":* ibid.
117. *"The kids were constantly . . . got a kick out of it":* Oppenheimer, *The Other Mrs. Kennedy*, p. 433.
117. *Ethel crouched into the backseat . . . standing, seemingly unafraid:* ibid.
117. *He had an abrasion over:* ibid., p. 434.
118. *"I'm not doing this in order . . . and let's win there":* "RFK part 1 Last Speech at the Ambassador Hotel," YouTube, www.youtube.com/watch?v=vXuHcQ1Mrqs.
118. *"Is everybody else all right?":* Thomas, *Robert Kennedy*, ch. 21.
119. *"Ethel Kennedy is standing by . . . tremendous amount of presence":* Goldsmith, *Seven American Deaths*, pp. 44–45.
119. *Five other people had been:* MSNBC, "Key Figures Associated with RFK's Assassination," NBCNews.com, July 9, 2013. Web, May 30, 2014. www.nbcnews.com/id/24895033/ns/us_news-rfk_40_years_later/t/key-figures-associated-rfks-assassination/#.U4vGmRZ2CVk.
119. *Two medics arrived . . . slipping into unconsciousness:* ibid.
119. *"he said something like":* Oppenheimer, *The Other Mrs. Kennedy*, p. 442.
119. *Surgeons tried to remove:* ibid., p. 443.
119. *When Bobby was finally wheeled:* Kennedy, *Ethel*, HBO, 2012.
120. *"And the news just kept coming":* Oppenheimer, *The Other Mrs. Kennedy*, p. 446.
120. *"If there's one thing about our faith":* ibid., p. 471.
120. *"Don't cry now":* ibid., p. 465.
120. *"a good and decent man, who":* Thomas, *Robert Kennedy*, ch. 21.
120. *"It was the only moment . . . resting against the casket":* ibid.
121. *She greeted nearly every:* ibid.; Oppenheimer, *The Other Mrs. Kennedy*, p. 473.
121. *A priest said a prayer, and . . . into the ground:* Oppenheimer, *The Other Mrs. Kennedy*, p. 476.

11. STILL HERSELF

122. *she observed the old-fashioned:* Flynn, Betty, "Ethel Year After: Still Herself," *Boston Globe*, May 25, 1969.
122. *The children were expected to:* Leamer, *Kennedy Women*,]p. 637.
122. *She took the kids on:* Flynn, "Ethel Year After: Still Herself."
122. *She poured significant energy:* Oppenheimer, *The Other Mrs. Kennedy*, p. 491.
122. *She endured bed rest:* Flynn, "Ethel Year After: Still Herself."
122–23. *"Ethel is the same person . . . as if he wasn't gone":* ibid.
123. *"frequent visitor to Hickory Hill . . . you can see the sorrow there":* ibid.

123. *"I got it because of my cooking"*: Oppenheimer, *The Other Mrs. Kennedy*, p. 497.

123. *"Ethel's mood swept from deep"*: Leamer, *Kennedy Women*, p. 636.

123. *The turnover for maids*: Leamer, *Kennedy Women*, p. 640.

123. *He pled with her, asked for . . . remained an issue*: Oppenheimer, *The Other Mrs. Kennedy*, p. 525.

123. *A rowdy bunch, they destroyed*: ibid., p. 524.

123–24. *"They untied boats from the docks . . . threw lit firecrackers into the house"*: Leamer, *Kennedy Women*, pp. 660–61.

124. *He and David escaped with minor*: Leamer, *Kennedy Women*, p. 662.

124. *He'd been in town to*: Leamer, *Kennedy Women*, p. 727.

124. *Warren Rogers of* Look *magazine*: Oppenheimer, *The Other Mrs. Kennedy*, pp. 537–47.

124–25. *"There have been so many times . . . last forty years"*: Kennedy, *Ethel*, HBO, 2012.

125. *"Because it was Rory who"*: Associated Press, "Ethel Kennedy, RFK's Widow, Is Subject of HBO Documentary," October 17, 2012.

PART III: JACKIE

1. BLACK JACK AND JANET

128. *His father's fortune*: Bradford, *America's Queen*, p. 2.

128. *"Jackie and her younger"*: ibid., p. 1.

128. *Like Black Jack, Jackie's . . . Janet and Black Jack wed*: ibid., p. 7.

129. *She was competing in equestrian*: ibid., pp. 8, 9.

129–30. *"almost irrational social climbing . . . and I would"*: Haslam, Nicky, "The Real Lee Radziwill," *New York Times*, February 7, 2013.

130. *"There was such relentless . . . which she always kept"*: Bradford, *America's Queen*, p. 13.

130. *"It was like for the years from ten to twenty"*: ibid.

131. *It was there that she made*: Smith, *Grace and Power*, p. xv.

131. *"Jackie was already a rebel"*: Bradford, *America's Queen*, p. 15.

131–32. *Jackie and Lee's new stepfather*: Haslam, "The Real Lee Radziwill."

132. *"My amiable, long-suffering"*: Vidal, *Palimpsest*, p. 7.

132. *"permanently susceptible to the"*: ibid., p. 205.

132. *"He was a kind man"*: Bradford, *America's Queen*, p. 21.

132. *"A house more Victorian . . . Caroline and Jacqueline"*: Haslam, "The Real Lee Radziwill."

132. *"dark, musty"*: .Bradford, *America's Queen*, p. 20.

132. *Jackie did not share*: ibid.

132. *large brick neo-Georgian*: ibid., p. 19.

132. *"the lawn and the woods beyond"*: Vidal, *Palimpsest*, p. 10.

133. *"I always love it so at Merrywood . . . those great steep hills"*: Perry, *Jacqueline Kennedy*, p. 25.

133. *"Jackie never once spoke of step-this"*: Bradford, *America's Queen*, p. 25.

133. *"I think he . . . counted on us totally"*: Bradford, *America's Queen*, p. 25.

133. *In 1944 Jackie and her horse Danseuse*: Glueckstein, *Of Men, Women and Horses*, p. 64.

133. *"had begun to concentrate":* Perry, *Jacqueline Kennedy*, p. 25.
134. *"the prototype of the dangerous":* Bradford, *America's Queen*, pp. 28–29.
134. *"What we liked to do was . . . dirty old man":* ibid., p. 27.
134. *"From its very start, in 1843":* Peretz, Evgenia, "The Code of Miss Porter's," *Vanity Fair*, July 2009.
135. *"She really had a very dirty sense of humor":* Bradford, *America's Queen*, p. 29.
135. *One advised her twelve-year-old sister:* Bradford, *America's Queen*, p. 29.
135. *"never be a housewife":* Perry, *Jacqueline Kennedy*, p. 26.
135. *"I remember that talking . . . enveloping you with this gaze":* ibid.

2. THAT DAMN VASSAR

136. *"I spent two years at Vassar":* Perry, *Jacqueline Kennedy*, p. 27.
136. *"I knew about her Deb of the Year title":* Heymann, *A Woman Named Jackie*, p. 70.
136–37. *"She was intellectually very curious . . . it was most flattering ":* ibid., p. 71.
137. *"I was struggling like mad . . . coach me through it":* Bradford, *America's Queen*, p. 36.
137. *"It was a transitory period . . . lawyers and stockbrokers":* Heymann, *A Woman Named Jackie*, p. 72.
137. *"Jackie was learning the American geisha . . . she honed to perfection":* Bradford, *America's Queen*, p. 37.
137. *"beetle-browed bores":* Heymann, *A Woman Named Jackie*, p. 72.
138. *"She couldn't tolerate weak":* Bradford, *America's Queen*, p. 38.
138. *"I suppose it won't be long . . . she has nothing":* Heymann, *A Woman Named Jackie*, pp. 73–74.
138. *"If I was dressed up . . . 'Play the game'":* Bradford, *America's Queen*, p. 36.
138. *"You just remember, Jacqueline . . . obligation to warn us":* ibid., p. 37.
138. *In January of 1948:* ibid., p. 32.
138. *The turmoil was not only:* Heymann, *A Woman Named Jackie*, pp. 74–75.
138. *"The precipitate decline of the Bouviers' fortunes":* Bradford, *America's Queen*, p. 33.
139. *"glamour, glitter and rush":* ibid., p. 40.
139. *"I've had a glimpse . . . soak it all up":* Heymann, *A Woman Named Jackie*, p. 76.
139. *"the high point of my life":* ibid., p. 80.
139. *"Like most French residences . . . trooper in the truest sense of the word":* ibid.
139–40. *"The most wonderful thing here is . . . that is playing":* Bradford, *America's Queen*, p. 41.
140. *"it was just too luxurious and":* ibid., p. 42.
140. *"Don't you ever plan to come home?"* ibid, p.42.
140. *"You may hate the thought . . . half as bad as you think":* ibid., pp. 41–42.
140. *"Jackie's favorite activity was . . . stories they had to tell":* Heymann, *A Woman Named Jackie*, p. 83.
141. *"She was an extremely . . . didn't need to take my classes":* Perry, *Jacqueline Kennedy*, p. 29.
141. *"an autobiography; technical":* ibid., p. 30.
141. *"As to physical appearance":* Bradford, *America's Queen*, p. 46.
141. *"poets and idealists who could":* ibid.
142. *The whirlwind trip was:* ibid., pp. 48–49.

142. *"After the dinner, why, I walked . . . couldn't join him for a drink":* Bartlett, JFK Oral History #1, pp. 20–21.

3. THE CAREER WOMAN AND THE DISTINGUISHED GENTLEMAN

143. *"Perhaps her mother and stepfather":* Perry, *Jacqueline Kennedy,* p. 31.

143. *An encounter with a flamboyantly gay staff:* Bradford, *America's Queen,* p. 4.9

143. *Jackie, trained in the use of a professional:* Perry, *Jacqueline Kennedy,* p. 32.

144. *"You could make the column . . . capture how they talked":* Smith, *Grace and Power,* pp. 25–26.

144. *"Do you think a wife should . . . young man's slave":* Bradford, *America's Queen,* p. 53; Smith, *Grace and Power,* p. 26.

144. *There are a differing accounts:* Perry, *Jacqueline Kennedy,* p. 32; Heymann, *A Woman Named Jackie,* p. 92; Bradford, p. 56.

144. *"tall, well-built, urbane, very":* Heymann, *A Woman Named Jackie,* p. 91.

144. *"She didn't say much and neither . . . much you could say":* ibid., p. 108.

144. *And Jackie confided her fears:* Bradford, *America's Queen,* p. 57.

145. *"If you didn't get on the offensive":* Kennedy, *Historic Conversations,* First Conversation.

145. *For example, steroids prescribed for digestive:* Perry, *Jacqueline Bouvier,* p. 33, citing Dallek, *Unfinished Life.*

146. *"A remarkable combination of informality":* Bernstein, JFK Oral History, pp. 2–5.

4. A SPORADIC COURTSHIP, A CELEBRITY WEDDING

147–48. *"He had no facility for":* Perry, *Jacqueline Kennedy,* p. 34.

148. *"He saw her as a kindred spirit":* Dallek, *Unfinished Life,* p. 193.

148. *"He'd call me from some oyster bar":* Perry, *Jacqueline Kennedy,* p. 35.

148. *She took part in his intellectual:* Heymann, *A Woman Named Jackie,* p. 114.

148. *"How can I explain these people?":* ibid., p.115.

149. *"when they have nothing else to":* ibid., p. 116.

149. *"Joe Kennedy not only condoned . . . 'A politician has to . . . we've ever seen around here.'":* ibid., p. 117.

149. *"I remember the first time . . . won them over pretty quickly.":* Haslam, Nicky, "The Real Lee Radziwill," *New York Times,* February 7, 2013.

149. *"He really brightened . . . not true of many women":* Dallek, *Unfinished Life,* p. 193.

150. *"The year before we were married . . . on crutches more than not":* Kennedy, *Historic Conversations,* First Conversation.

150. *"She wasn't sexually attracted . . . terribly obvious Freudian situations":* Dallek, *Unfinished Life,* p. 194.

150. *"she would never have married":* Bradford, *America's Queen,* p. 67.

150. *"Articles excellent but you are missed":* Perry, *Jacqueline Kennedy,* p. 36.

150. *The engagement hit the papers:* ibid., p. 37.

150. *The wedding was, at Joe's direction:* ibid., p. 37.

151. *"something traditional and old-fashioned":* Heymann, *A Woman Named Jackie,* p. 130.

151. *"Joe reportedly was particularly pleased":* Perry, *Jacqueline Kennedy,* p. 37.

151. *"He was on his best behavior . . . went straight to the bar":* Vidal, *Palimpsest*, pp. 18–19.
151. *"The only time I ever. . . . was a nightmare":* Haslam, "The Real Lee Radziwill."
151–52. *"This is the most beautiful place . . . how unbelievably heavenly Jack is":* JBK to Joe and Rose Kennedy, 1953, RFKP, Box 14.
152. *"at last I know the true meaning":* Dallek, *Unfinished Life*, p. 194.
152. *As early as a couple of weeks into:* Heymann, *A Woman Named Jackie*, p. 135.

5. JACK'S DARK SIDE

153. *"I had designs on John . . . most eligible bachelor in New England":* Coit, JFK Oral History, p. 1.
153. *"overwhelming impression was . . . small stubby fingered hands.":* ibid., p. 2.
154. *"I gave a gulp":* ibid., p. 3.
154. *"glamour-boy pictures . . . had gone home":* ibid., pp. 3–4
154. *"a little open topless":* ibid., p. 4.
154–55. *"Where I made my mistake. . . 'But I can't wait . . . haven't any time'":* ibid., pp. 4–5.
155. *"He was so cold":* ibid., p. 5.
155. *"he frightened me more":* ibid.
155. *"I was afraid":* ibid., p. 6.
155. *"I don't think there are any men":* Dallek, *Unfinished Life*, p. 194.
156. *"after the first year they were":* Dallek, *Unfinished Life*, pp. 194–95.

6. THE SENATOR'S WIFE

157. *"I was taken immediately . . . have dinner at the Ritz":* Kennedy, *Historic Conversations*, First Conversation.
157. *"It just seems it was suitcases":* ibid.
157. *"It was terrifically nomadic":* ibid.
157. *While Jack and Fay attended:* Bradford, *America's Queen*, p. 76.
158. *"a nearly permanent houseguest":* Perry, *Jacqueline Kennedy*, p. 43.
158. *"Almost immediately, all the Kennedys":* Heymann, *A Woman Named Jackie*, p. 137.
158. *"I don't think she ever felt . . . play touch football":* Bradford, *America's Queen*, p. 91.
158. *Not only did she not fit into:* ibid.
158. *"So he loved the Irish . . . don't feel any jealousy":* Kennedy, *Historic Conversations*, First Conversation.
158. *"I was alone almost . . . no home life whatsoever":* Dallek, *Unfinished Life*, p. 194.
159. *"prepared for the humiliation":* ibid.
159. *"After their marriage his suits . . . an immaculate dresser":* Perry, *Jacqueline Kennedy*, pp. 40–41.
159. *"[Jack] tended to talk on and on":* Heymann, *A Woman Named Jackie*, p.168.
159. *"He consulted an ear, nose":* Dallek, *Unfinished Life*, p. 195.
160. *"had become almost unbearable . . . descend stairs sideways":* ibid., p. 196.
160. *"Jack was determined to have . . . paralyzed by pain":* ibid.
160. *"Jackie was magnificent with him . . . distract him from the pain":* Heymann, *A Woman Named Jackie*, p. 171.
161. *"huge, open, oozing . . . had to have backbone":* ibid., p. 173.

161. *"the winter of [Jack's] back"*: Kennedy, *Historic Conversations*, First Conversation.

161. *"Jack did more on the book . . . of any one person"*: Dallek, *Unfinished Life*, p. 199.

161. *"whose help during all the days"*: Perry, *Jacqueline Kennedy*, pp. 44–45.

161. *"I thought it would be a place"*: Kennedy, *Historic Conversations*, First Conversation.

162. *She also broke her ankle*: Perry, *Jacqueline Kennedy*, p. 46.

162. *Speaking engagements had Jack*: Kennedy, *Historic Conversations*, First Conversation.

162. *During this time and through the end of 1959*: Heymann, *A Woman Named Jackie*, p. 180.

162. *"hiked up her dress and broke"*: Maxine Cheshire, quoted in ibid., p. 186.

162. *As far as Jackie knew, Jack was relaxing with his dad*: Kennedy, *Historic Conversations*, First Conversation.

162. *Jack was enjoying himself enough"*: Heymann, *A Woman Named Jackie*, p. 190.

163. *Only after Smathers warned him*: ibid., pp. 190–91.

163. *"Everything is getting better . . . make you a grandmother yet"*: Letter from JBK to Rose, undated, Box 12, RFKP.

163. *"I didn't want to live there"*: Kennedy, *Historic Conversations*, First Conversation.

163. *Built in 1812, the three-story*: Perry, *Jacqueline Kennedy*, p. 48.

163. *"I remember that when she got . . . red chintz one week"*: Janet Auchincloss, JFK Oral History #1, p. 11.

164. *"They had an entirely average marriage"*: Heymann, *A Woman Named Jackie*, p. 203.

164. *"We were having dinner"*: Janet Auchincloss, JFK Oral History #1, p. 11.

164. *Buried next to his mother*: Bradford, *America's Queen*, p. 113.

7. THE CAMPAIGNER

166. *"as robust as a sumo"*: Heymann, *A Woman Named Jackie*, p. 200.

166. *"I will always remember the sweet expression"*: Perry, *Jacqueline Kennedy*, p. 49.

166. *"was more emotional about Caroline's"*: ibid.

166. *"There was cook Pearl"*: Bradford, *America's Queen*, p. 121.

167. *"I don't like to buy"*: Heymann, *A Woman Named Jackie*, p. 201.

167. *"When Jackie opened her mouth"*: Perry, *Jacqueline Kennedy*, p. 50.

167. *"simply invaluable"*: ibid.

167. *Jack handily won*: ibid.

168. *"Bonjour, mes amis"*: Bradford, *America's Queen*, p. 123.

168. *"You could just hear the screaming . . . embarrassment on my part"*: ibid.

169. *"candidates' spouses in the 1960 election"*: Perry, *Jacqueline Kennedy*, p. 57.

169. *"answer any questions they may have"*: ibid., p. 61.

169. *"there were over three million"*: Leamer, *Kennedy Women*, p. 503.

169. *"underneath a veil of lovely"*: Perry, *Jacqueline Kennedy*, p. 51.

169. *"judgment of people . . . she didn't conceal it"*: Bradford, *America's Queen*, pp. 129–30.

170. *"About the fifth day out"*: Kennedy, *Historic Conversations*, First Conversation.

170. *"All the talk over what"*: Perry, *Jacqueline Kennedy*, p. 60.

170. *"the longest night"*: Leamer, *Kennedy Women*, p. 509.

170. *Though the Secret Service quietly*: Heymann, *A Woman Named Jackie*, p. 244.

170. *"303 electoral votes to Nixon's 219"*: Dallek, *Unfinished Life*, p. 294.

170. *Almost a month premature:* Bradford, *America's Queen*, pp.141–42.

171. *"behind a door somewhere, out of sight":* ibid., p.142.

171. "two-hour crying jag": ibid., p.143.

171. *"The month after the baby's birth . . . couldn't hold any food down":* JBK to Rose, Box 14, RFKP. This letter was written to Rose in 1973, to help Rose as she assembled her memoirs.

171. *"I said Mrs. Truman . . . my babies and their father":* ibid.

171. *"I felt the President's house":* ibid.

172. *"From her bed [Jackie] is trying . . . the Library of Congress":* "1961: January 4-5, Jackie, Avedon, Hairdressers." Box 4, RFKP.

172. *Unfortunately, JFK was allergic:* "Times to Remember background materials," Box 12, RFKP.

172. *"The common misconception . . . influence on fashion":* Heymann, *A Woman Named Jackie*, p. 255.

172. *The designer Halston:* ibid.

173. *"You will be there . . . given with maximum politeness":* Bradford, *America's Queen*, p. 148.

173. *"I won't give any interviews":* ibid.

173. *Tish was prone to gaffes:* ibid., p. 144.

174. *"I did not wish to hurt her . . . church or someplace later":* Leamer, *Kennedy Women*, p. 515.

174. *The Secret Service, having:* Hill, *Mrs. Kennedy and Me*, p. 36.

174. *"[It] was not a happy time in my:* JBK to Rose, June 1973, RFKP Box 14.

174. *An exhausted Jackie had:* Heymann, *A Woman Named Jackie*, pp. 256–57.

174. *Pat Nixon, who sat next:* Bradford, *America's Queen*, p. 165.

175. *"the Kennedys, Fitzgeralds, and Bouviers":* Leamer, *Kennedy Women*, p. 521.

175. *"Jesus Christ":* Bradford, *America's Queen*, p. 166.

175. *"I missed all the gala things . . . one rises to it":* ibid.

8. THE QUEEN OF THE RESTORATION

176. *"My first impression of Mrs. Kennedy . . . learned it rapidly and gracefully":* Avery, JFK Oral History, p. 4.

176. *"a gaunt, unloved mansion":* Bradford, *America's Queen*, p. 169.

176. *"the peculiar combination of vomit":* Alsop, *"I've Seen the Best of It,"* pp. 434–35.

176. *The two preferred to eat together:* Bradford, *America's Queen*, pp. 170–71.

176. *"there was not a kitchen":* West, JFK Oral History, p. 3.

177. *"Because the process of gutting":* Perry, *Jacqueline Kennedy*, p. 101.

177. *"It was filled with":* West, JFK Oral History, p. 3.

177. *The Eisenhowers hadn't felt the need:* Heymann, *A Woman Named Jackie*, p. 262.

177. *"for the first time we were faced":* Avery, JFK Oral History, pp. 2–3.

177. *"Mrs. Kennedy came in frequently . . . you'd get the phone call":* ibid., p. 4.

178. *"Jackie's wish, murmured with a":* Heymann, *A Woman Named Jackie*, p. 264.

178. *Between the paces she put:* Bradford, *America's Queen*, p. 174.

178. *"When I learned I would be living . . . nothing in it earlier than 1948":* Perry, *Jacqueline Kennedy*, p. 95.

178. *"We've got a lot of work ahead . . . this into a grand house":* Smith, *Grace and Power,* pp. 89–90.
178. *"I know we're out of money . . . antiques into this house":* Bradford, *America's Queen,* p. 174.
178. *"I would write 50 letters to 50 musuem":* Perry, *Jacqueline Kennedy,* p. 102.
178. *"I knew funds would be needed . . . if not impossible":* ibid., p. 104.
178. *"It would be a sacrilege merely":* ibid., p. 102.
179. *"authentic furniture of the date":* Bradford, *America's Queen,* p. 175.
179. *The 175-room mansion:* Smith, *Grace and Power,* p. 94.
179. *"extensive curatorial and/or collecting experience":* Perry, *Jacqueline Kennedy,* p. 105.
179. *"To furnish the White House":* ibid., p. 109.
180. *"Without question,"* Barbara Perry wrote: ibid., p. 103.
180. *"her classic country . . . her work was primarily":* ibid., pp. 109–111.
180–81. *"the inspiration that [Jackie] was":* Boggs, JFK Oral History, p. 13.

9. LIFE AT THE WHITE HOUSE, AND AWAY

182. *To welcome three-year-old Caroline:* Hill, *Mrs. Kennedy and Me,* p. 46.
182. *"She is going to have to . . . treat her differently":* Perry, *Jacqueline Kennedy,* p. 70.
182–83. *"It is partly because . . . all bad for her":* Leamer, *Kennedy Women,* pp. 539–41.
183. *"Some of the most enduring images of the Kennedy years":* Smith, *Grace and Power,* p. 110.
183. *"She usually had her youngsters . . . great shock to me":* ibid., p. 106.
183. *The playgroup was run cooperatively:* ibid., pp. 106–7.
183. *By the fall of 1962, the nursery:* Perry, *Jacqueline Kennedy,* p. 71.
183–84. *"Jackie was not ready to . . . most public and important functions":* Leamer, *Kennedy Women,* p. 531.
184. *in Jackie's first year at the White House:* Heymann, *A Woman Named Jackie,* p. 268.
184. *Janet Auchincloss, Rose, Ethel:* Smith, *Grace and Power,* p. 111.
184. *"mostly alone or with the children":* Bradford, *America's Queen,* p. 201.
184. *Nancy Tuckerman remembered Jackie:* Tuckerman & Turnure, JFK Oral History, p. 12.
184. *Glen Ora was a seven-bedroom:* Heymann, *A Woman Named Jackie,* p. 268.
184. *"Middleburg was just plain boring . . . press hated Middleburg":* Hill, *Mrs. Kennedy and Me,* p. 49.
184. *The two spent ten thousand dollars on everything:* Bradford, *America's Queen,* p. 152.
185. *"Kennedy had affairs . . . call girls paid by Dave Powers":* Dallek, *Unfinished Life,* p. 476.
185. *"You were on the most elite":* Sabato, *The Kennedy Half-Century,* ch. 6.
186. *As they passed the secretary . . . Pierre Salinger's aides:* ibid.; Dallek, *Unfinished Life,* p. 477.
186. *"I think that Jack . . . not what she needed":* Leamer, *Kennedy Women,* p. 538.
186. *"[Jack] never wanted to have the . . . sort of light":* Kennedy, *Historic Conversations,* First Conversation.
187. *"a mixture of cabinet and friends from New York . . . walked around, puffing his cigar:* ibid.
187. *"Best parties I've ever attended . . . prettiest and the nicest":* ibid.

187. *"They set a feeling of warmth . . . attractive people and pretty surroundings":* Baldridge-Hollensteiner, JFK Oral History, p. 29.
187. *She arranged a performance:* Smith, *Grace and Power*, p. 237.
188. *It was through Malraux:* ibid., p. 275.
188. *"A logistical nightmare":* Hill, *Mrs. Kennedy and Me*, p. 95.
188. *"One of the worst headaches":* Baldridge-Hollensteiner, JFK Oral History, p. 23.
188. *"including Tish Baldridge's staff":* Hill, *Mrs. Kennedy and Me*, p. 96.
188–89. *"We had to have [the Marine Band]":* Baldridge-Hollensteiner, JFK Oral History, pp. 24–25.
189. *"It just so happened that . . . part of her master plan":* Hill, *Mrs. Kennedy and Me*, p. 97.
189. *And she was abroad a lot:* Perry, *Jacqueline Kennedy*, p. 76.
190. *United States forces managed to rescue:* Bradford, *America's Queen*, p. 192.
190. *"Within the privacy of his office" . . . crying in his bedroom":* Dallek, *Unfinished Life*, p. 366. (Jackie is referring to Jack's 1954 back surgery.)
191. *"I do not think it altogether inappropriate":* Hill, *Mrs. Kennedy and Me*, pp. 71–72.
191. *"Thanks in large part to Jackie":* Bradford, *America's Queen*, p. 197.
191. *"If you want war":* ibid., p. 198.
191. *"He savaged me . . . impervious to his charm":* ibid.
191. *"I think [Jack] was quite depressed . . . worse than he thought":* Kennedy, *Historic Conversations*, Fifth Conversation.
192. *"I'd just read* The Sabres of Paradise*":* ibid.
192. *"And by God, we were back":* ibid.
192. *"Every move, every comment":* Perry, *Jacqueline Kennedy*, p. 89.

10. PATRICK

194. *"Tucky" and Jackie had known each other:* Perry, *Jacqueline Kennedy*, pp. 167–68.
194. *She prepared scrapbooks:* ibid., p. 169.
195. *The four-pound, one-ounce boy:* Heymann, *A Woman Named Jackie*, pp. 385–86.
195. *"She was devastated . . . in such emotional pain":* Hill, *Mrs. Kennedy and Me*, p. 246.
195. *"which seemed to boost":* ibid.
195. *"With press photographers snapping . . . around them all the time":* ibid., p. 248.
196. *Those in attendance again:* Bradford, *America's Queen*, p. 253.
196. *And so, with Kennedy's blessing:* ibid., p. 255.

11. DALLAS

197. *Further, the Democratic Party:* Dallek, *Unfinished Life*, pp. 691–92.
197. *"Two years ago I introduced myself . . .":* Perry, *Jacqueline Kennedy*, p. 177.
198. *"Mr. President":* ibid.
198. *Turning to look at her husband:* Dallek, *Unfinished Life*, p. 694.
198. *"She was reaching for something . . . piece of the president's head":* Hill, *Mrs. Kennedy and Me*, p. 291.
198. *"My God! They have shot his":* ibid.
198. *"Jack," she said. "Jack, what have":* ibid., p. 292.
199. *"She still hadn't said a word, but":* ibid., p. 293.

12. AFTERMATH

200. *"She and I spoke for nearly . . . after he was hit":* Heymann, *A Woman Named Jackie,* p. 418.
201. *"I saw myself in the mirror . . . should have kept the blood on":* Swanson, *End of Days.*
201. *"I'm not going to":* Smith, *Grace and Power,* p. 443.
202. *"I don't want the church . . ."* ibid., pp. 443–451.
202. *Robert McNamara convinced:* ibid., pp. 443–51.
202. *"Her face covered . . . did not know about at the time":* ibid., pp. 453–54.
202. *When Hannan read passages . . . handed her his handkerchief:* ibid., p. 454.
202. *"fifty air force and navy jets":* ibid., p. 457.
203. *"Only bitter old men write . . . political theory or political science":* Heymann, *A Woman Named Jackie,* p. 418.
203. *"That's when she came out . . . 'Don't let it be forgot . . . known as Camelot'":* ibid., pp. 418–19.
203. *"was a misreading of history":* ibid., p. 419.

13. THE MANY LIVES OF JACKIE KENNEDY

204. *"I don't have much to live for":* Smith, *Grace and Power,* p. 457.
204. *She also served:* Perry, *Jacqueline Kennedy,* pp. 190–91.
205. *After years of attempting:* ibid., p. 192.
205. *Jackie was present when:* ibid.
205. *Jackie worked closely with:* ibid., pp. 192–93.
205. *"There won't be one shred of his . . . snooping through those rooms now":* ibid., p. 194.
206. *Many Americans thought less:* ibid., pp. 195–96.
206. *Though the $200,000 a year:* ibid., p. 187.
206. *"Jackie and Ari did . . . love of Greek mythology":* ibid., p. 197.
207. *"He was dynamic . . . But fascinating":* Haslam, Nicky, "The Real Lee Radziwill," *New York Times,* February 7, 2013.
207. *After a court battle:* Leamer, *Kennedy Women,* p. 689.
208. *Caroline became a lawyer:* Perry, *Jacqueline Kennedy,* p. 199.

PART IV: JOAN

1. THE MUSIC

211. *"Those are some of my . . . those are poignant memories":* Author interview, April 3, 2014.
211. *Her father, Harry Wiggin Bennett:* Chellis, *Living with the Kennedys,* p. 20.
211. *Joan was educated in Catholic schools:* www.mville.edu/about/fast-facts.html.
211. *She was a solid seamstress:* David, *Joan: The Reluctant Kennedy,* p. 28.
211. *"My father was an . . . when I was about ten":* Kennedy, *Joy of Classical Music,* ch. 1.
212. *"If the radio wasn't on . . . to go out in the evening":* ibid.
212. *"The radio and the phonograph . . . which seemed limitless":* ibid.
213. *"When I heard the velvety":* ibid.

213. *"I had Joan and Candy . . . not to do it again" She hung the brush . . . girls to behave:* Palm Beach Post, "Ugly Duckling," http://news.google.com/newspapers?nid=1964&dat= 19690401&id=5r4iAAAAIBAJ&sjid=ZrUFAAAAIBAJ&pg=4757,35313.

213. *"I sensed that . . . mother was an alcoholic":* Chellis, *Living with the Kennedys*, p. 21.

213. *"Both parents were drinkers . . . doesn't exist":* Tarraborrelli, *Jackie, Ethel, Joan* p. 83.

213. *"Just her presence . . . felt terrible for her":* ibid., p. 84.

214. *"It struck me as odd":* ibid., p. 83.

214. *"I called them Harry":* Kennedy, *Joy of Classical Music*, ch. 1.

214. *"I had as cloistered a background . . . much like myself":* Peters, William, "Teddy Kennedy," *Redbook*, June 1962.

214. *"I was a loner . . . I was a late bloomer":* Chellis, *Living with the Kennedys*, p. 22.

214. *In fact, she had so:* Kennedy, *Joy of Classical Music*, ch. 2.

215. *"Have I got a girl . . . God's gift to the modeling business":* David, *Joan, The Reluctant Kennedy*, p. 44.

215. *"She had fine facial":* ibid., pp. 44–45.

215. *Joan was booked by:* Palm Beach Post, "Ugly Duckling."

215. *Jones noted that Joan:* David, *Joan, The Reluctant Kennedy*, p. 45.

215. *"float a little more . . . light on her feet":* ibid., p. 47.

215. *Joan's first modeling:* ibid., p. 46.

215. *Joan got jobs in print:* ibid., p. 45.

215. *"She was one of those rare . . . Ingrid Bergman when she was Joan's age":* ibid.

215. *"Television was in its infancy . . . landed a few jobs":* Kennedy, *Joy of Classical Music*, ch. 2.

216. *"I was also one of the gang . . . saddle shoes and poodle skirts":* ibid.

216. *"Drinking Coke for a national . . . 'Don't you burp, young lady!'":* ibid.

216. *"It was Jack, not me":* Kennedy, *True Compass*, p. 117.

216. *"I was totally unimpressed . . . castle with the nuns":* Clymer papers.

217. *"Then I couldn't go":* Clymer, *Edward M. Kennedy: A Biography*, p. 22.

217. *"I arrived at the party with not one but two dates":* David, *Joan, The Reluctant Kennedy*, p. 50.

217. *Now, months later, Jean:* ibid.

217. *"I'll never forget that . . . darn good-looking":* ibid.

217. *"I definitely wanted to see":* Kennedy, *True Compass*, p. 117.

2. MARRYING THE KENNEDYS

218. *While she'd had many:* Chellis, *Living with the Kennedys*, p. 25.

218. *"I just took no interest . . . never even heard of the Kennedys":* David, Joan, *The Reluctant Kennedy*, p. 50.

218. *"I had to be chaperoned . . . if you were a Manhattanville girl":* Klein, *Ted Kennedy*, p. 35.

218. *He had a well-known:* Leamer, *Kennedy Men*, ch. 18.

219. *"She asked me about Bronxville . . . mostly our piano":* Leamer, *Kennedy Women*, p. 471.

219. *Rose, still protective of her youngest child, called Manhattanville:* Clymer, *Edward M. Kennedy: A Biography*, p. 23.

219. *They decided to turn it:* Clymer, papers.

219. *"I was keen to join my brothers . . . to be a family man":* Kennedy, *True Compass*, p. 183.

220. *"Apparently, he had brought other girls home":* Leamer, *Kennedy Women*, p. 471.

220. *" It was too good to be true":* ibid.

220. *"What do you think . . . What do we do next?":* Leamer, *Kennedy Men*, ch. 18.

220. *"Do you love my son? . . . make you feel at ease":* ibid., ch. 18.

220. *"She came home and told me . . . manner to which she was accustomed":* Sadler, Christine, *McCall's*, "Coming of Age of Joan Kennedy," February 1965.

221. *"I had no idea what I was getting into":* Chellis, *Living with the Kennedys*, pp. 26–27.

221. *"That was my introduction":* Kennedy, *Joy of Classical Music*, ch. 3.

221. *The only other time the:* Leamer, *Kennedy Men*, ch. 18.

221. *Ted finally brought Joan:* Clymer, *Edward M. Kennedy: A Biography*, p. 23.

221. *He didn't make time to:* Leamer, *Kennedy Men*, ch. 18.

221. *"My parents thought":* Clymer papers.

222. *"a place of Champagne bubbles":* "Chateau in the Sky," *New York Times*, December 3, 2006. www.nytimes.com/2006/12/03/nyregion/thecity/03pier.html?pagewanted=all&_r=0.

222. *PLEASE HAVE THE PIANO:* Joseph P. Kennedy Personal Papers, JFK Library.

222. *Joan had wanted to be married:* Chellis, *Living with the Kennedys*, p. 27.

223. *"wanted to invite every political":* Leamer, *Kennedy Women*, p. 477.

223. *Before the ceremony, Jack and Ted seemed:* Clymer, *Edward M. Kennedy: A Biography*, p. 24.

223. *Ted's law-school schedule:* Kennedy, *True Compass*, p. 126.

223. *"The truth is that Joan and I . . . definitely not standout cuisine":* ibid., p. 126.

223. *"We were dumped there . . . it was a nightmare":* Leamer, *Kennedy Men*, ch. 18.

223. *"I had to clean house":* ibid., ch. 18.

224. *"She grew adept in an . . . inns that had no heat":* Kennedy, *True Compass*, p. 127.

224. *"every state was critical":* ibid., p. 127.

224. *"Politics took over our lives almost":* Chellis, *Living with the Kennedys*, p. 27.

3. CAMPAIGNING WITH THE KENNEDYS

225. *Joan gave birth to the couple's first child:* Associated Press, October 22, 1962.

225. *"I have never seen Ted . . . two new words—my daughter":* Leamer, *Kennedy Men*, ch. 19.

225. *"He wants nine . . . I wouldn't have him":* David, *Joan, The Reluctant Kennedy*, p. 88.

225. *Joan later described it as a whirl:* Kennedy, *Joy of Classical Music*, ch. 3.

225. *"I felt rather like a tourist":* ibid.

226. *"I never felt any anger of being . . . lot to talk about":* Peters, William, "Teddy Kennedy," *Redbook*, June 1962.

226. *"I felt accepted as a little . . . greatest signs of friendliness there is":* ibid.

226. *When Joan went to Washington:* Bradford, *America's Queen*, pp. 126–28.

226. *"We'd chat, talk about campaigning":* ibid, p.128.

227. *"I remember [Jackie] saying to me, 'Stay very close to . . . she's his sister.'":* ibid., p. 128.

227. *"That night Frank is having a dinner party . . . so pissed off":* Leamer, *Kennedy Women*, p. 507.

227. *"She acted like Rose":* Chellis, *Living with the Kennedys,* p. 33.
228. *"If Jack could win there":* Kennedy, *Joy of Classical Music,* ch. 3.
228. *"look nice and be friendly":* ibid.
228. *"got whistled at by the miners":* ibid.
228. *"It turned into a bit of a joke":* ibid.
228. *Despite the Kennedys' displeasure:* Cannelos, *Last Lion,* p. 79.
229. *"I don't know if I'll know":* Leamer, *Kennedy Women,* p. 506.
229. *Soon after, Ted and Joan joined:* Kennedy, *True Compass,* p. 158.
229. *Jack had been allowed to:* ibid., p. 159.

4. CATCHING UP

230. *But with the Massachusetts Senate:* Clymer papers.
231. *"You can have a serious":* Kennedy, *True Compass,* p. 162.
231. *"I'd worshipped my father . . . to catch up":* ibid.
231. *"Ted was the obvious choice":* Kennedy, *Joy of Classical Music,* ch.3.
231. *"passionately . . . interested in arms control.":* Kennedy, Edward, *True Compass,* p. 163.
231–32. *"Yes. Go [to Africa] and see what's . . . independence from Belgium":* ibid.
232. *If Ted left that night, he could catch:* ibid., p. 163–64.
232. *It was a gorgeous brick building, built:* ibid.
232. *"Remember your own":* ibid., p. 435.
232. *"This time, we were on our . . . grassroots round ourselves":* Kennedy, *Joy of Classical Music,* ch. 3.
232. *"We went to every little town":* Leamer, *Kennedy Women,* p. 559.
232. *"If Ted was in Boston, then I tried to":* Liston, Carol, "Joan Kennedy Too Busy to Be Shy," *Boston Globe,* December 23, 1965.
232–33. *"everyone is curious about what the . . . you got a crowd":* Clymer papers.
233. *"It was just a bunch of . . . us against the world":* ibid.
233. *"I'd get the hostess to tell me what":* Kennedy, *Joy of Classical Music,* ch. 4.
233. *"I say we need a senator with a conscience":* www.youtube.com/watch?v=G6H0LTyaC94.
233. *"Yes, I minded . . . but I":* Finney, Ruth, *New York Word Telegram and Sun,* November 26, 1962.
234. *The article focused on the many:* Henshaw, Tom, Associated Press, October 22, 1962.
234. *"All the way to Brookline . . . afraid I'd mispronounce it":* ibid.
234. *"My role, as I see it . . . about politics too":* Peters, William, "Teddy Kennedy," *Redbook,* June 1962.
235. *"Really, I'm quite fortunate":* Henshaw, Tom, Associated Press, October 22, 1962.

5. THE SUPPORTIVE WIFE

236. *"My father's illness hit . . . almost more than I could bear":* Kennedy, *True Compass,* p. 178.
236. *"In Boston, Mrs. Kennedy isn't . . . elegant as the First Lady":* Chapman, Priscilla, "At Home with Mrs. Kennedy," 1963.
237. *"an immense mail for a freshman":* Falacci, Frank, "The Senator's Image Emerges," *Boston Globe,* September 15, 1963.

237. *"He is diligently working":* ibid.

237. *"She's going to be the youngest Senate wife":* Finney, Ruth, *New York World–Telegram and Sun*, November 26, 1962.

238. *The final paragraph referenced:* "Joan Kennedy Loses Baby," *Boston Globe*, May 17, 1963.

238. *The baby's remains were flown:* "Joan Kennedy Loses Baby by Miscarriage," *Boston Globe*, June 2, 1964.

238. *"We've been married four years":* David, *Joan, The Reluctant Kennedy*, p. 88.

238. *"It was discouraging and depressing for . . . whatever of physical health":* ibid., p. 104.

238. *The island took its name from a squaw:* "Kennedy in Court Fight Opposing Squaw Island Subdivision," *Boston Globe*, January 26, 1973.

238–39. *"Teddy's away so much . . ." So she got to work . . . antiques that Joan adored:* Hoffman, Betty Hannah, "What It's Like to Marry a Kennedy," *Ladies Home Journal*, October 1962.

239. *"Jackie would say":* Leamer, *Kennedy Women*, p. 539.

239. *"In the summers, everybody else in":* Bradford, *America's Queen*, pp. 126–28.

239. *"She was very, very good . . . almost nobody knew about it":* Leamer, *Kennedy Women*, p. 539.

239. *She was there when Jack:* Chellis, *Living with the Kennedys*, p. 34.

240. *"My first overwhelming sense . . . the president was dead":* Kennedy, *True Compass*, p. 208.

240. *"She adored Jack":* ibid., p. 209.

240. *She begged Candy to stay:* Manchester, *Death of a President*, ch. 6.

240. *"People kept drifting in all evening . . . shut myself upstairs in my room and cry":* Hoffman, Betty Hannah, "Joan Kennedy's Story," *Ladies Home Journal*, July 1970.

240. *"Joan found the mere contemplation":* Manchester, *Death of a President*, ch. 8.

241. *"In the end, the best way to honor":* Kennedy, Edward, *True Compass*, p. 214.

241. *"as a knife, slicing open . . . my friend Ed Moss":* ibid., p. 216.

241. *"I tried to get some response . . . he grabbed it":* "Ted Half-Sitting, Half-Standing in Plane, Bayh Says," *Boston Globe*, June 21, 1964.

241. *Ted was badly hurt:* Kennedy, *True Compass*, p. 220.

241–42. *The Bayhs courageously helped:* "Ted Half-Sitting, Half-Standing in Plane, Bayh Says," *Boston Globe*,

242. *"Nine cars passed them . . . Birch had pulled me from the plane":* Kennedy, *True Compass*, p. 221.

242. *She was sped to Cooley:* Linscott, Seymour, "Kennedy's Plane Crashes; Senator's Condition 'Fair,'" *Boston Globe*, June 20, 1964.

242. *"He's going to":* Taraborrelli, *Jackie, Ethel, Joan*, p. 284.

242. *"Hi, Joansie. Don't":* Kennedy, *True Compass*, p. 221.

242. *"Kennedy's injuries were not":* Linscott, "Kennedy's Plane Crashes; Senator's Condition 'Fair.'"

242. *"My life hung in the balance":* Kennedy, *True Compass*, p. 221.

242–43. *"Whipping his head . . . vertebrae to heal naturally":* ibid., p. 222.

6. THE PRETTIEST STAND-IN

244. *"A man never had":* "Joan Launches Ted's Campaign," *Boston Globe*, September 15, 1964.

244. *"I am no doctor":* ibid.

244. *"I'd hit a VFW . . . best to give it some spin":* Kennedy, *The Joy of Classical Music*, ch. 3.

244. *Bobby, the attorney general, had given up his seat:* Negri, Gloria, "Delegate Joan Lovely, Lonely," *Boston Globe*, August 26, 1964.

245. *"Joan, who had crumpled when":* Clymer, *Edward M. Kennedy: A Biography*, p. 61.

245. *"a very busy patient . . . fine spirits":* "Joan Launches Ted's Campaign," *Boston Globe*.

245. *"Still, I was on the road":* Kennedy, *Joy of Classical Music*, ch. 3.

245. *"He's getting awful":* Canellos, *Last Lion*, p. 109.

7. "NOBODY, NOTHING"

246. *Joan managed for a long time:* Canellos, *Last Lion*, p. 118.

246. *She stayed as busy as ever:* "Joan Visits Retarded Classes," *Boston Globe*, December 11, 1965.

246. *cheer up soldiers wounded in Vietnam:* Liston, Carol, "Radiant Joan Kennedy Spreads Cheer on Tour," *Boston Globe*, December 10, 1965.

246. *When Ted buried the hatchet:* "Ted's Wife on Political Bandwagon," *Boston Globe*, September 21, 1966.

246. *And she was by her husband's side:* Riddell, Janet, "Memorial Building Solemnly Dedicated," *Boston Globe*, September 10, 1966.

246. *"The timing was ironic . . . clan cronies, Dean Markham":* Cheshire, Maxine, "Kennedys Wary of the 'Caroline,'" July 13, 1967.

247. *He was baptized by Cardinal Cushing:* Negri, Gloria, "Cardinal Baptizes Patrick," *Boston Globe*, July 30, 1967.

247. *"The house was always full of cooks . . . nothing, not needed":* Chellis, *Living with the Kennedys*, p. 30.

247. *"He thinks you're a wonderful wife . . . just has this addiction":* Canellos, *Last Lion*, p. 119.

247. *"When one grows up feeling":* Chellis, *Living with the Kennedys*, p. 39.

248. *"My dear . . . chase after politicians":* Clymer papers.

248. *"I tried telling myself":* Chellis, *Living with the Kennedys*, p. 39.

248. *"The only thing I was sure of":* ibid.

248. *"Joan Kennedy wore a glittering . . . Blue Room in the White House":* "Joan Stuns Nixons in Mini-Dress," United Press International, March 13, 1969.

248. *In 1968 she again was:* Canellos, *Last Lion*, p. 111.

248. *he worried that his brother:* ibid., p. 127.

248. *Bobby's theme was:* Kennedy, *Joy of Classical Music*, ch. 3.

249. *"I have never, ever . . . beyond grief and agony":* Canellos, *Last Lion*, p. 134.

249. *"She disappeared, and no one knew":* Chellis, *Living with the Kennedys*, p. 36.

249. *"He looked slightly heavier":* Murphy, Jeremiah, "Tragedy Ages Ted, Darkens His Mood," *Boston Globe*, August 22, 1968.

249. *"Gone, perhaps forever, is the Teddy Kennedy":* ibid.

249. *"It wasn't my personality . . . things didn't hurt so much":* Chellis, *Living with the Kennedys*, pp. 36–37.

250. *"a flurry of awed whispers—'She is pretty! She is pretty!'":* Caldwell, Jean, "Joan's a Real Kennedy; She Enjoys Campaigning," *Boston Globe*, September 14, 1968.

250. *Not two weeks later:* Cheshire, Maxine, "Joan Kennedy Will Campaign for Bayh," *Boston Globe*, September 24, 1968.

250. *Whatever grief she felt . . . non-answers to both:* Caldwell, "Joan's a Real Kennedy."

250. *"I drank socially at first":* Chellis, *Living with the Kennedys*, p. 40.

250. *"I tried to talk about it . . . nobody would really talk about it":* Leamer, *Kennedy Women*, p. 699.

251. *She stayed at the couple's Cape house:* Chellis, *Living with the Kennedys*, p. 37.

251. *"It's too early to predict anything . . . his decision, not mine":* Blackman, Ann, "And a Time for Solitude and Thought," *Boston Globe*, March 23, 1969.

8. CHAPPAQUIDDICK

252. *after serious contemplation, Ted decided:* Canellos, *Last Lion*, p. 146.

252. *"Don't run for President . . . Stop him":* Dedman, Bill, "Ted Kennedy FBI File Reveals Death Threats," MSNBC.com, June 14, 2010. www.nbcnews.com/id/34248485/ns/us_news-life/t/ted-kennedy-fbi-file-reveals-threats.

252. *almost 80 percent of whom:* Canellos, *Last Lion*, p. 146.

252. *"The feeling of momentum":* ibid.

253. *Afterward, he visited a:* ibid., pp. 148–49.

253. *"Politics was her life":* ibid., p. 149.

253. *"The next thing I recall":* Shaffer, *Left to Die*, p. 54.

253. *He said he dove repeatedly:* Leamer, *Kennedy Women*, p. 647.

254. *He didn't report the accident:* Canellos, *Last Lion*, pp. 155–57.

254. *"No one told me":* Chellis, *Living with the Kennedys*, p. 90.

254. *Joan had a miscarriage:* "Joan Kennedy Resting in Hospital," *Boston Globe*, August 30, 1969.

254. *About this time, she also learned:* Leamer, *Kennedy Women*, p. 651.

254. *On November 18, 1969, he died:* Kennedy, *True Compass*, pp. 292–93.

255. *"For a few months everyone . . . when I truly became an alcoholic":* Leamer, *Kennedy Women*, p. 651.

9. "THE BEGINNING OF THE END"

256. *"We remained together . . . perhaps fear of change":* Kennedy, *True Compass*, pp. 183–84.

256. *"the beginning of the end":* Chellis, *Living with the Kennedys*, p. 38.

256. *"I believe everything Ted said . . . alive at all":* "'I Worry All the Time Whether Ted Will Be Shot,' Says Joan Kennedy," Associated Press, June 30, 1970.

256. *Joan later recalled:* Kennedy, *Joy of Classical Music*, ch. 4.

257. *"repeat the performance":* Cheshire, Maxine, "TV Shows Chase Joan Kennedy," *Washington Post*, December 9, 1970.

257. *"It took a lot out of me":* Chellis, *Living with the Kennedys*, p. 41.

257. *Sometimes she'd leave the children:* ibid., p. 43.

257. *"My mom struggled mightily . . . aren't available to many people":* Kennedy, Patrick. Telephone interview with author, April 2014.

257. *"What family? . . . never wanted Ted to be President. Never":* "'I Worry All the Time Whether Ted Will Be Shot,' Says Joan Kennedy," Associated Press.

257. *"subjecting my family to fears . . . it's too early.":* "Kennedy Says Fear of Assassin Halted '72 Run," United Press International, July 27, 1971.

258. *"He grudgingly admitted":* Kennedy, *True Compass*, p. 305.

258. *He'd have to have his right:* ibid., p. 307.

258. *"Ted would bring in the whole . . . and I was the traffic cop":* Leamer, *Kennedy Women*, p. 676.

258. *Joan had been treated in private:* MacPherson, Myra, "Joan Kennedy—The Trying Years," *Boston Globe*, November 16, 1975.

259. *"has reached an agreement that":* Cheshire, Maxine, "Joan to Make Few Appearances If Ted Runs," September 9, 1973.

259. *In April 1976, Joan's mother:"* Joan Kennedy's Mother Found Dead in Florida," Associated Press, April 9, 1976.

259. *"I couldn't help her . . . for my own survival":* Chellis, *Living with the Kennedys*, p. 47.

259. *"I'd been told that an alcoholic . . . have some time for myself":* ibid.

259. *"public life has not been kind":* "Nation: The Vulnerable Soul of Joansie," *Time*, November 5, 1979.

259. *She relapsed badly:* ibid.

260. *"If Joan did not campaign . . . if Joan could forgive him, so could they":* Chellis, *Living with the Kennedys*, p. 70.

260. *She kept up with the grueling pace:* Dowd, Maureen, "Not a Launching But a Scuttling," *Time*, December 13, 1982.

260. *This was buoyed by her:* Taylor, Benjamin, "A Pledge from Joan Kennedy," *Boston Globe*, February 16, 1980.

260. *"I'm learning what it is like . . . never been doing better in my entire life":* "Joan Kennedy's Life Alone," Associated Press, March 3, 1982.

10. STILL A KENNEDY

261. *"She didn't pick being a . . . that they weren't alone":* Kennedy, Patrick. Personal interview with author. April 2014.

261. *"had a number of good years . . . more churches and castles":* ibid.

261. *Three years later, she was:* McPhee, Michele, and Dave Wedge, "The Fall of Joan," *Boston Magazine*, August 2005.

262. *"She was conscious . . . that it was anything special":* ibid.

262. *Though Joan didn't appear drunk:* ibid.

262. *The agreement stipulated that:* Ellement, John, and Maria Sacchetti, "Joan Kennedy, Children Reach Agreement; Medical, Financial Team, Rehab Cited," *Boston Globe*, June 13, 2005.

262. *His new wife, Vicki, was by his side:* Newton-Small, Jay, "A Family Gathers to Say Farewell to Ted Kennedy," *Time*, August 26, 2009.

262. *Ted stepped in and helped:* Donaldson, Susan James, "Kara Kennedy's Heart May Have Taken 'Direct Hit' by Cancer Cure," ABC News, September 20, 2011.

262–63. *"Her disease sidelined her . . . second chance with her, so to speak":* Author interview with Patrick Kennedy, April 2014.

263. *"I was aghast":* ibid.

PART V: VICKI

1. A DIFFERENT TYPE

266. *"What's wrong? . . . Dream on, Kennedy":* Kennedy, *True Compass*, p. 423.

266. *"Oh, don't talk to":* Clymer papers.

267. *"Up close, the face is a shock":* Kelly, Michael, "Ted Kennedy on the Rocks," *GQ*, February 1990.

267. *A criminal investigation:* Jordan, Mary, "Jury Finds Smith Not Guilty of Rape," *Washington Post*, December 12, 1991.

267. *Ted's approval ratings:* Kennedy, *True Compass*, p. 434.

267. *But as Ted chatted:* Clymer papers.

267. *he felt more relaxed:* Kennedy, *True Compass*, p. 423.

267. *Edmund Reggie, Vicki's father:* Reggie, Edmund, Oral history, JFK Library.

267. *"There was a film made about the Democratic Party":* Marquard, Bryan, *Boston Globe*, "Edmund M. Reggie, 87; Louisiana stalwart for Kennedy campaigns became Edward M. Kennedy's father-in-law," *Boston Globe*, November 19, 2013.

268. *"I was really taken . . . praying for [Jack's] success":* Reggie, Edmund, Oral history, JFK library.

268. *"I could never vote for":* Canellos, *Last Lion*, p. 282.

268. *"I have six children":* Reggie, Edmund, Oral history, JFK library.

268. *Victoria, Vicki for short, was:* Canellos, *Last Lion*, p. 283.

268. *"Where Life Is Rice and Easy":* Crowley city website, www.crowley-la.com.

268. *At one time, the city:* Canellos, *Last Lion*, p. 283.

268. *"but it wasn't a sprawling . . . to be just like Vicki Reggie":* Thomas, Jack, "The Next Kennedy: Folks Back in Crowley, La., Have Nothing But Good Things to Say about Her—It's Ted Who Gets the Mixed Reviews," *Boston Globe*, April 2, 1992.

268. *"There was a jukebox":* ibid.

268. *The Reggie family was of Lebanese:* Reggie, Edmund, Oral history. JFKL.

269. *"very sweet and very polite":* Thomas, "The Next Kennedy."

269. *"There were conversational boundaries . . . with each other":* Kennedy, *True Compass*, p. 400.

269. *Despite some missed classes:* Thomas, "The Next Kennedy."

269. *"What I remember about her":* ibid.

269. *"[She wasn't] bratty smart":* ibid.

269. *Some friends noted:* ibid.

269. *In a blue pinstripe suit with pocket hankie:* ibid.

269. *One picture showed Jack Kennedy:* ibid.

270. *After high school:* ibid.

270. *"I met him for the photo . . . evidence of it"*: Clymer papers.
270. *"No? . . . it didn't dawn on me"*: Kennedy, Vicki, "HWA Speakers Bureau—The Power of Choice," YouTube, February 28, 2013, www.youtube.com/watch?v=FBpxyo8iwgo.
271. *With Taplin's encouragement:* Thomas, "The Next Kennedy."
271. *"There is nothing good"*: Kennedy, "HWA Speakers Bureau."
271. *She also got their Nantucket:* Thomas, "The Next Kennedy."
271. *Everything was to be "very casual":* ibid.
271. *"But as much as Vicki"*: Kennedy, *True Compass*, p. 423.
271. *"Did I just say* yes?" Thomas, "The Next Kennedy."

2. THE WOMANIZING ENDS

273. *"As the former girlfriend"*: Kelly, Michael, "Ted Kennedy on the Rocks," *GQ*, February 1990.
273. *"so outrageous that I can't imagine"*: Kennedy, *True Compass*, p. 421.
274. *"position on offshore drilling"*: Worthington, Christa, "The Curse of the Kennedys," *The Independent*, May 25, 1997.
274. *"I've known Ted Kennedy a lot of years . . . when does"*: Thomas, "The Next Kennedy."
274. *"That's a relief, because I"*: Kennedy, *True Compass*, p. 424.
274. *"They were a little older"*: Clymer papers.
274. *Ted began keeping up on football:* Kennedy, *True Compass*, p. 424.
275. *"I remember one night I said . . . run upstairs five times" . . . "He said, 'No . . . beautiful sound in the world.'"*: Clymer papers.
275. *"There is no way"*: Kennedy, *True Compass*, p. 426.
275. *"I won't say that I was hurt"*: ibid.
275. *"Well, listen, I was just thinking, uh"*: ibid.
275. *"We certainly had not spent . . . each other as a married couple"*: ibid., p. 183.
276. *On January 14, 1992, Ted proposed:* ibid., p. 427.
276. *"He said, 'You know I love . . . ask you and Doris' . . . did it the proper way"*: Thomas, "The Next Kennedy."
276. *she shared the secret with a friend:* Kennedy, *True Compass*, p. 427.
276. *"If they've come to Crowley looking . . . Teddy Kennedy, with his past"*: Thomas, "The Next Kennedy."
276. *"So I swam down underwater"*: Clymer papers.
277. *"If anybody were looking to strategize . . . it's ludicrous"*: Thomas, "The Next Kennedy."
277. *"I knew I was right . . . knew the man"*: Kennedy, Vicki, "HWA Speakers Bureau—The Power of Choice," YouTube, February 28, 2013, www.youtube.com/watch?v=FBpxyo8iwgo.
277. *Ted gave his new bride an oil:* Kennedy, *True Compass*, p. 427.

3. BATTLING ROMNEY

278. *"If you don't stand up"*: Horowitz, Jason, "Romney's First Step Into Political Arena, vs. Ted Kennedy in 1994, Was a Cautious One," *Washington Post*, October 17, 2012, www.washington post.com/lifestyle/style/romneys-first-step-into-political-arena-vs-ted-kennedy-in-1994-was-a-cautious-one/2012/10/17/a81b35ca-0e5e-11e2-bb5e-492c0d30bff6_story.html.

278. *"was positioning himself . . . senior senator's outdated ways":* Kennedy, *True Compass,* p. 438.

278. *It was to be an expensive race:* Phillips, Frank, and Scot Lehigh, "Kennedy Borrows $2m for Campaign; Estate in Virginia Used as Collateral," *Boston Globe,* October 22, 1994.

278. *By Labor Day, a* Boston Globe *poll:* Goldman, Andrew, "Mitt Romney's War with the *Boston Globe,*" *New Republic,* October 5, 2012, www.newrepublic.com/article/politics/magazine/108184/mitt-romneys-war-the-boston-globe.

278. *In a move that highlighted :* Kennedy, *True Compass,* p. 439.

279. *"that there would be a lot":* Clymer papers.

279. *The firm uncovered slashed jobs:* Clymer, *Edward M. Kennedy: A Biography,* p. 536.

279. *"Do I still have my charisma?":* Howe, Peter, "Kennedy Blasts GOP Rival; Says Romney's Plan Attacks 'Poor Children,'" *Boston Globe,* June 18, 1994.

279. *"She was a natural . . . very good friends":* Kennedy, *True Compass,* p. 440.

279. *"No, thank you!":* ibid., p. 441.

280. *But this campaign, Ted called Mitt out:* ibid., p. 439.

280. *"It was important to talk about":* Clymer papers.

280. *"It doesn't ring true to me . . . what he really was doing":* ibid.

280. *"So, honey, is he good to you? . . . first time in my life":* Kennedy, *True Compass,* p. 441.

280. *"said he needed the help of Aerosmith":* "Vicki Kennedy Had Noteworthy Role in Speech," *Boston Globe,* September 13, 1994.

280–81. *"Well, this victory really isn't about me . . . Not your family. You.":* Kennedy, *True Compass,* p. 449.

4. NEW KIND OF KENNEDY

282. *"I was involved in every issue . . . with the love of my life":* Kennedy, Vicki, "HWA Speakers Bureau—The Power of Choice," YouTube, February 28, 2013, www.youtube.com/watch?v=FBpxyo8iwgo.

282. *Ted even respected:* Couric, Katie, "@KatieCouric: Vicki Reggie Kennedy & Ted Kennedy Jr.," YouTube, December 22, 2009, www.youtube.com/watch?v=9FCBm9kBpG8.

282. *Ted dressed as Ponce de Leon:* Bickelhaupt, Susan, "Ted Kennedy Makes Some Birthday Waves," *Boston Globe,* February 25, 1997.

282. *Vicki dressed as Anastasia:* Bickelhaupt, Susan, "'Joy' from the World," *Boston Globe,* December 20, 1997.

283. *"He's obviously been practicing":* Beggy, Carol, "King Tells All About His Accident," *Boston Globe,* October 30, 1999.

283. *"revealing the trademark Kennedy . . . Vicki, Vicki":* Milligan, Susan, "For Senator, a Positive Loss," *Boston Globe,* April 28, 2004.

283. *"Dear Teddy . . . but for our souls":* Kennedy, Edward, "Excerpts from eulogy by Sen. Kennedy," *New York Times,* January 25, 1995.

284. *"She was always there . . . in the way she did things":* Kennedy, *True Compass,* p. 476.

284. *Though John Jr. never ran:* Seelye, Katharine Q. "John F. Kennedy Jr., Heir to a Formidable Dynasty," *New York Times,* July 19, 1999.

284–85. *"He had every gift but length of years"*: Kennedy, "A Man with 'Every Gift but Length of Years,'" John F. Kennedy eulogy published in the *Boston Globe*, July 24, 1999.

285. *Not only did she have cancer:* Jacobs, Sally, "Kennedy, His Children, and Cancer," *Boston Globe*, May 25, 2008.

285. *We were told that every doctor:* Kennedy, *True Compass*, p. 5.

285. *Seven years after Kara's aggressive:* Kennedy, *True Compass*, p. 5.

285. *Some oncologists would speculate that:* Donaldson James, Susan, "Kara Kennedy's Heart May Have Taken 'Direct Hit' by Cancer Cure," ABC News, http://abcnews.go.com/Health/kara-kennedys-heart-attack-related-cancer-treatment/story?id=14558232.

285. *"One step at a time"*: Kennedy, *True Compass*, p. 5.

5. TIME TO SAIL

286. *They had coffee:* Kennedy, Vicki, "Vicki Kennedy's Final Remarks at UCSF Symposium," YouTube, November 24, 2011, www.youtube.com/watch?v=TcMY7MLYZ4k.

286. *He moved toward the door:* Kennedy, *True Compass*, p. 3.

286. *"You're going to be okay"*: ibid., p. 4.

286. *"I just knew it was"*: Kennedy, "Vicki Kennedy's Final Remarks at UCSF Symposium."

286. *"I went from concern to fear"*: ibid.

287. *"By the end of that day . . . they did"*: ibid.

287. *"Vicki and I privately were told"*: Kennedy, *True Compass*, p. 5.

287. *Only 30 percent:* "Glioblastoma," American Brain Tumor Association, May 27, 2014, www.abta.org/brain-tumor-information/types-of-tumors/glioblastoma.html.

287. *"It was our brain tumor . . . in every single way"*: Kennedy, "Vicki Kennedy's Final Remarks at UCSF Symposium."

287. *"His perspective was . . . stay ahead of the darkness, as he put it"*: ibid.

287–88. *"Everything seemed back to"*: Kennedy, *True Compass*, p. 7.

288. *More than a dozen experts:* Altman, Lawrence, "The Story behind Kennedy's Surgery," *New York Times*, July 29, 2008.

288. *In the meeting, the experts weighed:* ibid.

288. *"If I can show that there's hope"*: Kennedy, *True Compass*, p. 8.

288. *That preparation allowed them:* Kennedy, "Vicki Kennedy's Final Remarks at UCSF Symposium."

288. *"We had an unspoken pact . . . it was magnificent"*: ibid.

288–89. *"because the cancer was not . . . removed for the best chances"*: Altman, "The Story behind Kennedy's Surgery."

289. *It lasted a grueling three and:* Paul, Katie, "Ted Kennedy Kept Awake during Risky Brain Surgery," *Newsweek*, June 1, 2008.

289. *"But once you've started . . . some manipulation up there"*: ibid.

289. *"He needed me to be his advocate . . . was the fierce lioness"*: Kennedy, "Vicki Kennedy's Final Remarks at UCSF Symposium."

289. *"Medicare is in jeopardy! . . . I need to get back to Washington"*: ibid.

290. *"You can't go back . . . brain surgery"*: ibid.

290. *"It was a secret little":* ibid.
290. *"Immediately the roll call came to a":* Herszenhorn, David M. "Kennedy Returns to the Senate," *New York Times,* July 9, 2008, http://thecaucus.blogs.nytimes. com/2008/07/09/kennedy-returns-to-the-senate/?_php=true&_type=blogs&_r=0.
290. *The final tally was sixty-nine:* ibid.
290. *"There wasn't a person":* ibid.
290. *Ted called his friend:* Kennedy, *True Compass,* p. 9.
290. *"For all those whose cares":* Toobin, Jeffrey, "The Shrum Curse," *New Yorker,* August 20, 2007.
290. *"I knew essentially":* Kennedy, *True Compass,* p. 9.
291. *They weren't sure what kind:* Kennedy, "Vicki Kennedy's Final Remarks at UCSF Symposium."
291. *A minute in, he had:* Kennedy, *True Compass,* pp. 9–10.
291. *"You know, I really don't":* ibid.
291. *"If you give him pain . . . worked too hard for this night":* ibid., p. 10.
291. *"Vicki, shall we say":* ibid.
291. *"What do you think . . . with the family and wave":* ibid.
292. *Ted would have to play:* ibid., p. 11.
292. *Vicki was anxious and exhausted:* Kennedy, "Vicki Kennedy's Final Remarks at UCSF Symposium."
292. *"Nothing, nothing was going":* Kennedy, *True Compass,* p. 12.
292. *"They liked my speech!":* Kennedy, "Vicki Kennedy's Final Remarks at UCSF Symposium."
292. *Returning to his office in the:* ibid.
292. *Ted's mahogany desk had once:* Russell, Jenna, "As Showcase and Centerpiece of the Late Senator's Legacy, Edward M. Kennedy Institute in Boston Will Feature a Replica of His Office," *Boston Globe,* January 31, 2010.
292. *With Vicki by his side:* Milligan, Susan, "Kennedy Returns to Senate," *Boston Globe,* November 18, 2008.
292. *A banner reading "Welcome Back:* ibid.
293. *"You've never seen":* Kennedy, "Vicki Kennedy's Final Remarks at UCSF Symposium."

6. TO THE GRAVE

294. *Vicki knew those precious extra:* Kennedy, Vicki, "Vicki Kennedy's Final Remarks at UCSF Symposium," YouTube, November 24, 2011, www.youtube.com/ watch?v=TcMY7MLYZ4k.
294. *In true Ted fashion:* ibid.
294. *"There I was caring for . . . all going to be OK":* Hayes, Cathy, "Vicki Kennedy Rules Out Run for Political Office," *Irish Central,* August 16, 2010, www.irishcentral.com/ news/vicki-kennedy-rules-out-run-for-political-office-100751824-237710671.html.
294. *Even President Obama joined:* Miga, Andrew, "Obama Sings 'Happy Birthday' to Ted Kennedy at Tribute Concert," *Huffington Post,* March 8, 2009, www.huffingtonpost. com/2009/03/09/obama-sings-happy-birthda_n_172939.html.

295. *"I was gonna stay out there all day":* Kennedy, "Vicki Kennedy's Final Remarks at UCSF Symposium."

295. *"Sailing, for me, has always been":* Kennedy, *True Compass*, p. 6.

295. *He even had a diary from his First Communion:* Kennedy, "Vicki Kennedy's Final Remarks at UCSF Symposium."

295. *His publisher's delivery of manuscripts:* Couric, Katie, "@KatieCouric: Vicki Reggie Kennedy & Ted Kennedy Jr.," YouTube, December 22, 2009, www.youtube.com/watch?v=9FCBm9kBpG8.

295. *"That was the greatest gift . . . the way we lived it":* Kennedy, "Vicki Kennedy's Final Remarks at UCSF Symposium."

296. *The morning of the mass:* Balz, Dan, Keith B. Richburg, and Shailagh Murray, "'We loved this kind and tender hero,'" *Washington Post*, August 30, 2009.

296. *"Bells began to toll at 10:45 a.m.":* ibid.

SOURCES

Alsop, Joseph W. *"I've Seen the Best of It": Memoirs*. New York: Norton, 1992.

Avedon, Richard. *The Kennedys: Portrait of a Family*. New York: Collins Design, 2007.

Avery, Isaac. Recorded interview by Pamela Turnure and Nancy Tuckerman, May 12, 1964. John F. Kennedy Library Oral History Program.

Baldridge-Hollensteiner, Letitia. Recorded interview by Mrs. Wayne Fredericks, April 24, 1964. John F. Kennedy Library Oral History Program.

Bartlett, Charles. Recorded interview by Fred Holborn, January 6, 1965. John F. Kennedy Library Oral History Program. (#1)

Bernstein, Leonard. Recorded interview by Nelson Aldrich, July 21, 1965. John F. Kennedy Library Oral History Program.

Boggs, Corinne "Lindy." Recorded interview by Bill Hartigan, April 1, 1976. John F. Kennedy Library Oral History Program.

Bouvier, Lee, and Jacqueline Bouvier. *One Special Summer 1974*. New York: Delacorte Press, 1974.

Bradford, Sarah. *America's Queen: The Life of Jacqueline Kennedy Onassis*. New York: Penguin, 2000.

Canellos, Peter S., ed. *Last Lion: The Fall and Rise of Ted Kennedy*. New York: Simon & Schuster, 2009.

Cassidy, Tina. *Jackie After O: One Remarkable Year When Jacqueline Kennedy Onassis Defied Expectations and Rediscovered Her Dreams*. New York: It Books, 2012.

Cavanaugh, John. Recorded interview by Joseph E. O'Connor, March 27, 1966. John F. Kennedy Library Oral History Program.

Chellis, Marcia. *Living with the Kennedys: The Joan Kennedy Story*. New York: Jove Books, 1985.

Clymer, Adam. *Edward M. Kennedy: A Biography*. New York: William Morrow, 1999.

Dallek, Robert. *An Unfinished Life: John F. Kennedy, 1917–1963*. New York: Back Bay Books, 2003.

David, Lester. *Ethel: The Story of Mrs. Robert F. Kennedy*. New York: World Publishing, 1971.

———. *Joan, The Reluctant Kennedy*. New York: Funk & Wagnalls, 1974.

Glueckstein, Fred. *Of Men, Women and Horses*. Bloomington, IN: Xlibris, 2006.

Goldsmith, Kenneth. *Seven American Deaths and Disasters*. Brooklyn: powerHouse Books, 2013.

Hennessey, Luella. Recorded interview by Ed Martin, November 26, 1964. John F. Kennedy Library Oral History Program. (#1)

Hennessey-Donovan, Luella. Recorded interview by Ed Martin, September 25, 1991. John F. Kennedy Library Oral History Program. (#2)

Hersh, Seymour M. *The Dark Side of Camelot*. New York: Back Bay Books, 1997.

Heymann, C. David. *A Woman Named Jackie: An Intimate Biography of Jacqueline Bouvier Kennedy Onassis*. New York: Lyle Stuart, 1989.

Hill, Clint, with Lisa McCubbin. *Mrs. Kennedy and Me*. New York: Gallery Books, 2012.

Kennedy, Edward M. *My Senator and Me: A Dog's-Eye View of Washington, D.C.* New York: Scholastic, 2006.

———. *True Compass: A Memoir*. New York: Twelve, 2009.

Kennedy, Jacqueline. *Historic Conversations on Life with John F. Kennedy*. New York: Hyperion, 2011. Electronic edition.

Kennedy, Joan. *The Joy of Classical Music: A Guide for You and Your Family*. New York: Nan A. Talese, 1992. Electronic edition.

Kennedy, John F. *Profiles in Courage*. New York: Harper and Brothers, 1956.

Kennedy, Rory. *Ethel*, HBO, 2012.

Kennedy, Rose Fitzgerald. *Rose Fitzgerald Kennedy: Times to Remember*. New York: Doubleday, 1974.

The Rose Fitzgerald Kennedy Personal Papers (RFKP), housed at the John F. Kennedy Presidential Library and Museum, Boston MA.

Klein, Edward. *Ted Kennedy: The Dream that Never Died*. New York: Crown, 2009.

John F. Kennedy Library Foundation. *Rose Kennedy's Family Album: From the Fitzgerald Kennedy Private Collection, 1878–1946*. New York: Grand Central, 2013.

Leamer, Laurence. *The Kennedy Men: 1901–1963*. New York: William Morrow, 2001.

———. *The Kennedy Women: The Saga of an American Family*. New York: Villard Books, 1994.

Manchester, William. *The Death of a President*. New York: Harper and Row, 1967.

Nasaw, David. *The Patriarch: The Remarkable Life and Turbulent Times of Joseph P. Kennedy*. New York: Penguin Press, 2012. Electronic edition.

Oppenheimer, Jerry. *The Other Mrs. Kennedy*. New York: St. Martin's Press, 1994.

Perry, Barbara A. *Jacqueline Kennedy: First Lady of the New Frontier*. Lawrence: University Press of Kansas, 2004.

———. *Rose Kennedy: The Life and Times of a Political Matriarch*. New York: W.W. Norton, 2013.

Sabato, Larry J. *The Kennedy Half-Century: The Presidency, Assassination, and Lasting Legacy of John F. Kennedy*. New York: Bloomsbury, 2013. Electronic edition.

Schlesinger, Arthur M. Jr. *A Thousand Days: John F. Kennedy in the White House*. Boston: Houghton Mifflin, 2005.

Shaffer, J. B., and Leslie Leland. *Left to Die*. New York: Strategic Book Publishing, 2009.

Smith, Sally Bedell. *Grace and Power: The Private World of the Kennedy White House*. New York: Random House, 2004.

Swanson, James L. *End of Days: The Assassination of John F. Kennedy*. New York: William Morrow, 2013.

Taraborrelli, J. Randy. *Jackie, Ethel, Joan: Women of Camelot*. New York: Warner Books, 2000.

Thomas, Evan. *Robert Kennedy: His Life*. New York: Simon & Schuster, 2000. Electronic edition.

SOURCES

Tuckerman, Nancy, and Pamela Turnure. Recorded interview by Mrs. Wayne Fredericks, 1964. John F. Kennedy Library Oral History Program.

Vidal, Gore. *Palimpsest: A Memoir*. New York: Random House, 1995.

West, J. Bernard. Recorded interview by Pamela Turnure and Nancy Tuckerman, 1967. John F. Kennedy Library Oral History Program.

INDEX

337

INDEX

ABOUT THE AUTHORS

Amber Hunt is a journalist who handles investigations for the *Enquirer of Cincinnati, Ohio*. She formerly worked as a crime reporter for the *Detroit Free Press* and was a 2011 Knight-Wallace Fellow at the University of Michigan, where she studied the importance of empathy in urban crime reporting. She has received numerous awards for her reporting from the Michigan Associated Press and won the 2005 Al Nakkula Award for Police Reporting. She has appeared in several television shows highlighting true crimes, including *Dateline NBC* and A&E's *Crime Stories*. She is the author of *Dead But Not Forgotten*; *All-American Murder*; and *See How Much You Love Me*.

David Batcher is a writer based in Minneapolis. He studied theology and literature at St. Olaf College.